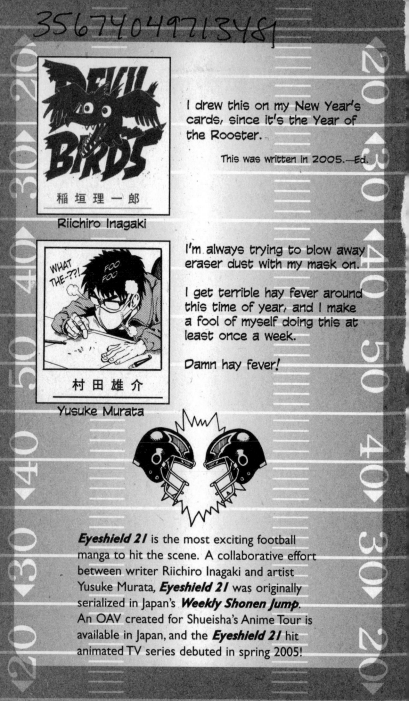

DEVIL BIRDS

稲垣理一郎

Riichiro Inagaki

I drew this on my New Year's cards, since it's the Year of the Rooster.

This was written in 2005. —Ed.

WHAT THE-??!

FOO FOO

村田雄介

Yusuke Murata

I'm always trying to blow away eraser dust with my mask on.

I get terrible hay fever around this time of year, and I make a fool of myself doing this at least once a week.

Damn hay fever!

Eyeshield 21 is the most exciting football manga to hit the scene. A collaborative effort between writer Riichiro Inagaki and artist Yusuke Murata, *Eyeshield 21* was originally serialized in Japan's *Weekly Shonen Jump*. An OAV created for Shueisha's Anime Tour is available in Japan, and the *Eyeshield 21* hit animated TV series debuted in spring 2005!

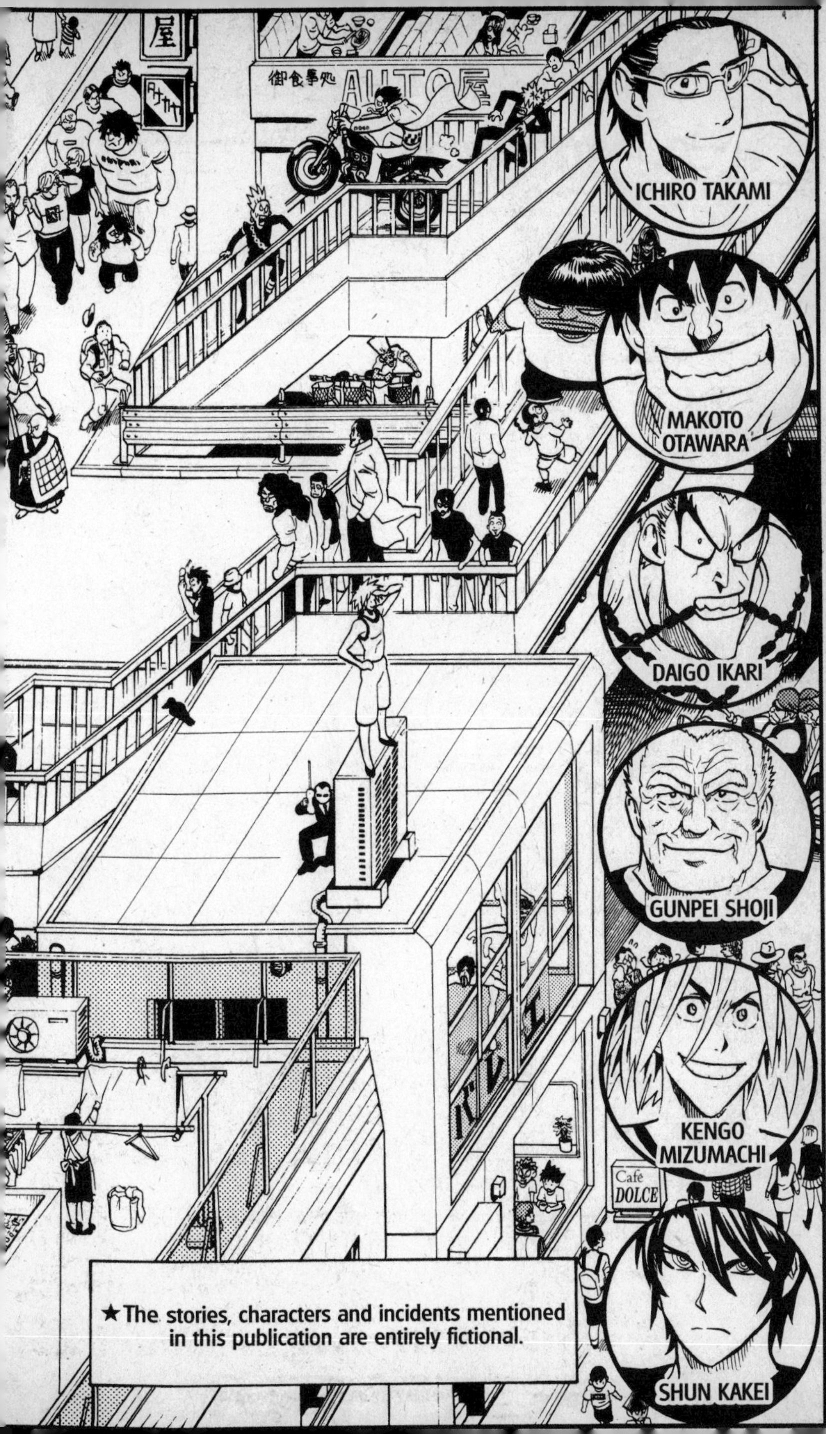

屋
御食事処
AUTO屋
ICHIRO TAKAMI
MAKOTO OTAWARA
DAIGO IKARI
GUNPEI SHOJI
KENGO MIZUMACHI
Café DOLCE
SHUN KAKEI
★The stories, characters and incidents mentioned in this publication are entirely fictional.

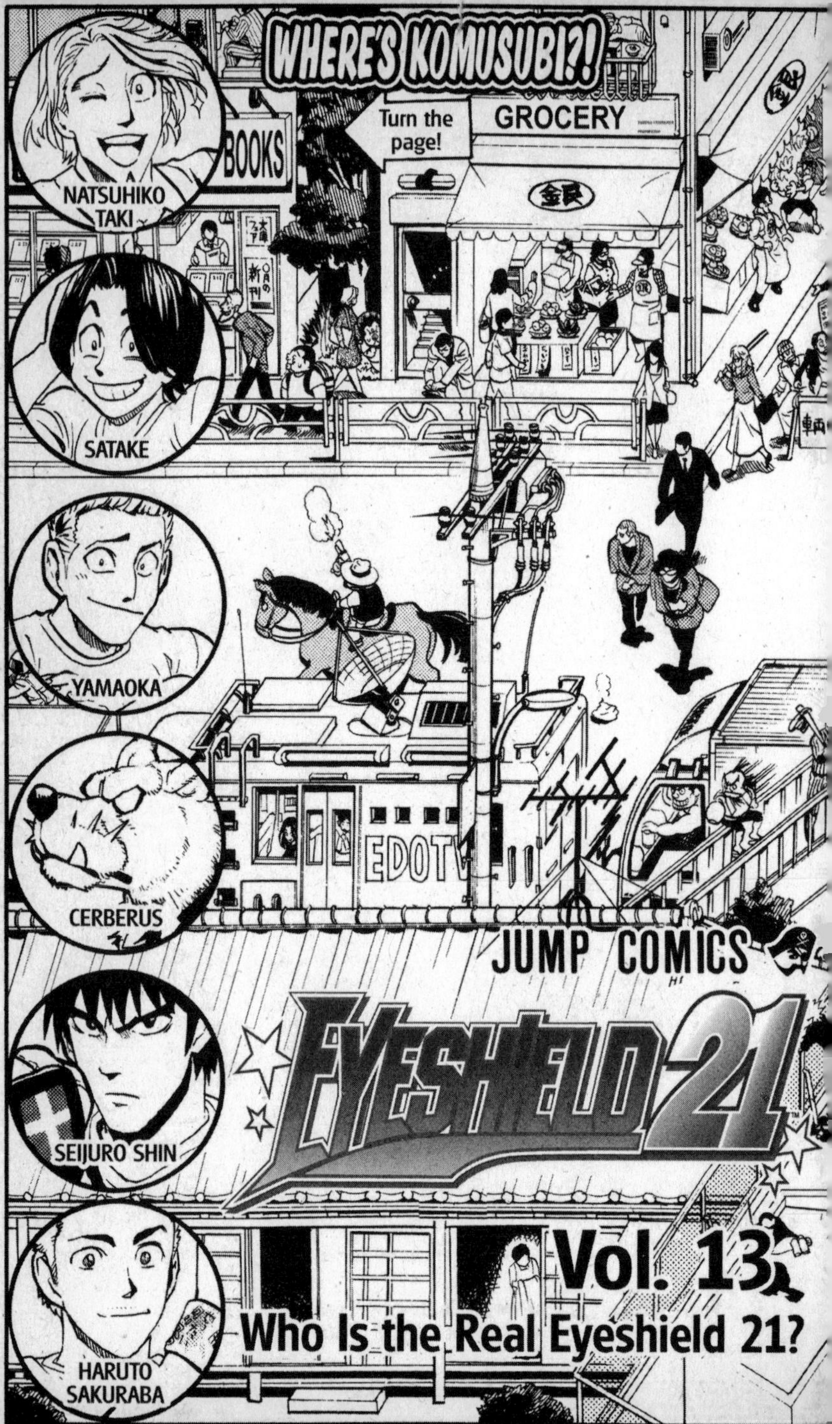
WHERE'S KOMUSUBI?!
Turn the page!
GROCERY
BOOKS
NATSUHIKO TAKI
SATAKE
YAMAOKA
CERBERUS
SEIJURO SHIN
HARUTO SAKURABA
EDOTV
JUMP COMICS
EYESHIELD 21
Vol. 13
Who Is the Real Eyeshield 21?

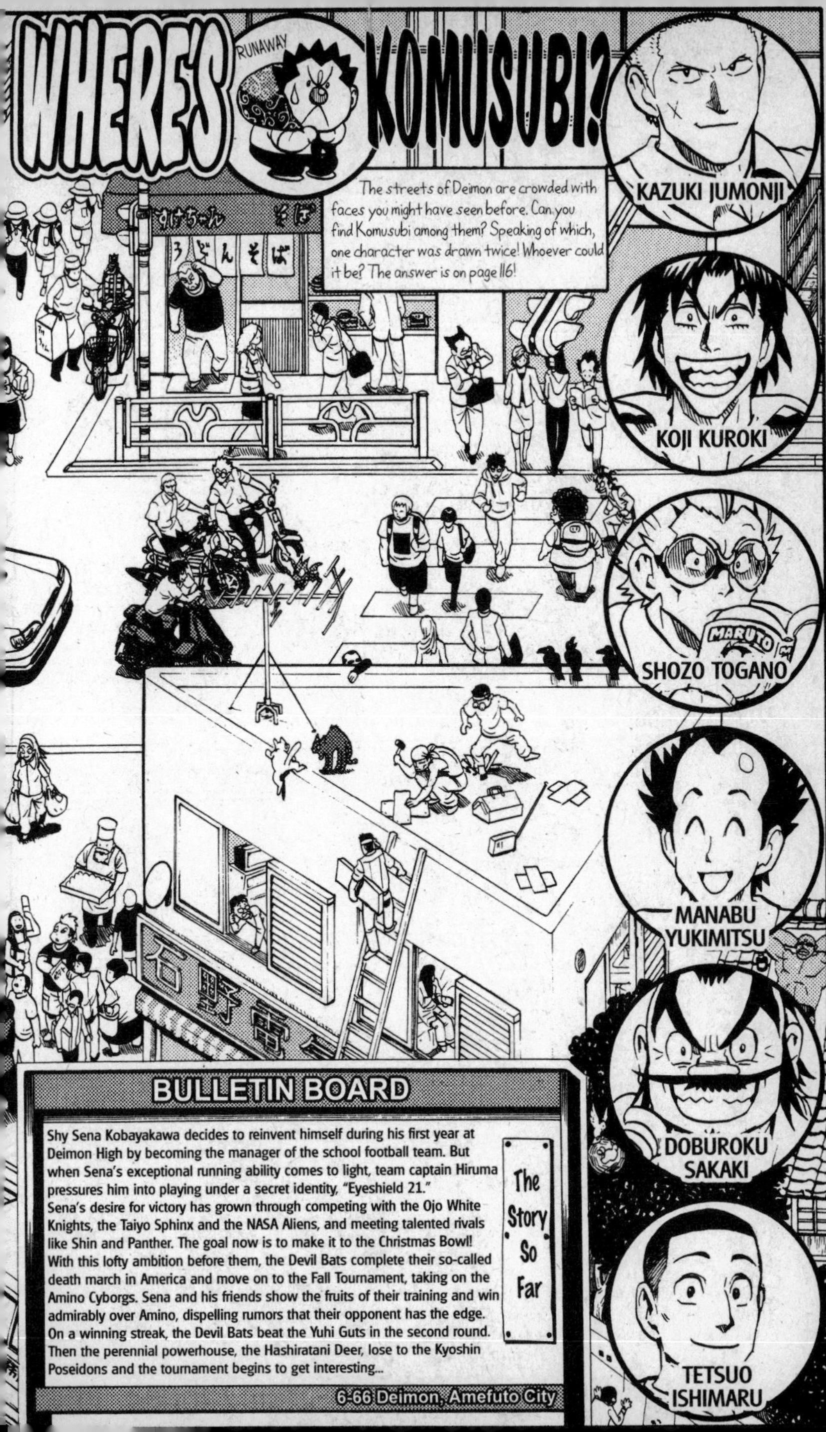
WHERE'S RUNAWAY KOMUSUBI?
The streets of Deimon are crowded with faces you might have seen before. Can you find Komusubi among them? Speaking of which, one character was drawn twice! Whoever could it be? The answer is on page 116!
KAZUKI JUMONJI
KOJI KUROKI
MARUTO
SHOZO TOGANO
MANABU YUKIMITSU
DOBUROKU SAKAKI
TETSUO ISHIMARU
BULLETIN BOARD
The Story So Far
6-66 Deimon, Amefuto City

Shy Sena Kobayakawa decides to reinvent himself during his first year at Deimon High by becoming the manager of the school football team. But when Sena's exceptional running ability comes to light, team captain Hiruma pressures him into playing under a secret identity, "Eyeshield 21."
Sena's desire for victory has grown through competing with the Ojo White Knights, the Taiyo Sphinx and the NASA Aliens, and meeting talented rivals like Shin and Panther. The goal now is to make it to the Christmas Bowl! With this lofty ambition before them, the Devil Bats complete their so-called death march in America and move on to the Fall Tournament, taking on the Amino Cyborgs. Sena and his friends show the fruits of their training and win admirably over Amino, dispelling rumors that their opponent has the edge. On a winning streak, the Devil Bats beat the Yuhi Guts in the second round. Then the perennial powerhouse, the Hashiratani Deer, lose to the Kyoshin Poseidons and the tournament begins to get interesting...

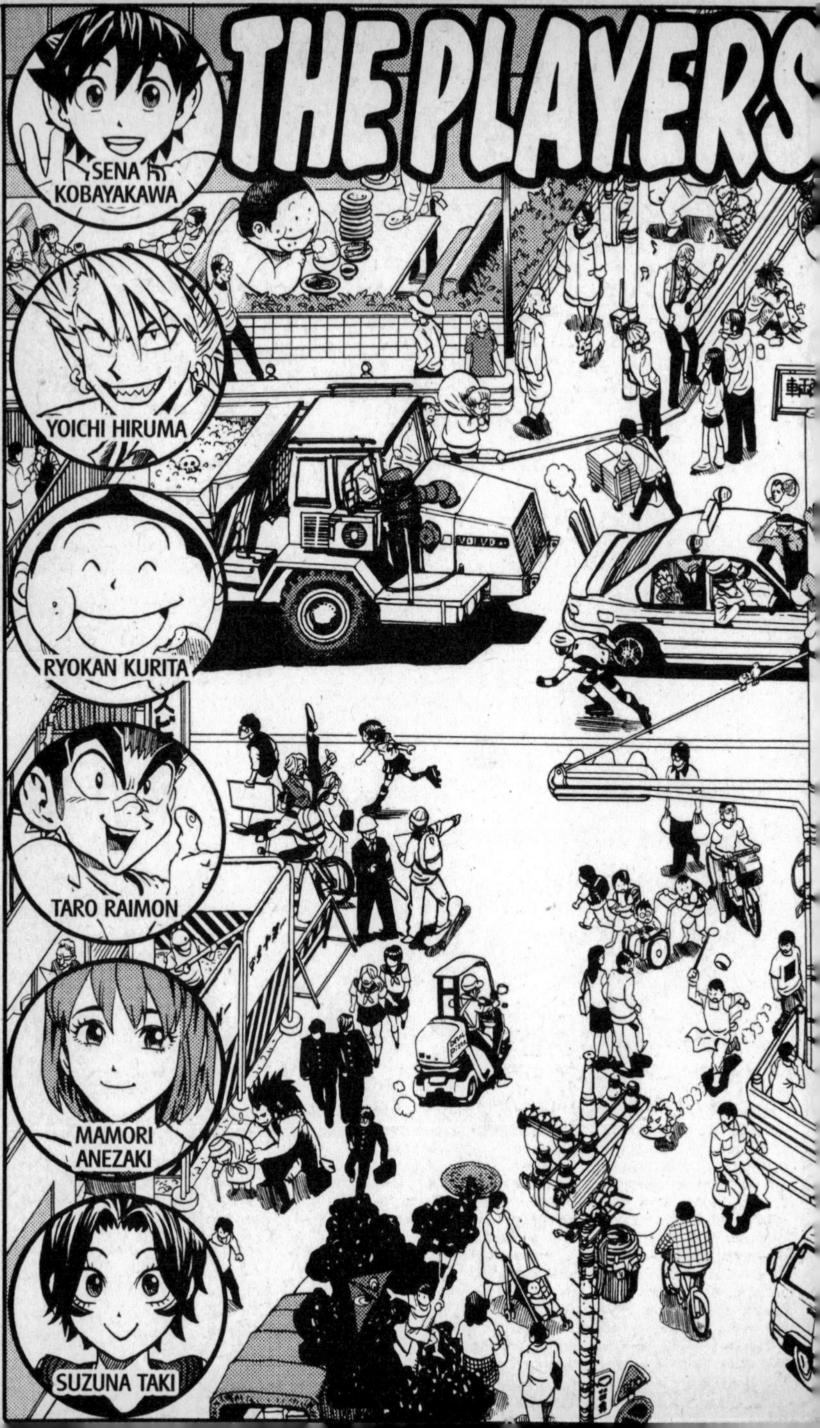
THE PLAYERS
SENA KOBAYAKAWA
YOICHI HIRUMA
RYOKAN KURITA
TARO RAIMON
MAMORI ANEZAKI
SUZUNA TAKI

EYESHIELD 21

Vol. 13
Who Is the Real Eyeshield 21?

CONTENTS

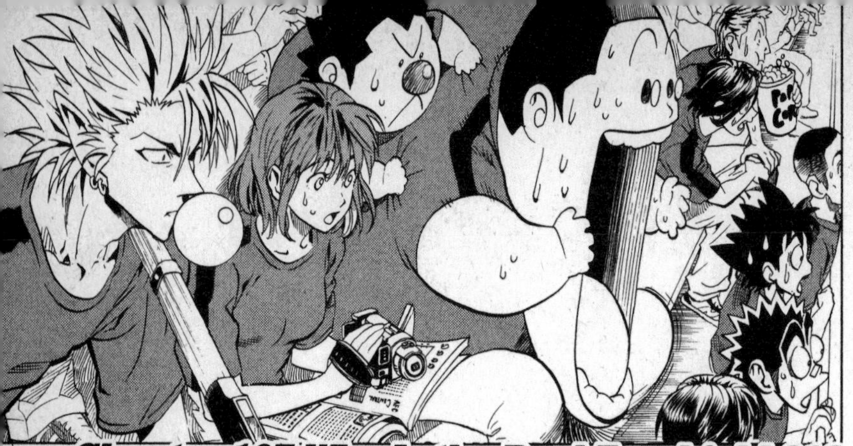

Chapter 107 Who Is the Real Eyeshield 21?

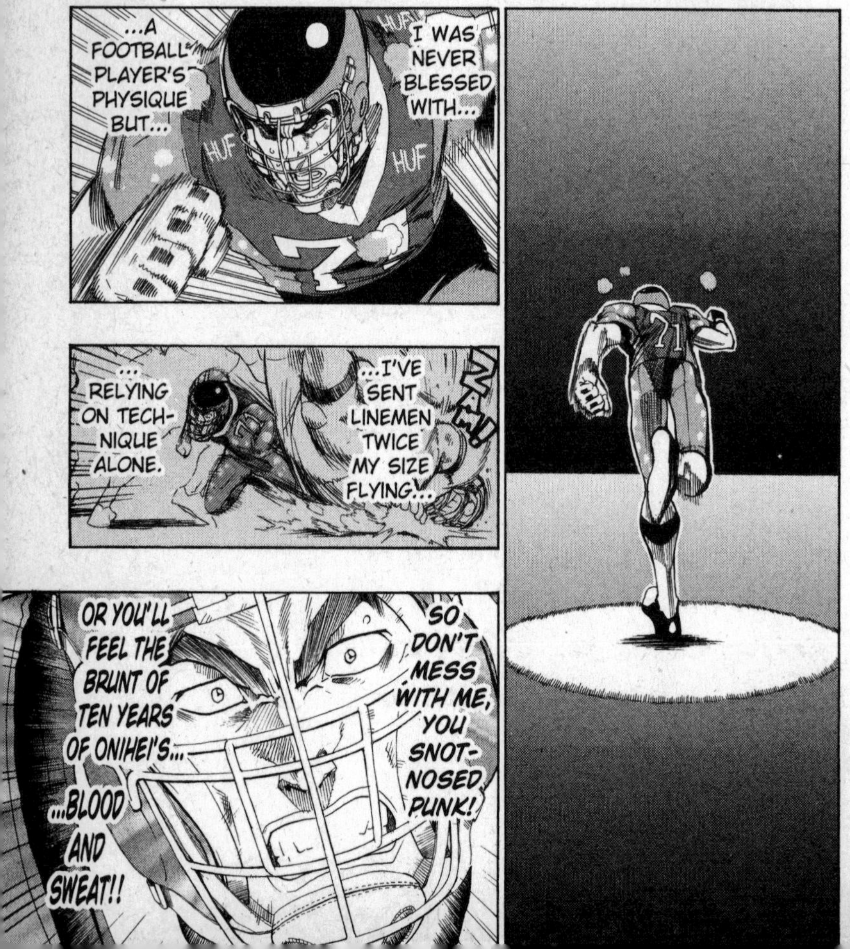
I WAS NEVER BLESSED WITH...
...A FOOTBALL PLAYER'S PHYSIQUE BUT...
HUF
HUF
HUF
HUF
...I'VE SENT LINEMEN TWICE MY SIZE FLYING...
...RELYING ON TECH-NIQUE ALONE.
SO DON'T MESS WITH ME, YOU SNOT-NOSED PUNK!
OR YOU'LL FEEL THE BRUNT OF TEN YEARS OF ONIHEI'S...
...BLOOD AND SWEAT!!

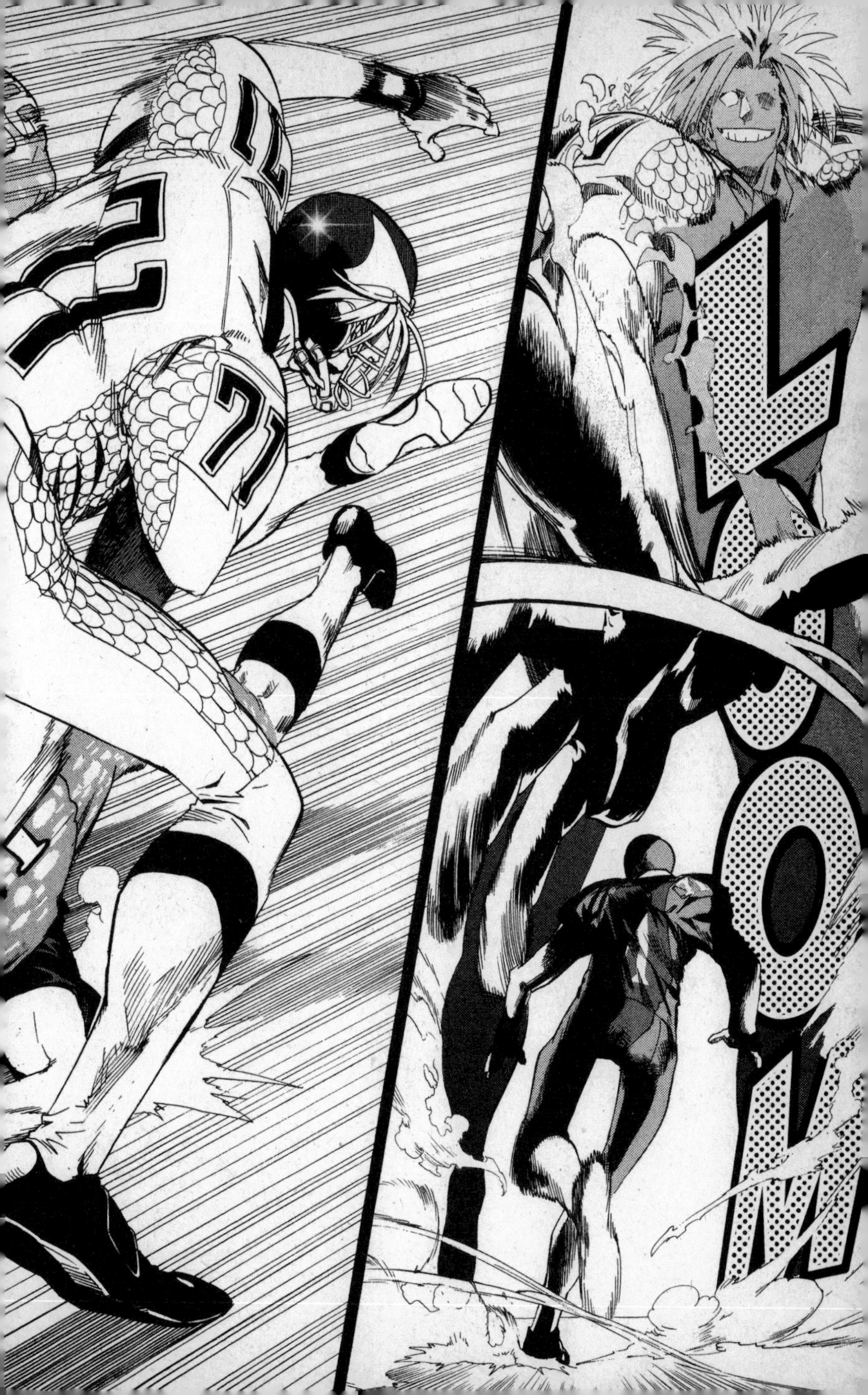
ZOOM

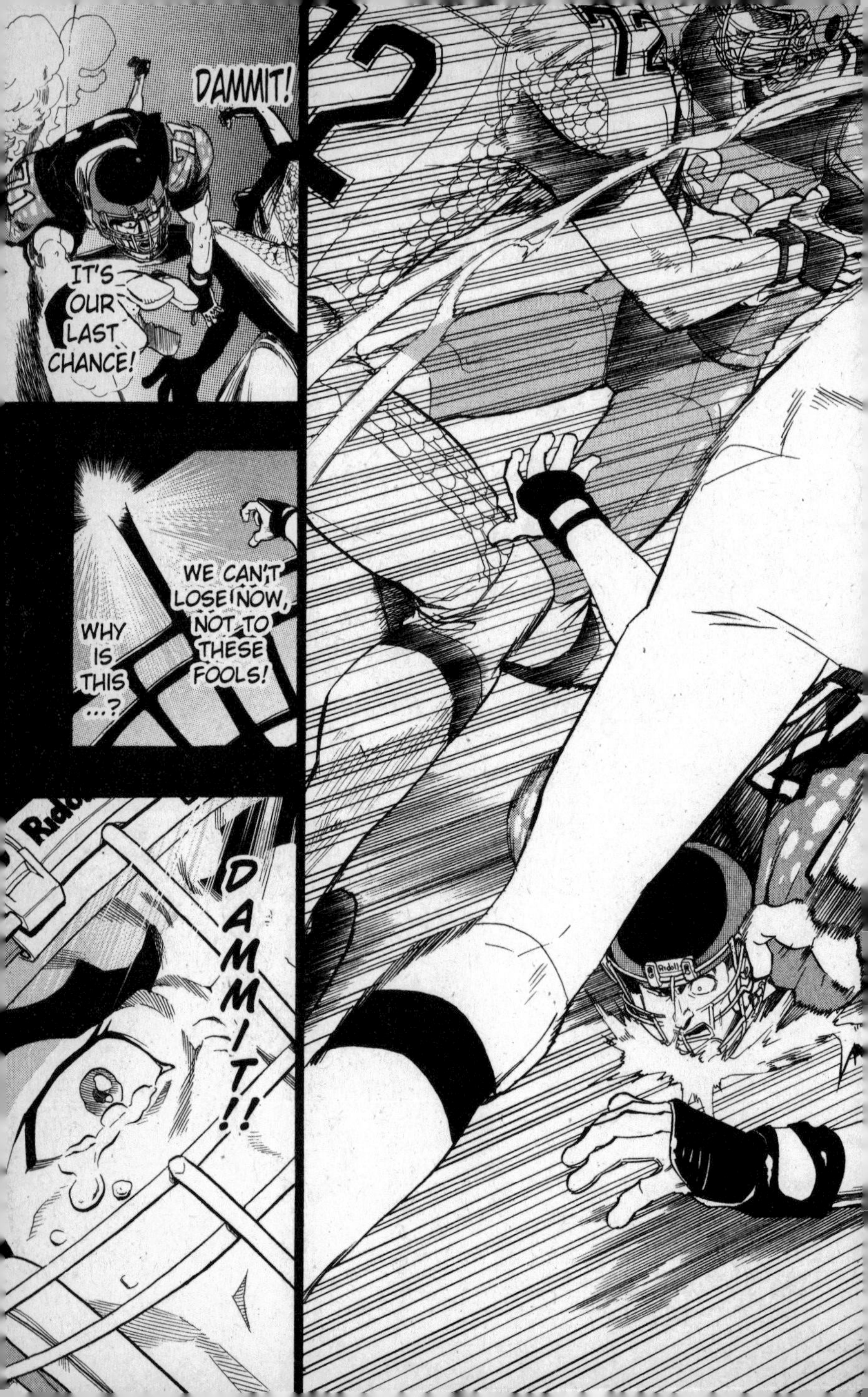
DAMMIT!
IT'S OUR LAST CHANCE!
WE CAN'T LOSE NOW, NOT TO THESE FOOLS!
WHY IS THIS ...?
DAMMIT!!

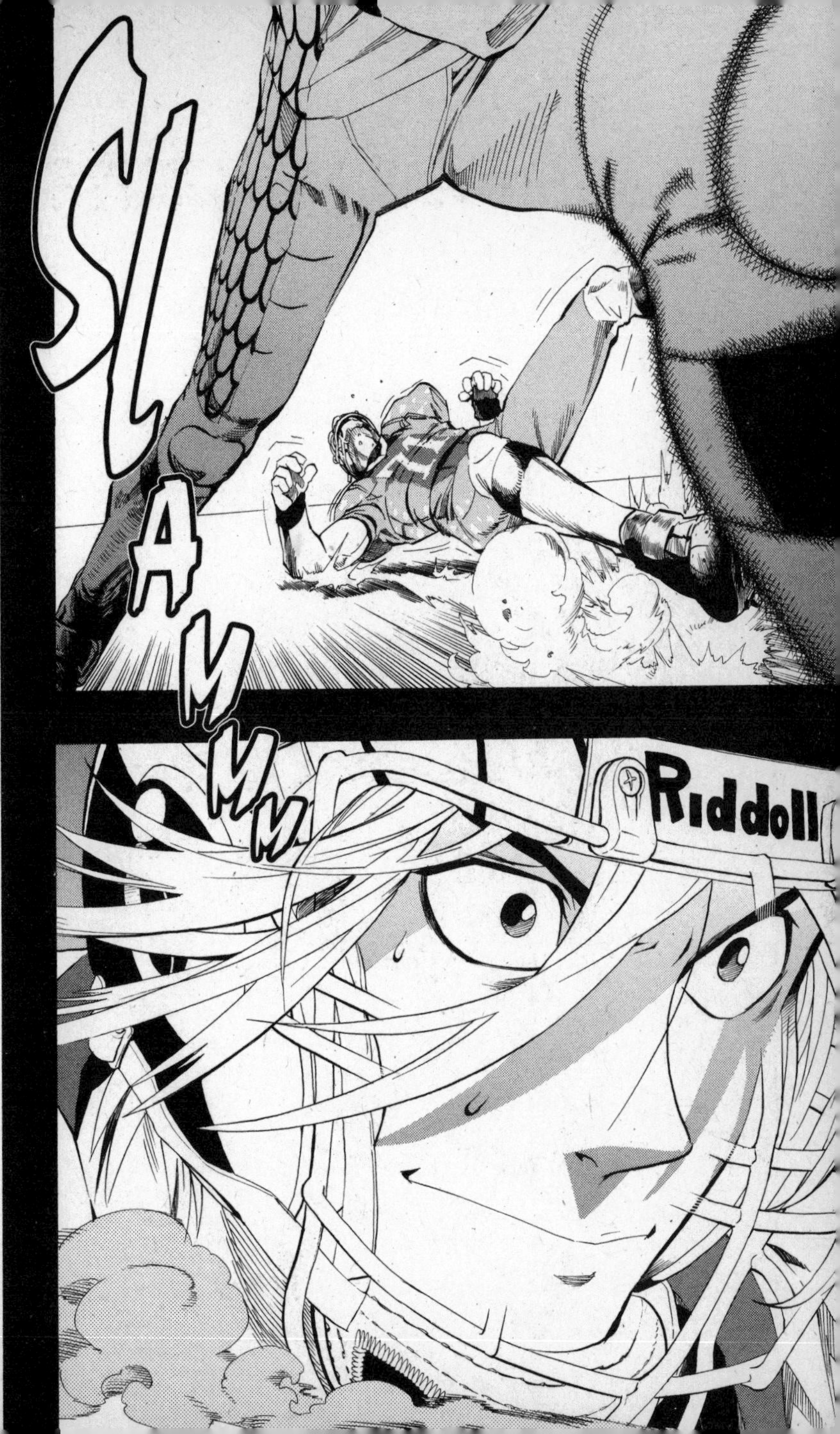
SLAMMMM
Riddoll

Chapter 107 Who Is the Real Eyeshield 21?

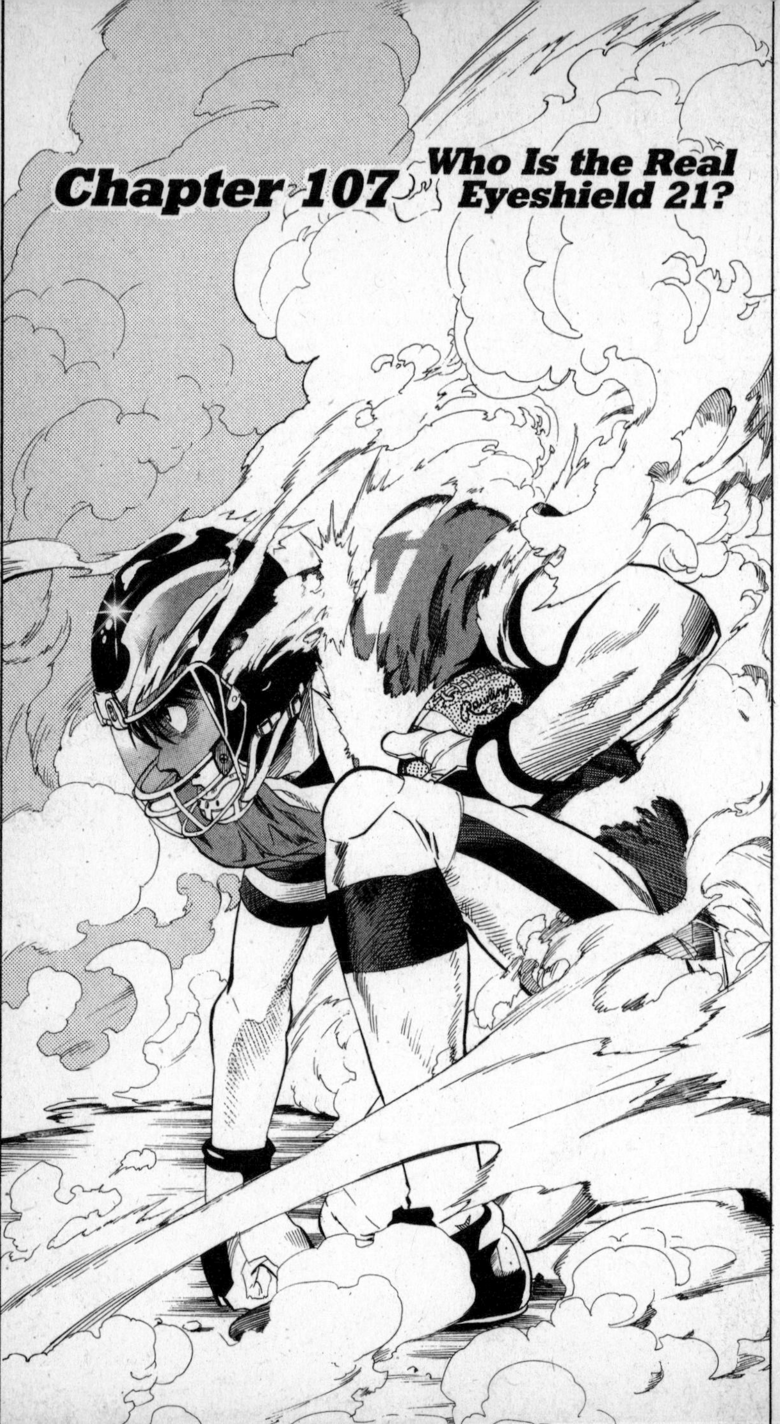

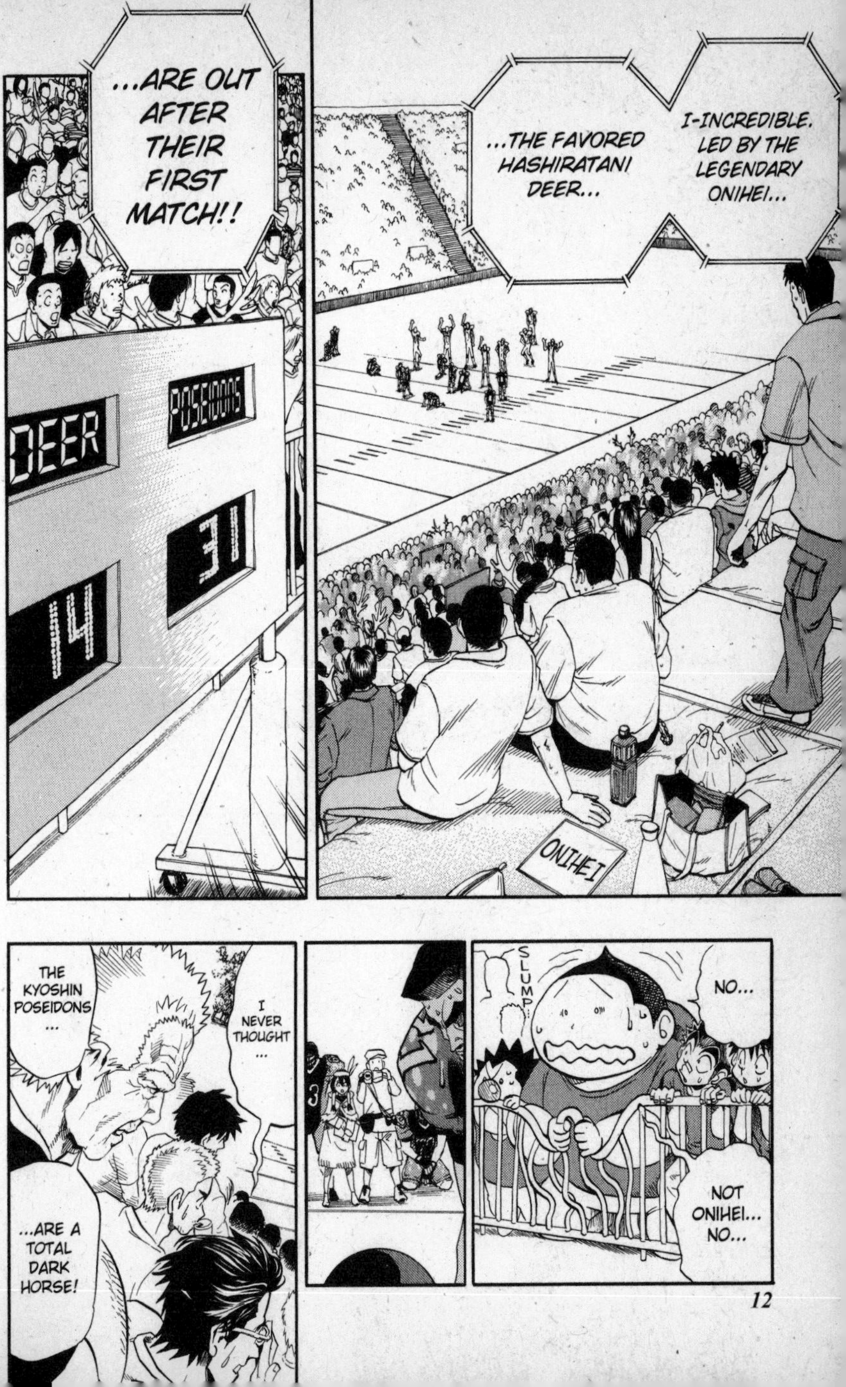
I-INCREDIBLE. LED BY THE LEGENDARY ONIHEI...
...THE FAVORED HASHIRATANI DEER...
ONIHEI
...ARE OUT AFTER THEIR FIRST MATCH!!
DEER
POSEIDONS
14
31
NO...
SLUMP...
NOT ONIHEI... NO...
THE KYOSHIN POSEIDONS...
I NEVER THOUGHT...
...ARE A TOTAL DARK HORSE!

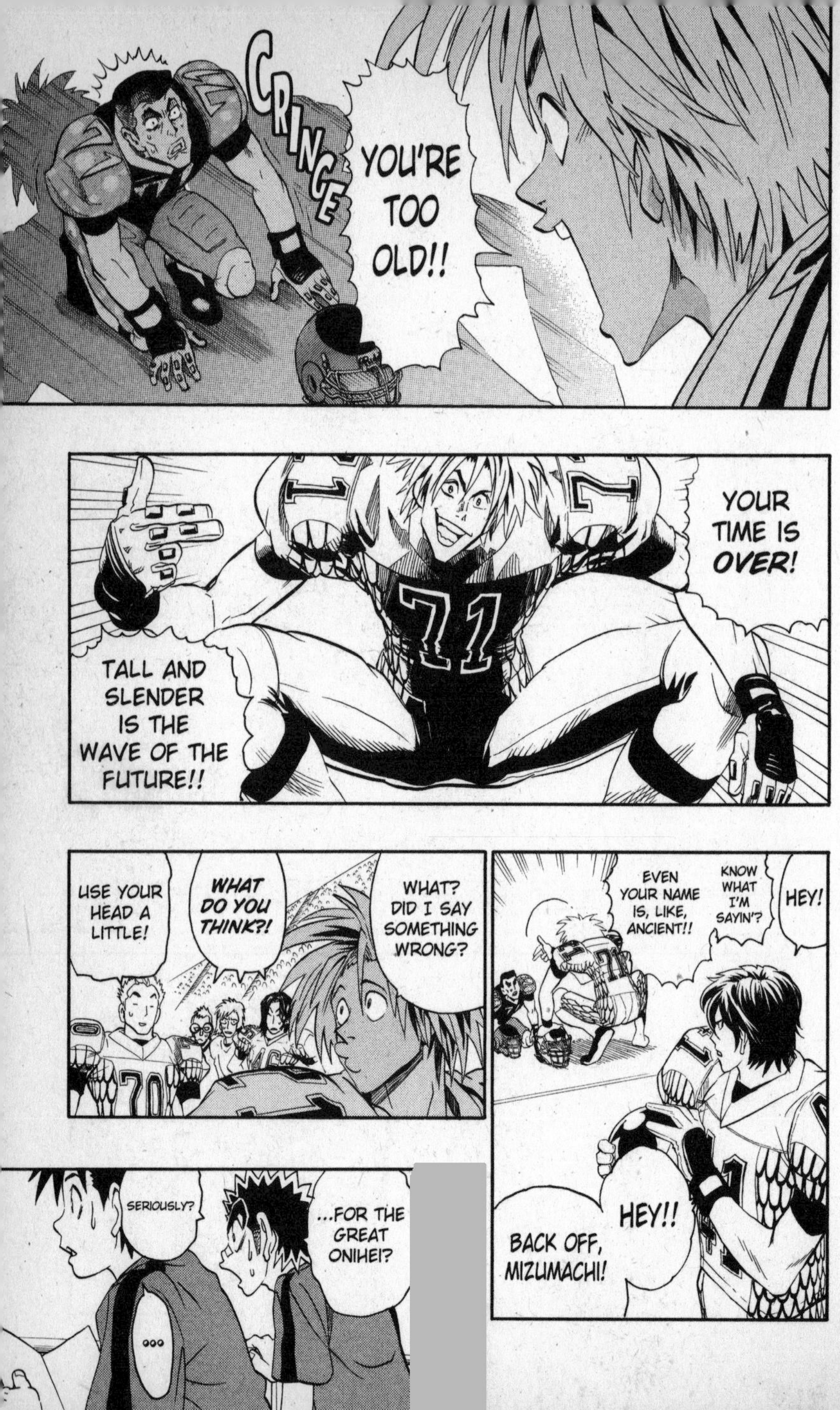

YOU'RE TOO OLD!!
CRINGE
YOUR TIME IS OVER!
TALL AND SLENDER IS THE WAVE OF THE FUTURE!!
HEY!
KNOW WHAT I'M SAYIN'?
EVEN YOUR NAME IS, LIKE, ANCIENT!!
HEY!!
BACK OFF, MIZUMACHI!
WHAT? DID I SAY SOMETHING WRONG?
WHAT DO YOU THINK?!
USE YOUR HEAD A LITTLE!
...FOR THE GREAT ONIHEI?
SERIOUSLY?
...

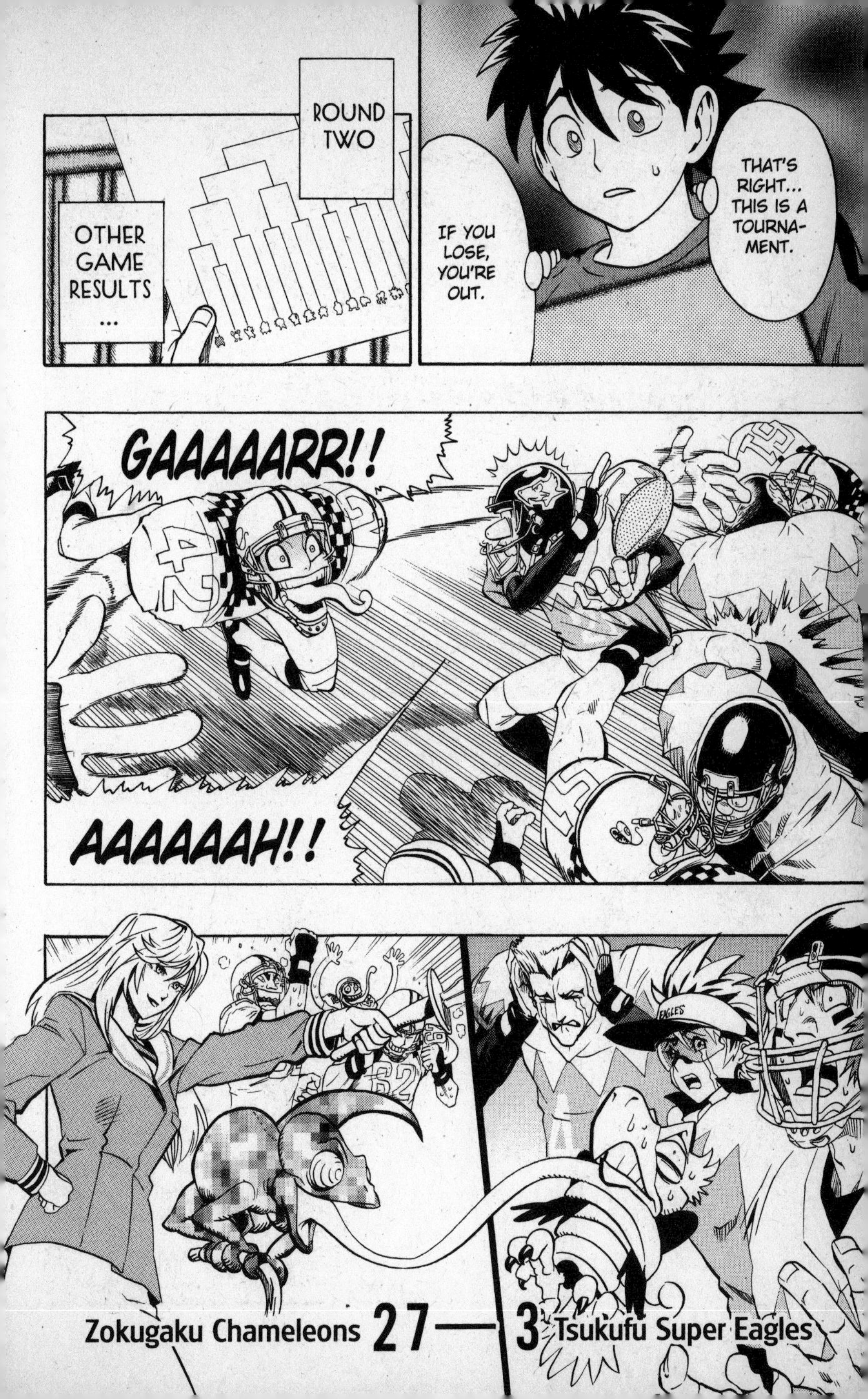
THAT'S RIGHT... THIS IS A TOURNAMENT.
IF YOU LOSE, YOU'RE OUT.
ROUND TWO
OTHER GAME RESULTS ...
GAAAAARR!!
AAAAAAH!!
EAGLES
Zokugaku Chameleons 27 — 3 Tsukufu Super Eagles

READ THIS WAY

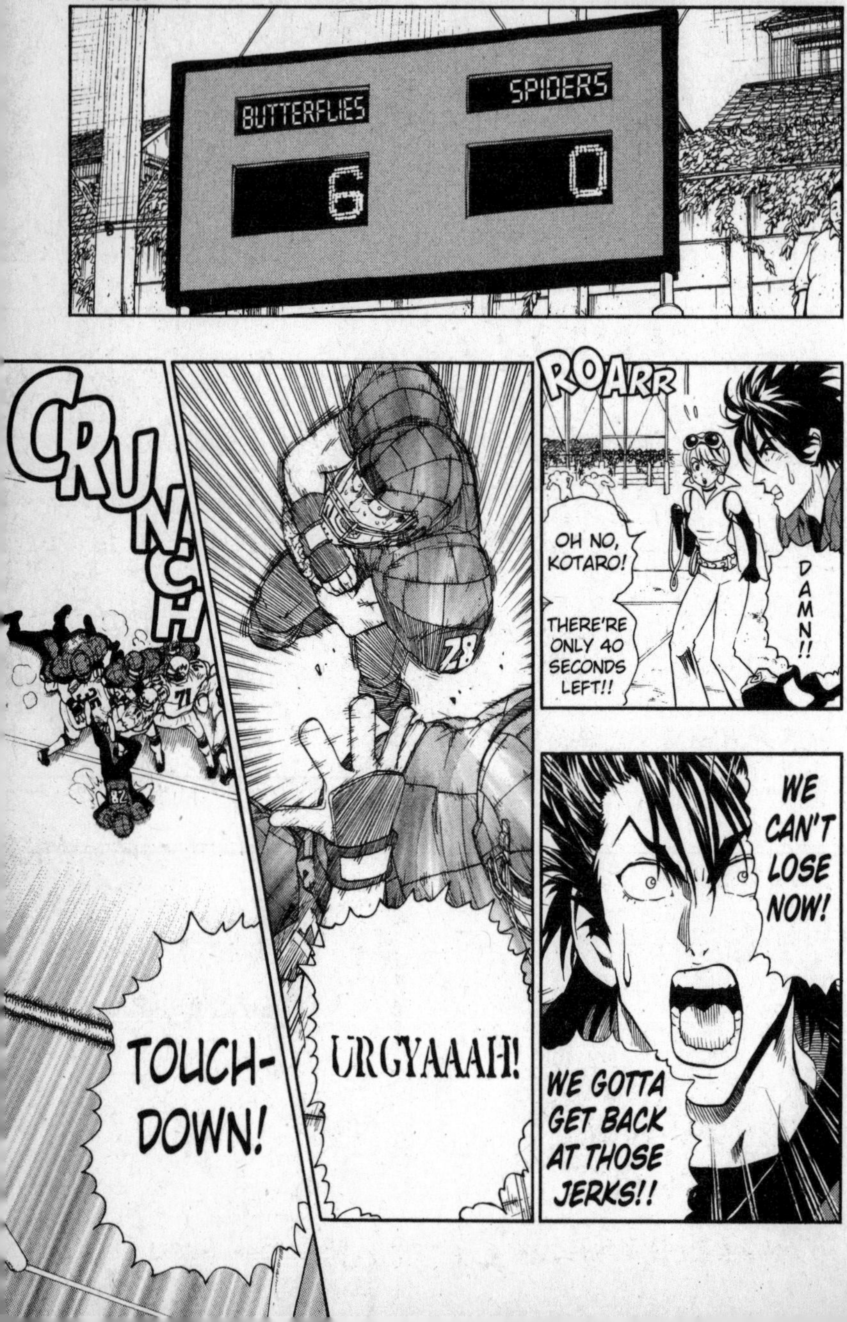
BUTTERFLIES
6
SPIDERS
0
ROARR
OH NO, KOTARO!
THERE'RE ONLY 40 SECONDS LEFT!!
DAMN!!
WE CAN'T LOSE NOW!
WE GOTTA GET BACK AT THOSE JERKS!!
URGYAAAH!
CRUNCH
TOUCH-DOWN!

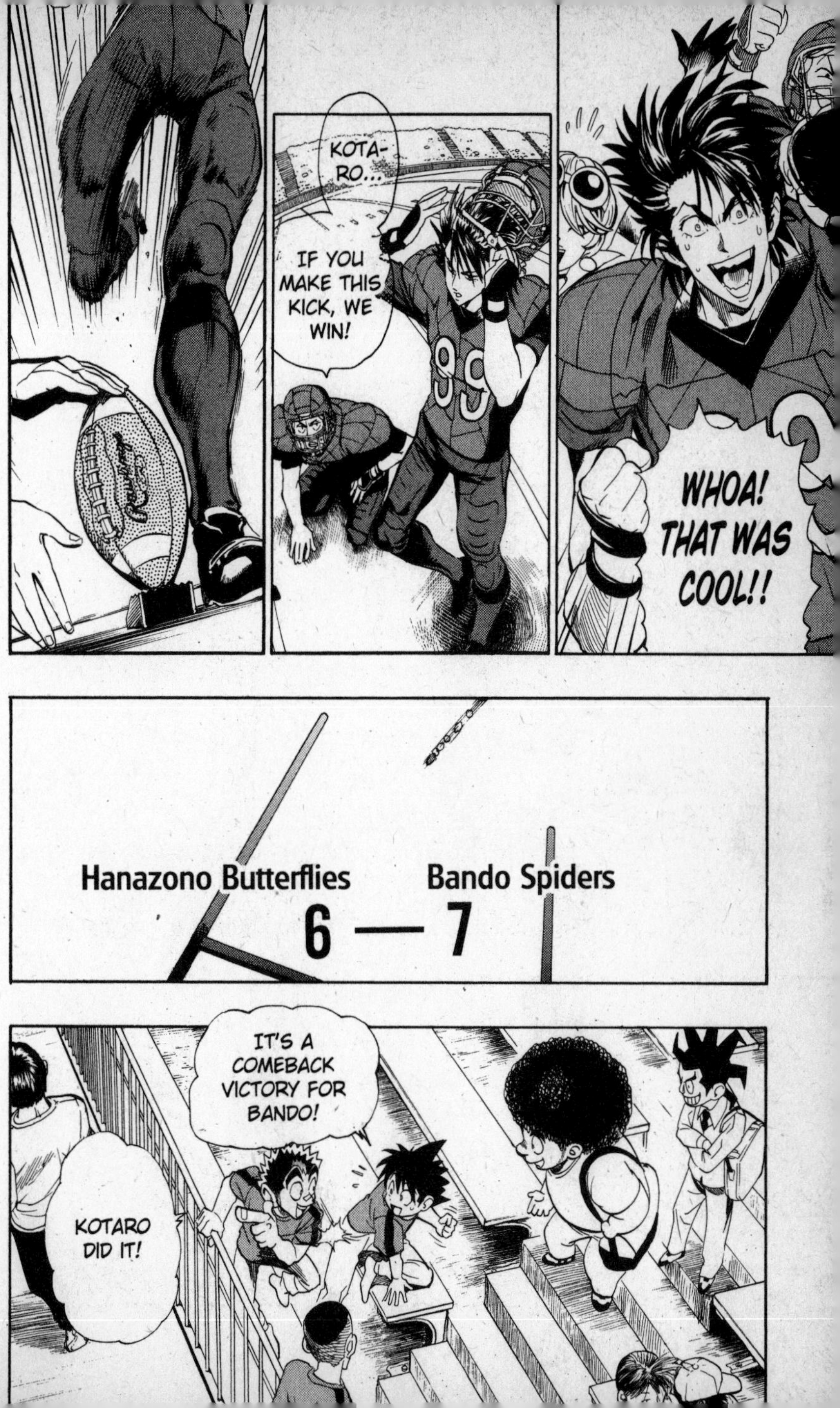
WHOA! THAT WAS COOL!!
KOTA-RO...
IF YOU MAKE THIS KICK, WE WIN!
Hanazono Butterflies
Bando Spiders
6 — 7
IT'S A COMEBACK VICTORY FOR BANDO!
KOTARO DID IT!

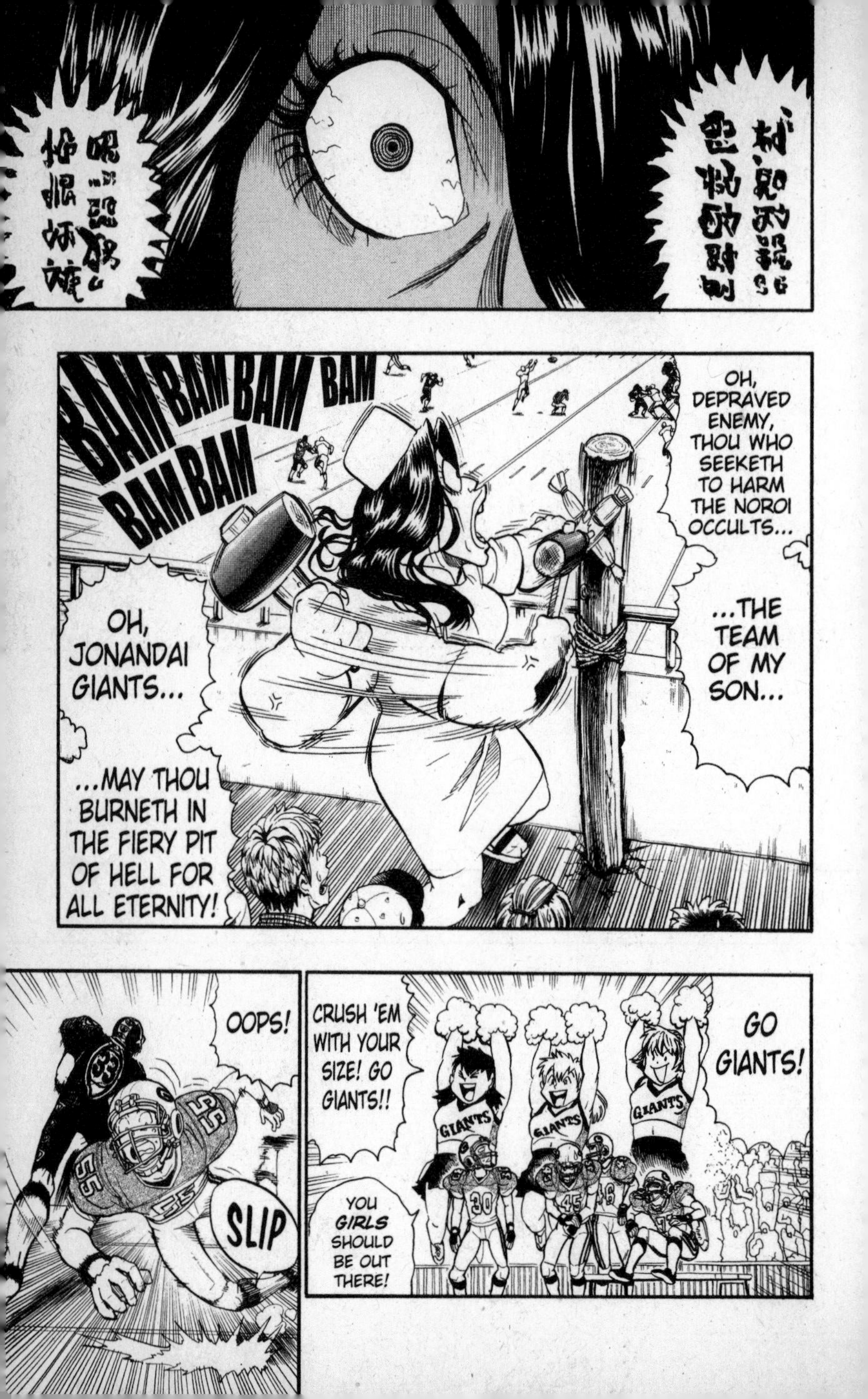
OH, DEPRAVED ENEMY, THOU WHO SEEKETH TO HARM THE NOROI OCCULTS...
...THE TEAM OF MY SON...
BAM BAM BAM BAM BAM BAM
OH, JONANDAI GIANTS...
...MAY THOU BURNETH IN THE FIERY PIT OF HELL FOR ALL ETERNITY!
GO GIANTS!
CRUSH 'EM WITH YOUR SIZE! GO GIANTS!!
YOU *GIRLS* SHOULD BE OUT THERE!
GIANTS
GIANTS
GIANTS
OOPS!
SLIP

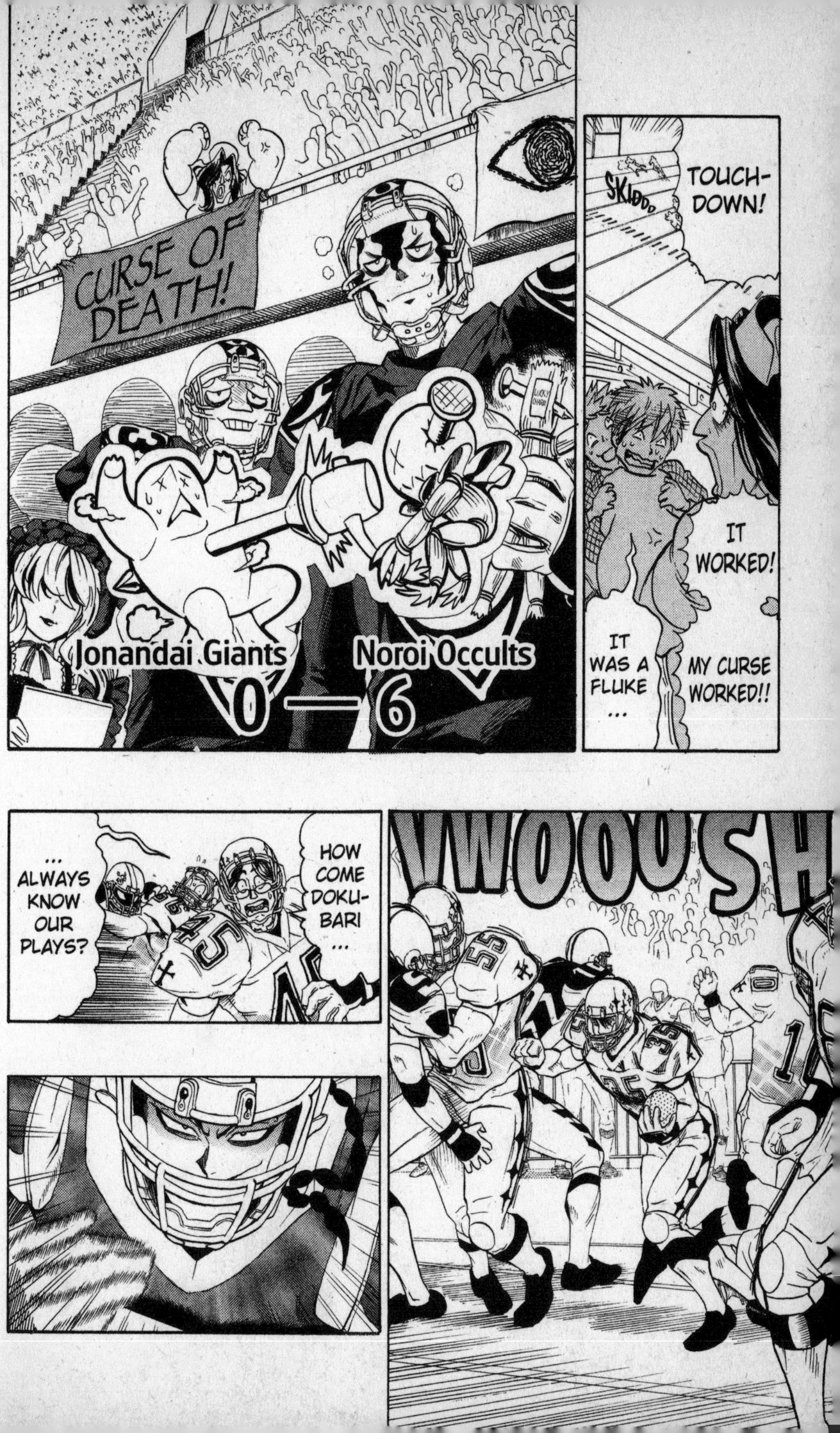
SKIDDD
TOUCH-DOWN!
IT WORKED!
MY CURSE WORKED!!
IT WAS A FLUKE ...
CURSE OF DEATH!
Jonandai Giants
Noroi Occults
0 — 6
VWOOOSH
HOW COME DOKU-BARI ...
... ALWAYS KNOW OUR PLAYS?

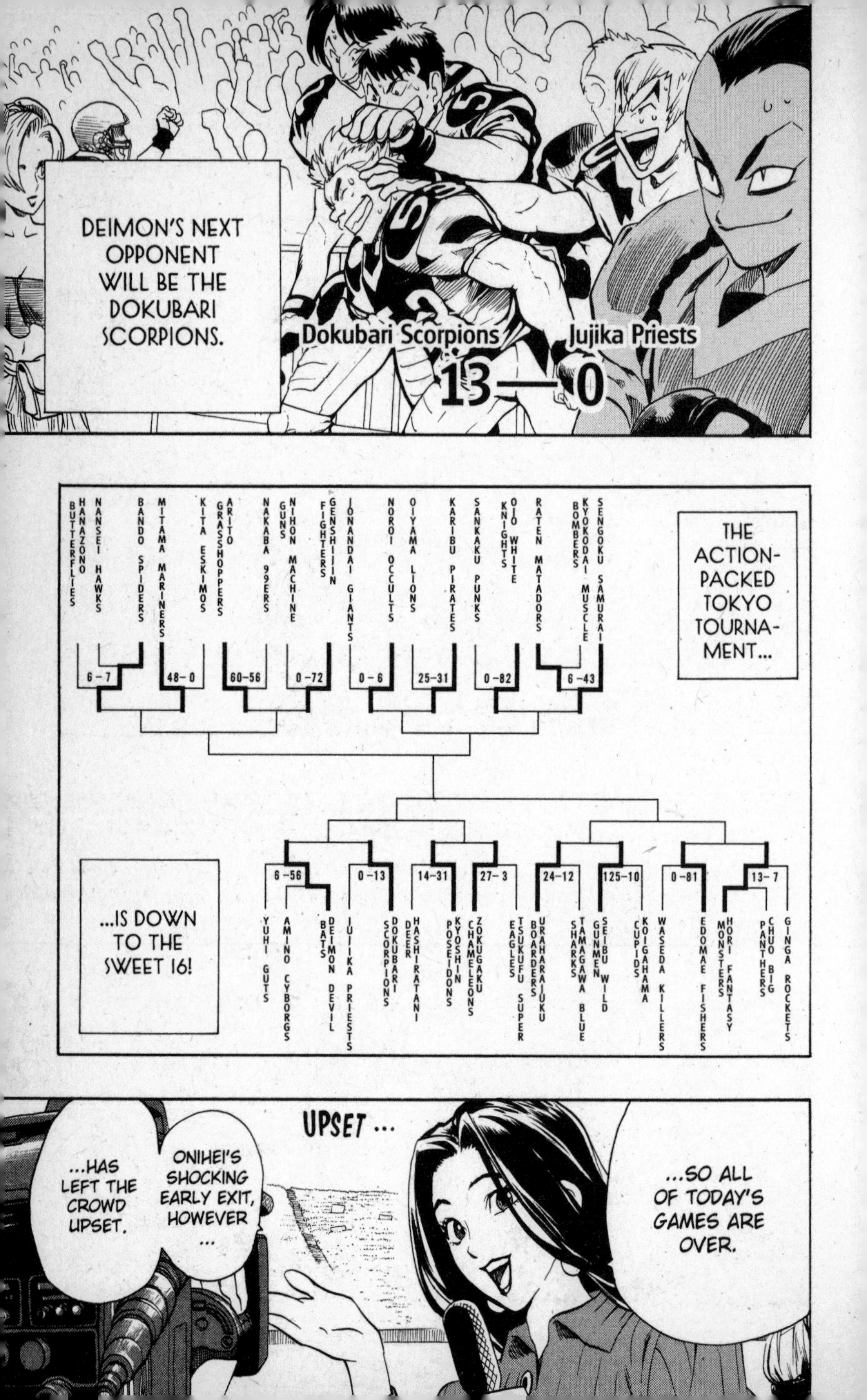
DEIMON'S NEXT OPPONENT WILL BE THE DOKUBARI SCORPIONS.
Dokubari Scorpions
Jujika Priests
13—0
THE ACTION-PACKED TOKYO TOURNAMENT...
...IS DOWN TO THE SWEET 16!
HANAZONO BUTTERFLIES
NANSEI HAWKS
BANDO SPIDERS
MITAMA MARINERS
KITA ESKIMOS
ARITO GRASSHOPPERS
NAKABA 99ERS
NIHON MACHINE GUNS
GENSHIJIN FIGHTERS
JONANDAI GIANTS
NOROI OCCULTS
OIYAMA LIONS
KARIBU PIRATES
SANKAKU PUNKS
OJO WHITE KNIGHTS
RATEN MATADORS
KYOKODAI MUSCLE BOMBERS
SENGOKU SAMURAI
6-7
48-0
60-56
0-72
0-6
25-31
0-82
6-43
6-56
0-13
14-31
27-3
24-12
125-10
0-81
13-7
YUHI GUTS
AMINO CYBORGS
DEIMON DEVIL BATS
JUJIKA PRIESTS
DOKUBARI SCORPIONS
HASHIRATANI DEER
KYOSHIN POSEIDONS
ZOKUGAKU CHAMELEONS
TSUKUFU SUPER EAGLES
URAHARAJUKU BOARDERS
TAMAGAWA BLUE SHARKS
SEIBU WILD GUNMEN
KOIGAHAMA CUPIDS
WASEDA KILLERS
EDOMAE FISHERS
HORI FANTASY MONSTERS
CHUO BIG PANTHERS
GINGA ROCKETS
...SO ALL OF TODAY'S GAMES ARE OVER.
UPSET ...
ONIHEI'S SHOCKING EARLY EXIT, HOWEVER ...
...HAS LEFT THE CROWD UPSET.

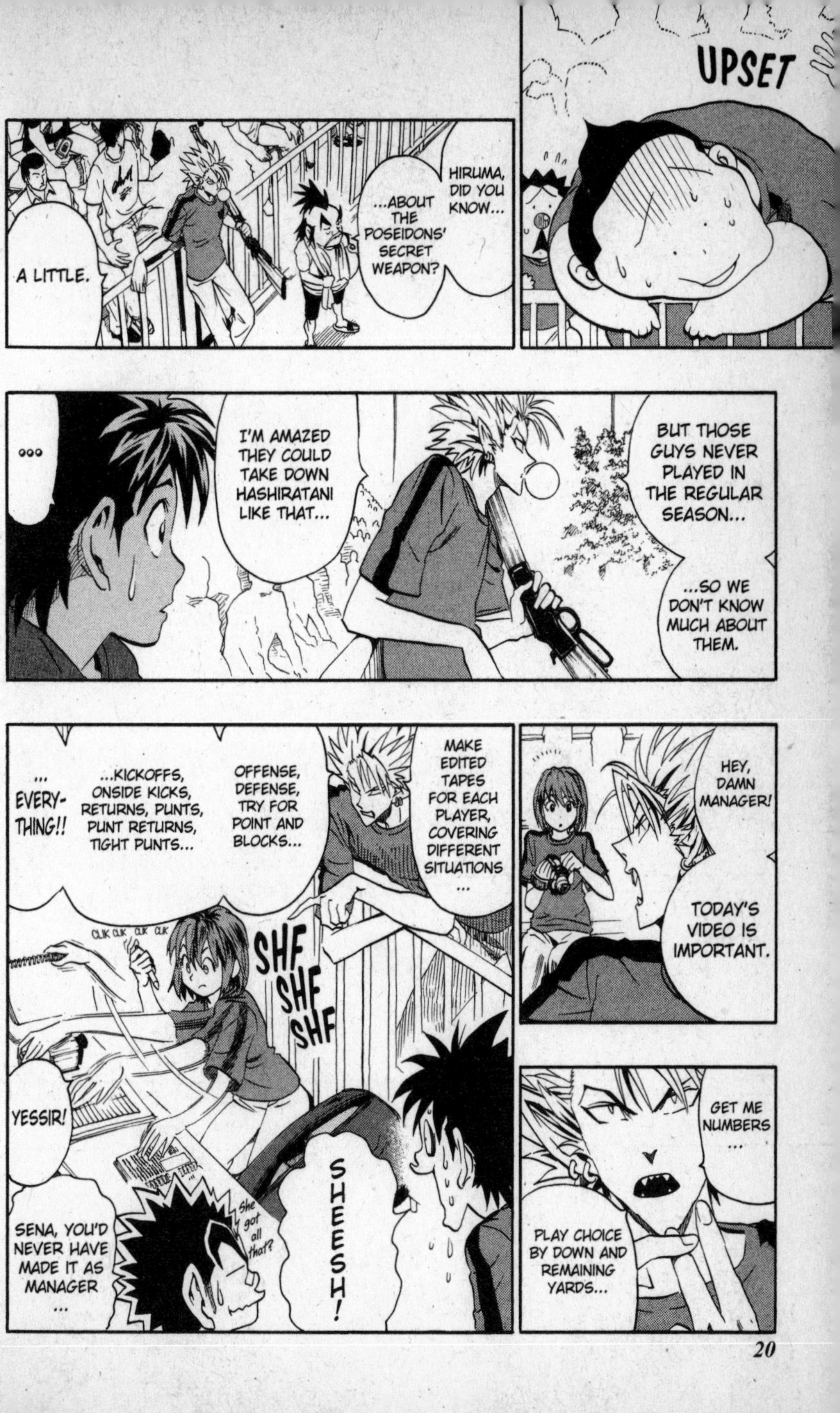
UPSET
HIRUMA, DID YOU KNOW...
...ABOUT THE POSEIDONS' SECRET WEAPON?
A LITTLE.
BUT THOSE GUYS NEVER PLAYED IN THE REGULAR SEASON...
...SO WE DON'T KNOW MUCH ABOUT THEM.
I'M AMAZED THEY COULD TAKE DOWN HASHIRATANI LIKE THAT...
...
HEY, DAMN MANAGER!
TODAY'S VIDEO IS IMPORTANT.
GET ME NUMBERS...
PLAY CHOICE BY DOWN AND REMAINING YARDS...
MAKE EDITED TAPES FOR EACH PLAYER, COVERING DIFFERENT SITUATIONS...
OFFENSE, DEFENSE, TRY FOR POINT AND BLOCKS...
...KICKOFFS, ONSIDE KICKS, RETURNS, PUNTS, PUNT RETURNS, TIGHT PUNTS...
...EVERY-THING!!
CLIK CLIK CLIK CLIK
SHF SHF SHF
YESSIR!
SHEESH!
She got all that?
SENA, YOU'D NEVER HAVE MADE IT AS MANAGER...

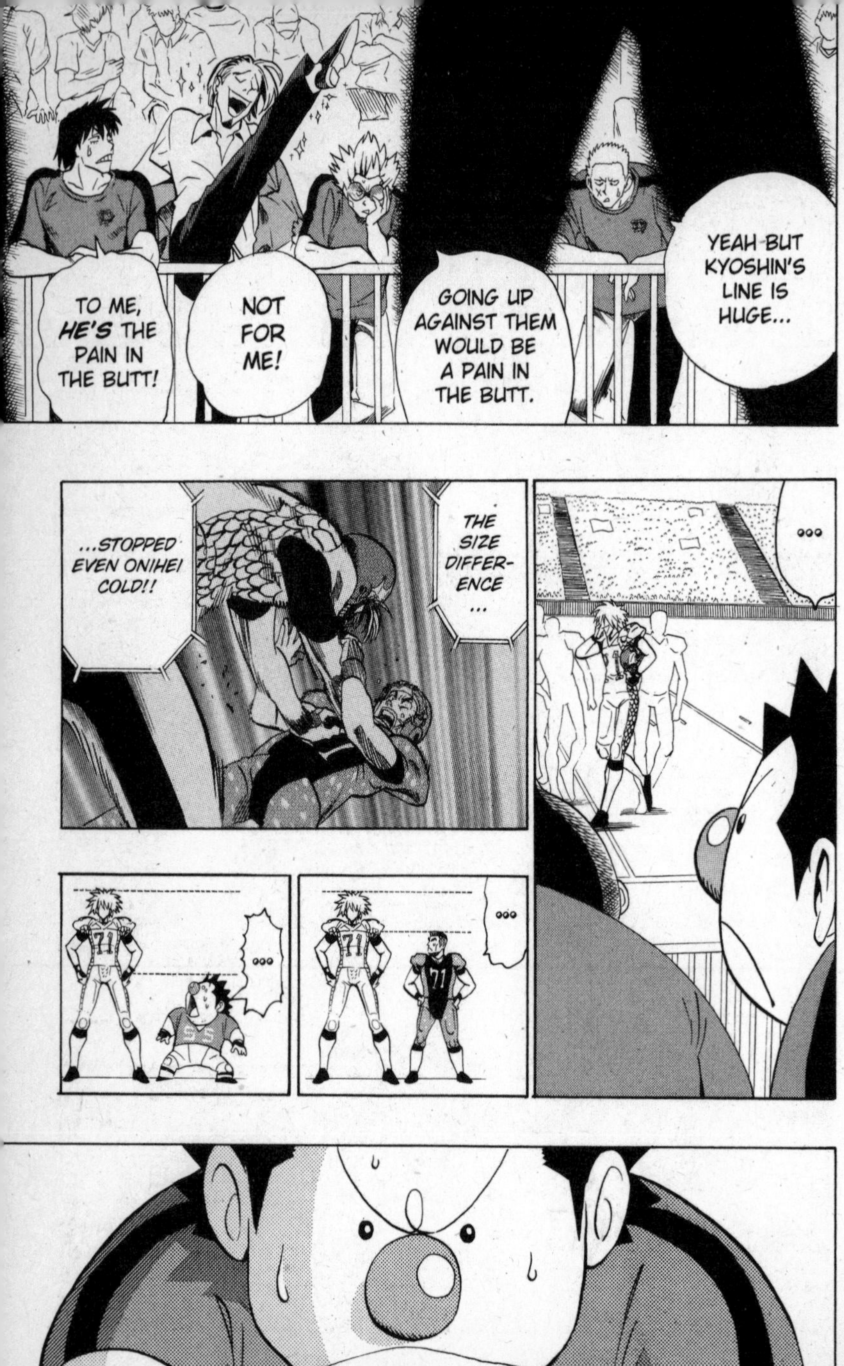
YEAH BUT KYOSHIN'S LINE IS HUGE...
GOING UP AGAINST THEM WOULD BE A PAIN IN THE BUTT.
NOT FOR ME!
TO ME, *HE'S* THE PAIN IN THE BUTT!
...
THE SIZE DIFFERENCE ...
...STOPPED EVEN ONIHEI COLD!!
...
...

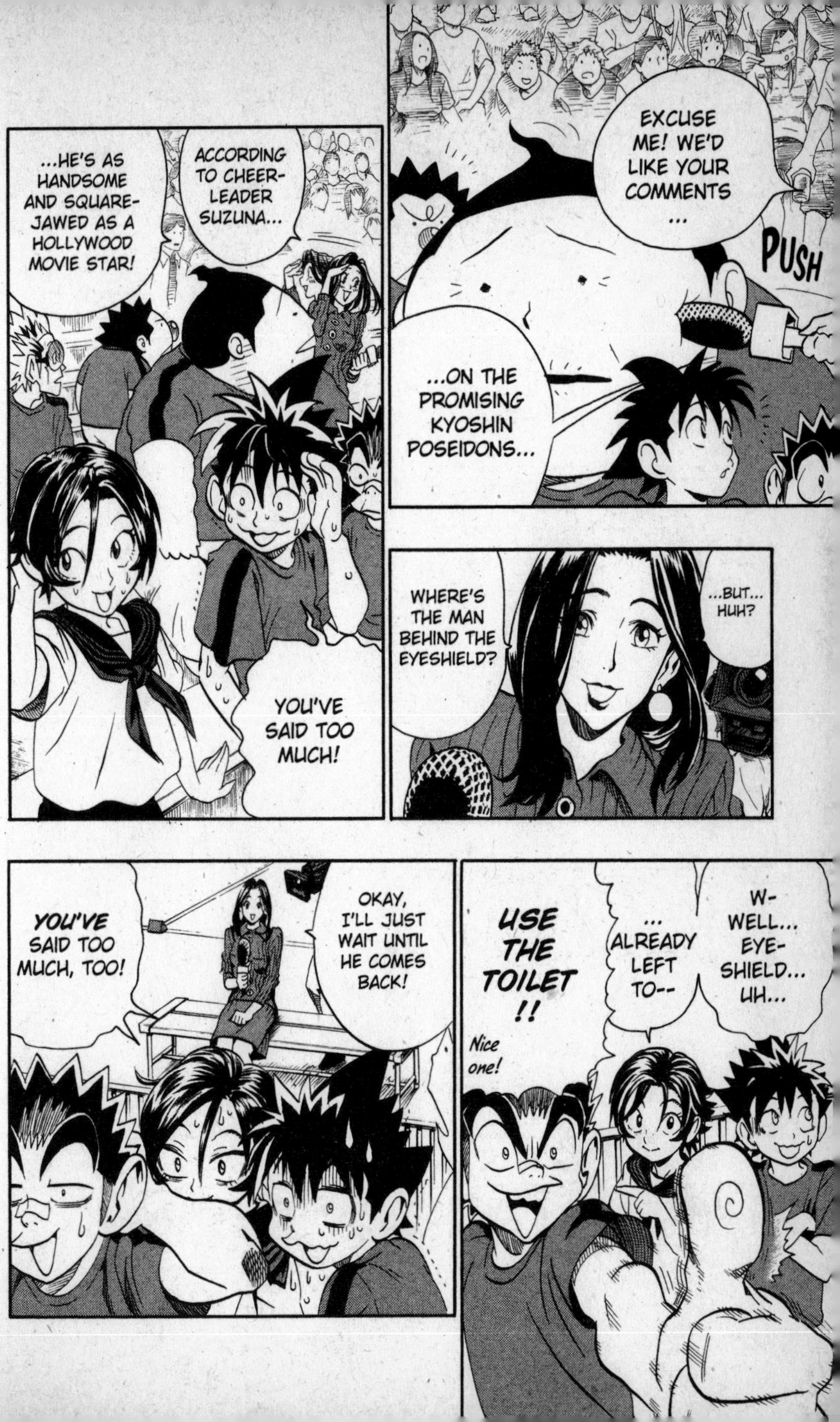
EXCUSE ME! WE'D LIKE YOUR COMMENTS ...
PUSH
...ON THE PROMISING KYOSHIN POSEIDONS...
...BUT... HUH?
WHERE'S THE MAN BEHIND THE EYESHIELD?
ACCORDING TO CHEER-LEADER SUZUNA...
...HE'S AS HANDSOME AND SQUARE-JAWED AS A HOLLYWOOD MOVIE STAR!
YOU'VE SAID TOO MUCH!
W-WELL... EYE-SHIELD... UH...
... ALREADY LEFT TO--
USE THE TOILET !!
Nice one!
OKAY, I'LL JUST WAIT UNTIL HE COMES BACK!
YOU'VE SAID TOO MUCH, TOO!

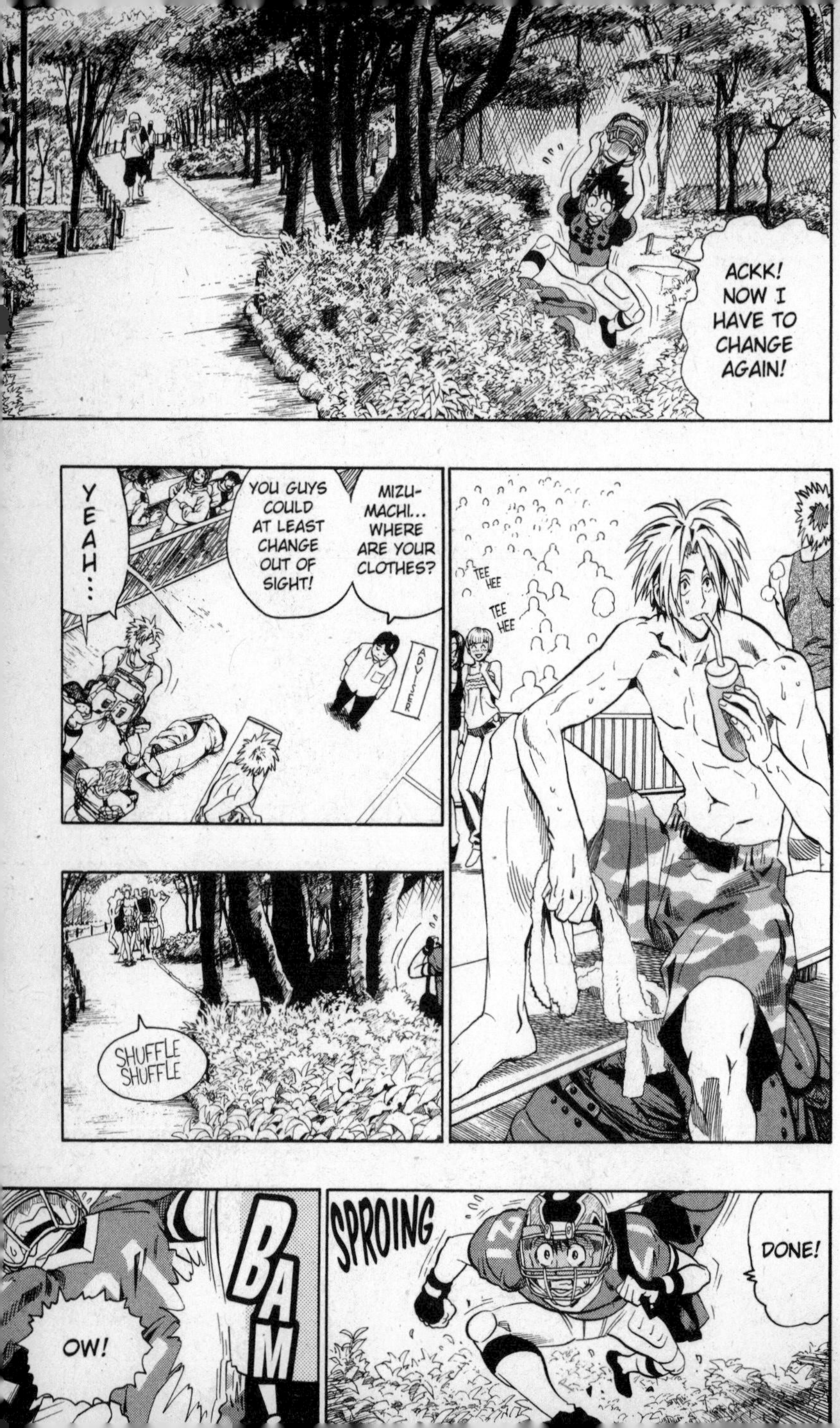
ACKK! NOW I HAVE TO CHANGE AGAIN!
TEE HEE
TEE HEE
MIZU-MACHI... WHERE ARE YOUR CLOTHES?
YOU GUYS COULD AT LEAST CHANGE OUT OF SIGHT!
YEAH...
ADVISER
SHUFFLE SHUFFLE
DONE!
SPROING
BAM!
OW!

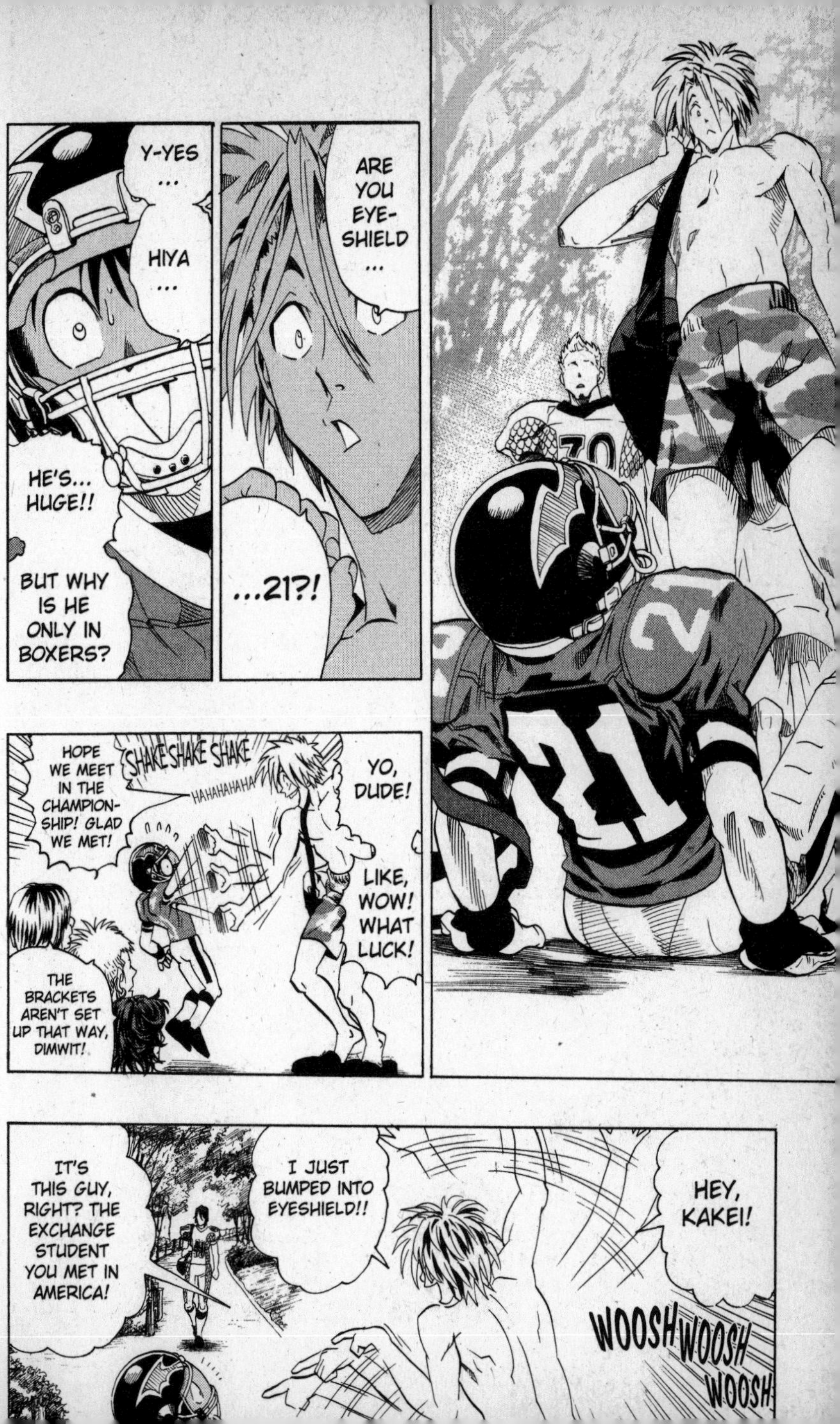
ARE YOU EYE-SHIELD ...
...21?!
Y-YES ...
HIYA ...
HE'S... HUGE!!
BUT WHY IS HE ONLY IN BOXERS?
YO, DUDE!
LIKE, WOW! WHAT LUCK!
SHAKE SHAKE SHAKE
HAHAHAHAHA
HOPE WE MEET IN THE CHAMPION-SHIP! GLAD WE MET!
THE BRACKETS AREN'T SET UP THAT WAY, DIMWIT!
HEY, KAKEI!
WOOSH WOOSH WOOSH
I JUST BUMPED INTO EYESHIELD!!
IT'S THIS GUY, RIGHT? THE EXCHANGE STUDENT YOU MET IN AMERICA!

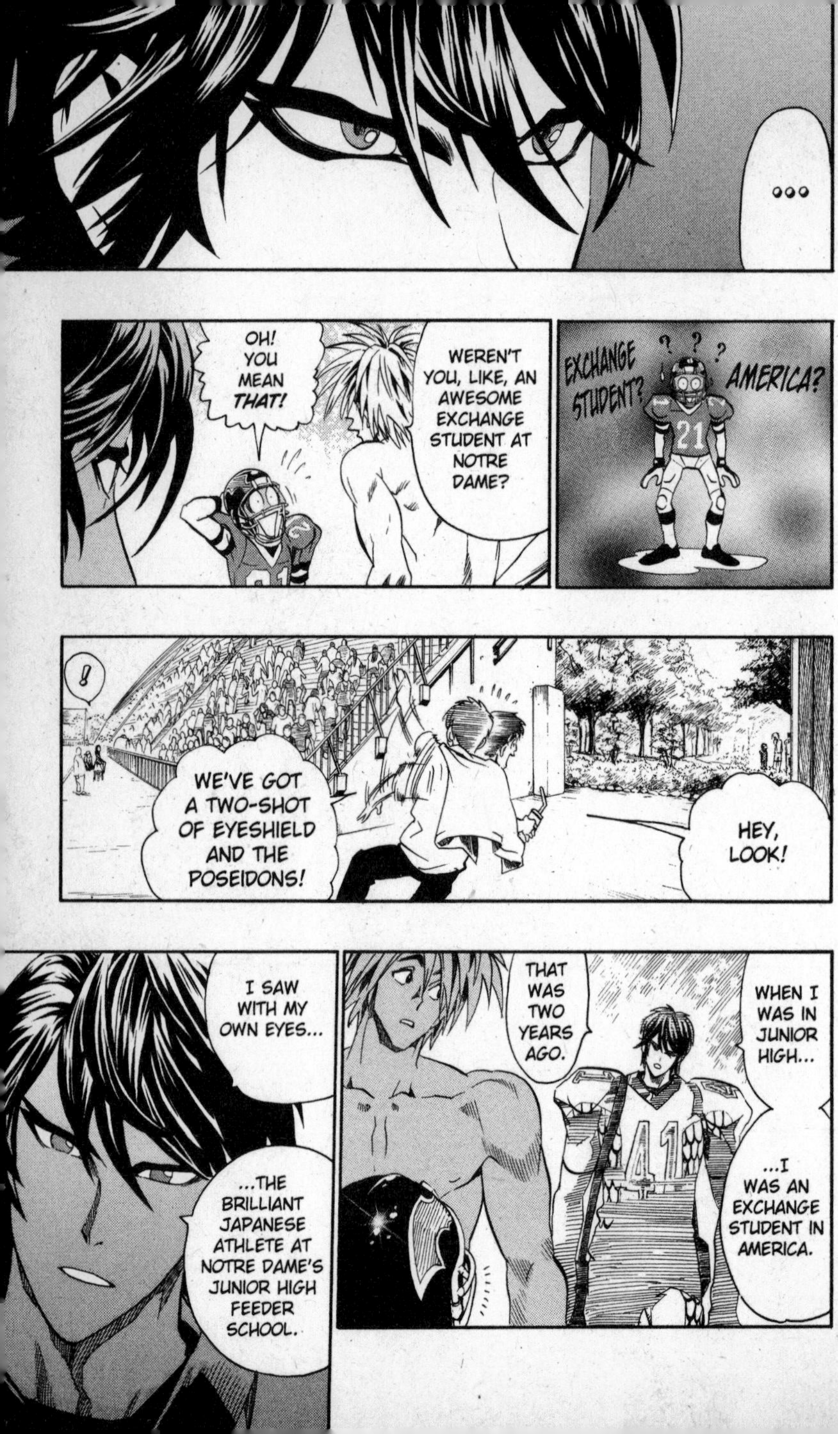
...
AMERICA?
EXCHANGE STUDENT?
WEREN'T YOU, LIKE, AN AWESOME EXCHANGE STUDENT AT NOTRE DAME?
OH! YOU MEAN THAT!
HEY, LOOK!
WE'VE GOT A TWO-SHOT OF EYESHIELD AND THE POSEIDONS!
!
WHEN I WAS IN JUNIOR HIGH...
THAT WAS TWO YEARS AGO.
...I WAS AN EXCHANGE STUDENT IN AMERICA.
I SAW WITH MY OWN EYES...
...THE BRILLIANT JAPANESE ATHLETE AT NOTRE DAME'S JUNIOR HIGH FEEDER SCHOOL.

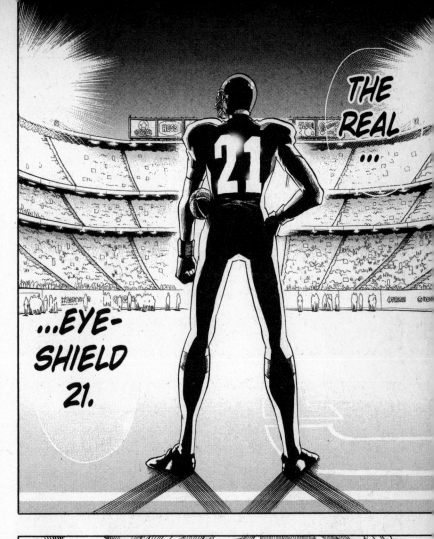

THE REAL
...

...EYE-
SHIELD 21.

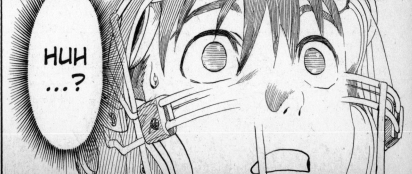

HUH
...?

READ THIS WAY

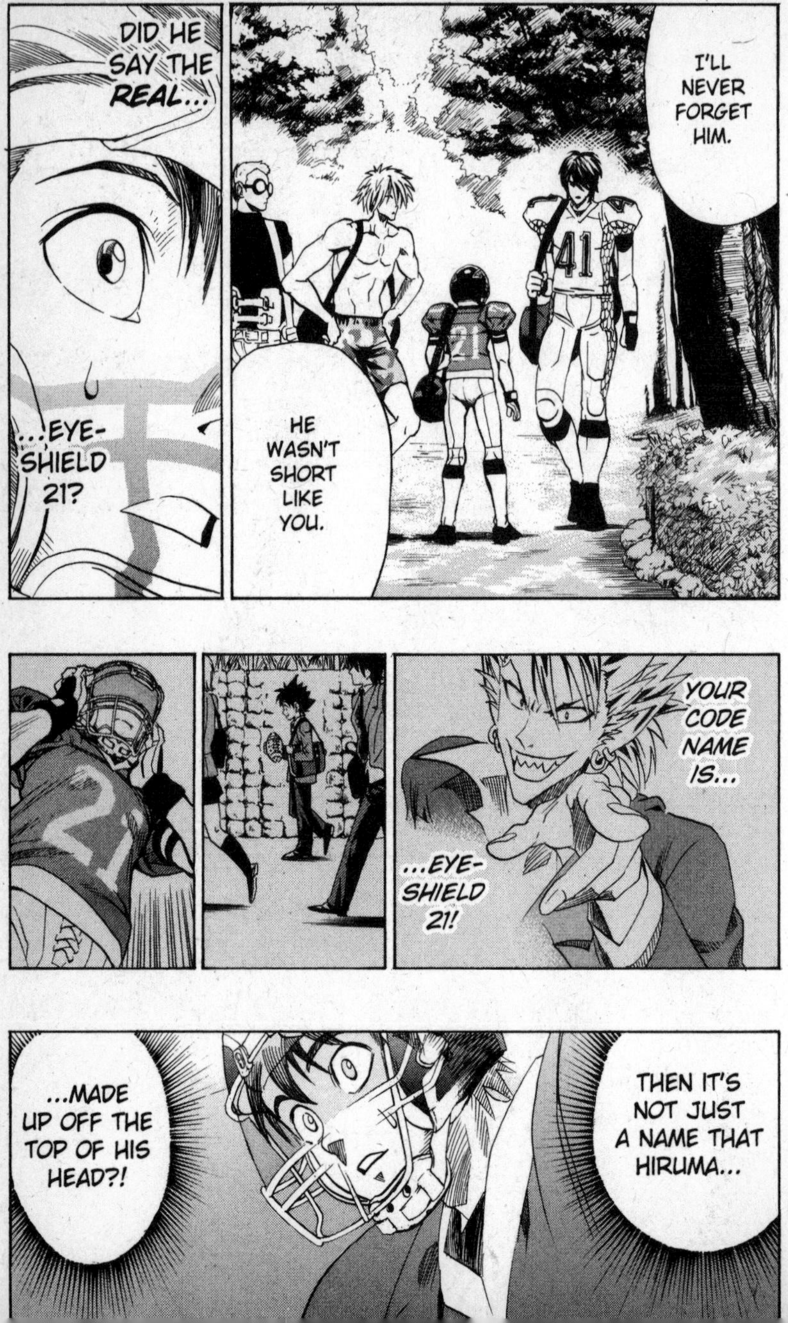
I'LL NEVER FORGET HIM.
HE WASN'T SHORT LIKE YOU.
DID HE SAY THE REAL...
...EYE-SHIELD 21?
YOUR CODE NAME IS...
...EYE-SHIELD 21!
THEN IT'S NOT JUST A NAME THAT HIRUMA...
...MADE UP OFF THE TOP OF HIS HEAD?!

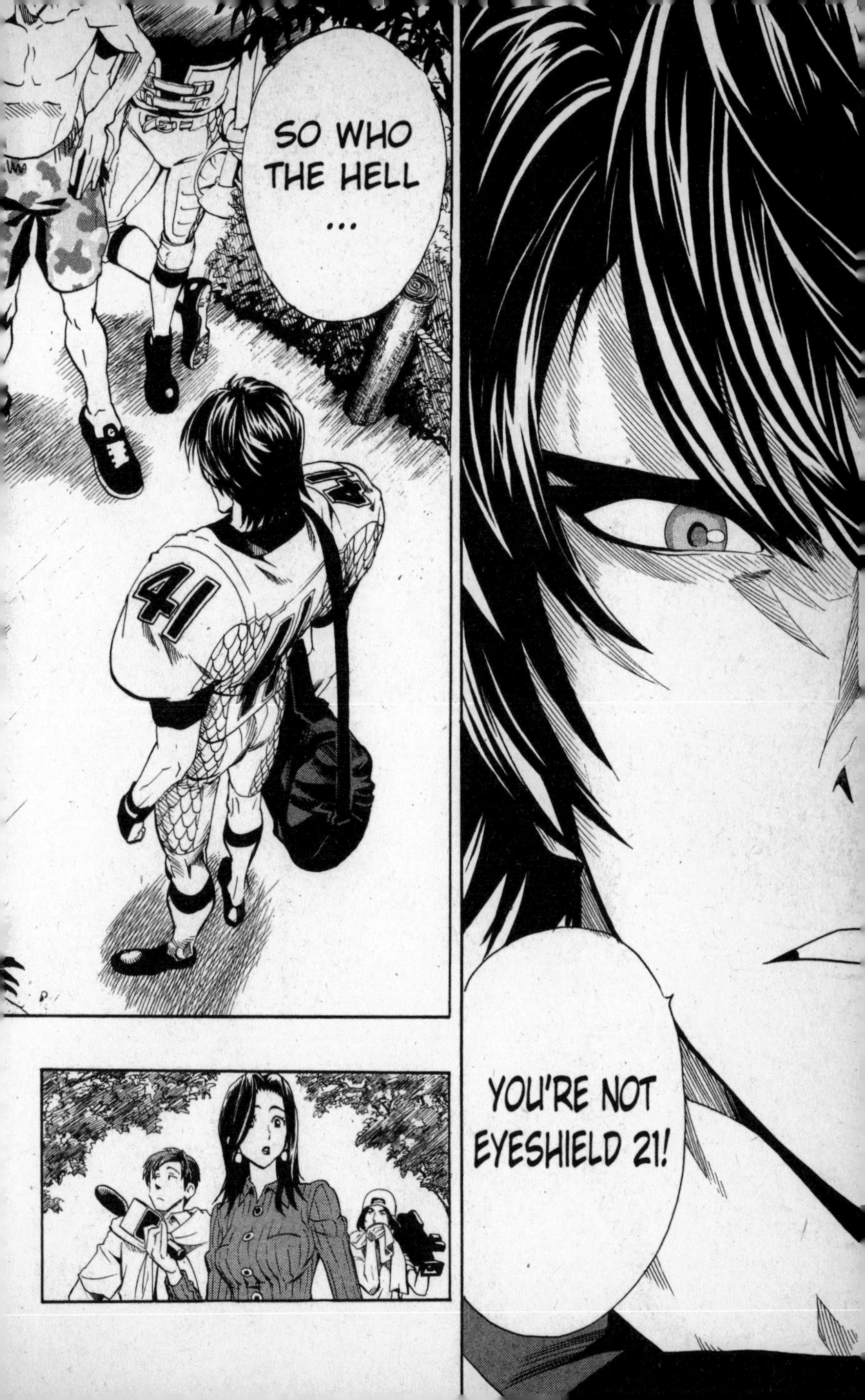
YOU'RE NOT EYESHIELD 21!
SO WHO THE HELL ...

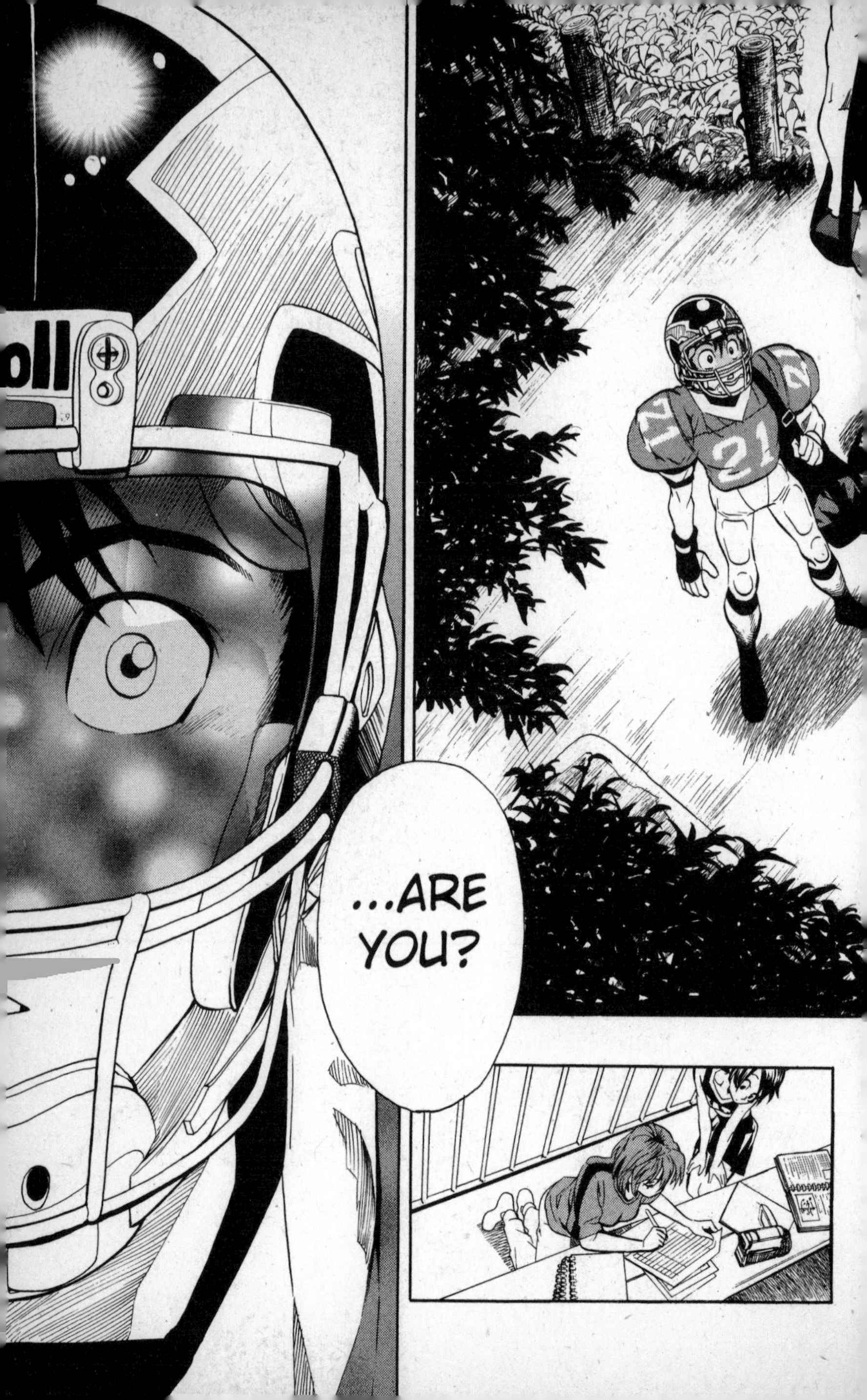
...ARE YOU?

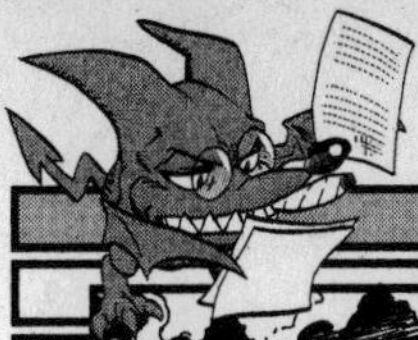

High School Selection Guidance for Prospective Applicants!

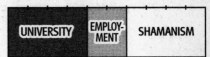

NOROI HIGH SCHOOL

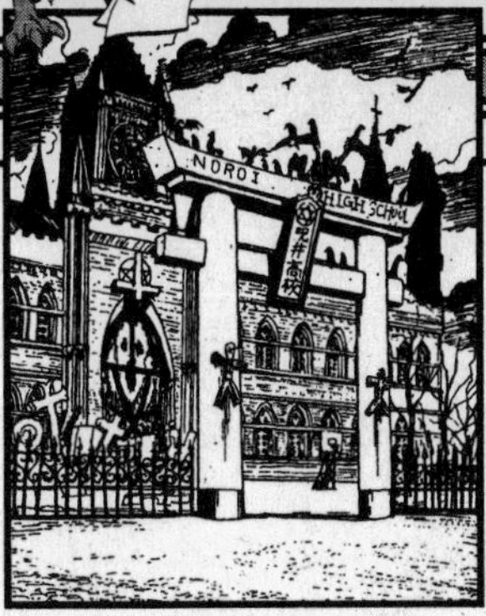
NOROI

Student Body: 481

Special Campus Facilities: Magic Circle

Major Career Options after Graduation

UNIVERSITY	EMPLOYMENT	SHAMANISM

The school's special Hoodoo curriculum accounts for half of all classes. Of course, this puts a strain on the other subjects, but as the students like to say, "Hex your teacher, and you can get any grade you want!"

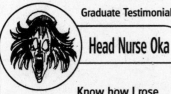

Graduate Testimonial

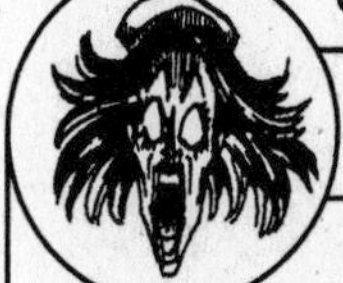

Head Nurse Oka

Know how I rose to be head nurse so quickly? I bet you thought **I put a curse on the hospital director!** Well, you're wrong! **I put a curse on myself**, one that would kill me if I didn't move up! That's the kind of spirit I learned at this school!

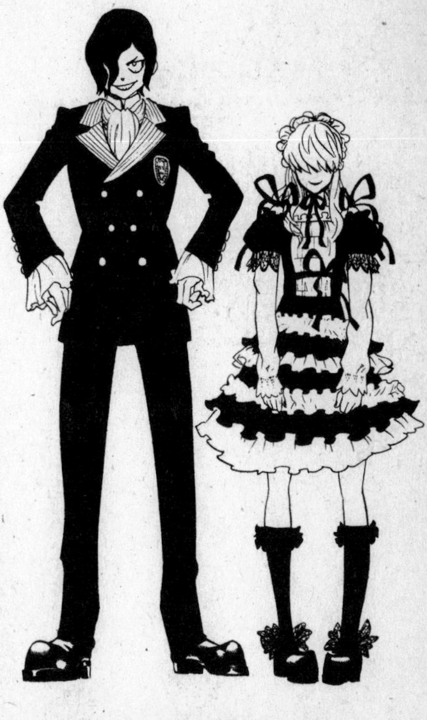

UNIFORM

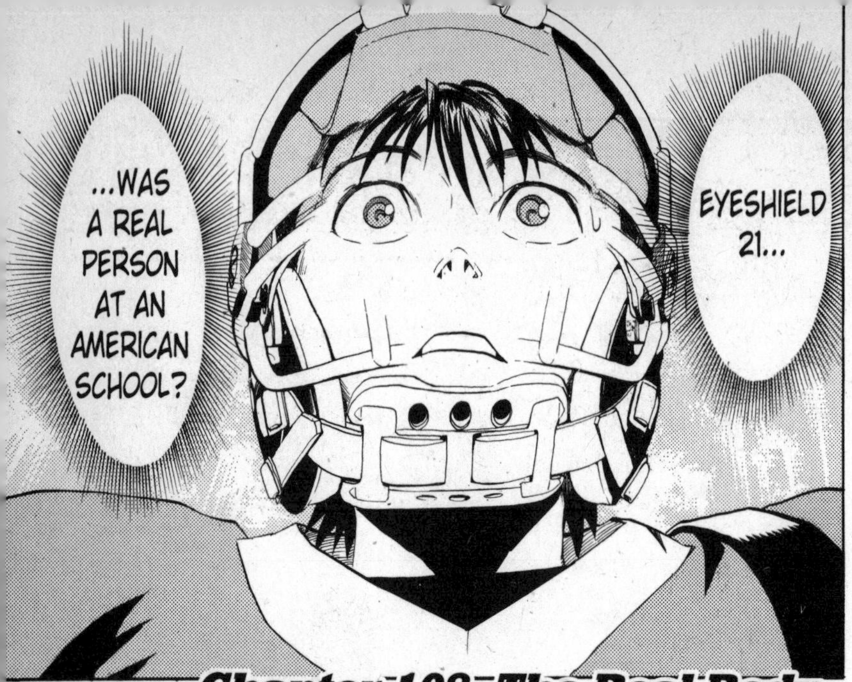
EYESHIELD 21...
...WAS A REAL PERSON AT AN AMERICAN SCHOOL?

Chapter 108 The Real Body

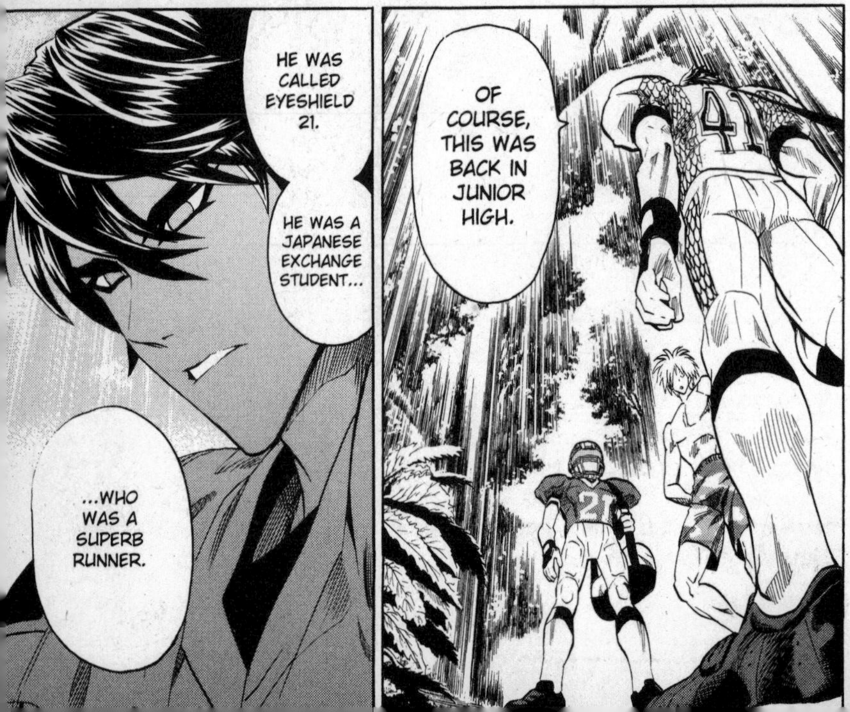
OF COURSE, THIS WAS BACK IN JUNIOR HIGH.
HE WAS CALLED EYESHIELD 21.
HE WAS A JAPANESE EXCHANGE STUDENT...
...WHO WAS A SUPERB RUNNER.

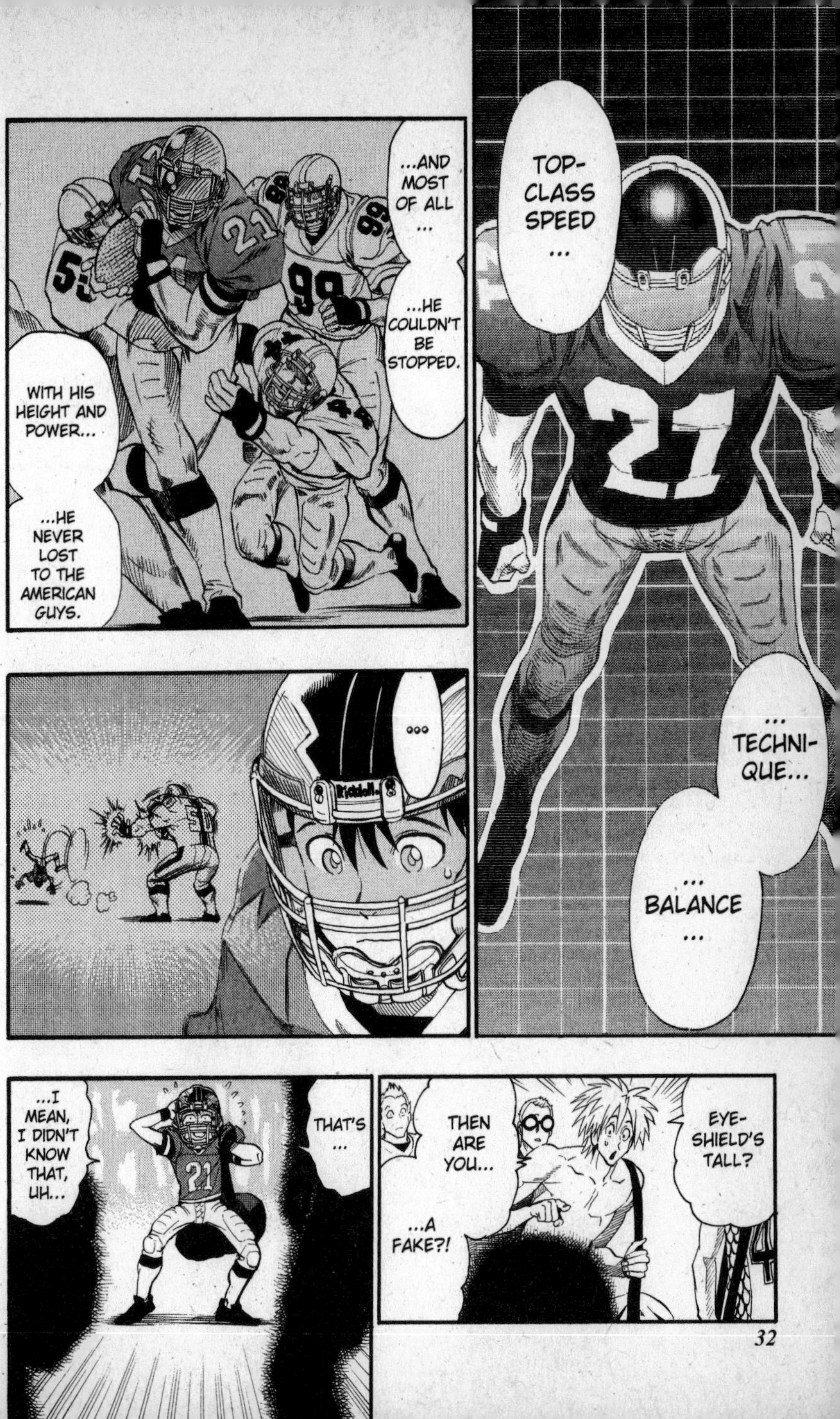
TOP-CLASS SPEED ...
... TECHNIQUE...
... BALANCE ...
...AND MOST OF ALL ...
...HE COULDN'T BE STOPPED.
WITH HIS HEIGHT AND POWER...
...HE NEVER LOST TO THE AMERICAN GUYS.
...
EYE-SHIELD'S TALL?
THEN ARE YOU...
...A FAKE?!
THAT'S ...
...I MEAN, I DIDN'T KNOW THAT, UH...

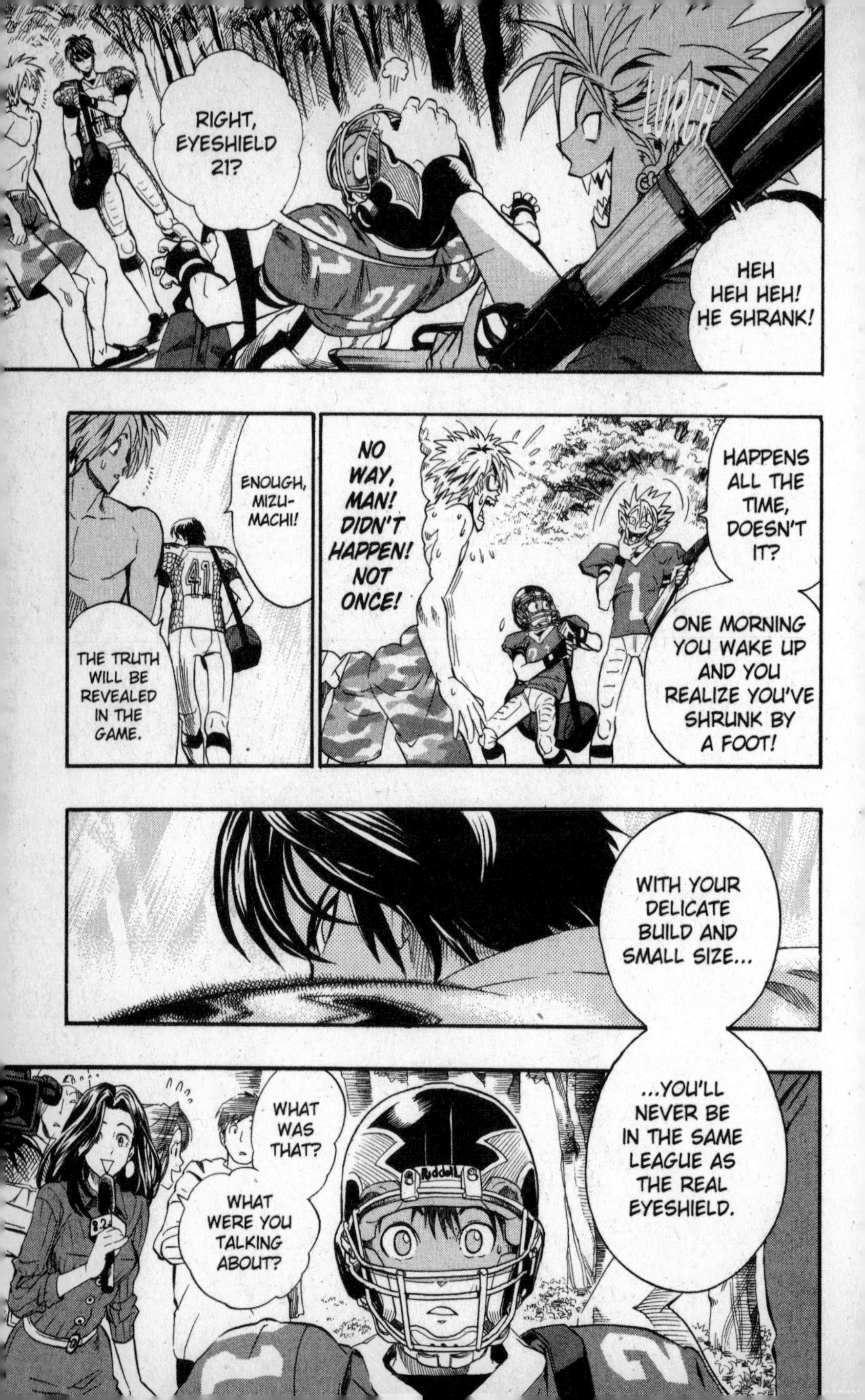
HEH HEH HEH! HE SHRANK!
LURCH
RIGHT, EYESHIELD 21?
HAPPENS ALL THE TIME, DOESN'T IT?
ONE MORNING YOU WAKE UP AND YOU REALIZE YOU'VE SHRUNK BY A FOOT!
NO WAY, MAN! DIDN'T HAPPEN! NOT ONCE!
ENOUGH, MIZUMACHI!
THE TRUTH WILL BE REVEALED IN THE GAME.
WITH YOUR DELICATE BUILD AND SMALL SIZE...
...YOU'LL NEVER BE IN THE SAME LEAGUE AS THE REAL EYESHIELD.
WHAT WAS THAT?
WHAT WERE YOU TALKING ABOUT?

Chapter 108 The Real Body

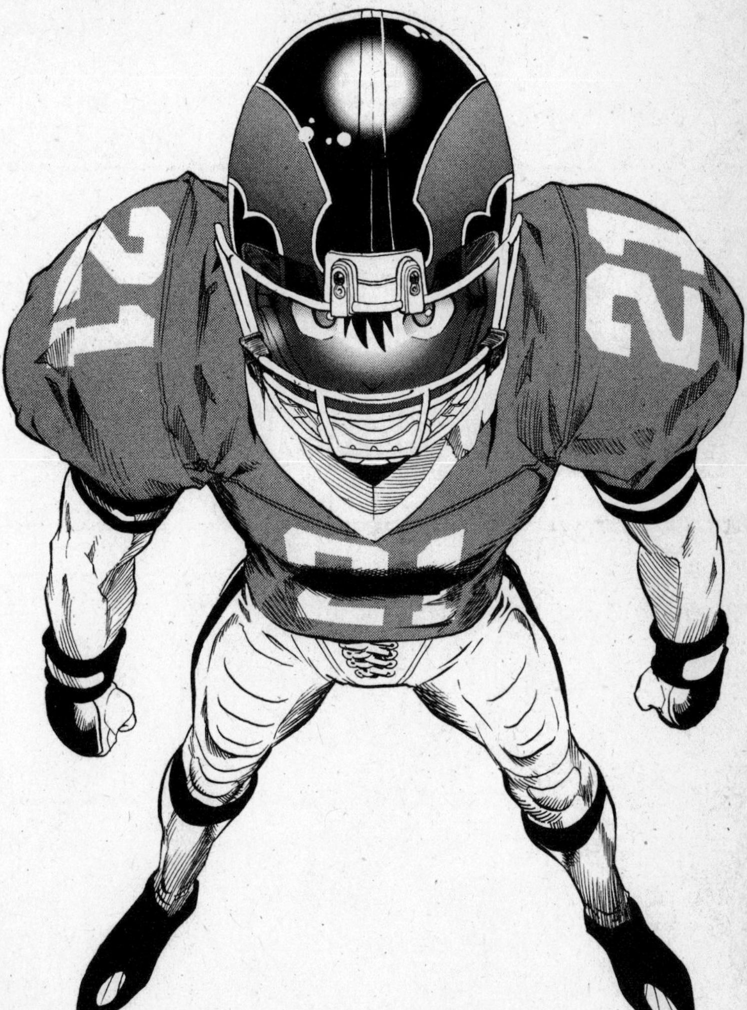

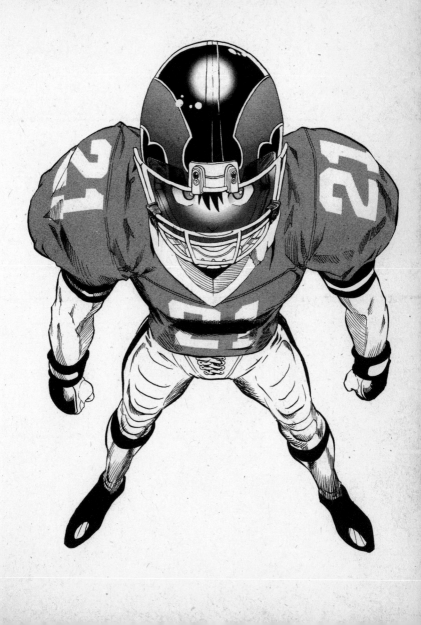

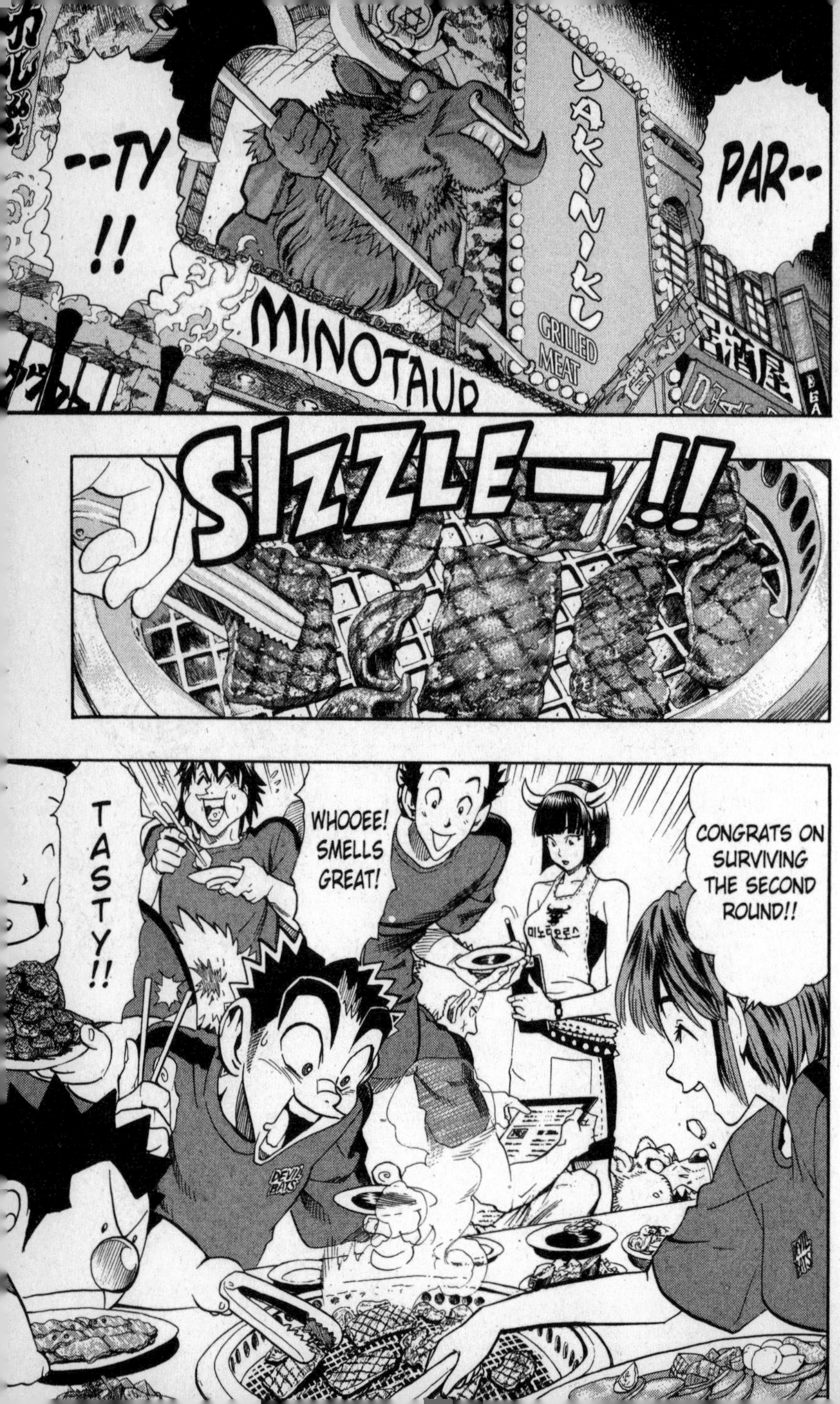
PAR--
--TY !!
YAKINIKU
GRILLED MEAT
MINOTAUR
SIZZLE—!!
CONGRATS ON SURVIVING THE SECOND ROUND!!
WHOOEE! SMELLS GREAT!
TASTY!!

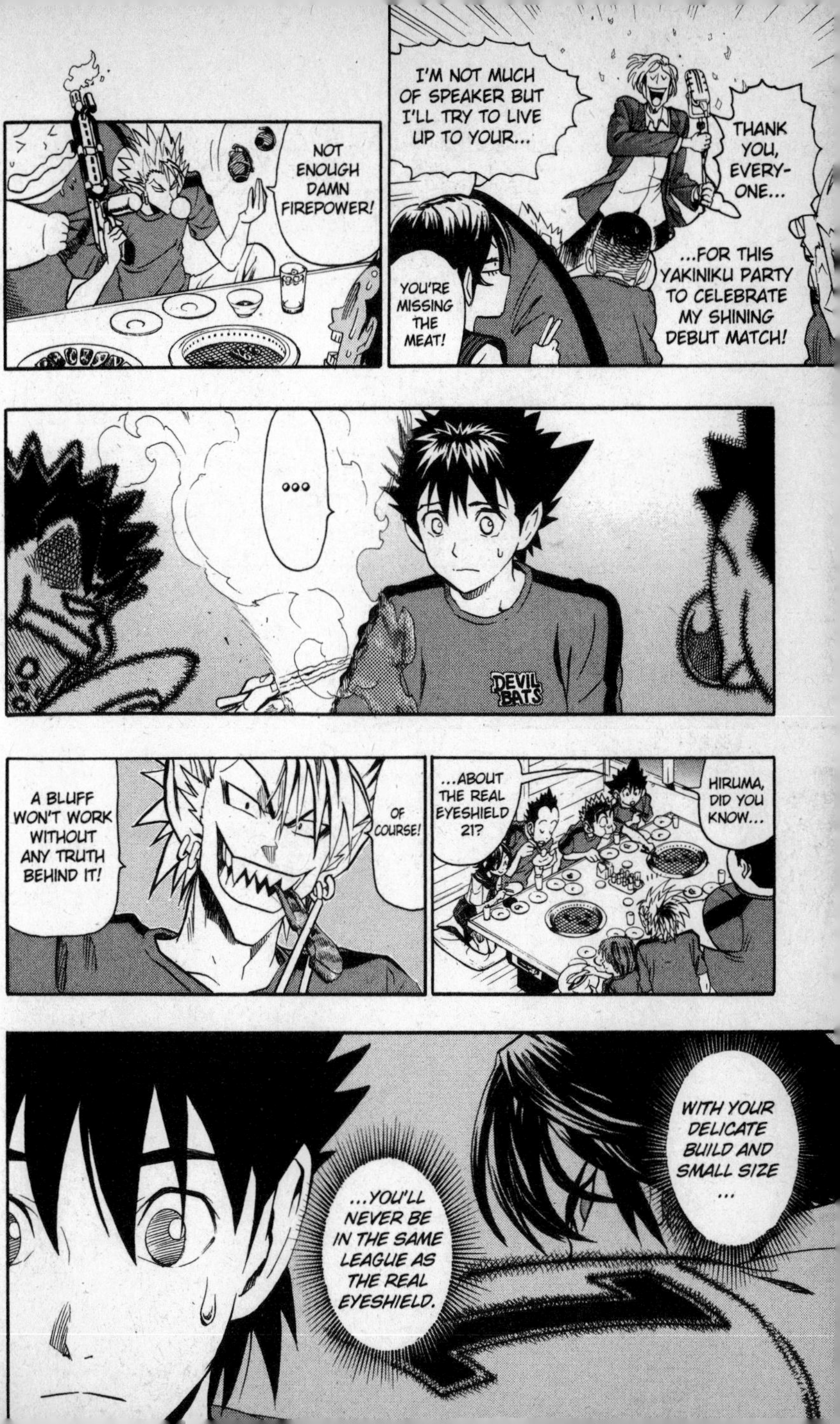
THANK YOU, EVERY-ONE...
...FOR THIS YAKINIKU PARTY TO CELEBRATE MY SHINING DEBUT MATCH!
I'M NOT MUCH OF SPEAKER BUT I'LL TRY TO LIVE UP TO YOUR...
YOU'RE MISSING THE MEAT!
NOT ENOUGH DAMN FIREPOWER!
...
DEVIL BATS
HIRUMA, DID YOU KNOW...
...ABOUT THE REAL EYESHIELD 21?
OF COURSE!
A BLUFF WON'T WORK WITHOUT ANY TRUTH BEHIND IT!
WITH YOUR DELICATE BUILD AND SMALL SIZE...
...YOU'LL NEVER BE IN THE SAME LEAGUE AS THE REAL EYESHIELD.

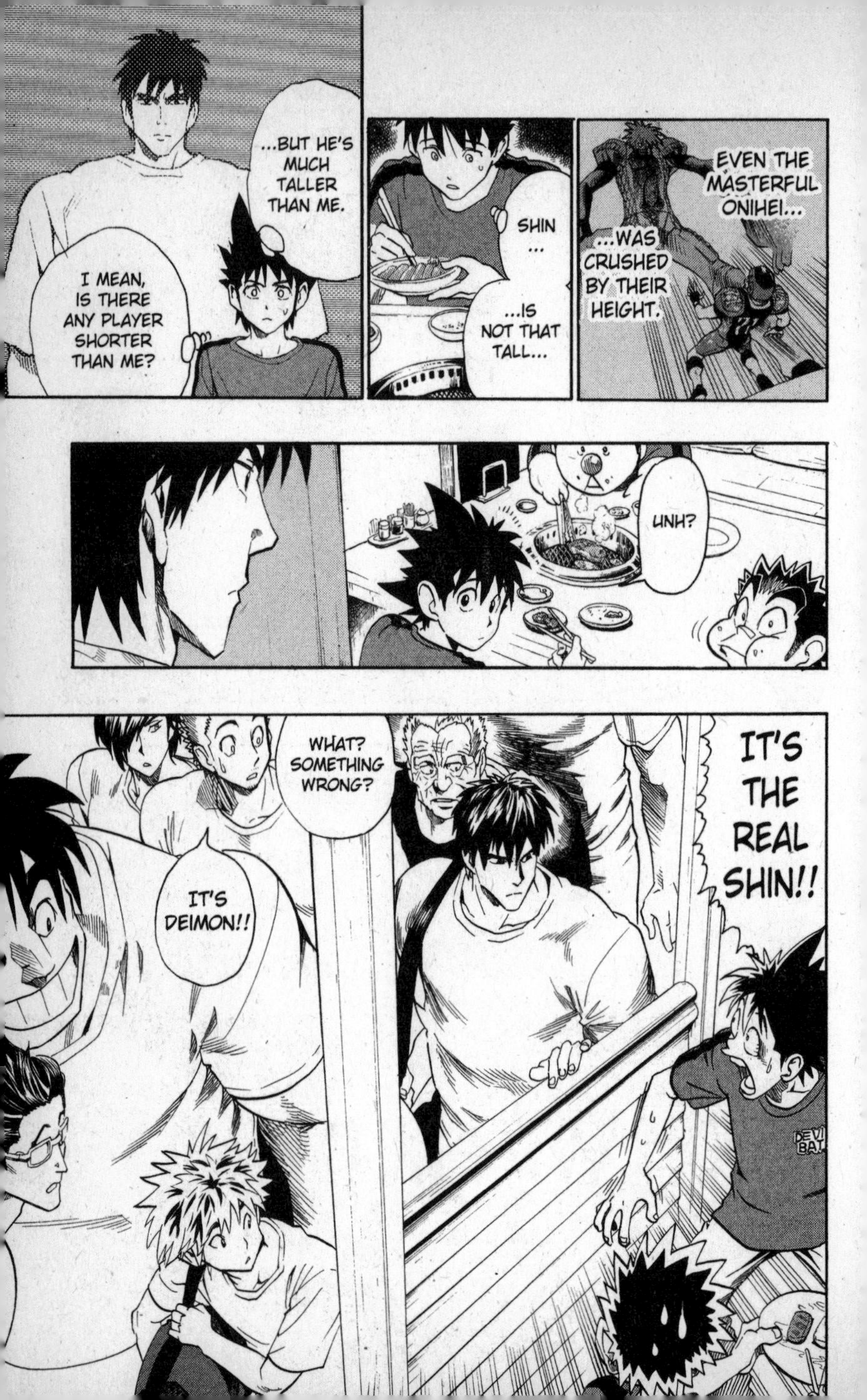
EVEN THE MASTERFUL ONIHEI...
...WAS CRUSHED BY THEIR HEIGHT.
SHIN ...
...IS NOT THAT TALL...
...BUT HE'S MUCH TALLER THAN ME.
I MEAN, IS THERE ANY PLAYER SHORTER THAN ME?
UNH?
IT'S THE REAL SHIN!!
WHAT? SOMETHING WRONG?
IT'S DEIMON!!

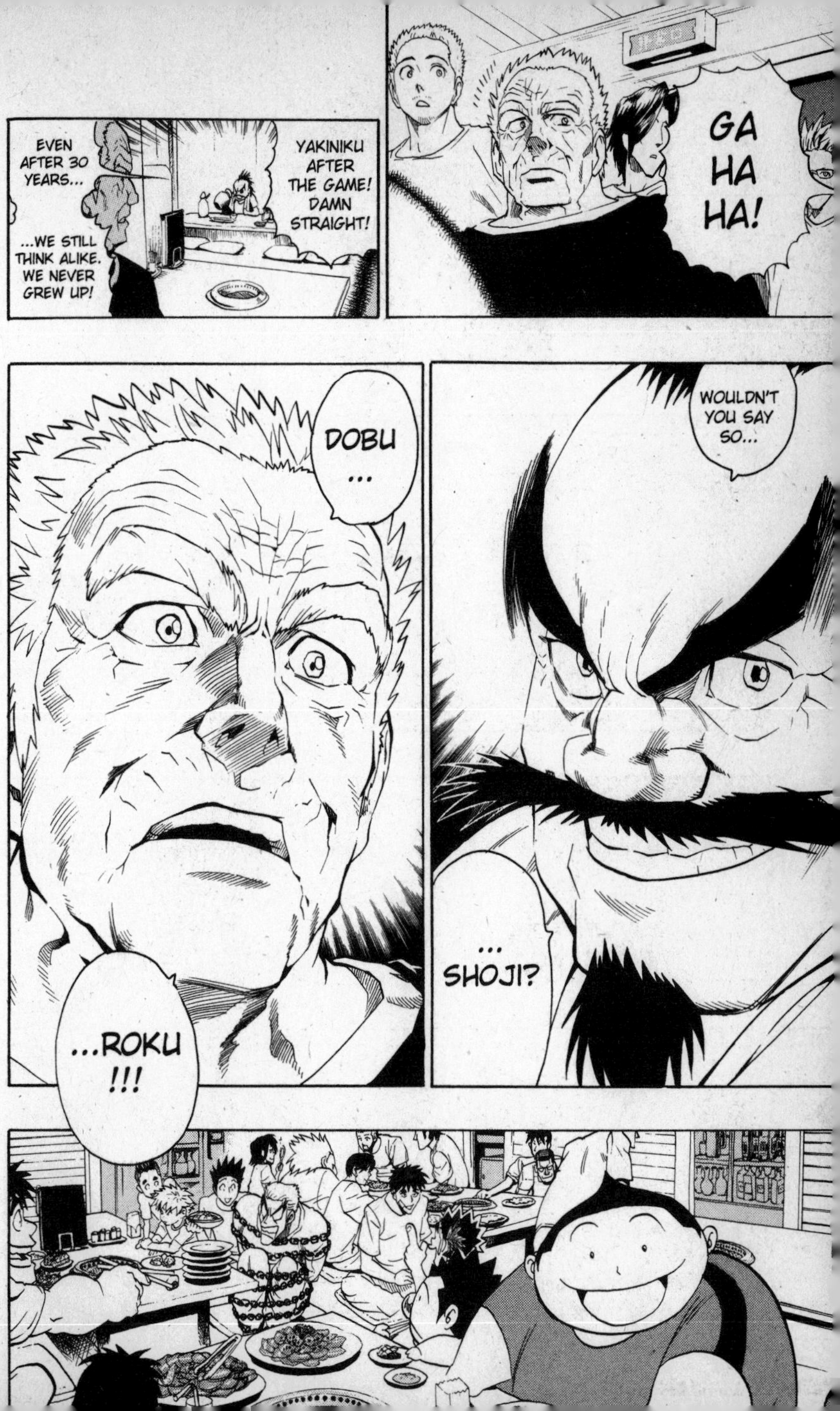
GA HA HA!
YAKINIKU AFTER THE GAME! DAMN STRAIGHT!
EVEN AFTER 30 YEARS...
...WE STILL THINK ALIKE. WE NEVER GREW UP!
WOULDN'T YOU SAY SO...
...SHOJI?
DOBU...
...ROKU!!!

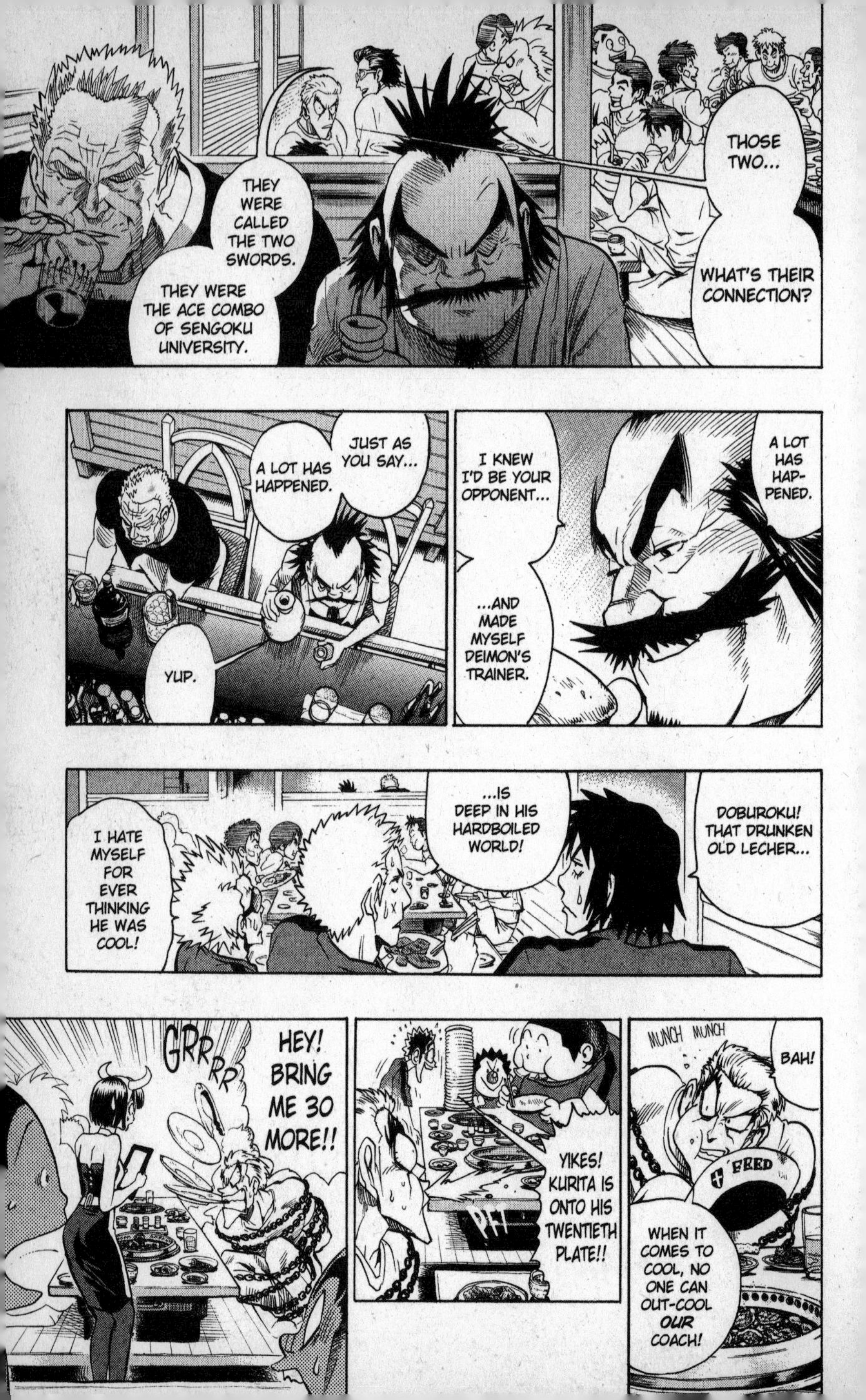
THOSE TWO...
WHAT'S THEIR CONNECTION?
THEY WERE CALLED THE TWO SWORDS.
THEY WERE THE ACE COMBO OF SENGOKU UNIVERSITY.
A LOT HAS HAP-PENED.
I KNEW I'D BE YOUR OPPONENT...
...AND MADE MYSELF DEIMON'S TRAINER.
JUST AS YOU SAY...
A LOT HAS HAPPENED.
YUP.
DOBUROKU! THAT DRUNKEN OLD LECHER...
...IS DEEP IN HIS HARDBOILED WORLD!
I HATE MYSELF FOR EVER THINKING HE WAS COOL!
MUNCH MUNCH
BAH!
FRED
WHEN IT COMES TO COOL, NO ONE CAN OUT-COOL OUR COACH!
YIKES! KURITA IS ONTO HIS TWENTIETH PLATE!!
HEY! BRING ME 30 MORE!!
GRRRR

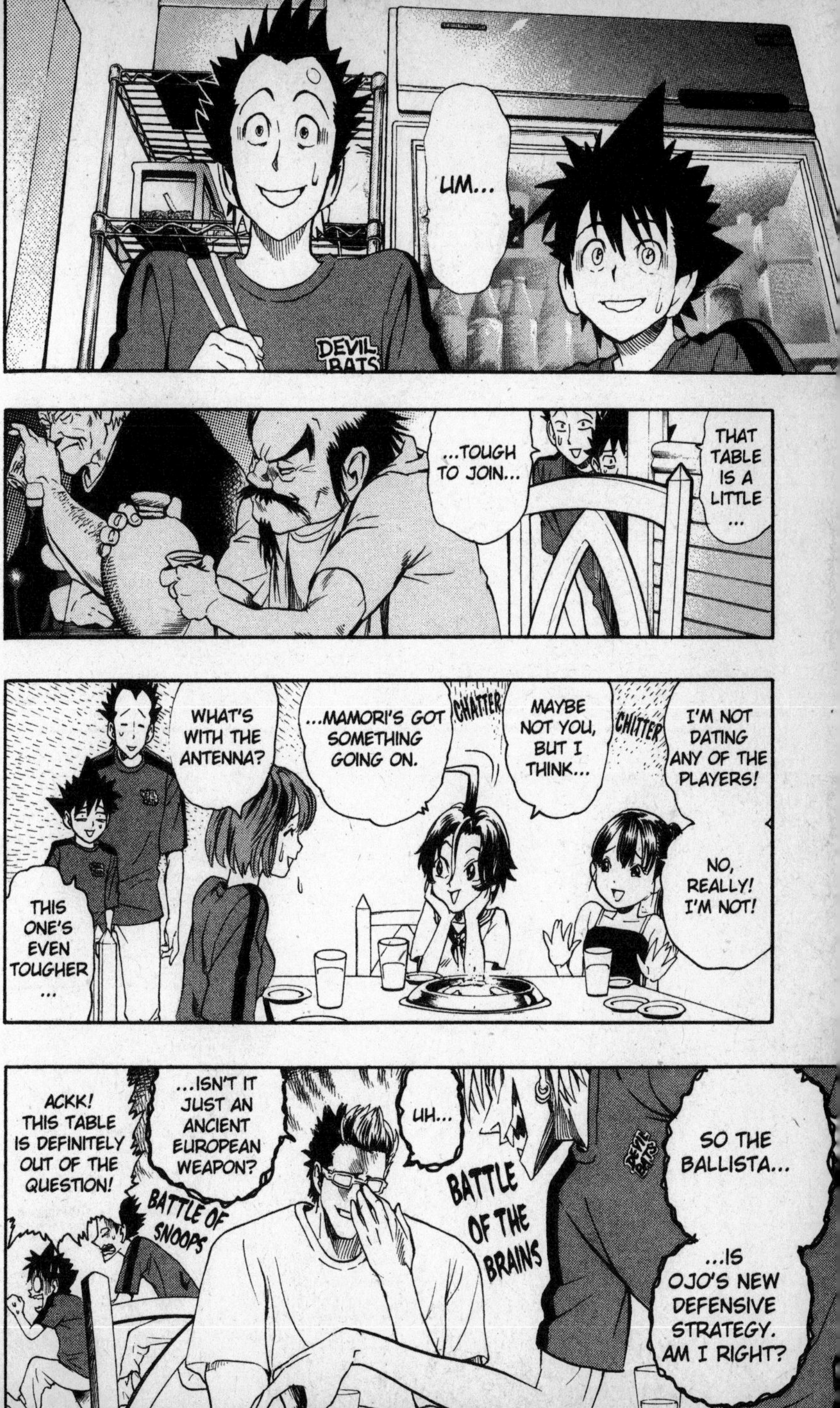
UM...
DEVIL BATS
THAT TABLE IS A LITTLE ...
...TOUGH TO JOIN...
I'M NOT DATING ANY OF THE PLAYERS!
CHITTER
MAYBE NOT YOU, BUT I THINK...
CHATTER
...MAMORI'S GOT SOMETHING GOING ON.
WHAT'S WITH THE ANTENNA?
NO, REALLY! I'M NOT!
THIS ONE'S EVEN TOUGHER ...
SO THE BALLISTA...
DEVIL BATS
BATTLE OF THE BRAINS
UH...
...ISN'T IT JUST AN ANCIENT EUROPEAN WEAPON?
ACKK! THIS TABLE IS DEFINITELY OUT OF THE QUESTION!
BATTLE OF SNOOPS
...IS OJO'S NEW DEFENSIVE STRATEGY. AM I RIGHT?

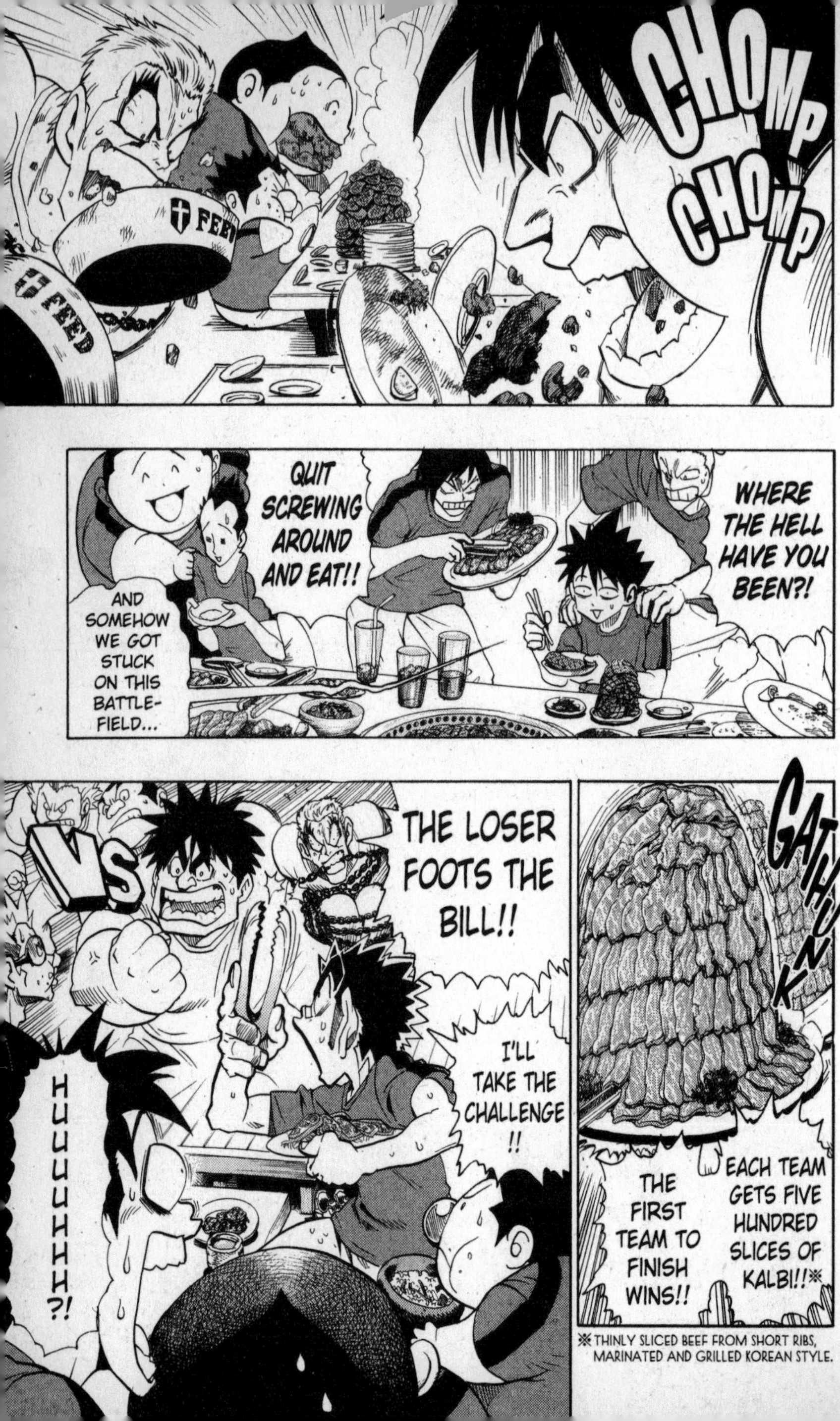
CHOMP
CHOMP
FEED
FEED
WHERE THE HELL HAVE YOU BEEN?!
QUIT SCREWING AROUND AND EAT!!
AND SOMEHOW WE GOT STUCK ON THIS BATTLE-FIELD...
GATHUNK
EACH TEAM GETS FIVE HUNDRED SLICES OF KALBI!!※
THE FIRST TEAM TO FINISH WINS!!
THE LOSER FOOTS THE BILL!!
VS
I'LL TAKE THE CHALLENGE!!
HUUUUUHHH?!

※THINLY SLICED BEEF FROM SHORT RIBS, MARINATED AND GRILLED KOREAN STYLE.

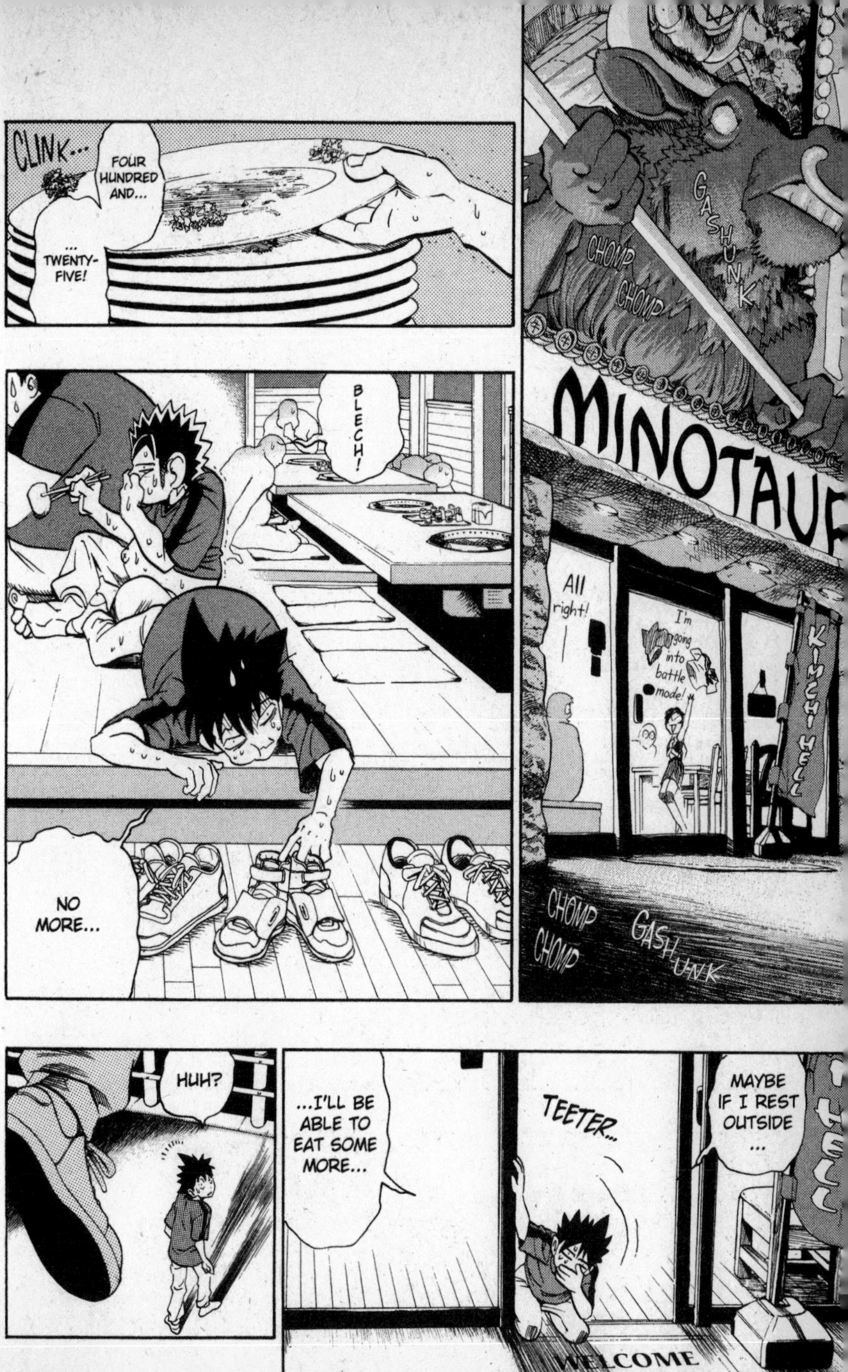
GASHUNK
CHOMP CHOMP
MINOTAU
All right!
I'm going into battle mode!
KIMCHI HELL
CHOMP CHOMP
GASHUNK
CLINK...
FOUR HUNDRED AND...
... TWENTY-FIVE!
BLECH!
NO MORE...
MAYBE IF I REST OUTSIDE ...
TEETER...
HELL
WELCOME
...I'LL BE ABLE TO EAT SOME MORE...
HUH?

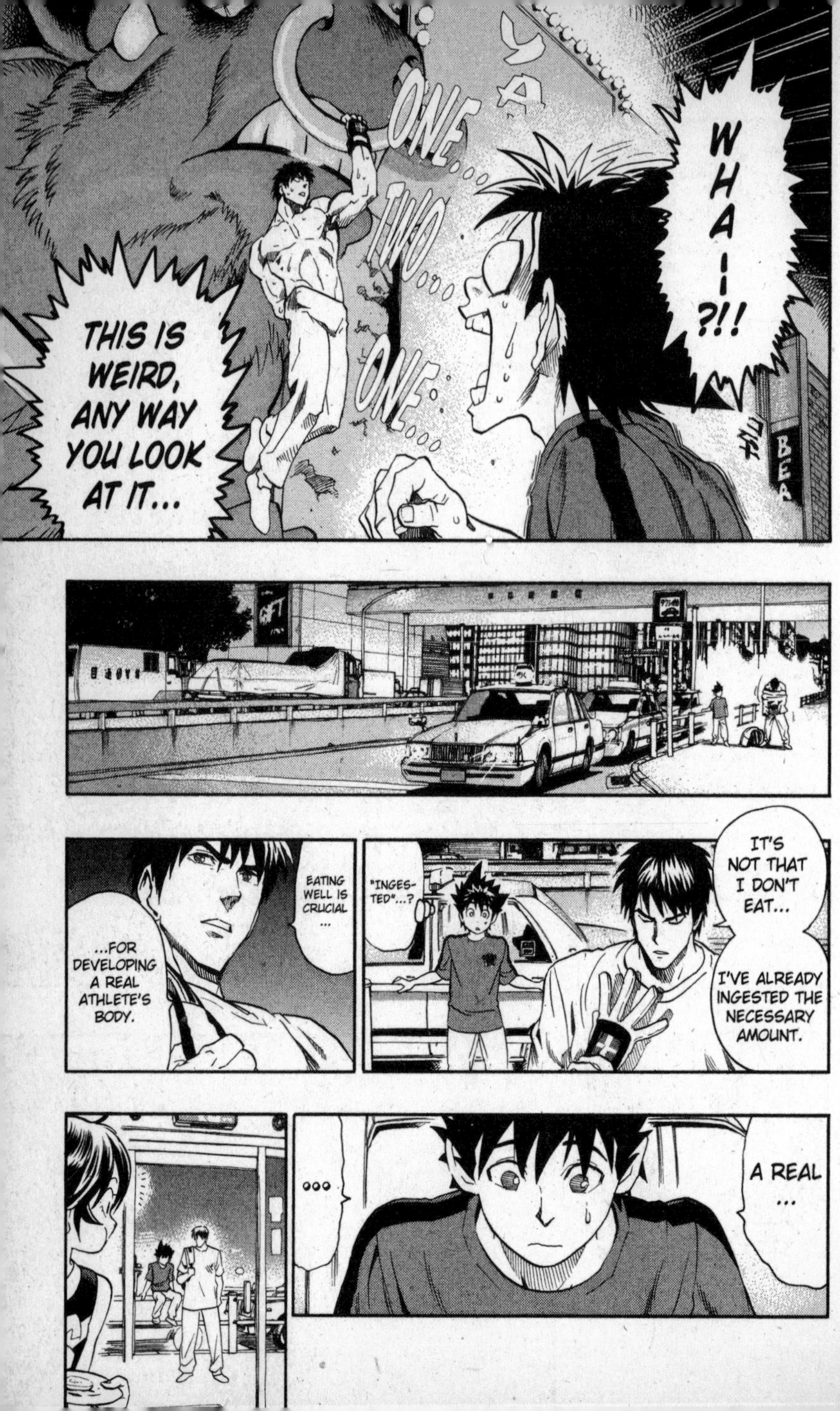
WHA I ?!!
YA
ONE... TWO... ONE...
BEA
THIS IS WEIRD, ANY WAY YOU LOOK AT IT...
IT'S NOT THAT I DON'T EAT...
I'VE ALREADY INGESTED THE NECESSARY AMOUNT.
"INGES-TED"...?
EATING WELL IS CRUCIAL ...
...FOR DEVELOPING A REAL ATHLETE'S BODY.
A REAL ...
...

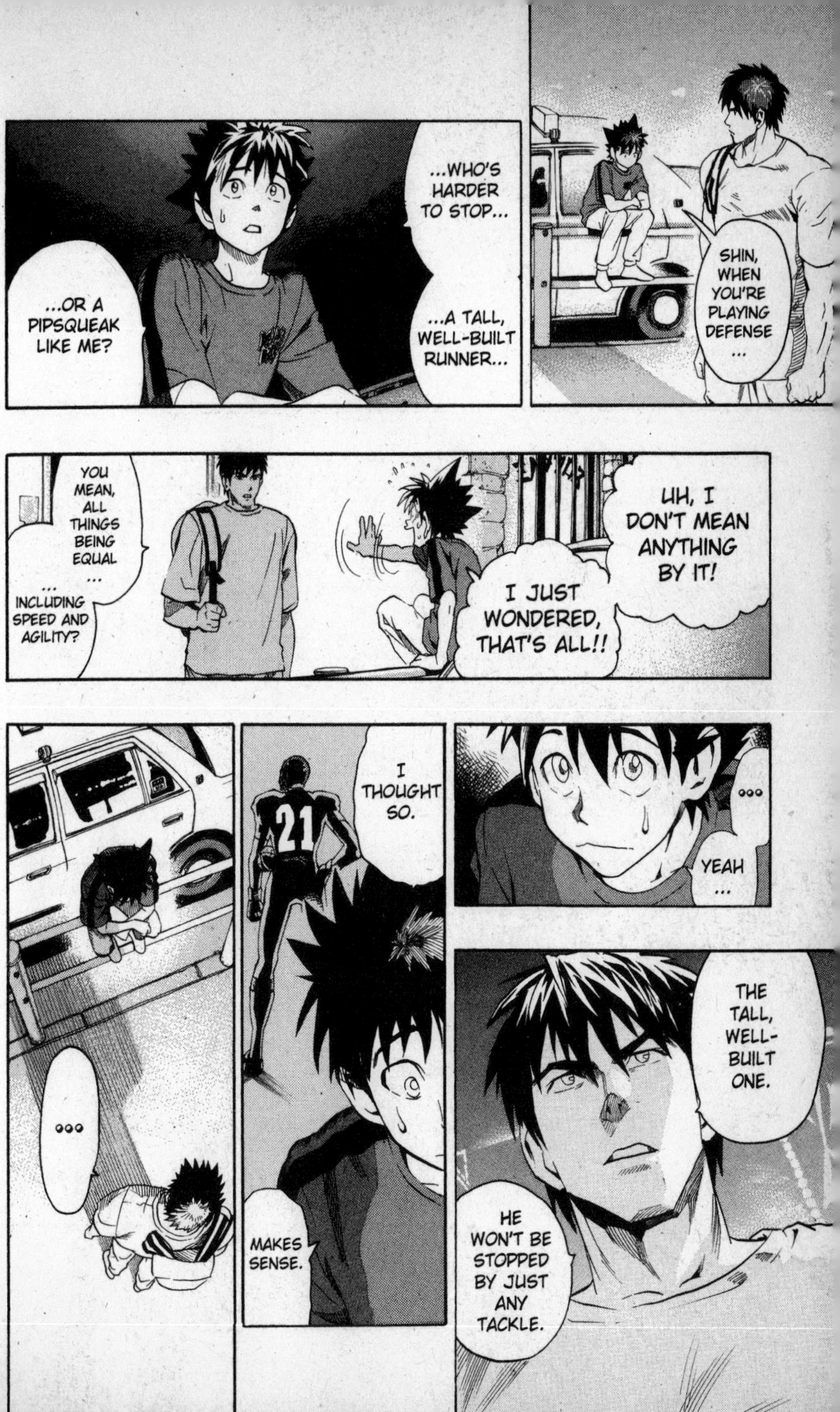
SHIN, WHEN YOU'RE PLAYING DEFENSE ...
...WHO'S HARDER TO STOP...
...A TALL, WELL-BUILT RUNNER...
...OR A PIPSQUEAK LIKE ME?
YOU MEAN, ALL THINGS BEING EQUAL ... INCLUDING SPEED AND AGILITY?
UH, I DON'T MEAN ANYTHING BY IT!
I JUST WONDERED, THAT'S ALL!!
...
YEAH ...
THE TALL, WELL-BUILT ONE.
HE WON'T BE STOPPED BY JUST ANY TACKLE.
I THOUGHT SO.
MAKES SENSE.
...

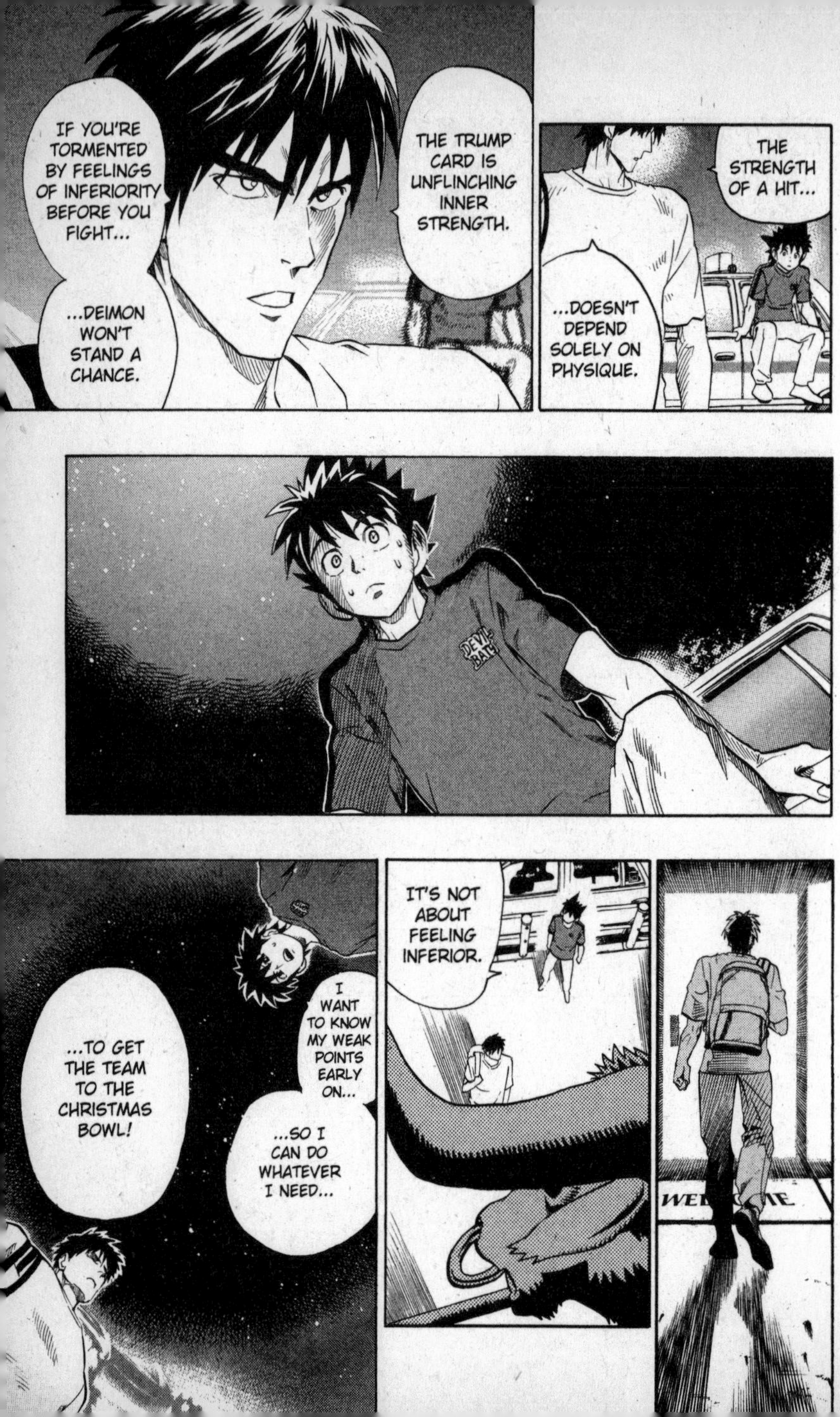
THE STRENGTH OF A HIT...
...DOESN'T DEPEND SOLELY ON PHYSIQUE.
THE TRUMP CARD IS UNFLINCHING INNER STRENGTH.
IF YOU'RE TORMENTED BY FEELINGS OF INFERIORITY BEFORE YOU FIGHT...
...DEIMON WON'T STAND A CHANCE.
IT'S NOT ABOUT FEELING INFERIOR.
I WANT TO KNOW MY WEAK POINTS EARLY ON...
...SO I CAN DO WHATEVER I NEED...
...TO GET THE TEAM TO THE CHRISTMAS BOWL!

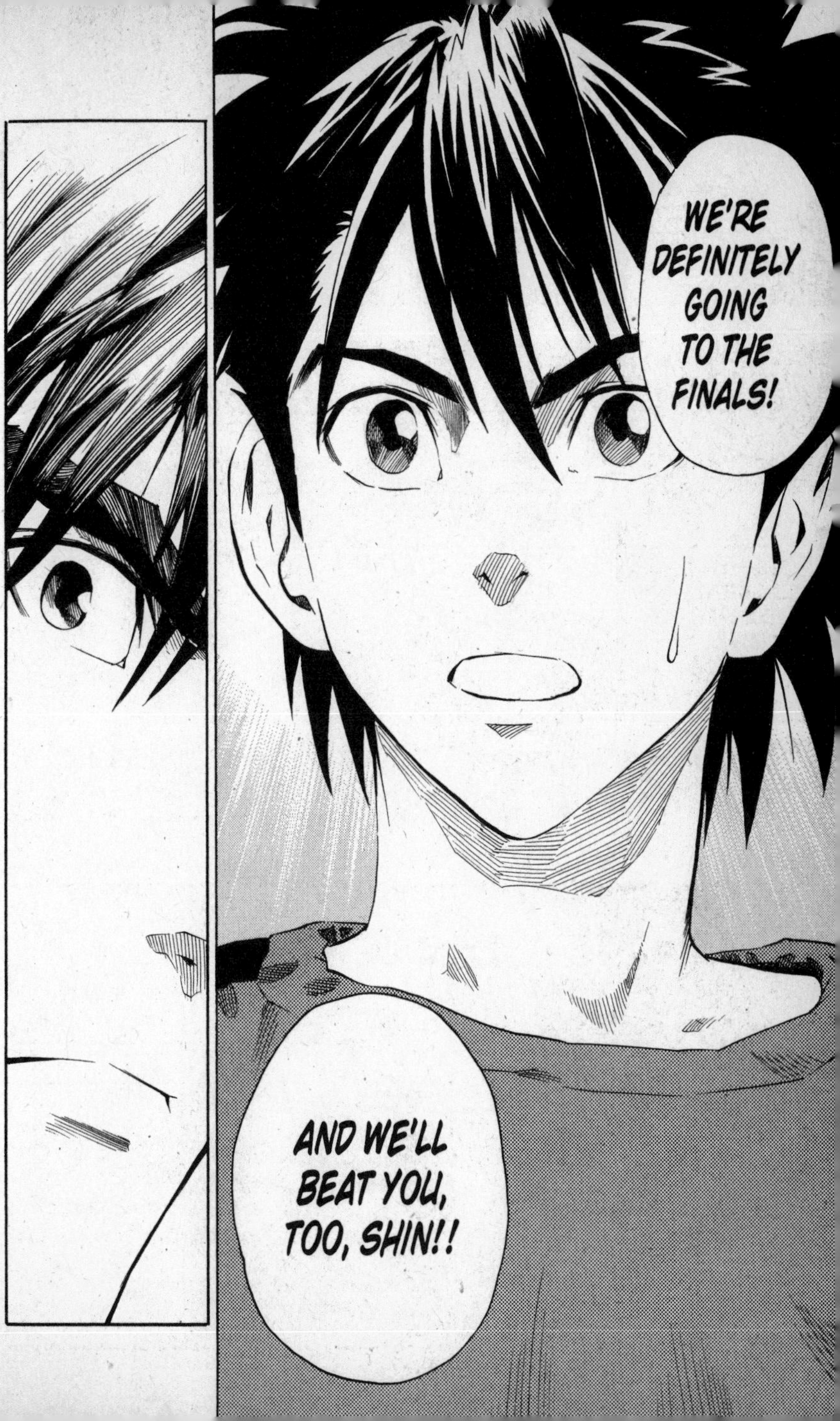
WE'RE DEFINITELY GOING TO THE FINALS!
AND WE'LL BEAT YOU, TOO, SHIN!!

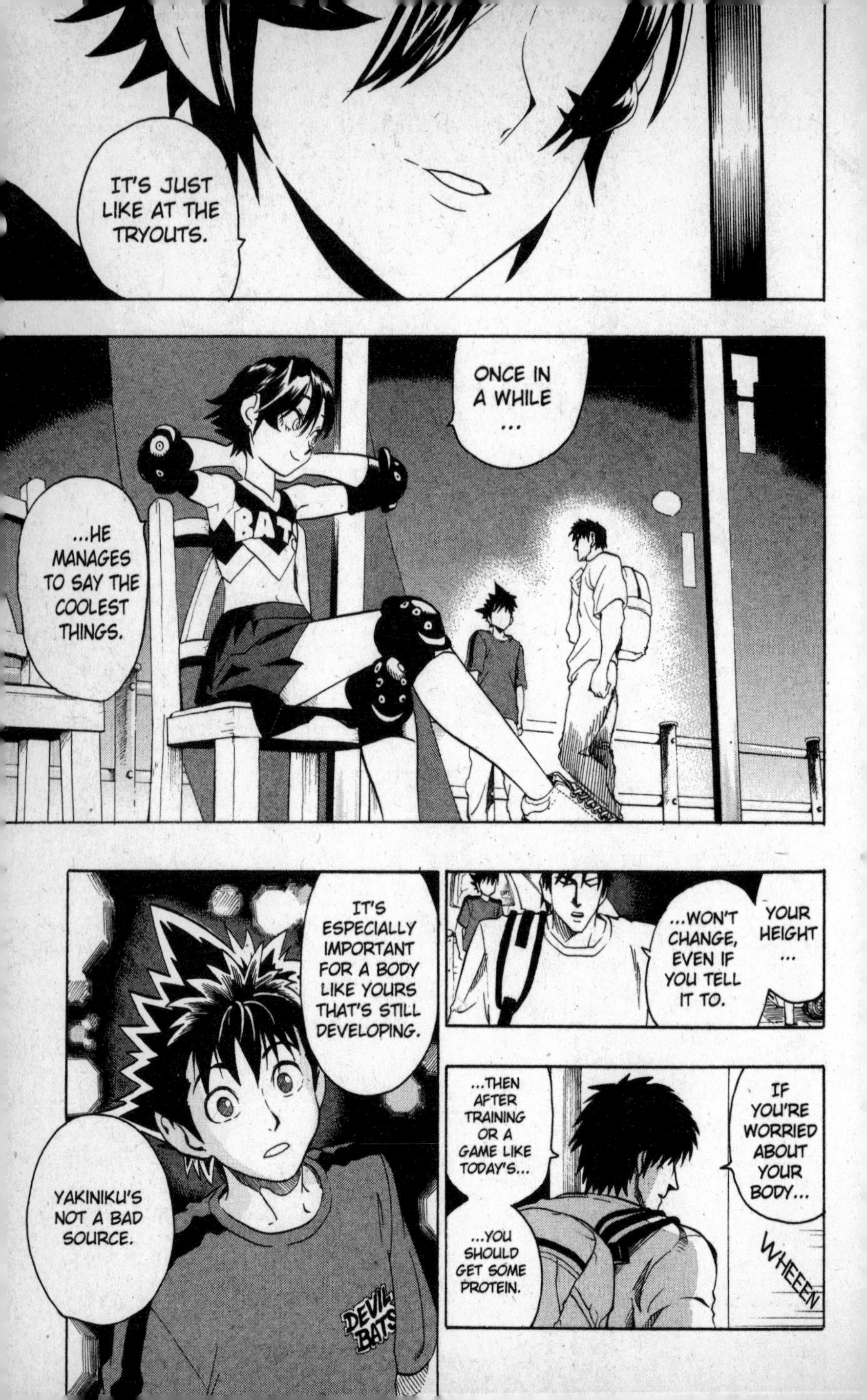
IT'S JUST LIKE AT THE TRYOUTS.
ONCE IN A WHILE ...
...HE MANAGES TO SAY THE COOLEST THINGS.
YOUR HEIGHT ...
...WON'T CHANGE, EVEN IF YOU TELL IT TO.
IF YOU'RE WORRIED ABOUT YOUR BODY...
...THEN AFTER TRAINING OR A GAME LIKE TODAY'S...
...YOU SHOULD GET SOME PROTEIN.
WHEEEN
IT'S ESPECIALLY IMPORTANT FOR A BODY LIKE YOURS THAT'S STILL DEVELOPING.
YAKINIKU'S NOT A BAD SOURCE.
DEVIL BATS

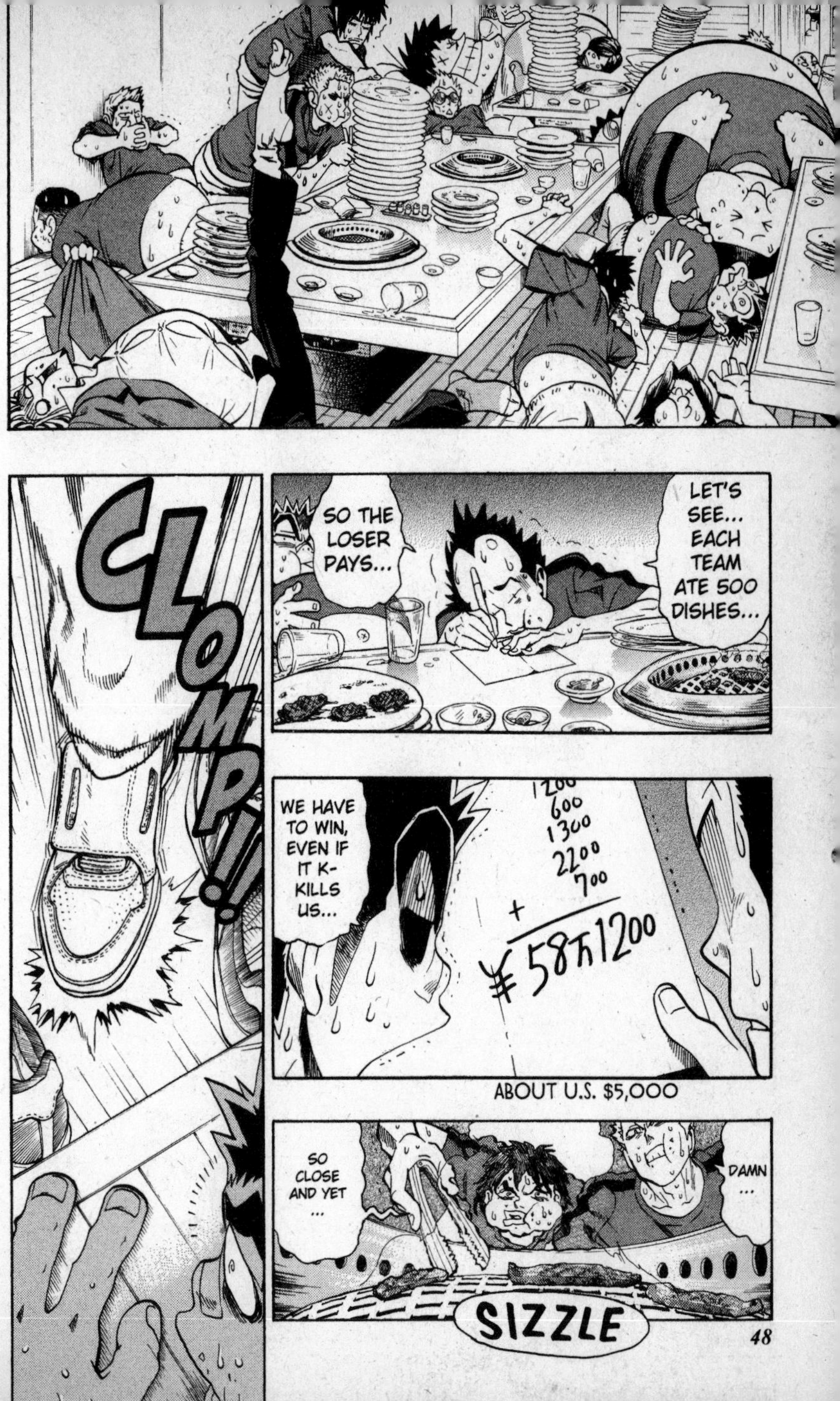
LET'S SEE... EACH TEAM ATE 500 DISHES...
SO THE LOSER PAYS...
1200
600
1300
2200
700
+
¥58万1200
WE HAVE TO WIN, EVEN IF IT K-KILLS US...
ABOUT U.S. $5,000
DAMN ...
SO CLOSE AND YET ...
SIZZLE
CLOMP!!

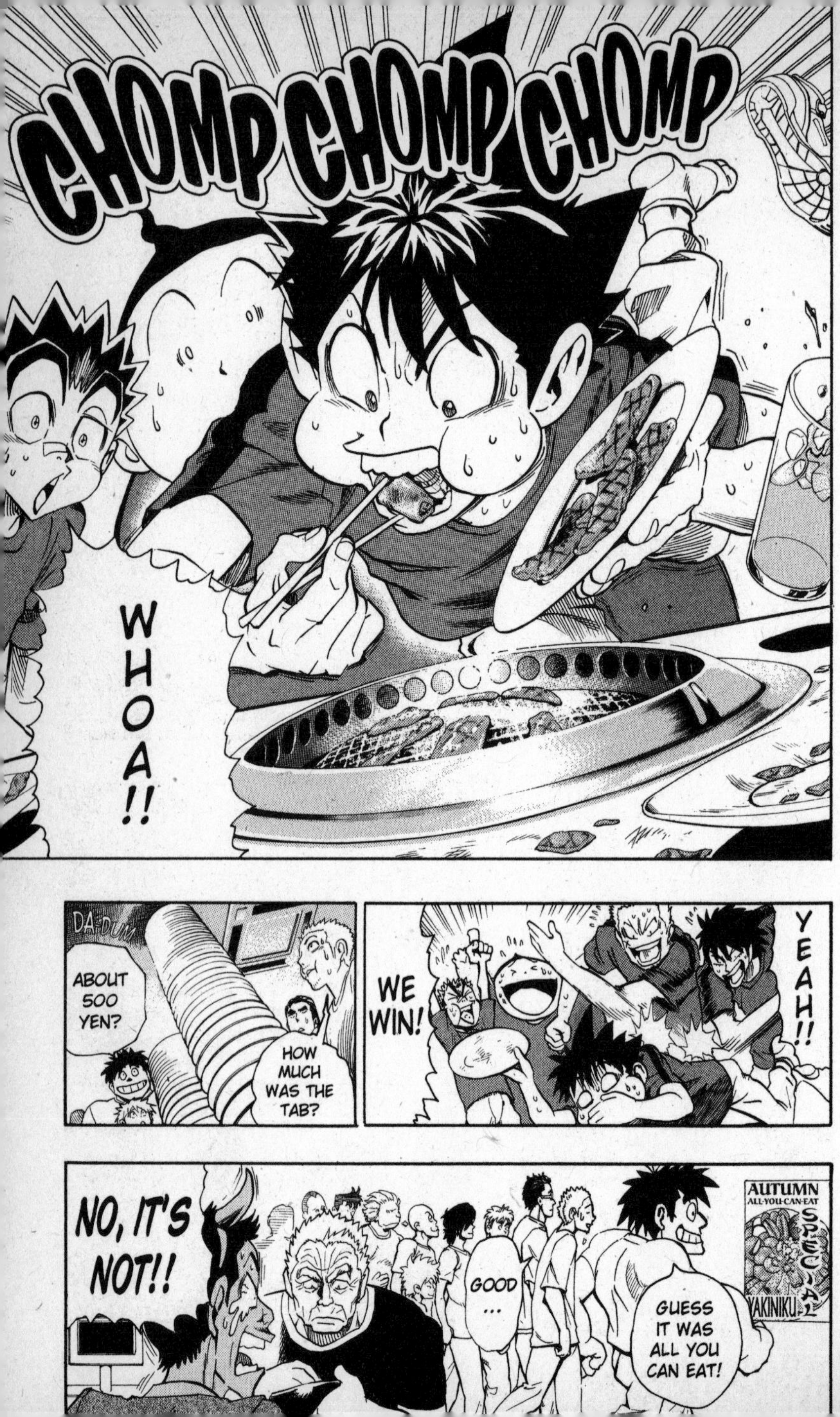
CHOMP CHOMP CHOMP
WHOA!!
YEAH!!
WE WIN!
DA-DUM
HOW MUCH WAS THE TAB?
ABOUT 500 YEN?
AUTUMN ALL-YOU-CAN-EAT YAKINIKU SPECIAL
GUESS IT WAS ALL YOU CAN EAT!
GOOD...
NO, IT'S NOT!!

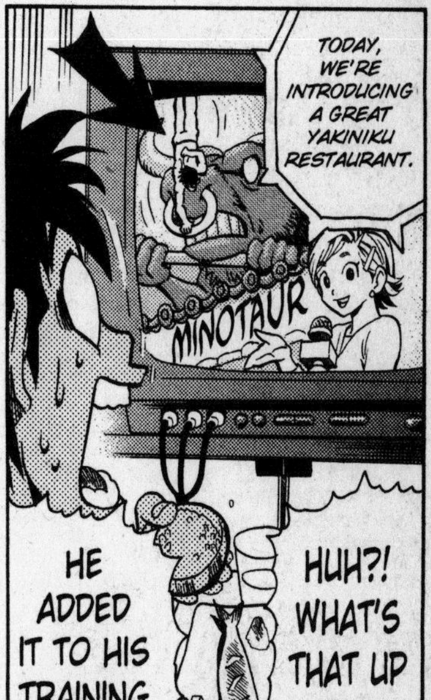
TODAY, WE'RE INTRODUCING A GREAT YAKINIKU RESTAURANT.
MINOTAUR
HUH?! WHAT'S THAT UP THERE?!
HE ADDED IT TO HIS TRAINING MENU!!

First published in *Jump GAG Special 2005 Extra*.

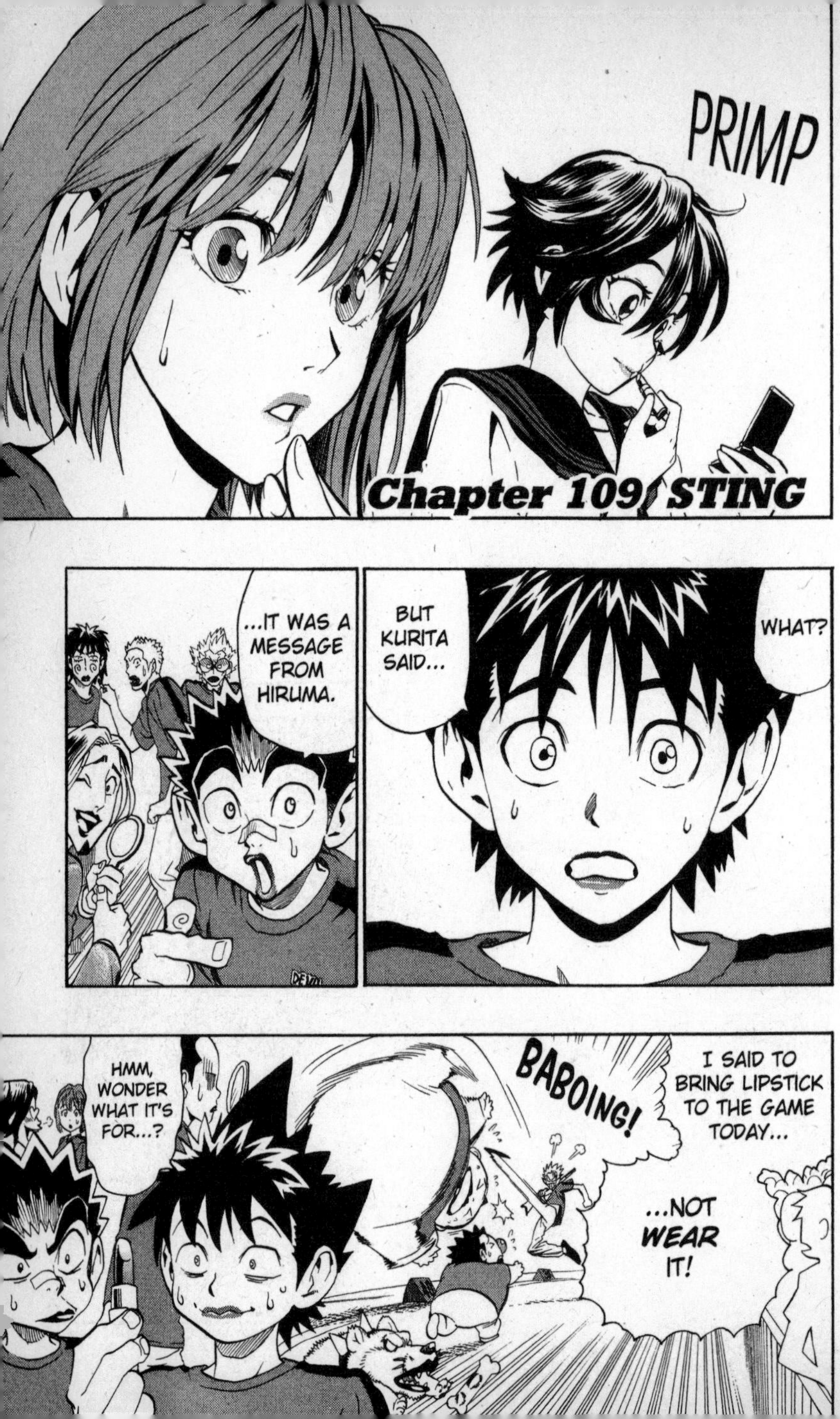
PRIMP
Chapter 109: STING
WHAT?
BUT KURITA SAID...
...IT WAS A MESSAGE FROM HIRUMA.
I SAID TO BRING LIPSTICK TO THE GAME TODAY...
BABOING!
...NOT WEAR IT!
HMM, WONDER WHAT IT'S FOR...?

Chapter 109 STING

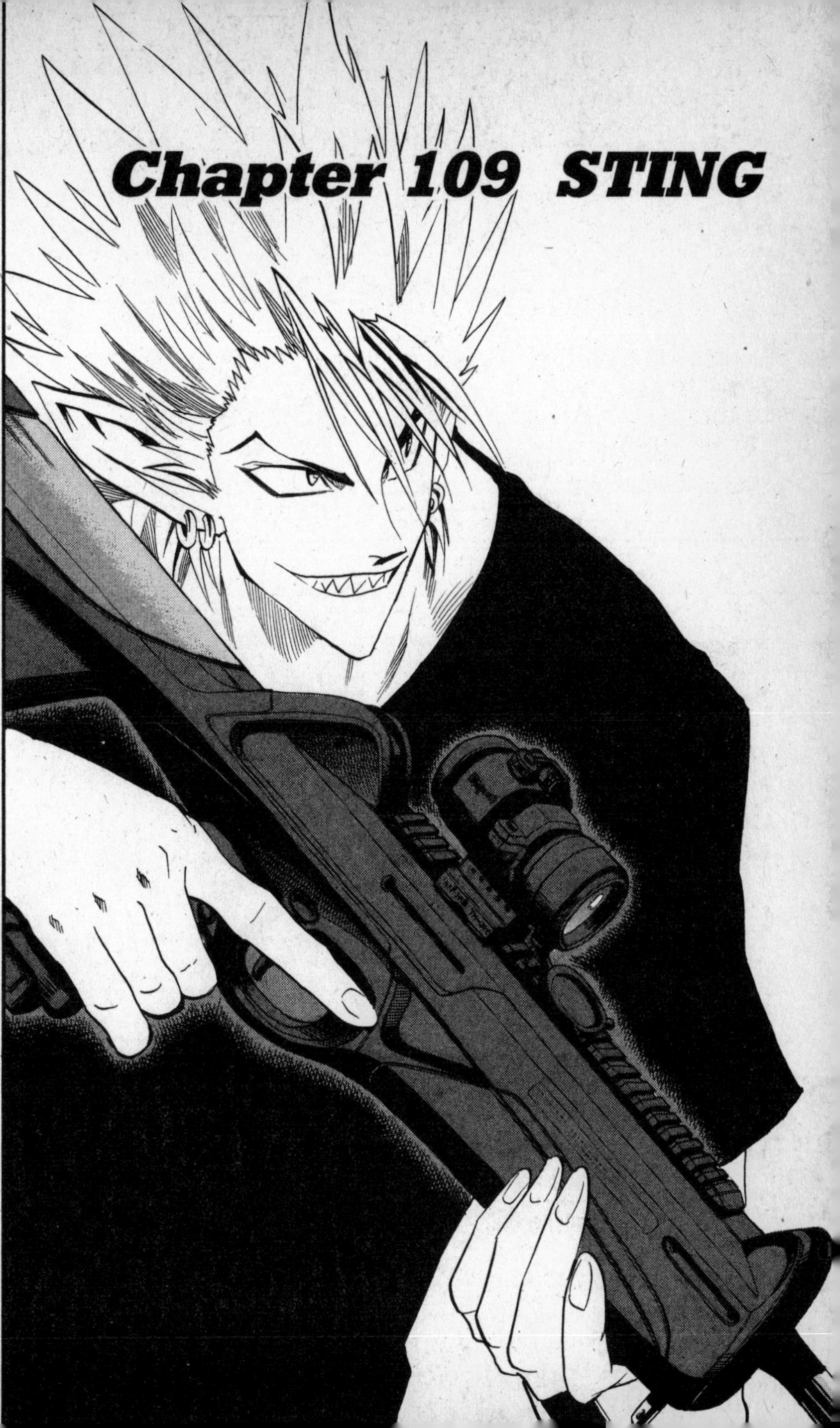

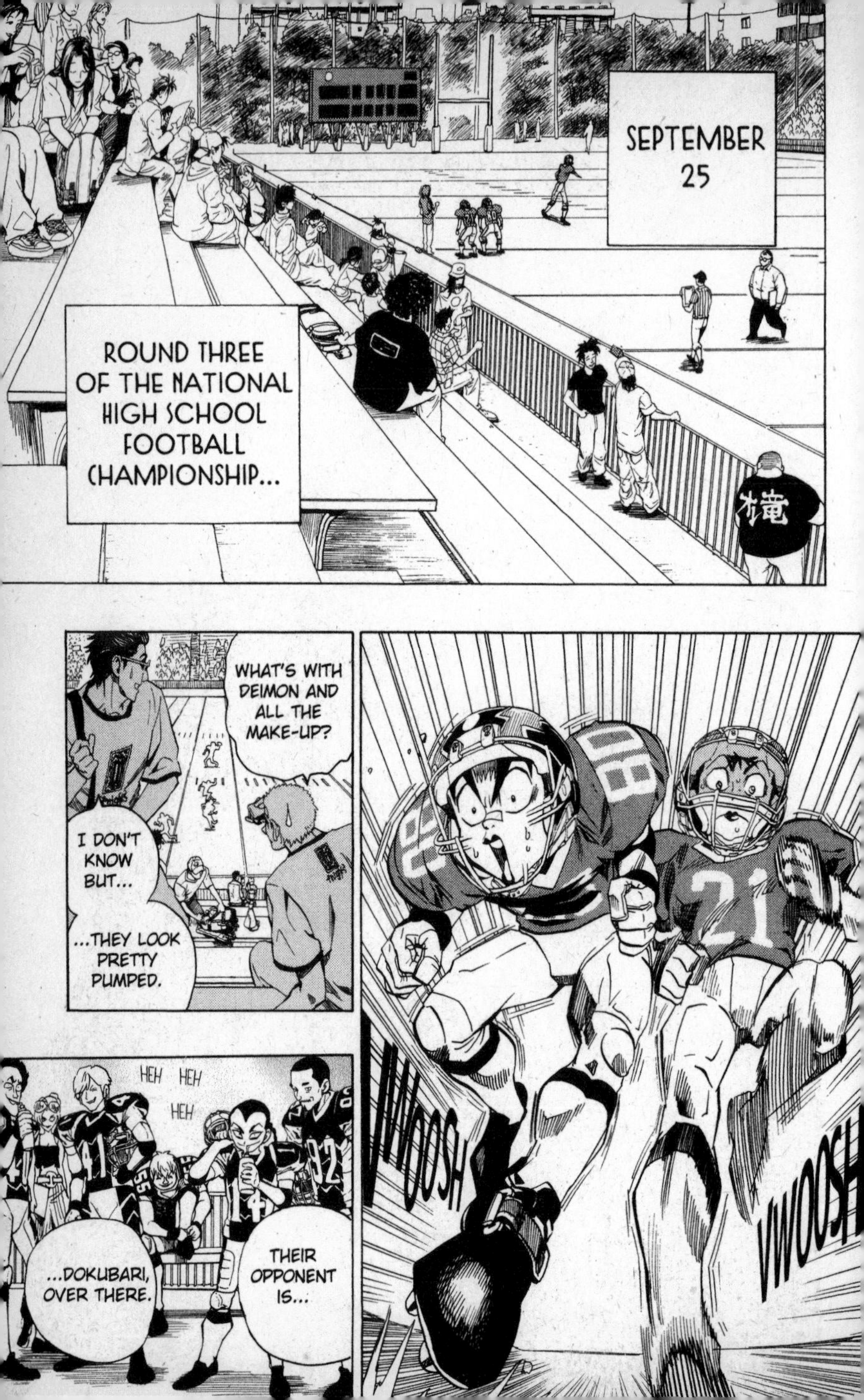
SEPTEMBER 25
ROUND THREE OF THE NATIONAL HIGH SCHOOL FOOTBALL CHAMPIONSHIP...
VWOOSH
VWOOSH
WHAT'S WITH DEIMON AND ALL THE MAKE-UP?
I DON'T KNOW BUT...
...THEY LOOK PRETTY PUMPED.
HEH HEH HEH
THEIR OPPONENT IS...
...DOKUBARI, OVER THERE.

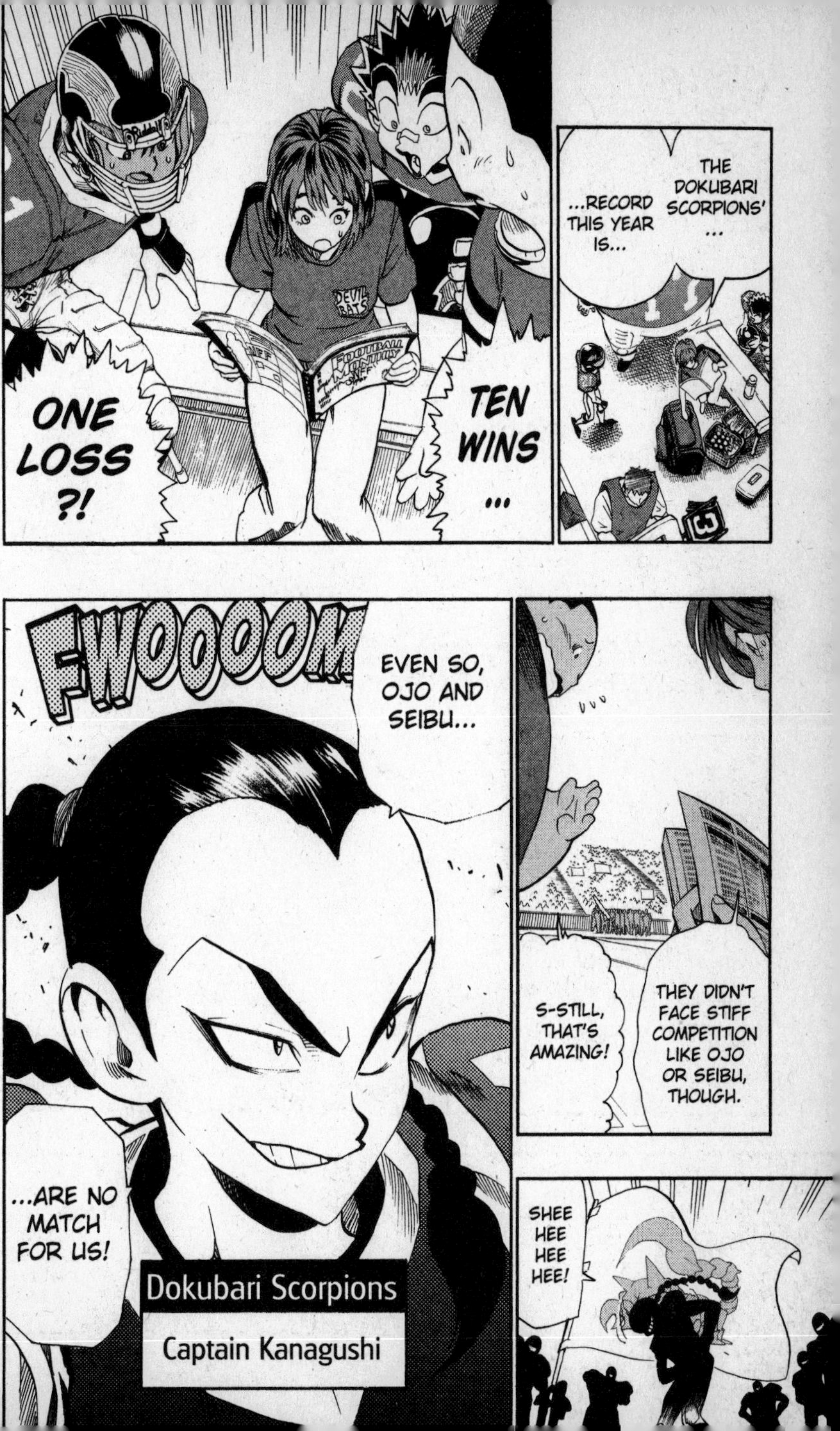
THE DOKUBARI SCORPIONS' ...
...RECORD THIS YEAR IS...
TEN WINS ...
ONE LOSS ?!
THEY DIDN'T FACE STIFF COMPETITION LIKE OJO OR SEIBU, THOUGH.
S-STILL, THAT'S AMAZING!
SHEE HEE HEE HEE!
FWOOOOM
EVEN SO, OJO AND SEIBU...
...ARE NO MATCH FOR US!
Dokubari Scorpions
Captain Kanagushi

READ THIS WAY

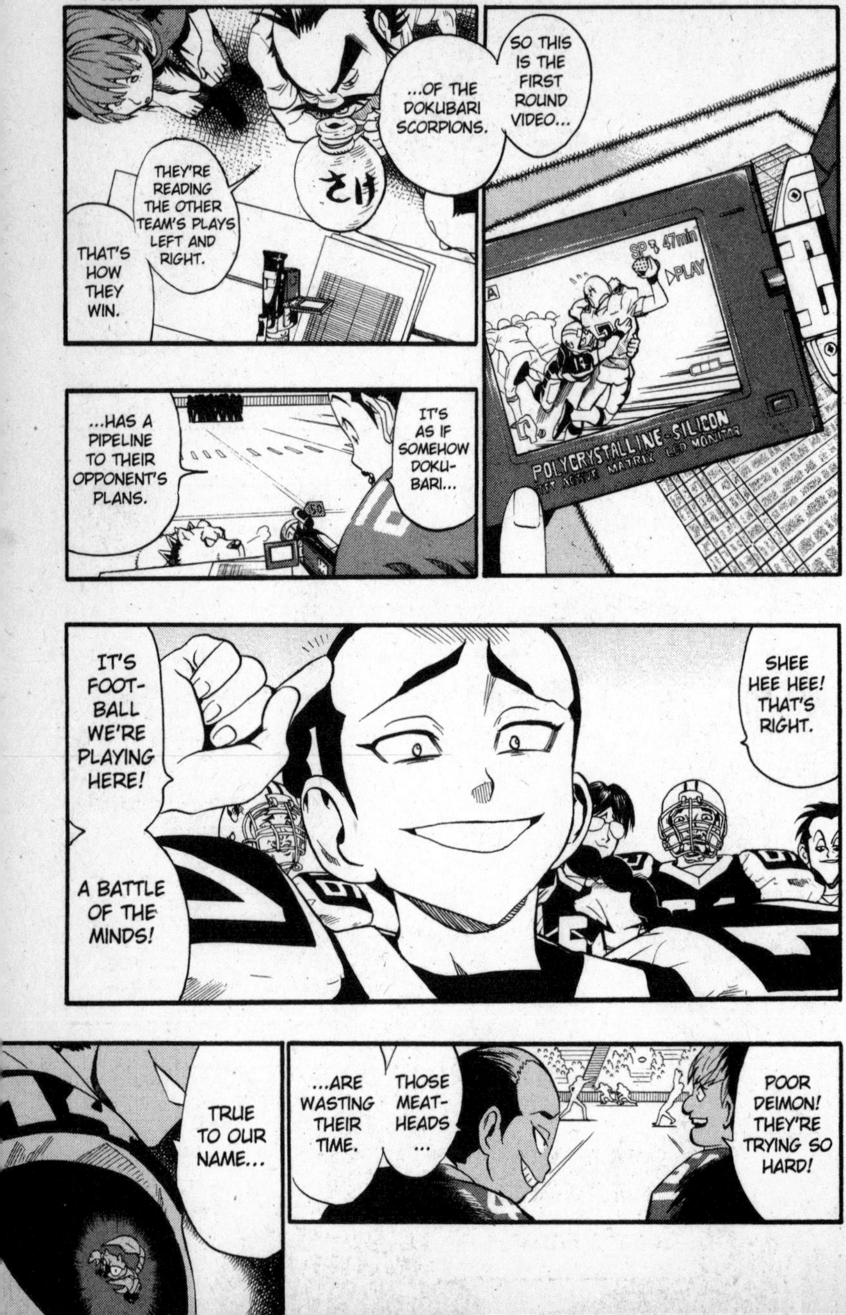
SO THIS IS THE FIRST ROUND VIDEO...
SP 47min
PLAY
POLYCRYSTALLINE-SILICON
TFT ACTIVE MATRIX LED MONITOR
...OF THE DOKUBARI SCORPIONS.
さけ
THEY'RE READING THE OTHER TEAM'S PLAYS LEFT AND RIGHT.
THAT'S HOW THEY WIN.
IT'S AS IF SOMEHOW DOKU-BARI...
...HAS A PIPELINE TO THEIR OPPONENT'S PLANS.
SHEE HEE HEE! THAT'S RIGHT.
IT'S FOOT-BALL WE'RE PLAYING HERE!
A BATTLE OF THE MINDS!
POOR DEIMON! THEY'RE TRYING SO HARD!
THOSE MEAT-HEADS...
...ARE WASTING THEIR TIME.
TRUE TO OUR NAME...

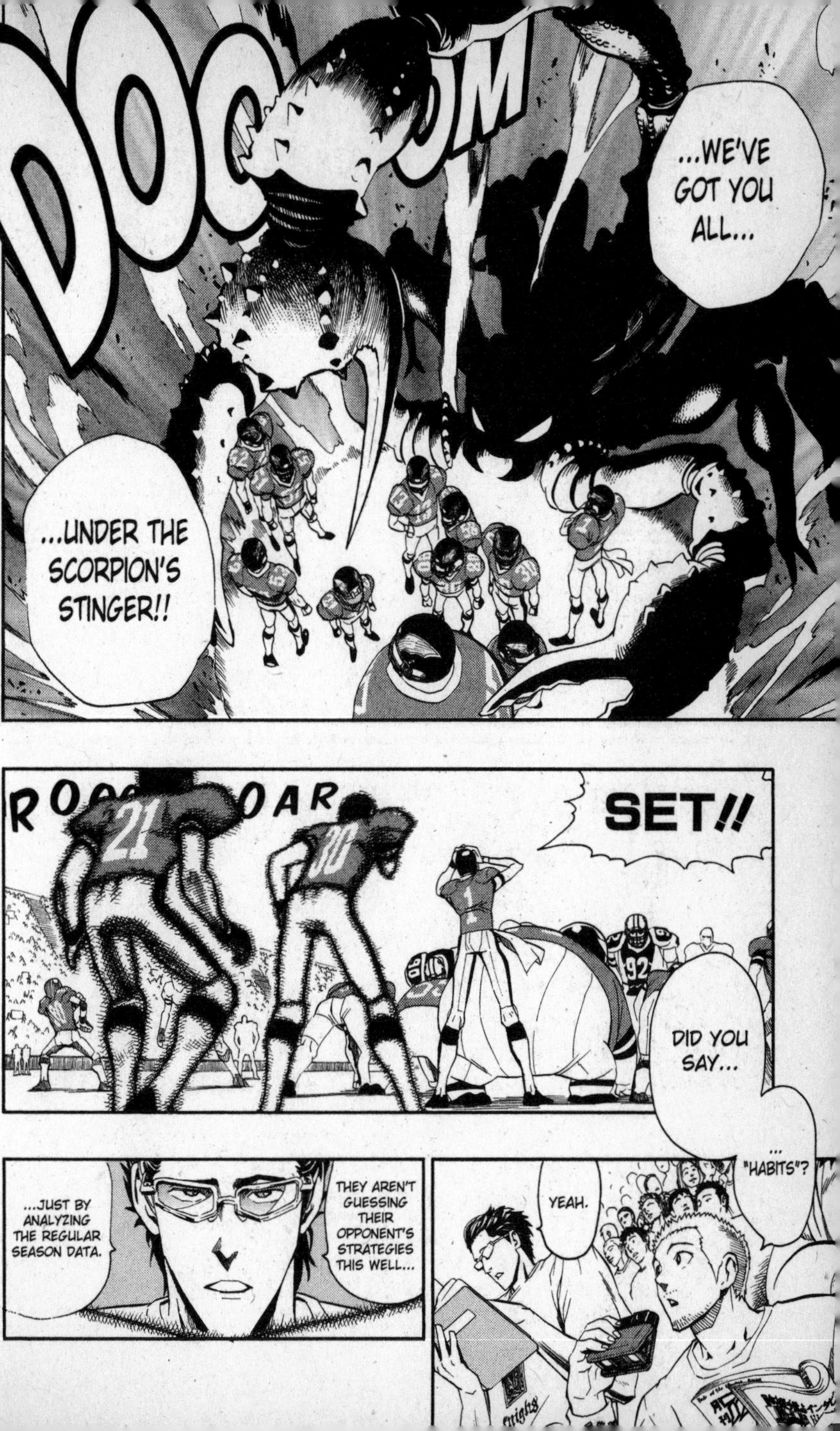
...WE'VE GOT YOU ALL...
DOO OM
...UNDER THE SCORPION'S STINGER!!
SET!!
RO OAR
DID YOU SAY...
... "HABITS"?
YEAH.
THEY AREN'T GUESSING THEIR OPPONENT'S STRATEGIES THIS WELL...
...JUST BY ANALYZING THE REGULAR SEASON DATA.

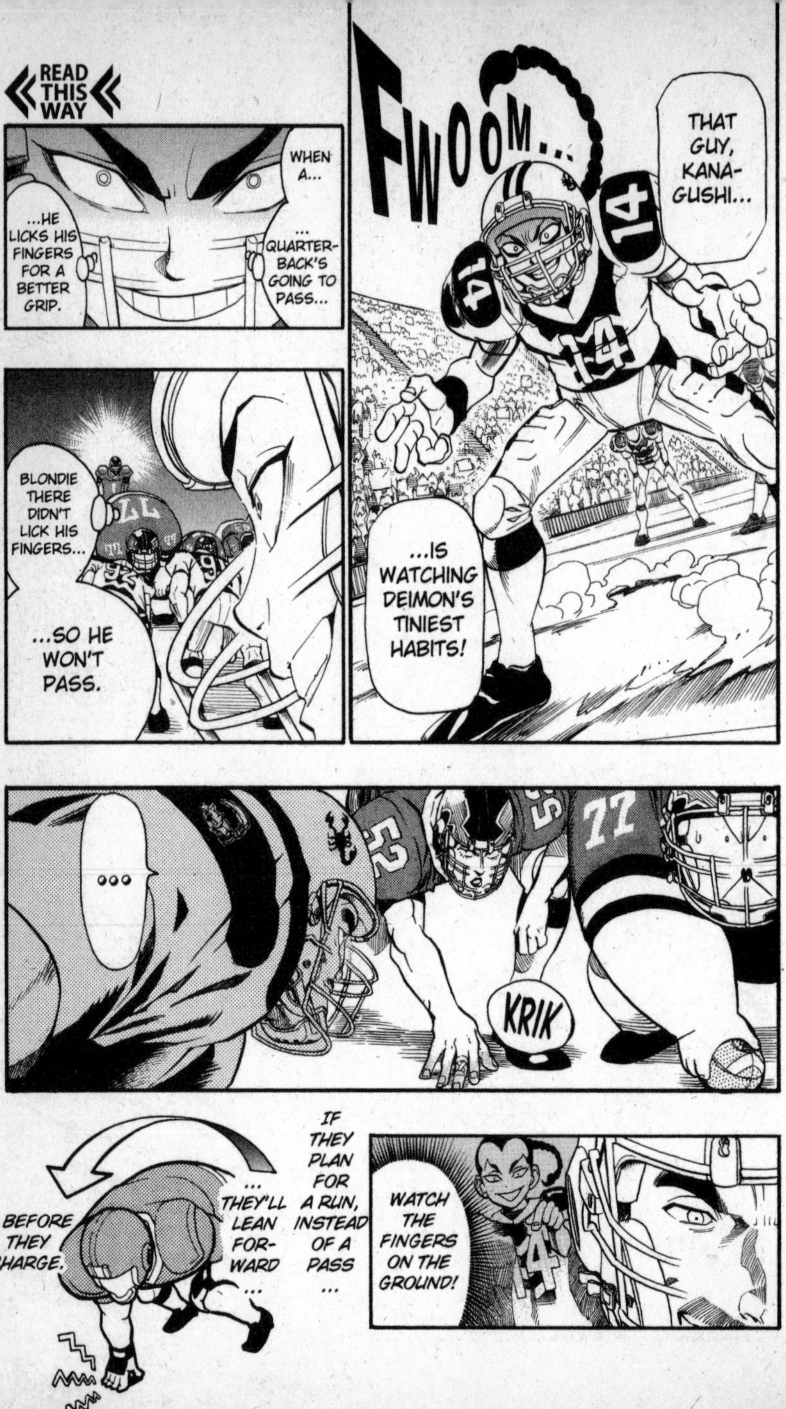
READ THIS WAY
FWOOM...
THAT GUY, KANA-GUSHI...
...IS WATCHING DEIMON'S TINIEST HABITS!
WHEN A...
...QUARTER-BACK'S GOING TO PASS...
...HE LICKS HIS FINGERS FOR A BETTER GRIP.
BLONDIE THERE DIDN'T LICK HIS FINGERS...
...SO HE WON'T PASS.
...
KRIK
WATCH THE FINGERS ON THE GROUND!
IF THEY PLAN FOR A RUN, INSTEAD OF A PASS...
...THEY'LL LEAN FOR-WARD...
...BEFORE THEY CHARGE.

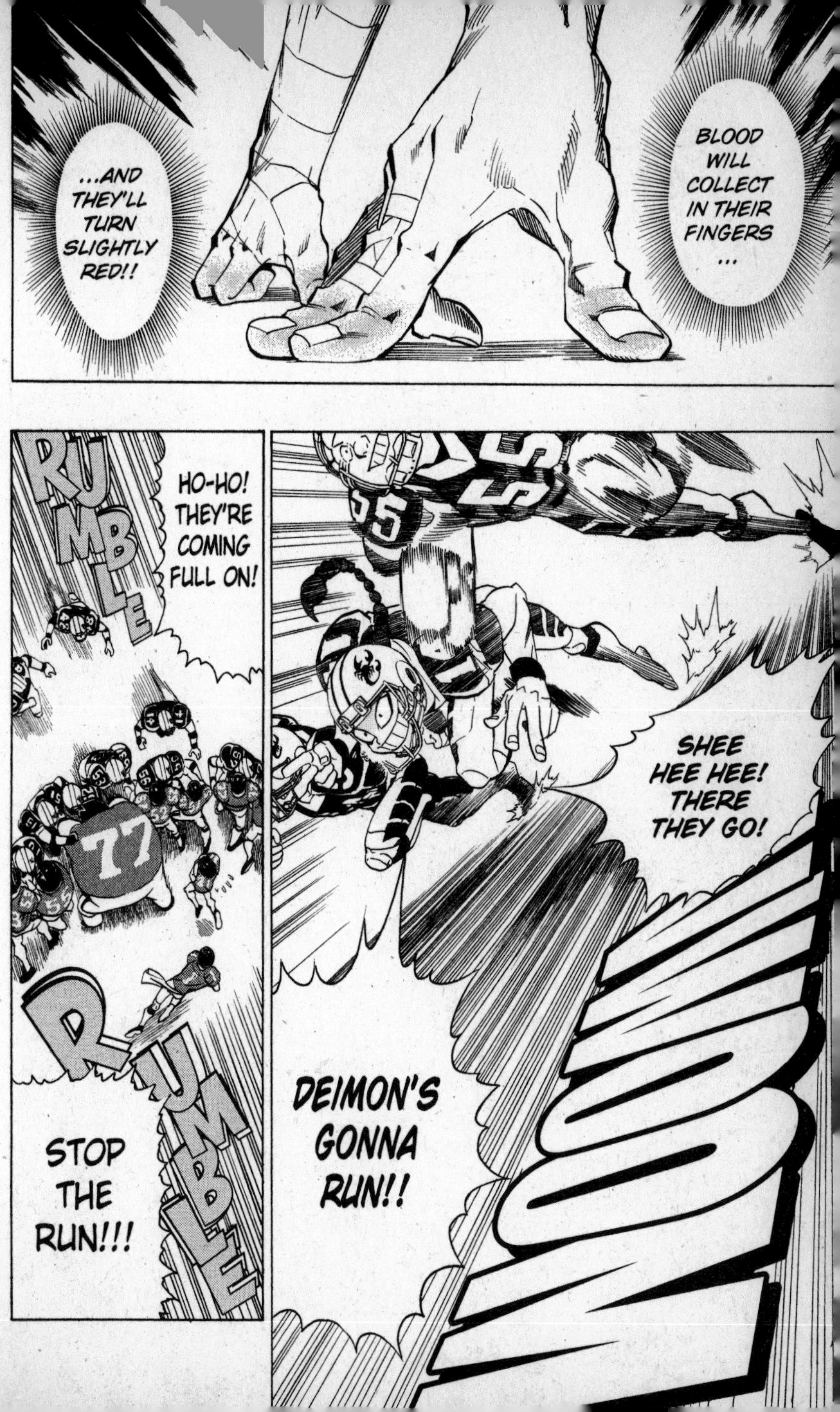
BLOOD WILL COLLECT IN THEIR FINGERS ...
...AND THEY'LL TURN SLIGHTLY RED!!
SHEE HEE HEE! THERE THEY GO!
DEIMON'S GONNA RUN!!
RUMBLE
HO-HO! THEY'RE COMING FULL ON!
RUMBLE
STOP THE RUN!!!

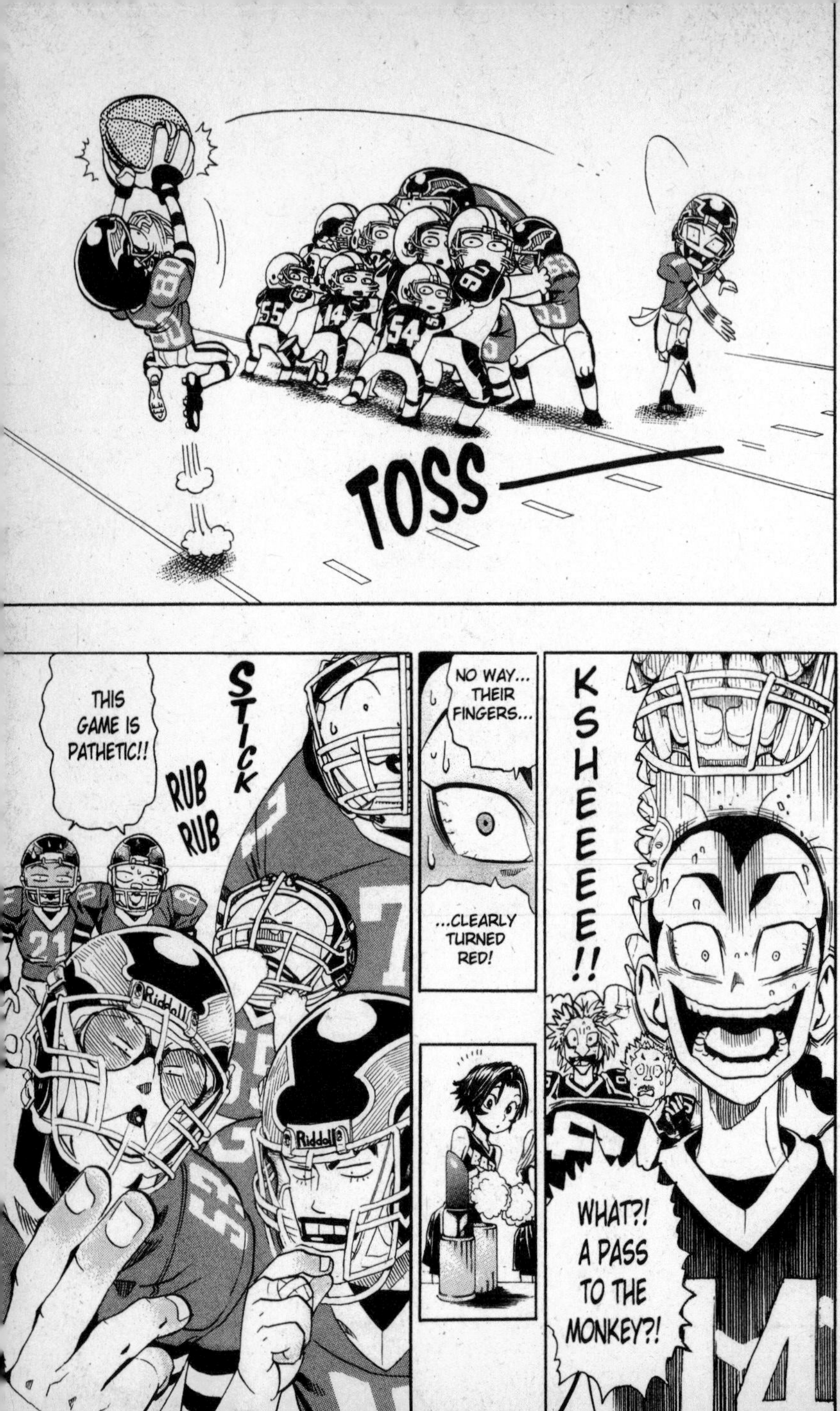
TOSS
KSHEEEEE!!
WHAT?! A PASS TO THE MONKEY?!
NO WAY... THEIR FINGERS...
...CLEARLY TURNED RED!
STICK
RUB RUB
THIS GAME IS PATHETIC!!

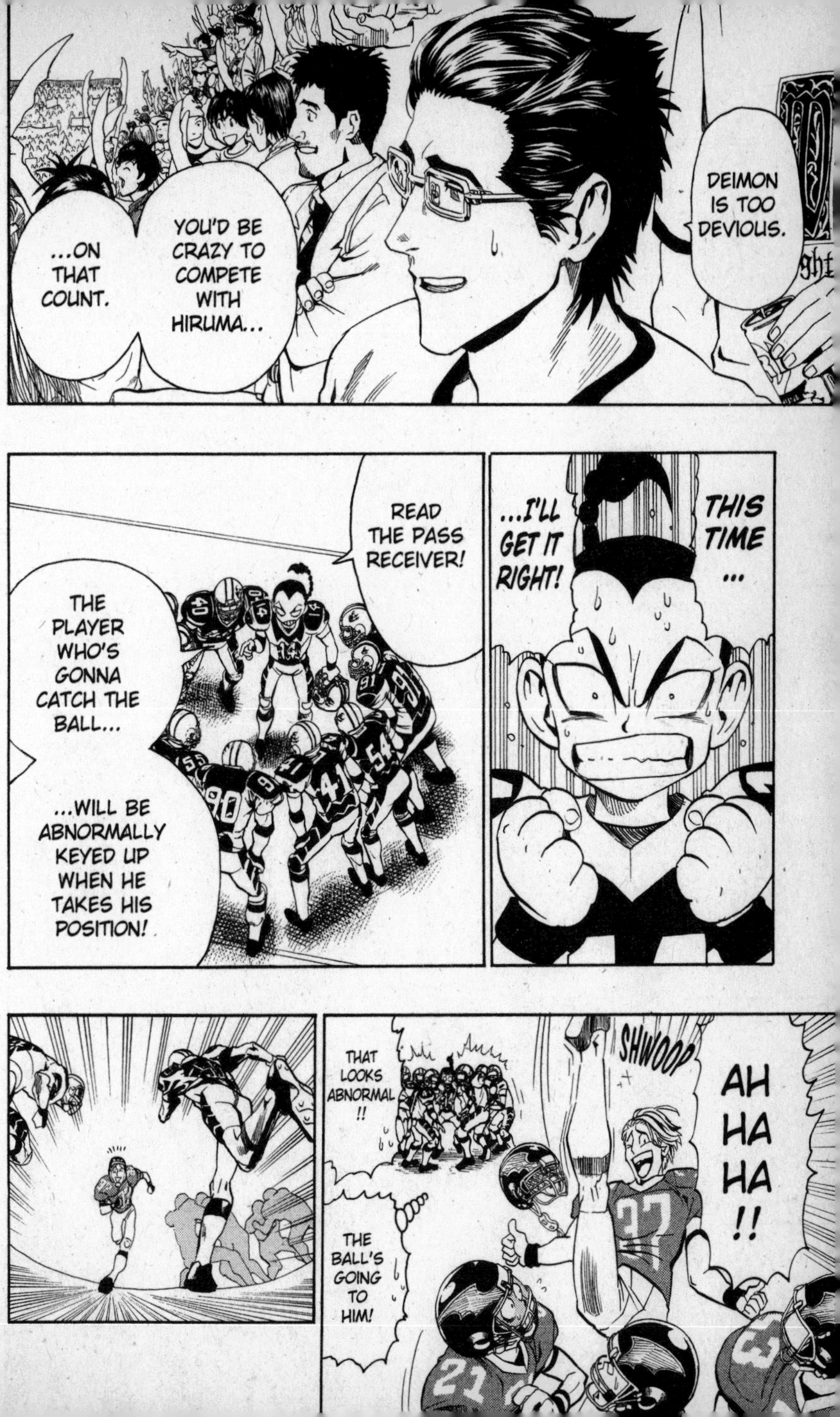
DEIMON IS TOO DEVIOUS.
YOU'D BE CRAZY TO COMPETE WITH HIRUMA...
...ON THAT COUNT.
THIS TIME...
...I'LL GET IT RIGHT!
READ THE PASS RECEIVER!
THE PLAYER WHO'S GONNA CATCH THE BALL...
...WILL BE ABNORMALLY KEYED UP WHEN HE TAKES HIS POSITION!
SHWOOP
AH HA HA HA!!
THAT LOOKS ABNORMAL!!
THE BALL'S GOING TO HIM!

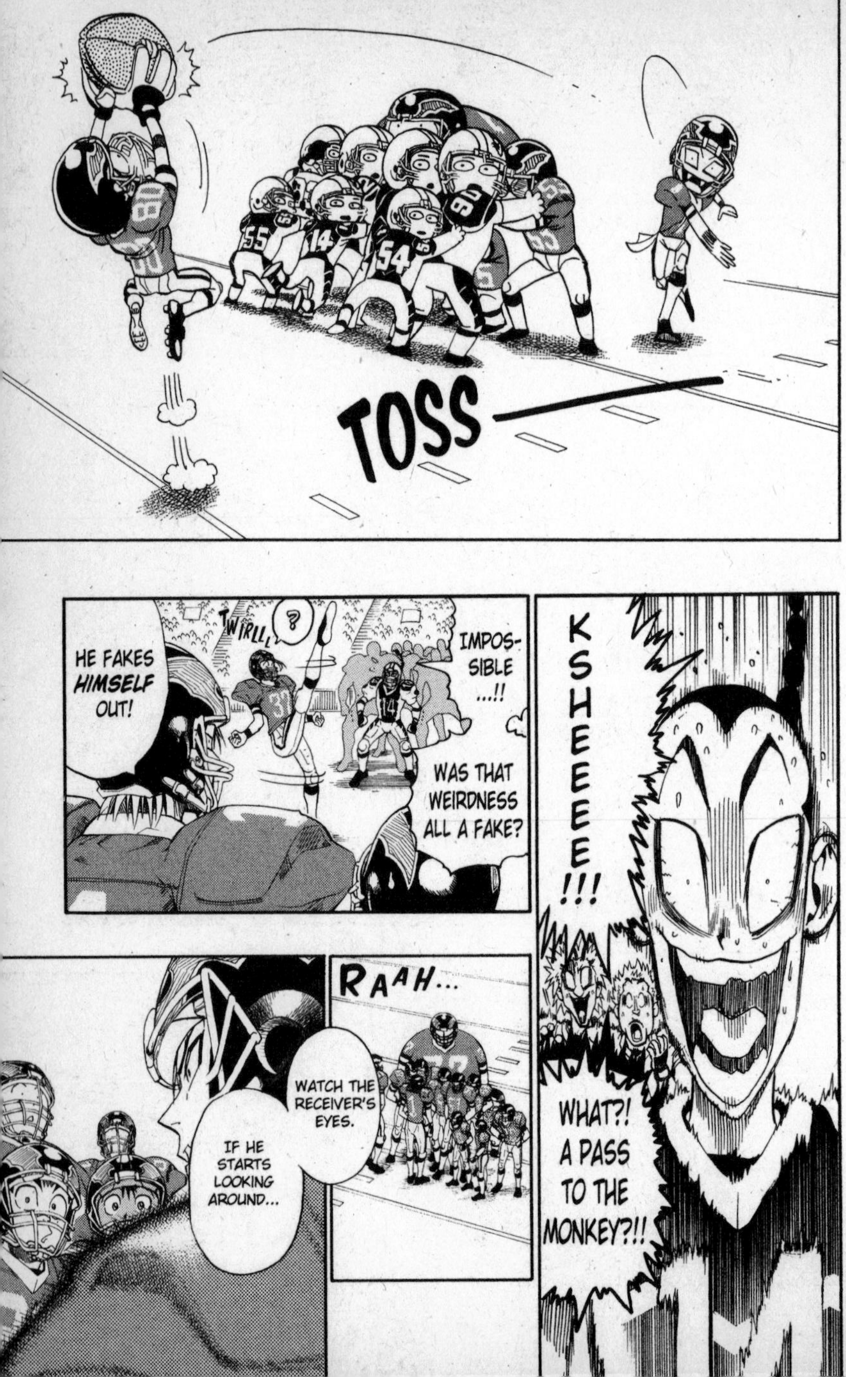
TOSS
KSHEEEE!!!
WHAT?! A PASS TO THE MONKEY?!!
IMPOS-SIBLE ...!!
?
TWIRLLL
HE FAKES HIMSELF OUT!
WAS THAT WEIRDNESS ALL A FAKE?
RAAH...
WATCH THE RECEIVER'S EYES.
IF HE STARTS LOOKING AROUND...

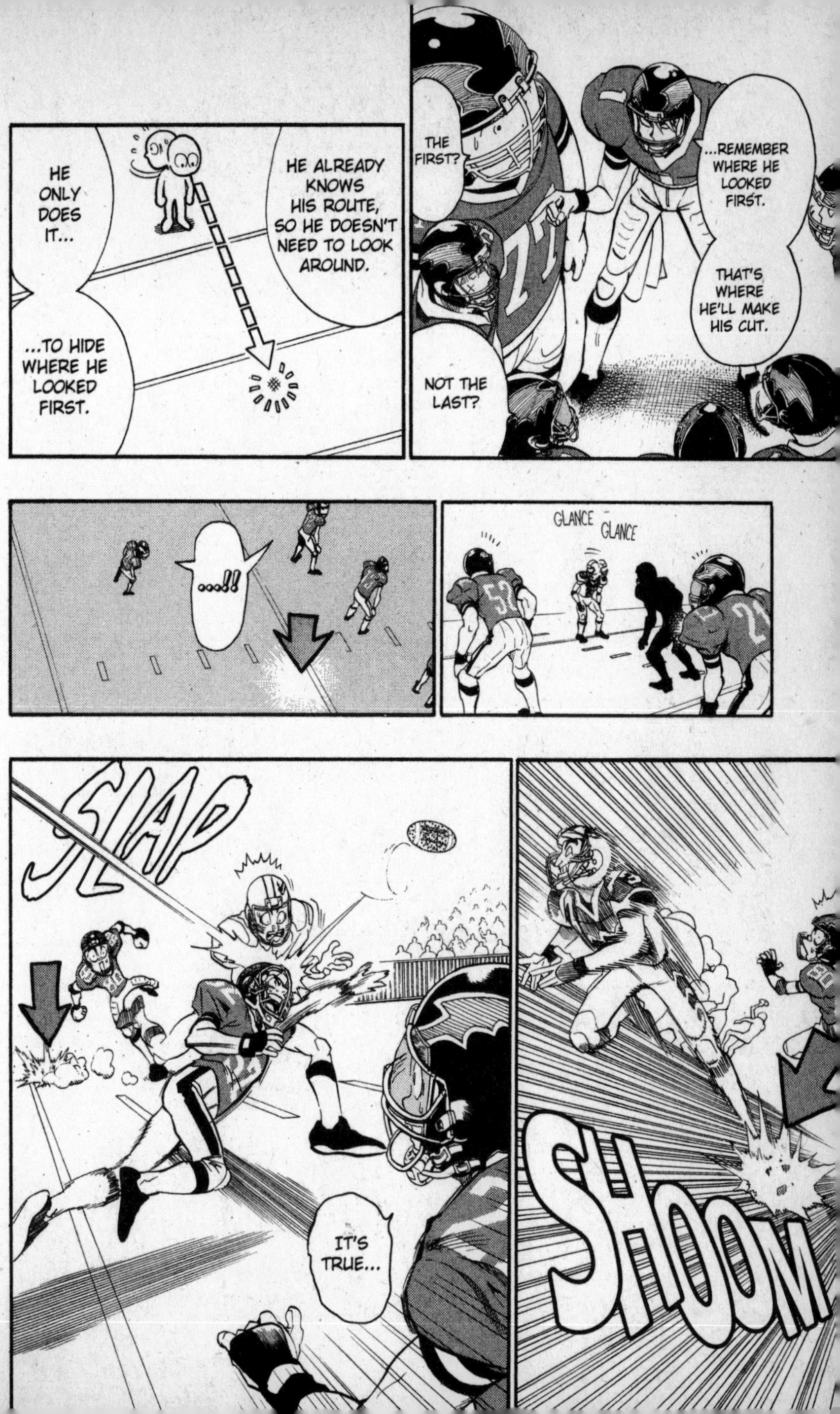
...REMEMBER WHERE HE LOOKED FIRST.
THE FIRST?
THAT'S WHERE HE'LL MAKE HIS CUT.
NOT THE LAST?
HE ALREADY KNOWS HIS ROUTE, SO HE DOESN'T NEED TO LOOK AROUND.
HE ONLY DOES IT...
...TO HIDE WHERE HE LOOKED FIRST.
GLANCE
GLANCE
...!!
SHOOOM
SLAP
IT'S TRUE...

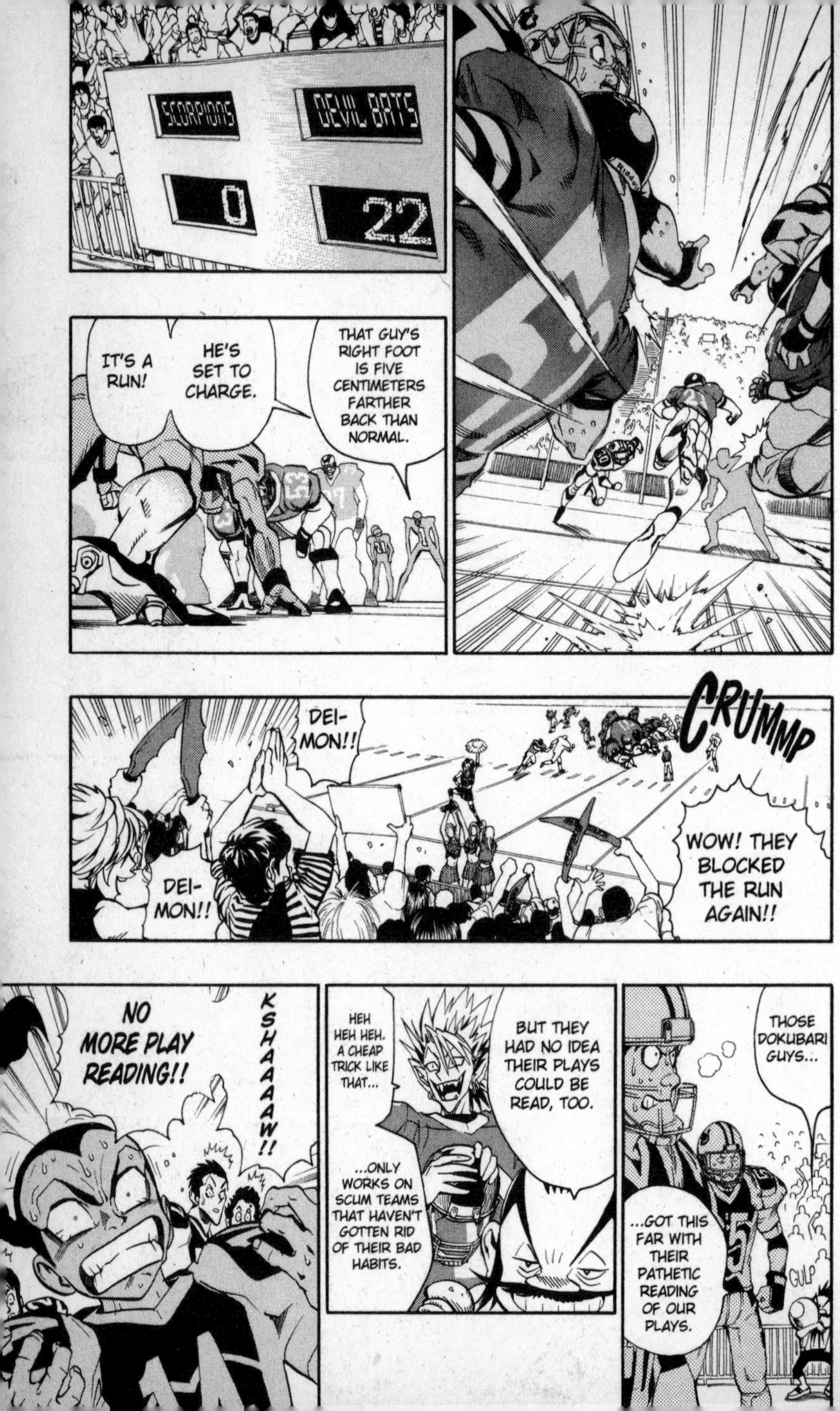
SCORPIONS
DEVIL BATS
0
22
THAT GUY'S RIGHT FOOT IS FIVE CENTIMETERS FARTHER BACK THAN NORMAL.
HE'S SET TO CHARGE.
IT'S A RUN!
CRUMMP
WOW! THEY BLOCKED THE RUN AGAIN!!
DEI-MON!!
DEI-MON!!
THOSE DOKUBARI GUYS...
...GOT THIS FAR WITH THEIR PATHETIC READING OF OUR PLAYS.
GULP
BUT THEY HAD NO IDEA THEIR PLAYS COULD BE READ, TOO.
HEH HEH HEH. A CHEAP TRICK LIKE THAT...
...ONLY WORKS ON SCUM TEAMS THAT HAVEN'T GOTTEN RID OF THEIR BAD HABITS.
KSHAAAAAW!!
NO MORE PLAY READING!!

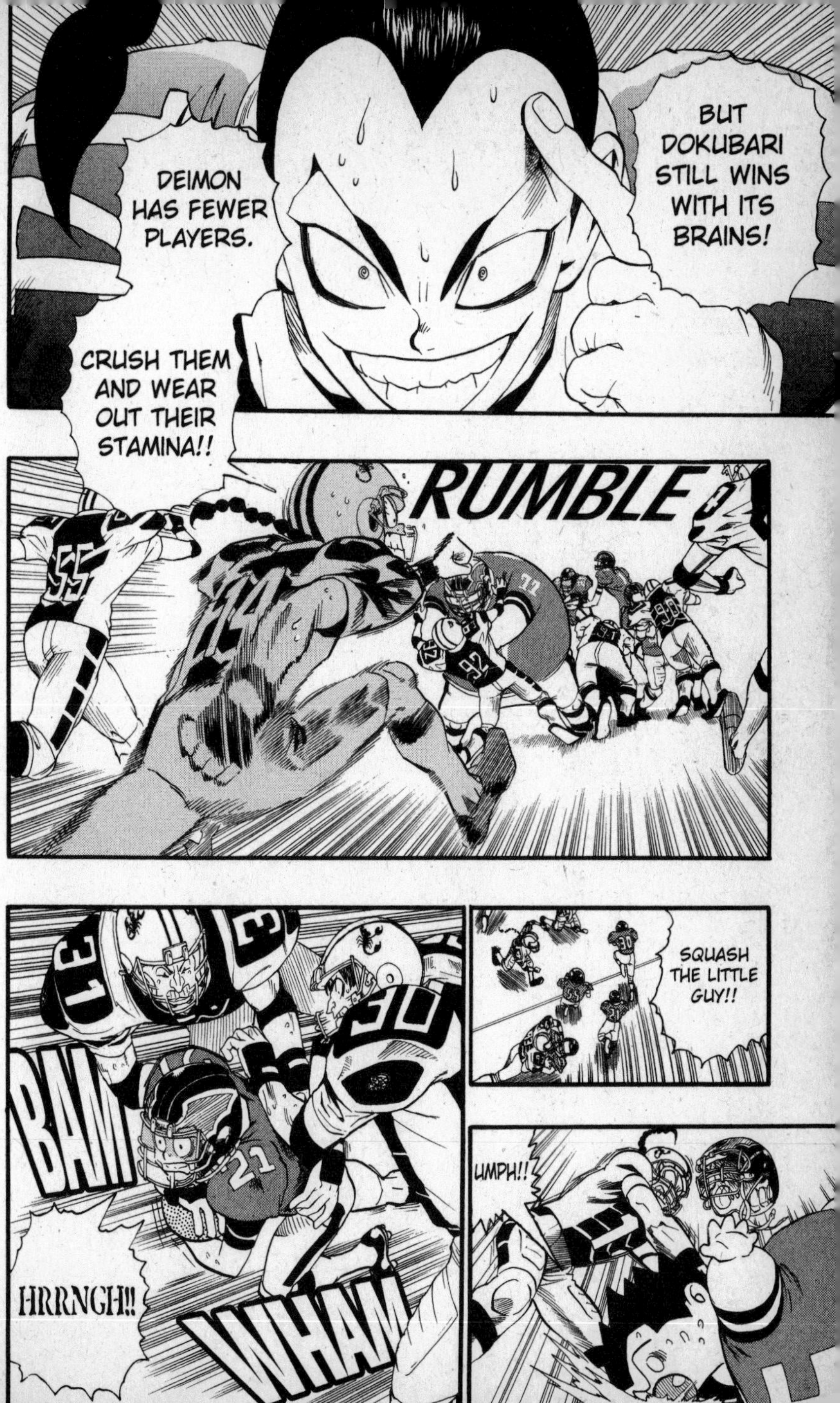
BUT DOKUBARI STILL WINS WITH ITS BRAINS!
DEIMON HAS FEWER PLAYERS.
CRUSH THEM AND WEAR OUT THEIR STAMINA!!
RUMBLE
SQUASH THE LITTLE GUY!!
UMPH!!
BAM
HRRNGH!!
WHAM

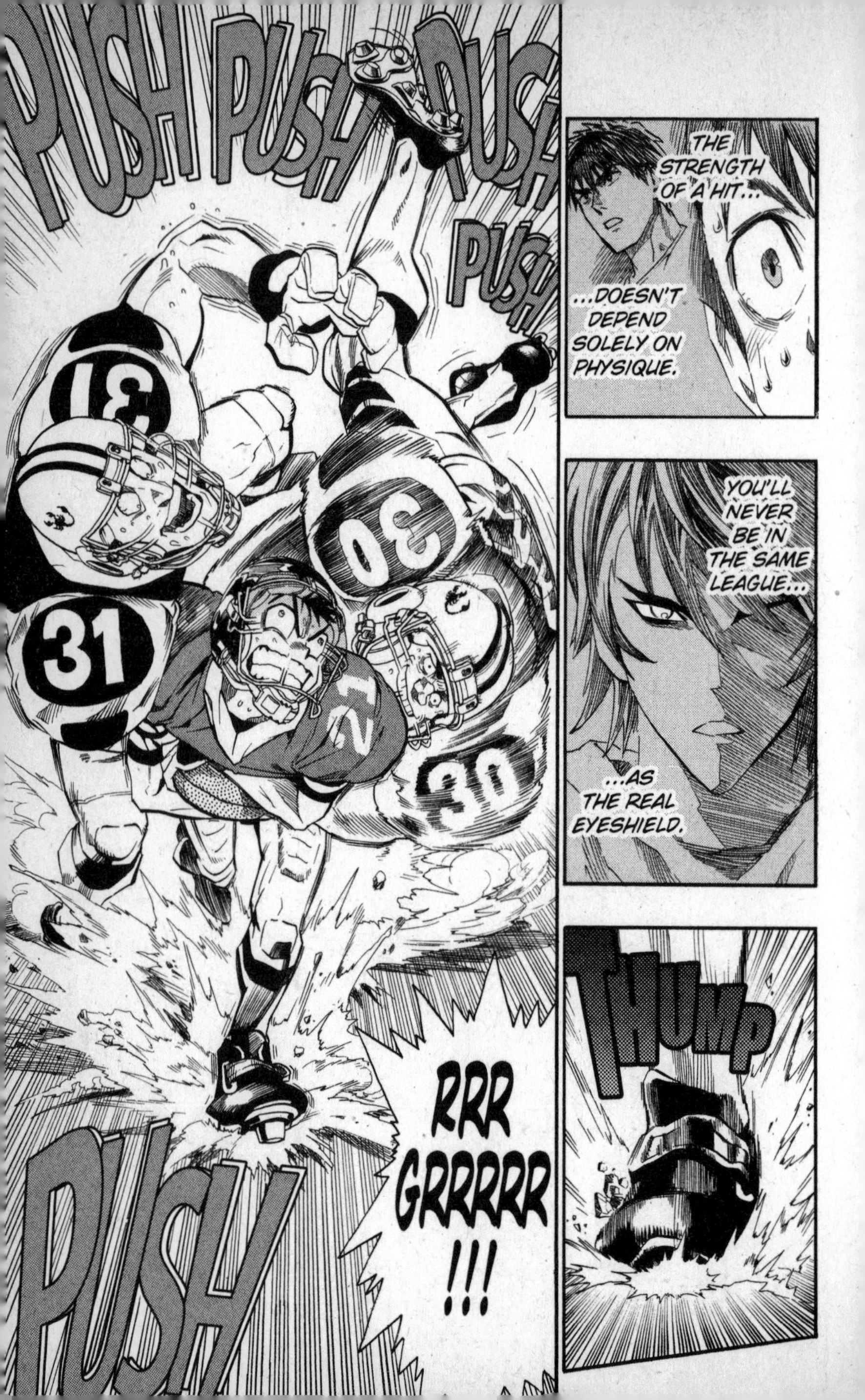
THE STRENGTH OF A HIT...
...DOESN'T DEPEND SOLELY ON PHYSIQUE.
YOU'LL NEVER BE IN THE SAME LEAGUE...
...AS THE REAL EYESHIELD.
THUMP
PUSH PUSH PUSH
PUSH
RRR GRRRRR !!!
PUSH

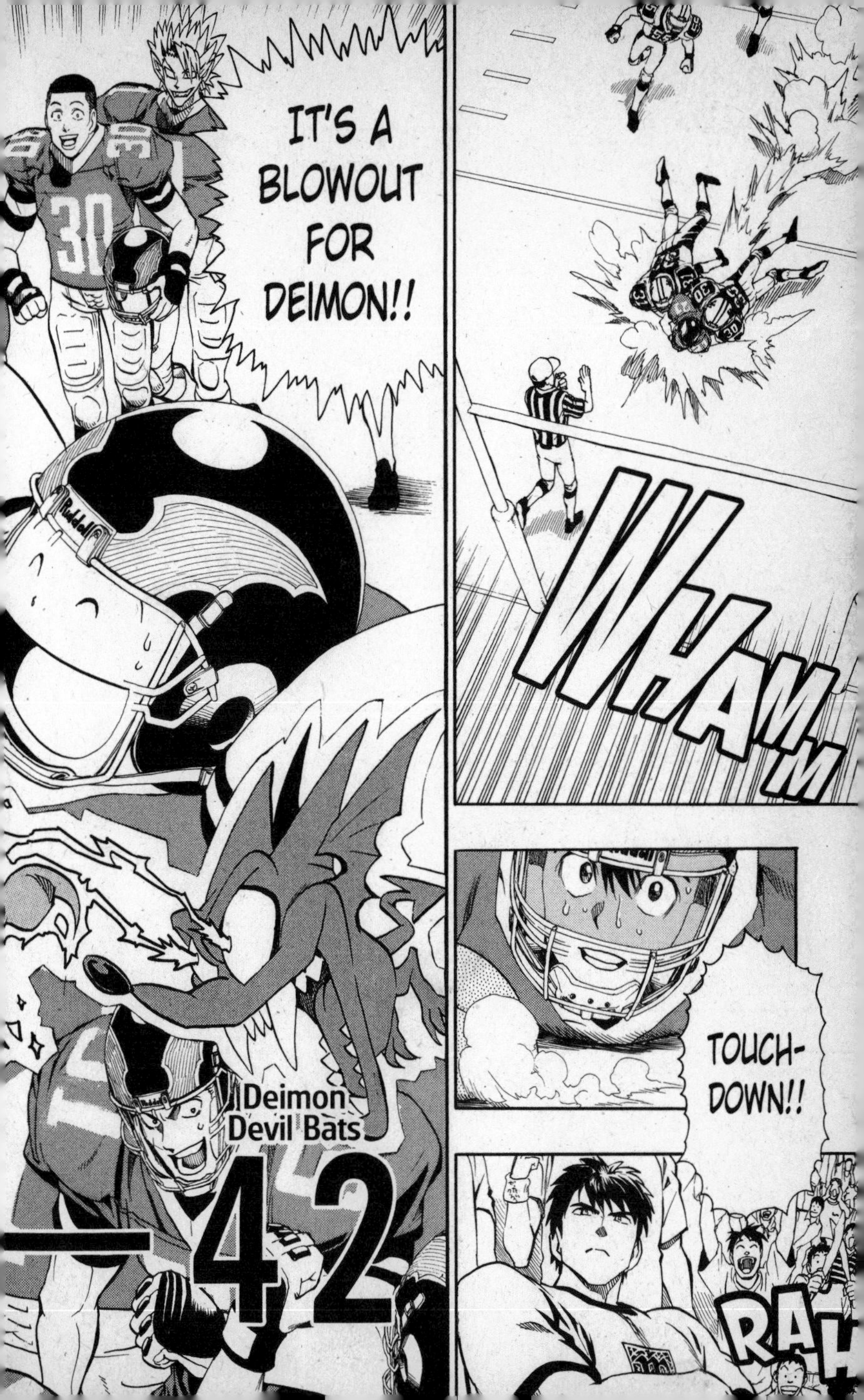
WHAMM
TOUCH-DOWN!!
RAH
IT'S A BLOWOUT FOR DEIMON!!
Deimon Devil Bats
42

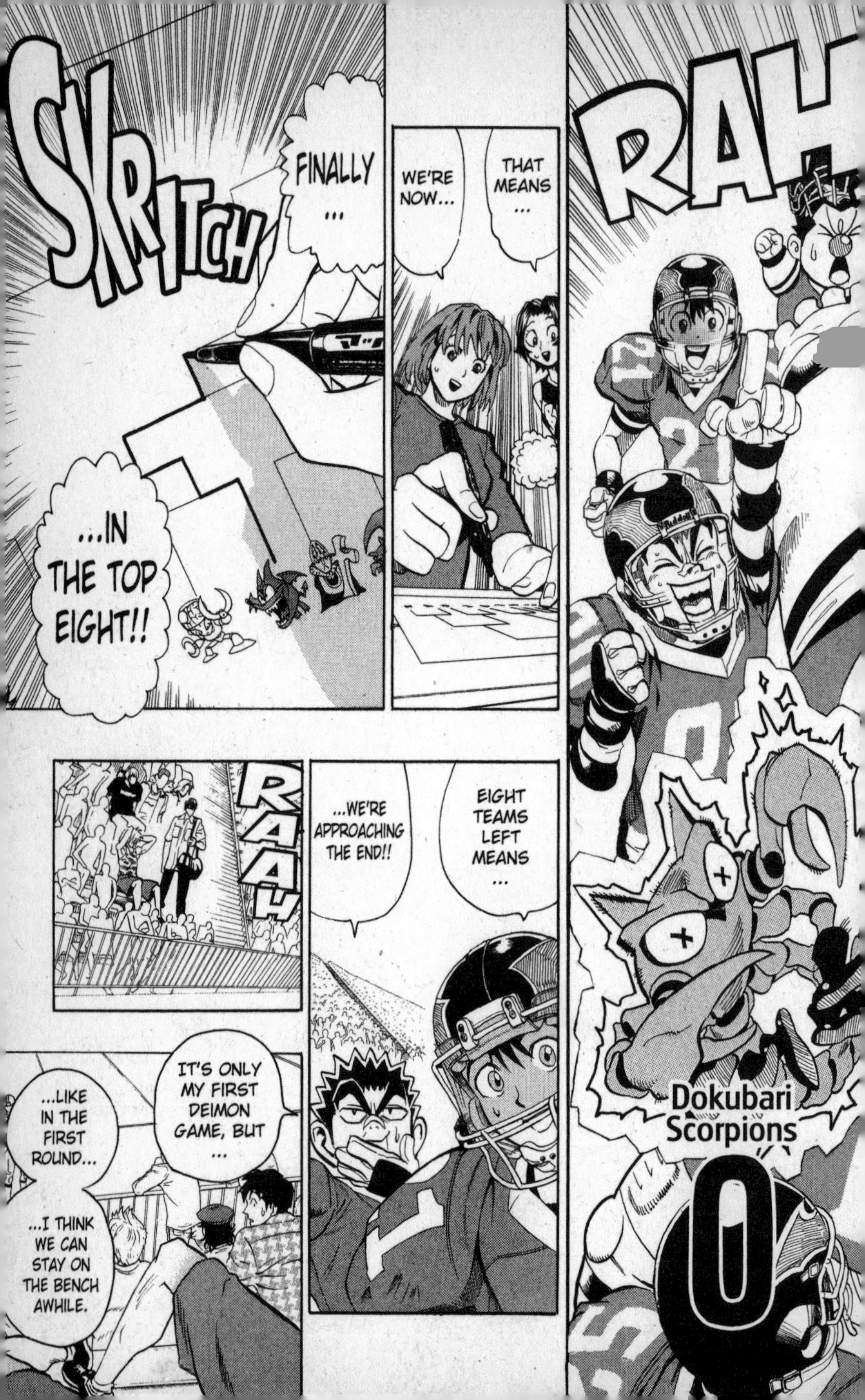
RAH
Dokubari Scorpions
0
THAT MEANS ...
WE'RE NOW...
SKRITCH
FINALLY ...
...IN THE TOP EIGHT!!
EIGHT TEAMS LEFT MEANS ...
...WE'RE APPROACHING THE END!!
RAAH
IT'S ONLY MY FIRST DEIMON GAME, BUT ...
...LIKE IN THE FIRST ROUND...
...I THINK WE CAN STAY ON THE BENCH AWHILE.

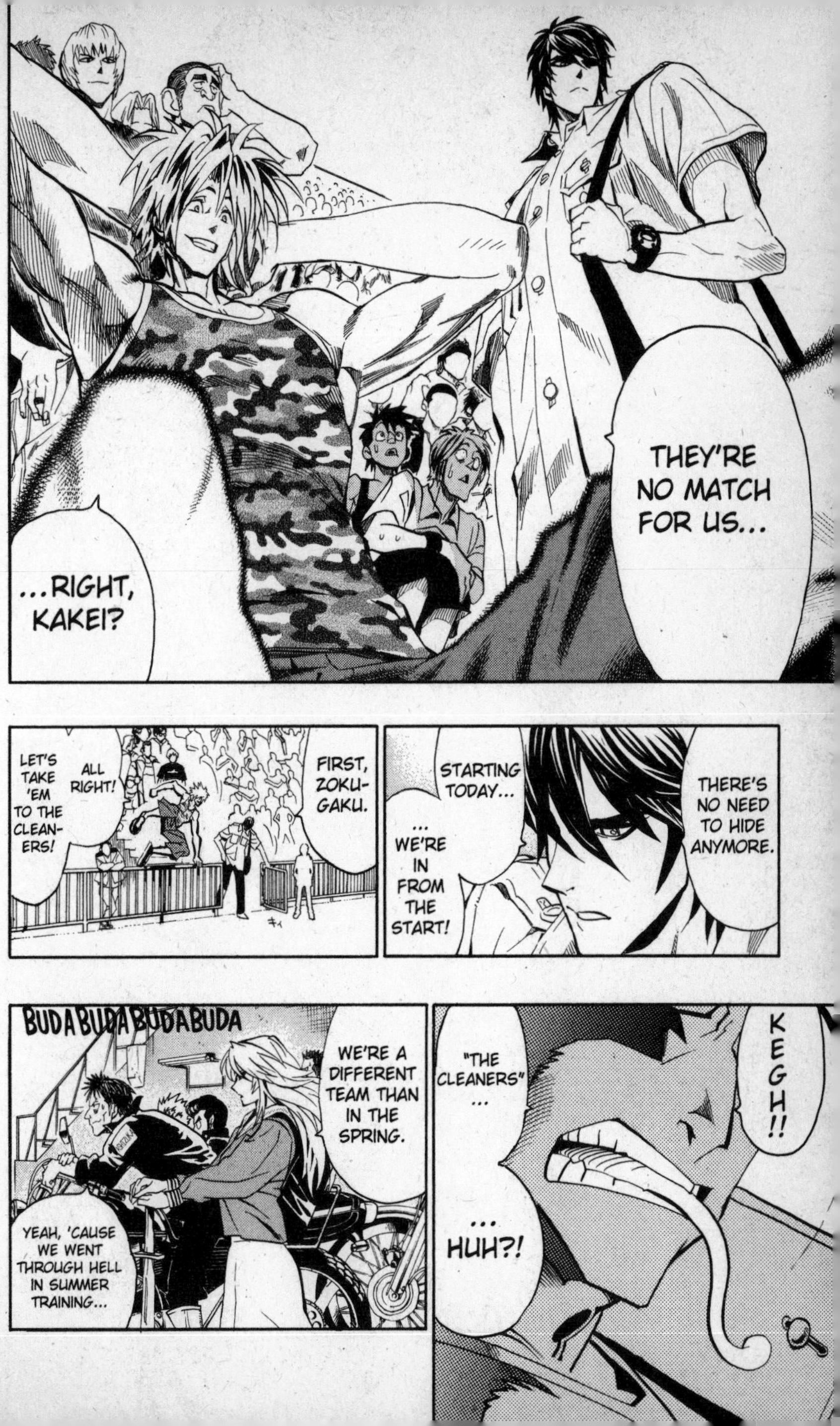

THEY'RE NO MATCH FOR US...
...RIGHT, KAKEI?
THERE'S NO NEED TO HIDE ANYMORE.
STARTING TODAY...
...WE'RE IN FROM THE START!
FIRST, ZOKU-GAKU.
ALL RIGHT!
LET'S TAKE 'EM TO THE CLEANERS!
キィ
KEGH!!
"THE CLEANERS"...
...HUH?!
BUDABUDABUDABUDA
WE'RE A DIFFERENT TEAM THAN IN THE SPRING.
YEAH, 'CAUSE WE WENT THROUGH HELL IN SUMMER TRAINING...

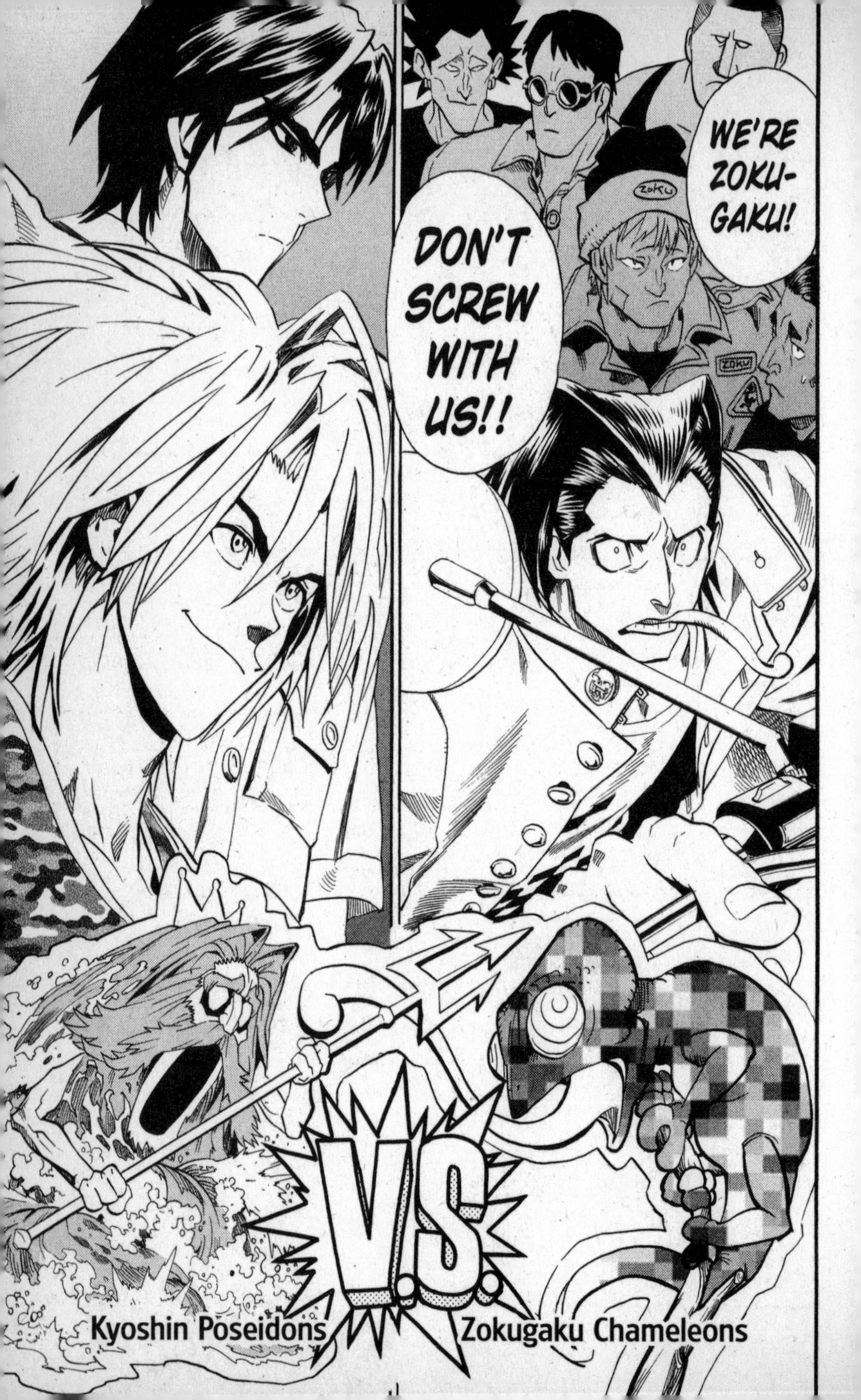
WE'RE ZOKU-GAKU!
DON'T SCREW WITH US!!
Kyoshin Poseidons
V.S.
Zokugaku Chameleons

High School Selection Guidance for Prospective Applicants!

ZOKUGAKU ACADEMY

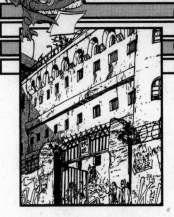

Student Body: 1,240

Special Campus Facilities: Gas Station

Major Career Options after Graduation

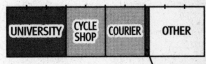

UNIVERSITY | CYCLE SHOP | COURIER | CIRCUS RIDING | OTHER

Whether you're in class or on a break, someone's always taking aim at the back of your skull with a baseball bat! Recommended for those seeking a survivalist lifestyle in high school!

Graduate Testimonial

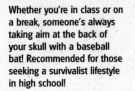

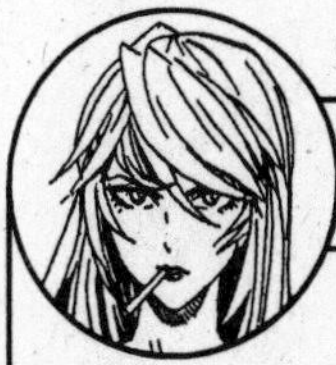

MEG TSUYUMINE

Join the football club, or I'll crush your balls!

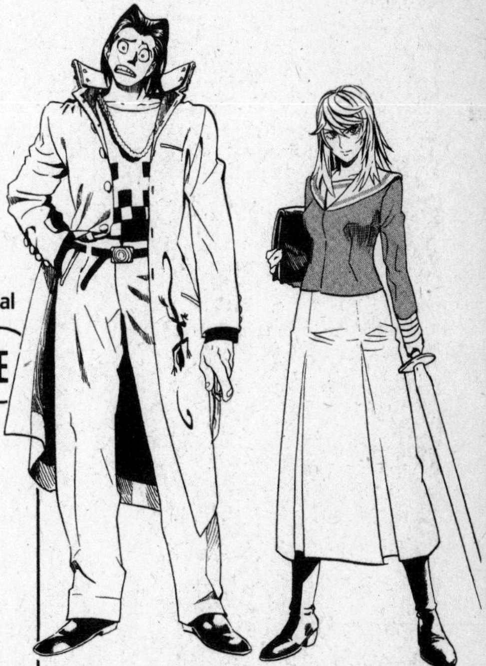

UNIFORM

Chapter 110 Ruled by Fear

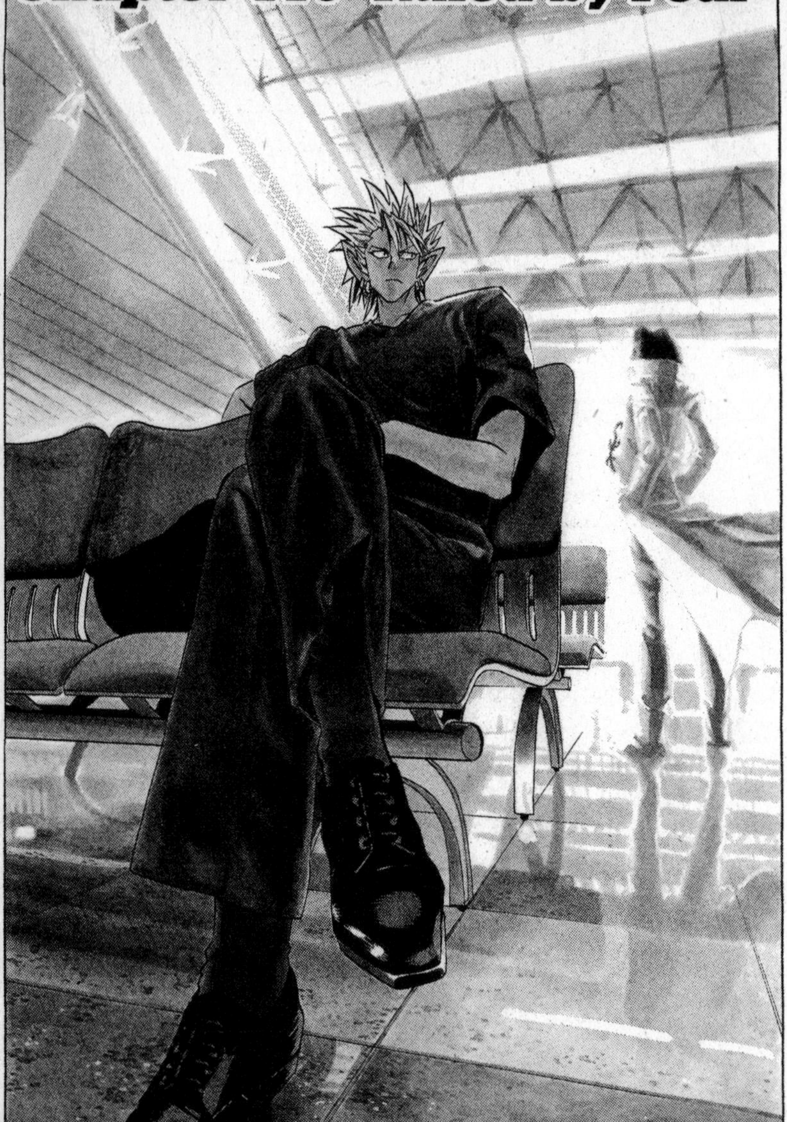

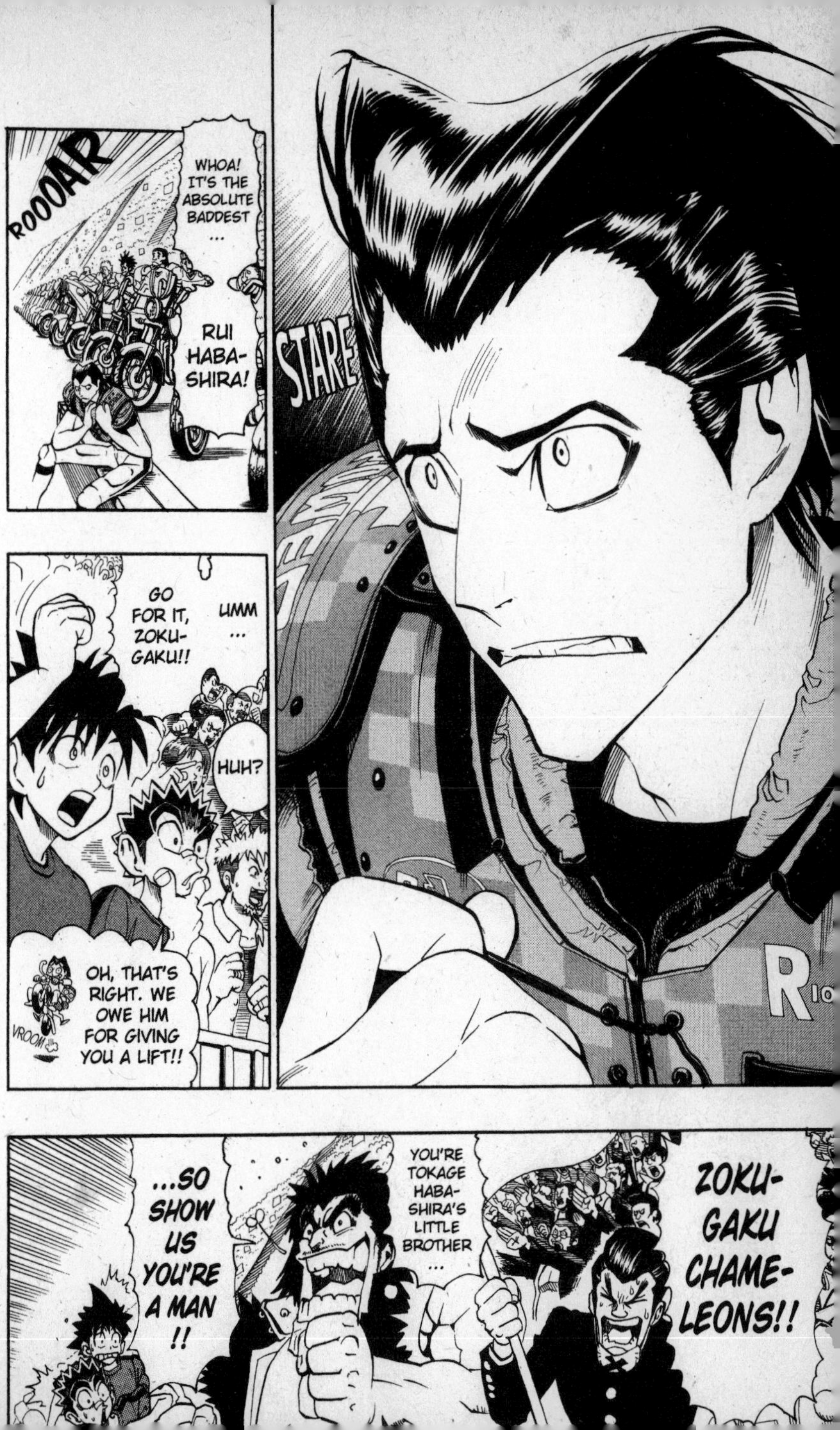
STARE
ROOOAR
WHOA! IT'S THE ABSOLUTE BADDEST …
RUI HABA-SHIRA!
UMM …
GO FOR IT, ZOKU-GAKU!!
HUH?
OH, THAT'S RIGHT. WE OWE HIM FOR GIVING YOU A LIFT!!
VROOM
ZOKU-GAKU CHAME-LEONS!!
YOU'RE TOKAGE HABA-SHIRA'S LITTLE BROTHER …
…SO SHOW US YOU'RE A MAN !!

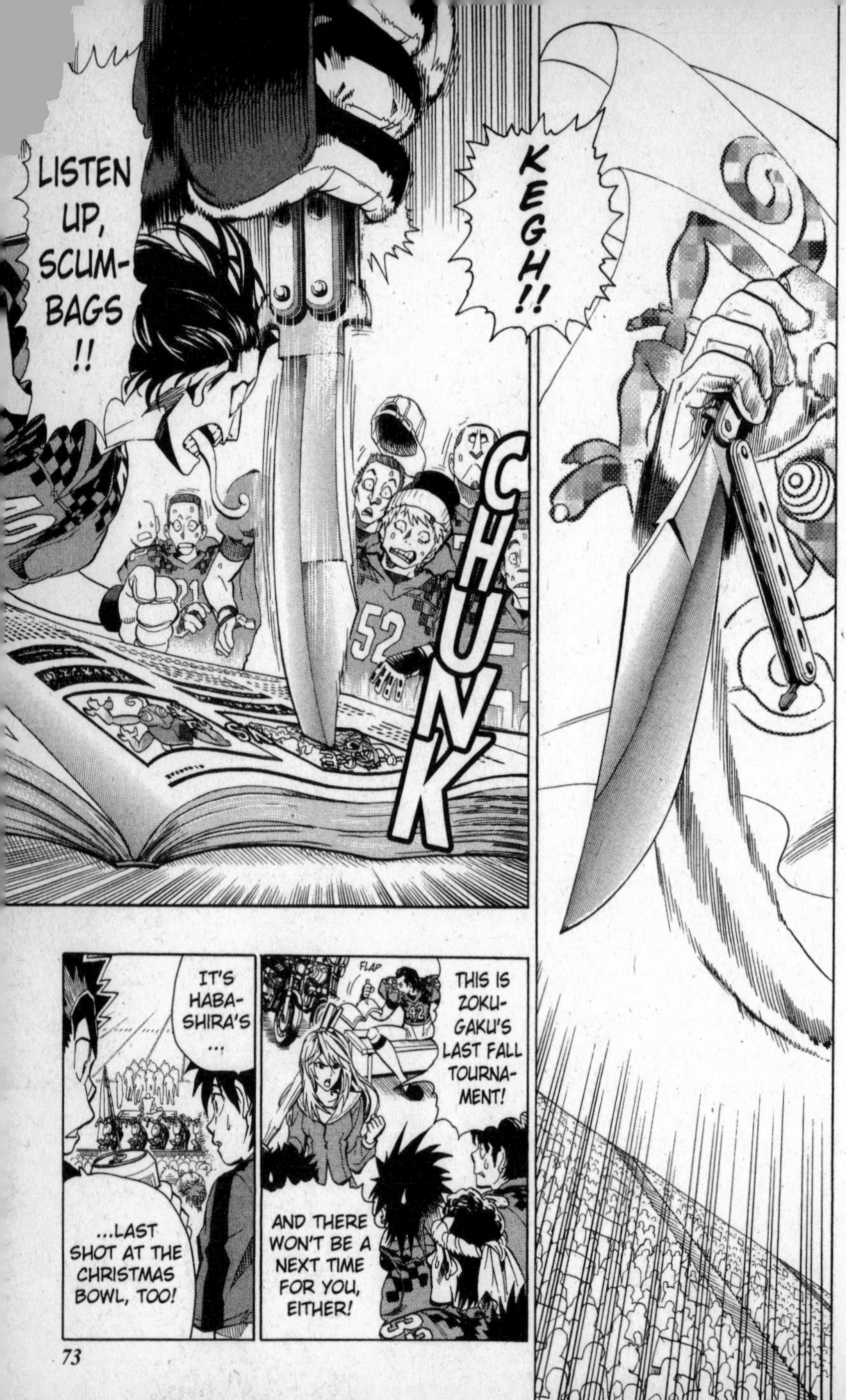
KEGH!!
LISTEN UP, SCUM-BAGS!!
CHUNK
FLAP
THIS IS ZOKU-GAKU'S LAST FALL TOURNAMENT!
AND THERE WON'T BE A NEXT TIME FOR YOU, EITHER!
IT'S HABA-SHIRA'S...
...LAST SHOT AT THE CHRISTMAS BOWL, TOO!

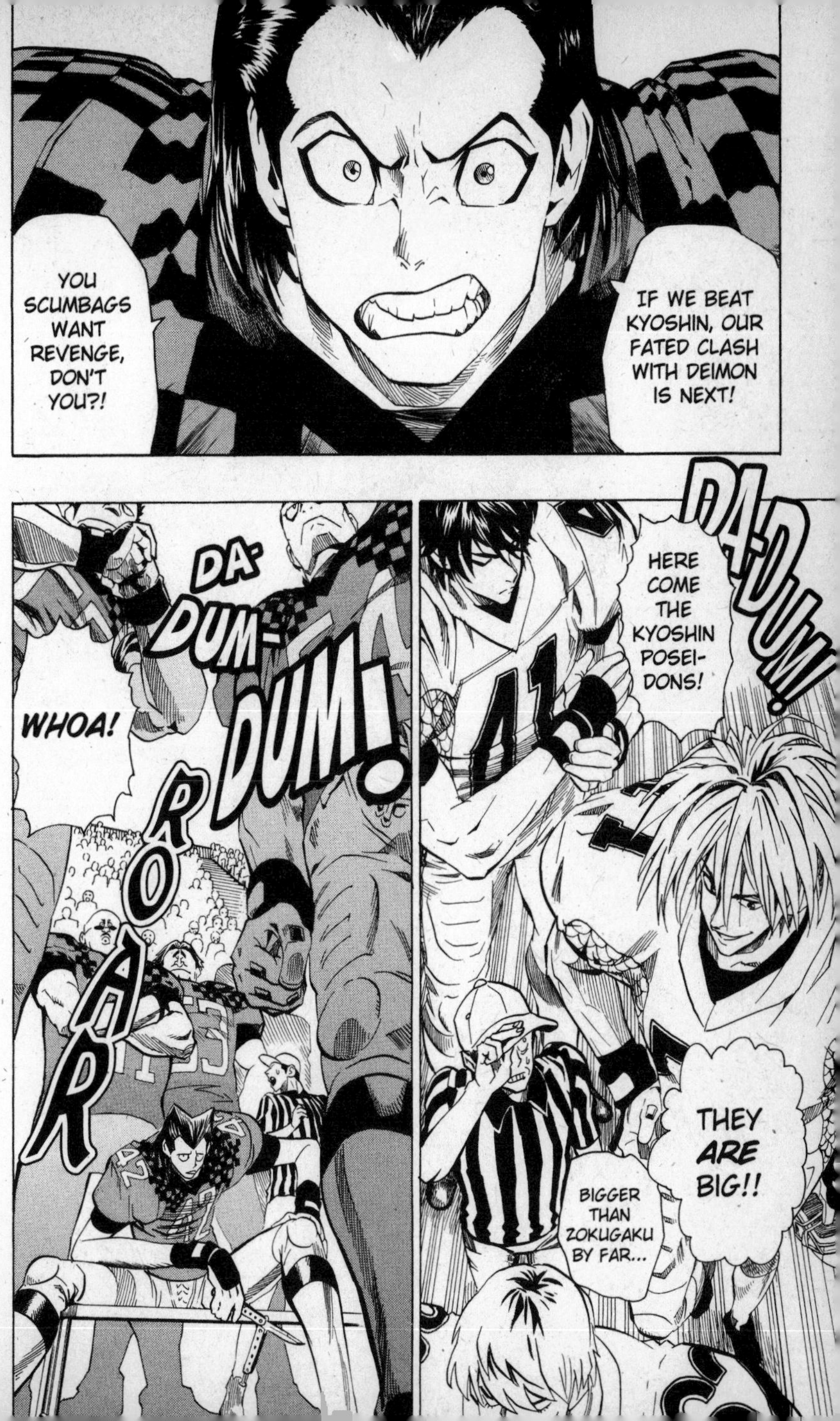
IF WE BEAT KYOSHIN, OUR FATED CLASH WITH DEIMON IS NEXT!
YOU SCUMBAGS WANT REVENGE, DON'T YOU?!
DA-DUM!!
HERE COME THE KYOSHIN POSEI-DONS!
THEY ARE BIG!!
BIGGER THAN ZOKUGAKU BY FAR...
DA-DUM-DUM!
WHOA!
ROAR

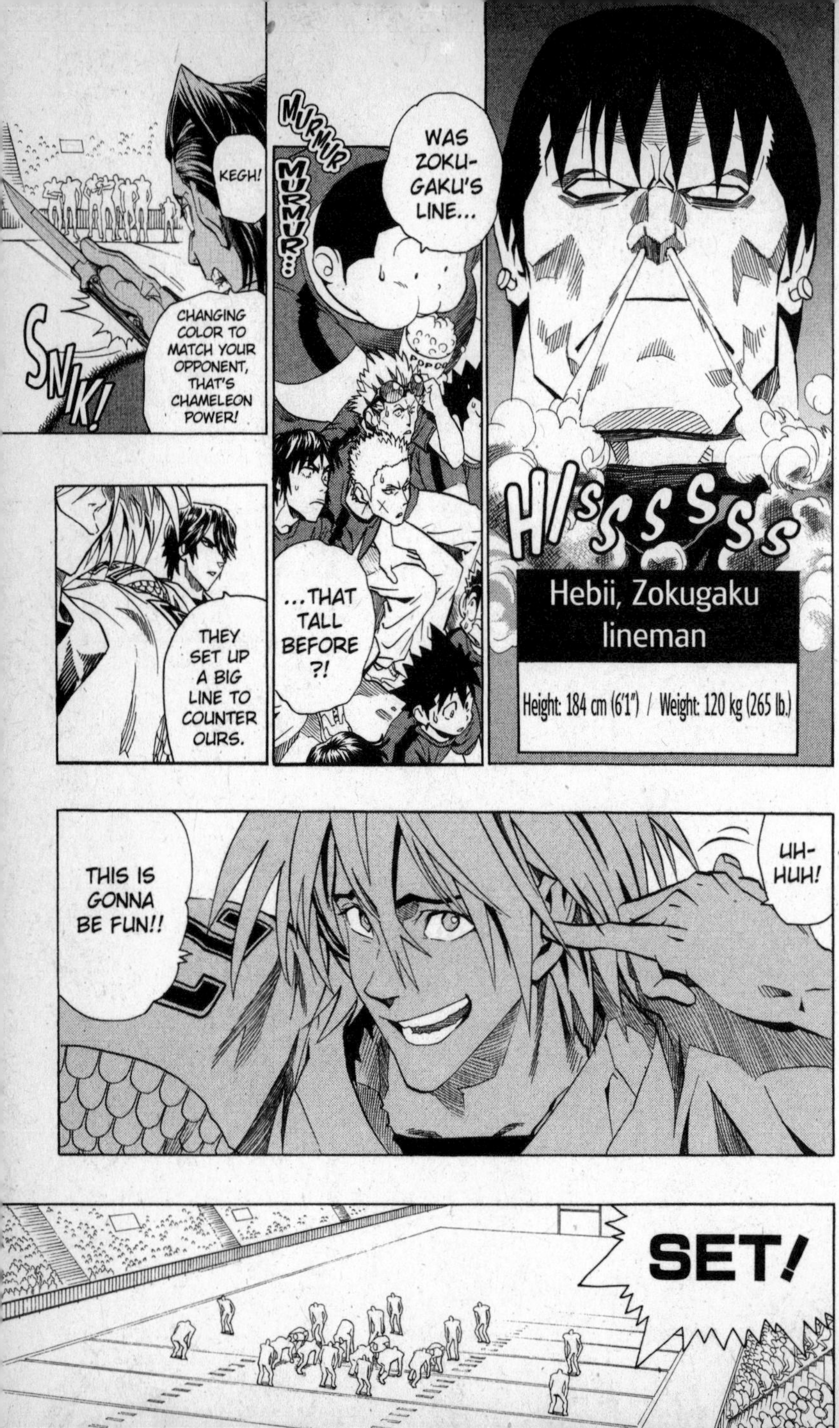
HISSSSSS
Hebii, Zokugaku lineman
Height: 184 cm (6'1") / Weight: 120 kg (265 lb.)
MURMUR
MURMUR...
WAS ZOKU-GAKU'S LINE...
...THAT TALL BEFORE?!
KEGH!
SNIK!
CHANGING COLOR TO MATCH YOUR OPPONENT, THAT'S CHAMELEON POWER!
THEY SET UP A BIG LINE TO COUNTER OURS.
UH-HUH!
THIS IS GONNA BE FUN!!
SET!

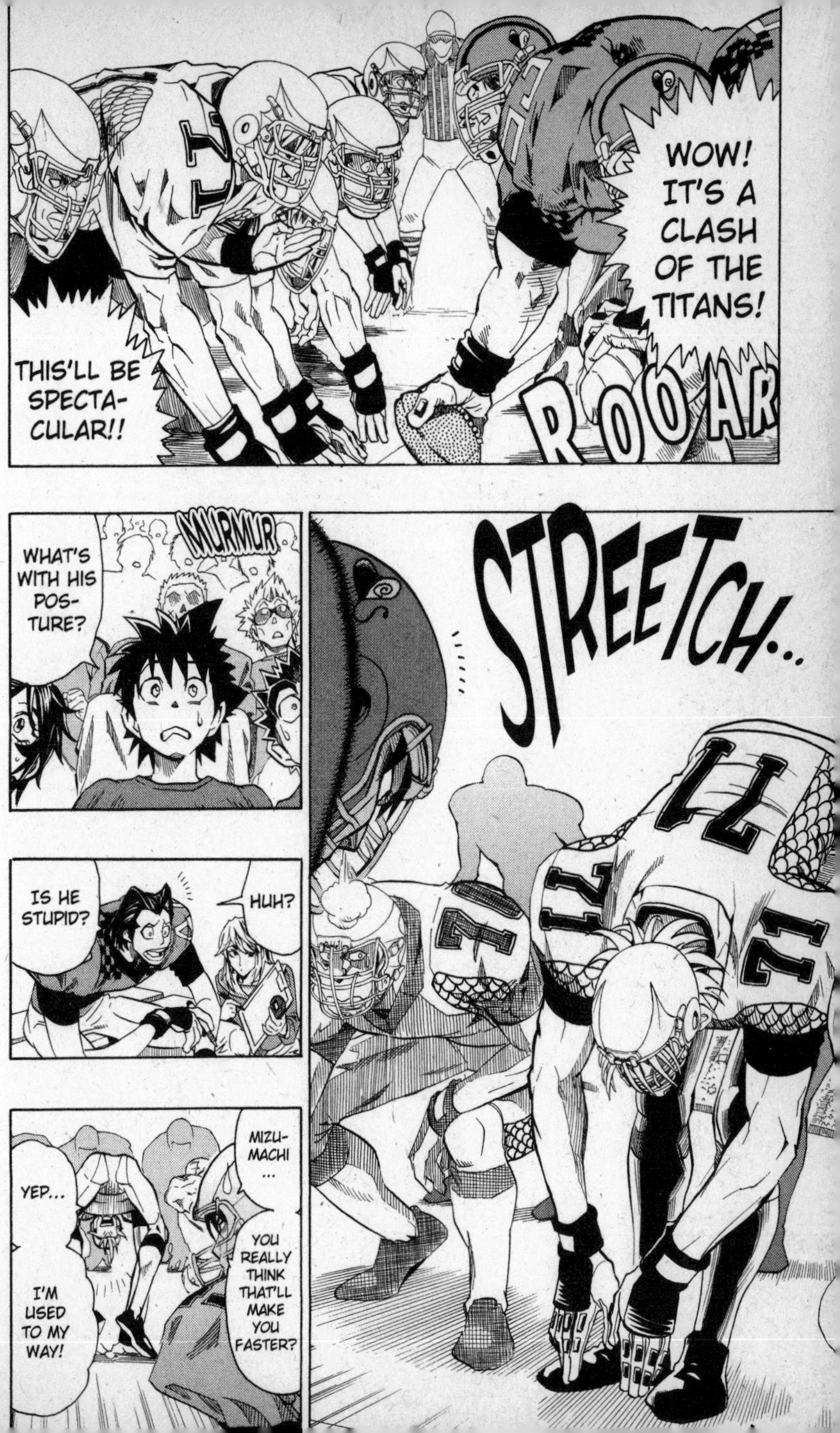
WOW! IT'S A CLASH OF THE TITANS!
ROOAR
THIS'LL BE SPECTACULAR!!
STREETCH...
MURMUR
WHAT'S WITH HIS POSTURE?
HUH?
IS HE STUPID?
MIZUMACHI...
YOU REALLY THINK THAT'LL MAKE YOU FASTER?
YEP...
I'M USED TO MY WAY!

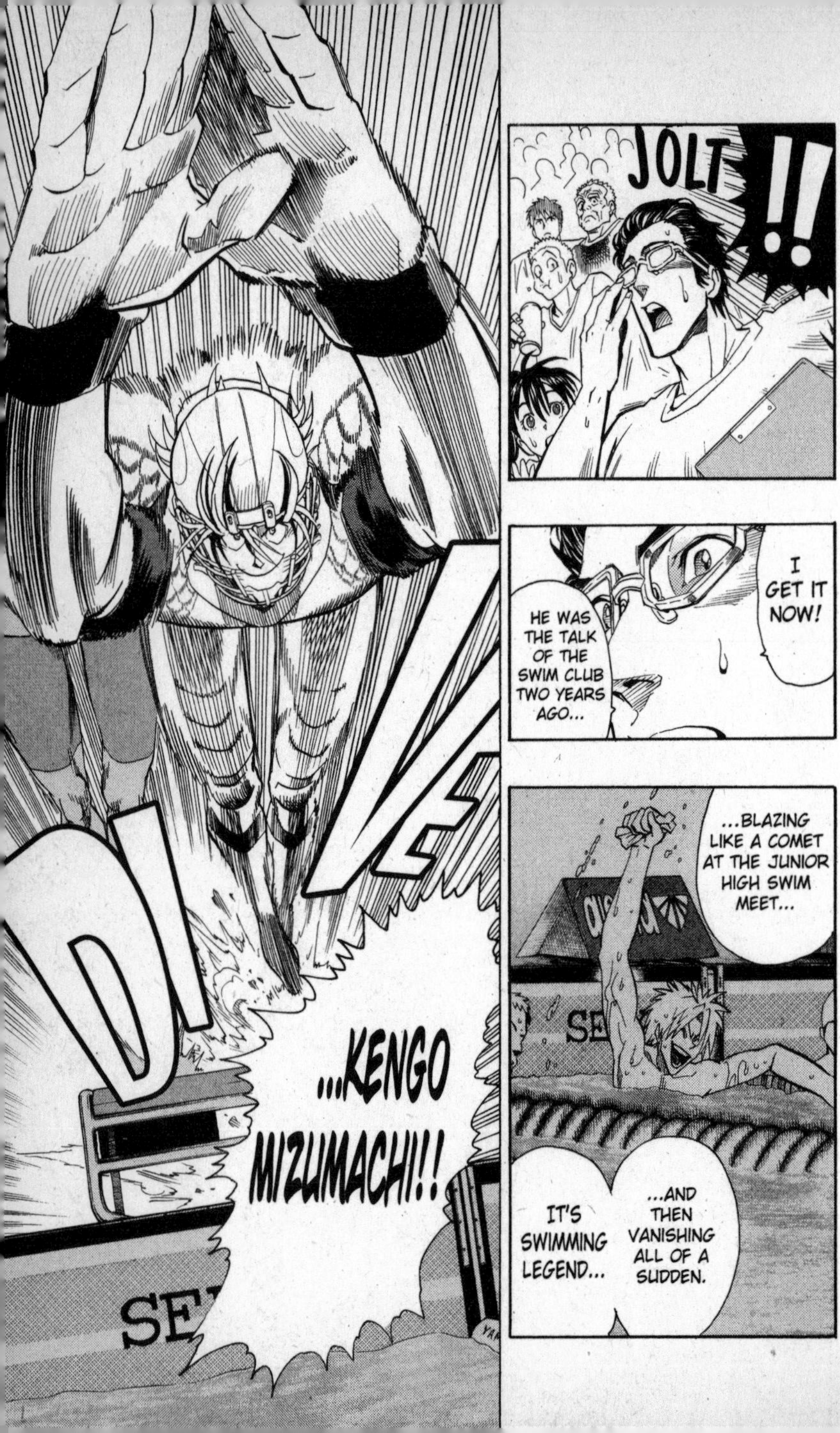
JOLT!!
I GET IT NOW!
HE WAS THE TALK OF THE SWIM CLUB TWO YEARS AGO...
...BLAZING LIKE A COMET AT THE JUNIOR HIGH SWIM MEET...
...AND THEN VANISHING ALL OF A SUDDEN.
IT'S SWIMMING LEGEND...
DIVE
...KENGO MIZUMACHI!!

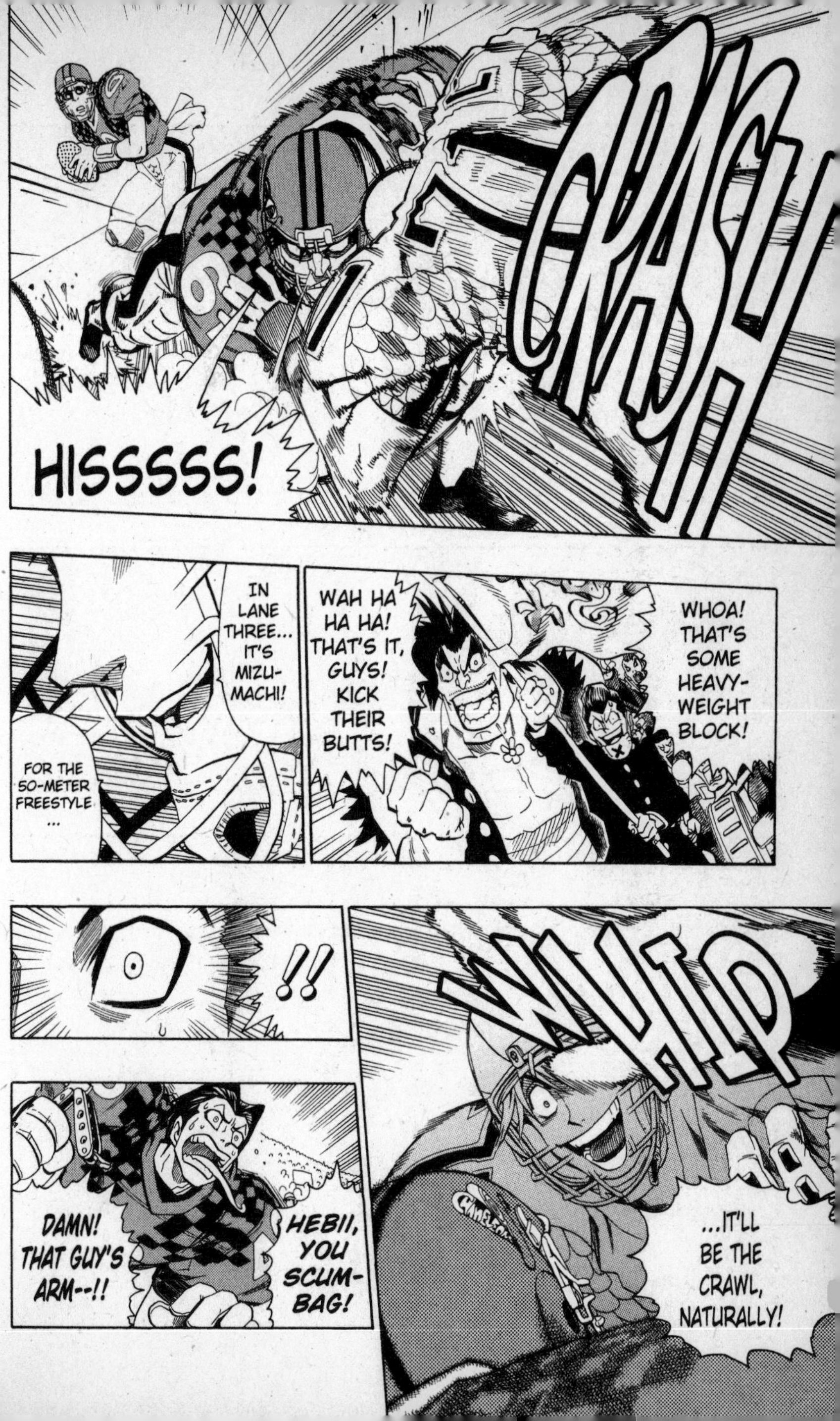
CRASH
HISSSSS!
WHOA! THAT'S SOME HEAVY-WEIGHT BLOCK!
WAH HA HA HA! THAT'S IT, GUYS! KICK THEIR BUTTS!
IN LANE THREE... IT'S MIZU-MACHI!
FOR THE 50-METER FREESTYLE...
WHIP
...IT'LL BE THE CRAWL, NATURALLY!
!!
HEBII, YOU SCUM-BAG!
DAMN! THAT GUY'S ARM--!!

READ THIS WAY

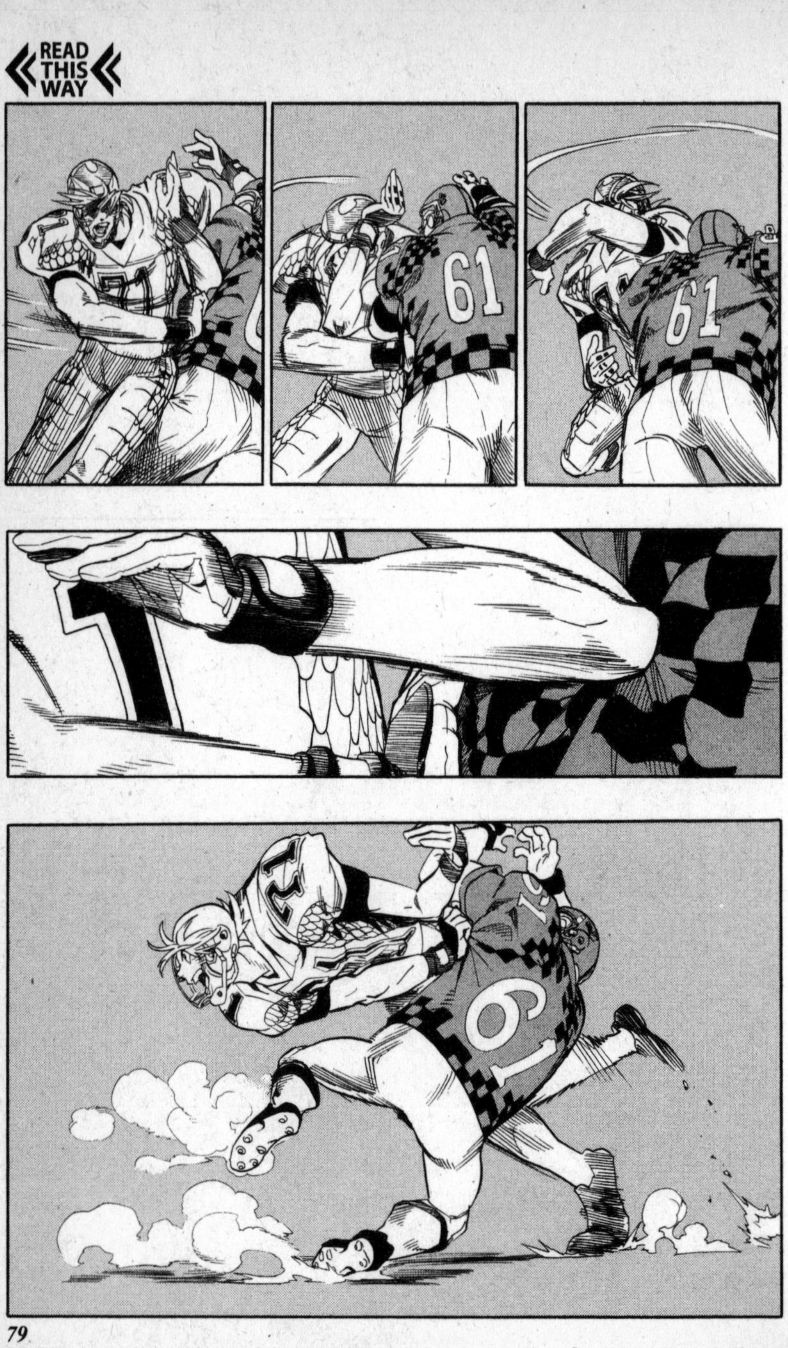

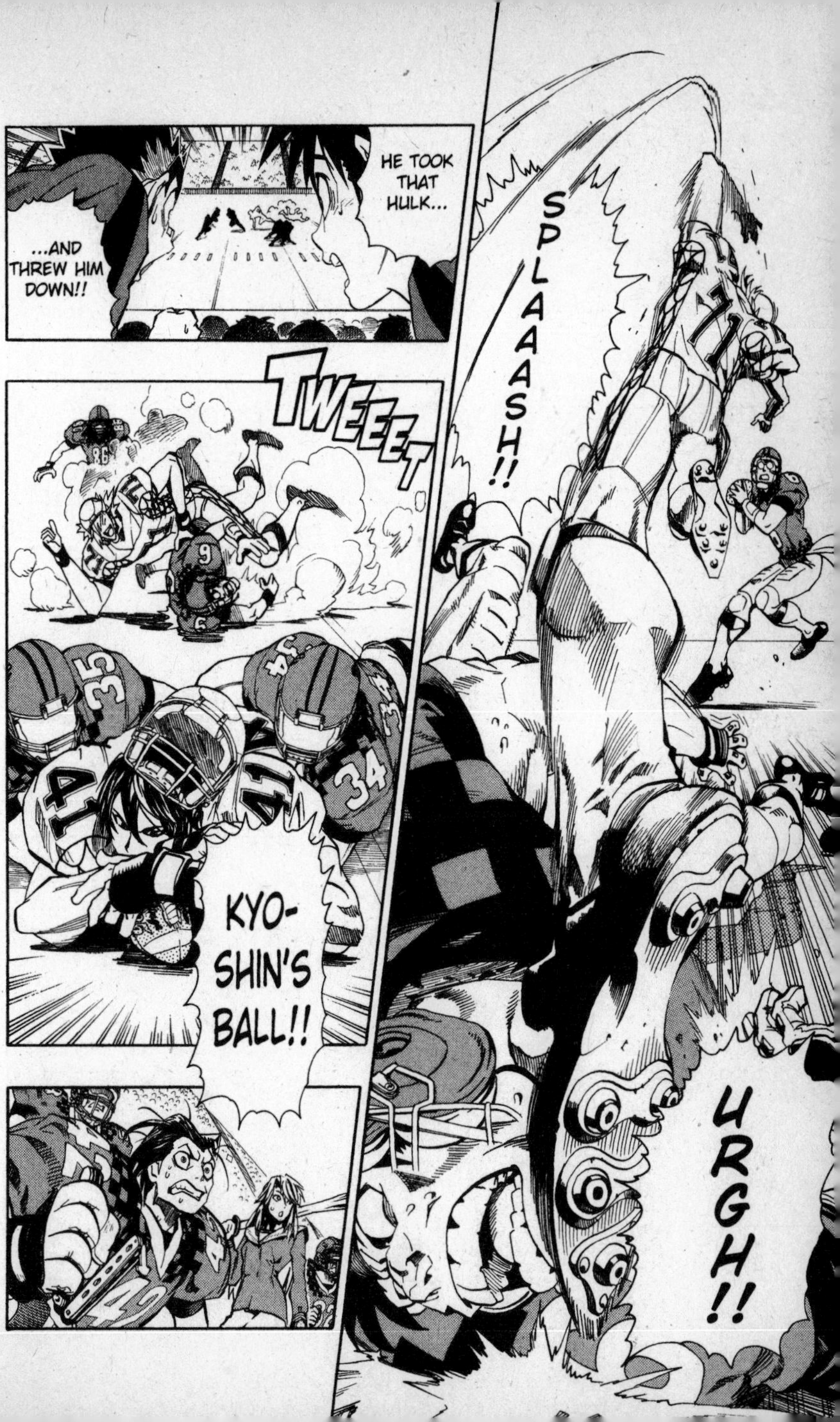
SPLAAAASH!!
URGH!!
HE TOOK THAT HULK...
...AND THREW HIM DOWN!!
TWEEEET
KYO-SHIN'S BALL!!

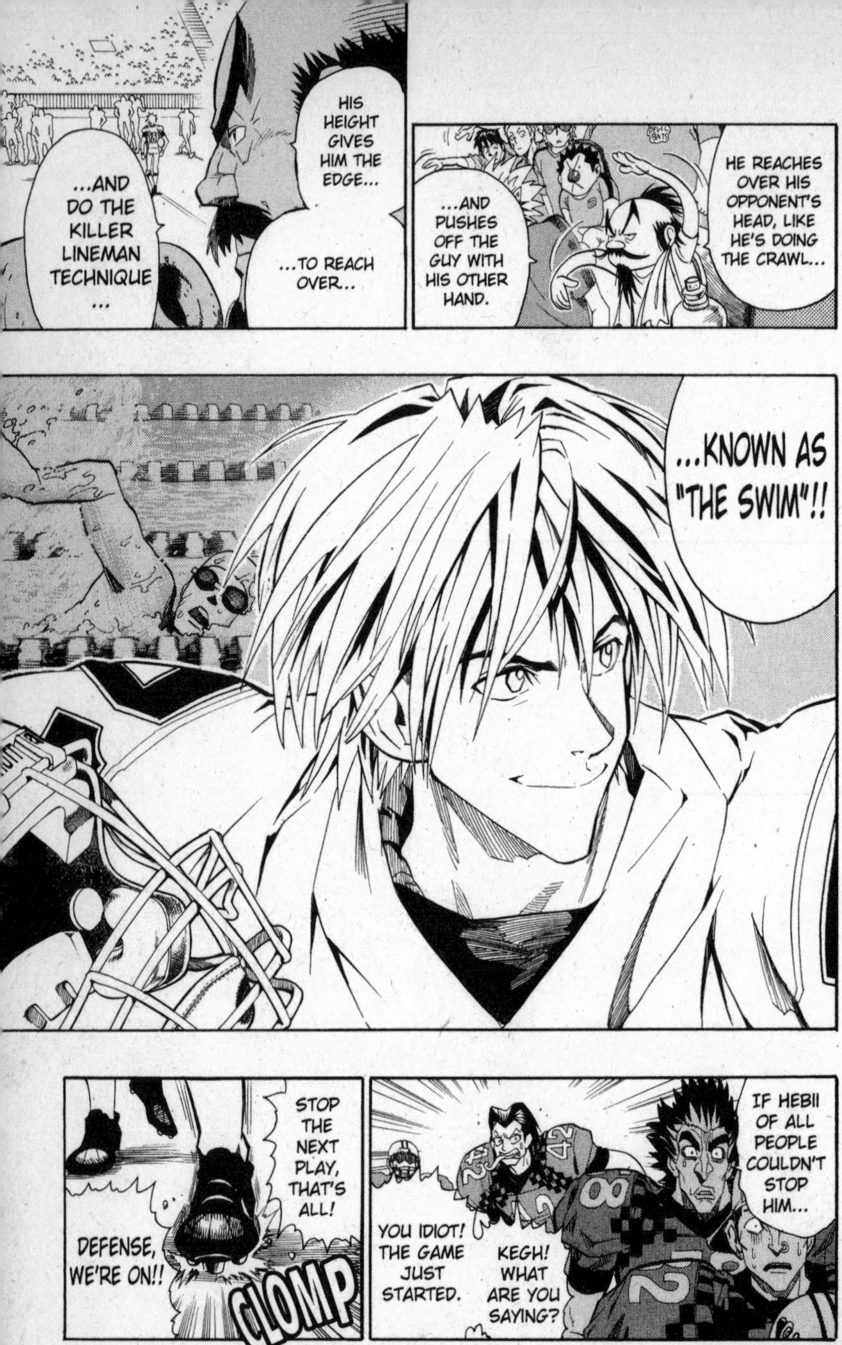
HE REACHES OVER HIS OPPONENT'S HEAD, LIKE HE'S DOING THE CRAWL...
...AND PUSHES OFF THE GUY WITH HIS OTHER HAND.
HIS HEIGHT GIVES HIM THE EDGE...
...TO REACH OVER...
...AND DO THE KILLER LINEMAN TECHNIQUE...
...KNOWN AS "THE SWIM"!!
IF HEBII OF ALL PEOPLE COULDN'T STOP HIM...
KEGH! WHAT ARE YOU SAYING?
YOU IDIOT! THE GAME JUST STARTED.
STOP THE NEXT PLAY, THAT'S ALL!
DEFENSE, WE'RE ON!!
CLOMP

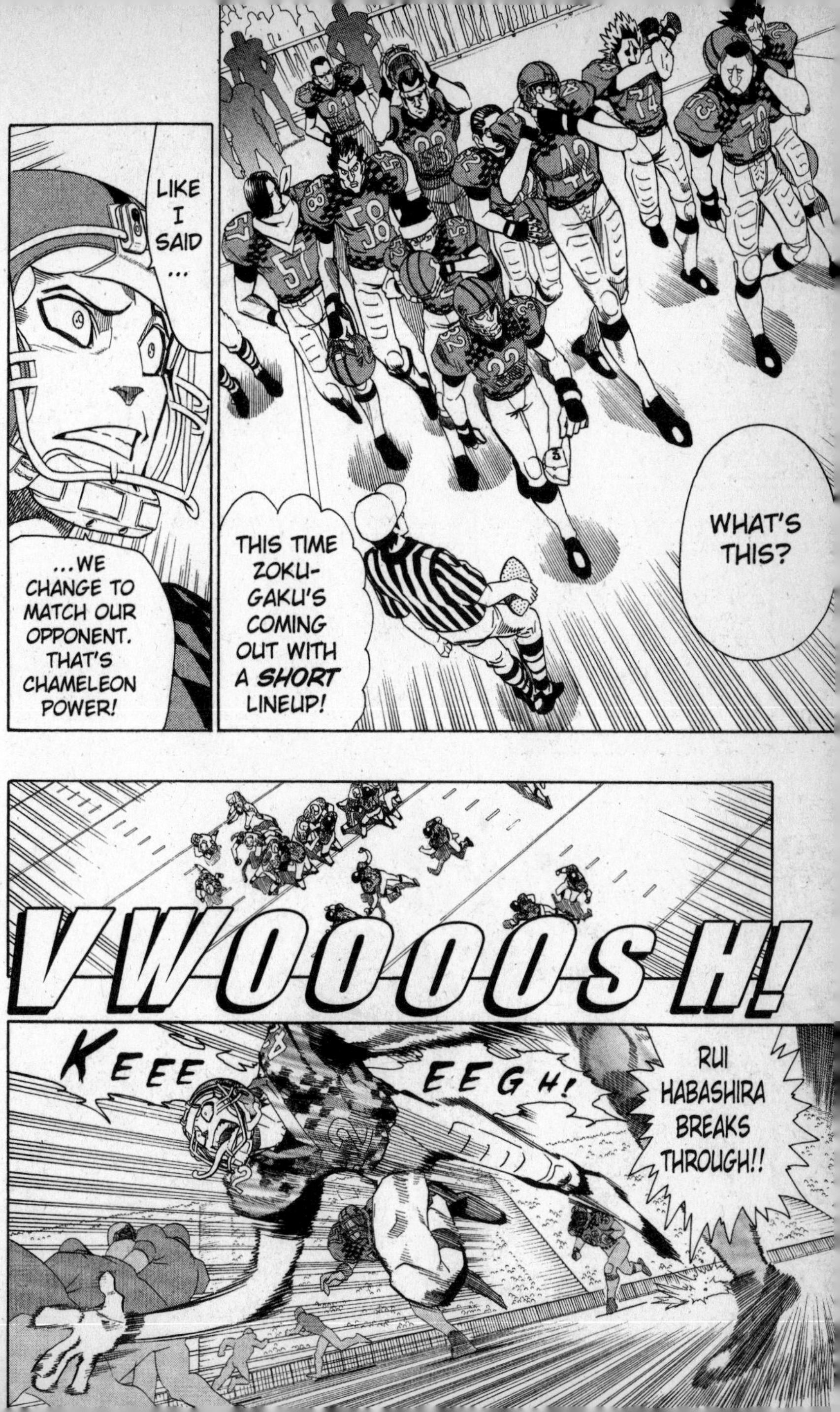
WHAT'S THIS?
THIS TIME ZOKU-GAKU'S COMING OUT WITH A SHORT LINEUP!
LIKE I SAID ...
...WE CHANGE TO MATCH OUR OPPONENT. THAT'S CHAMELEON POWER!
VWOOOOSH!
RUI HABASHIRA BREAKS THROUGH!!
KEEEEEGH!

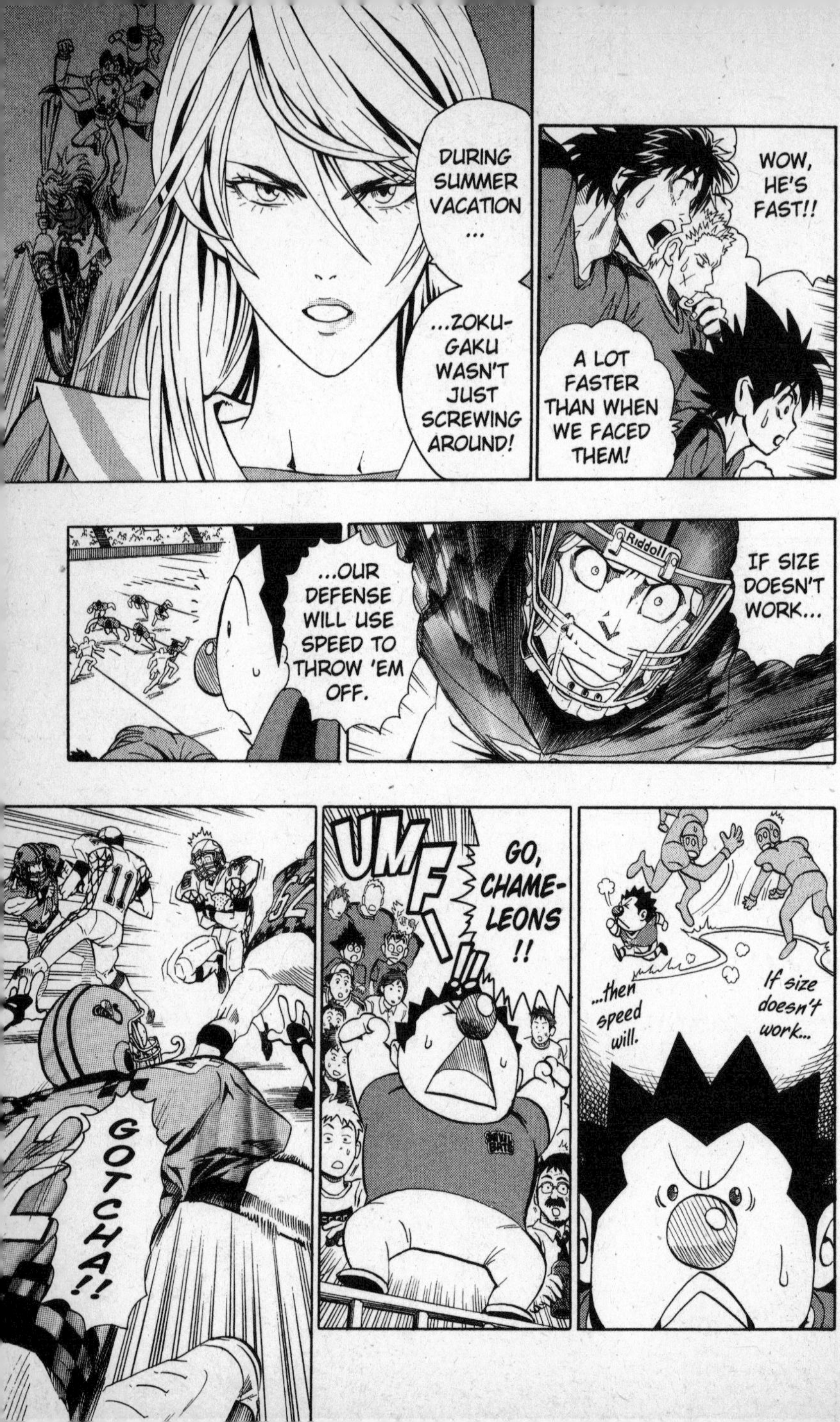
WOW, HE'S FAST!!
A LOT FASTER THAN WHEN WE FACED THEM!
DURING SUMMER VACATION...
...ZOKU-GAKU WASN'T JUST SCREWING AROUND!
IF SIZE DOESN'T WORK...
Riddoll
...OUR DEFENSE WILL USE SPEED TO THROW 'EM OFF.
If size doesn't work...
...then speed will.
GO, CHAME-LEONS!!
UMF!!
GOTCHA!!

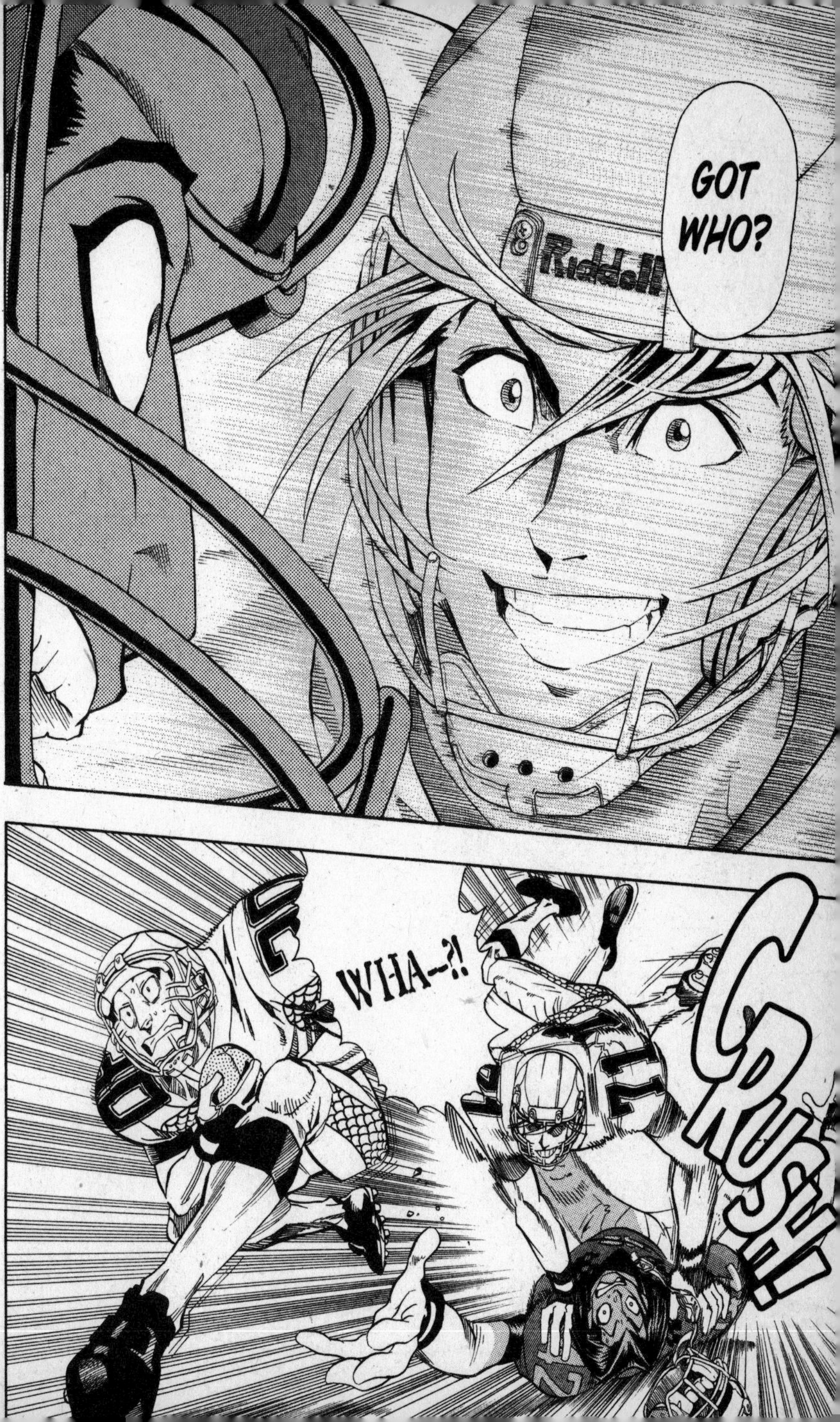
GOT WHO?
Riddell
WHA--?!
CRUSH!

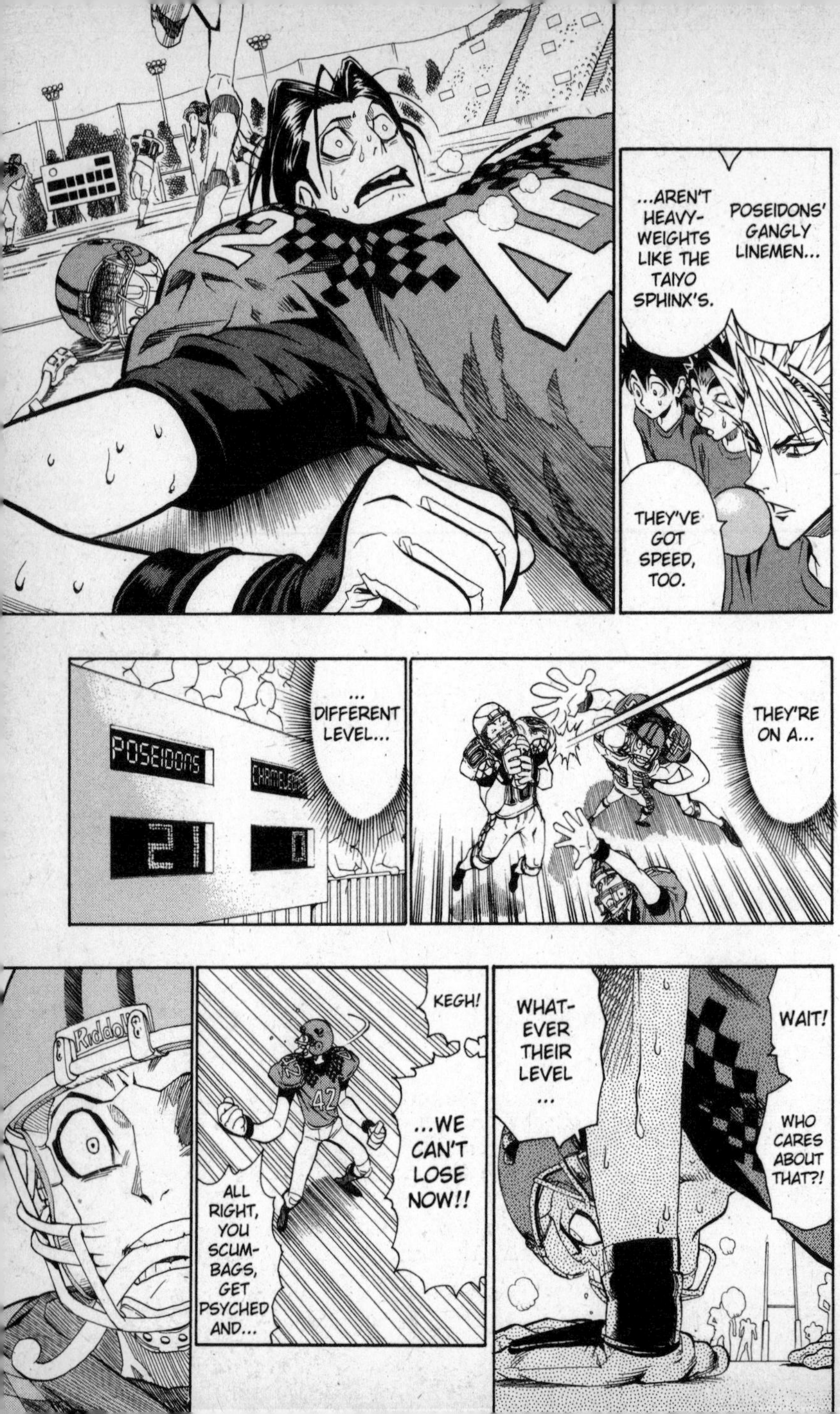
POSEIDONS' GANGLY LINEMEN...
...AREN'T HEAVY-WEIGHTS LIKE THE TAIYO SPHINX'S.
THEY'VE GOT SPEED, TOO.
THEY'RE ON A...
...DIFFERENT LEVEL...
POSEIDONS
21
0
WAIT!
WHO CARES ABOUT THAT?!
WHAT-EVER THEIR LEVEL ...
KEGH!
...WE CAN'T LOSE NOW!!
ALL RIGHT, YOU SCUM-BAGS, GET PSYCHED AND...

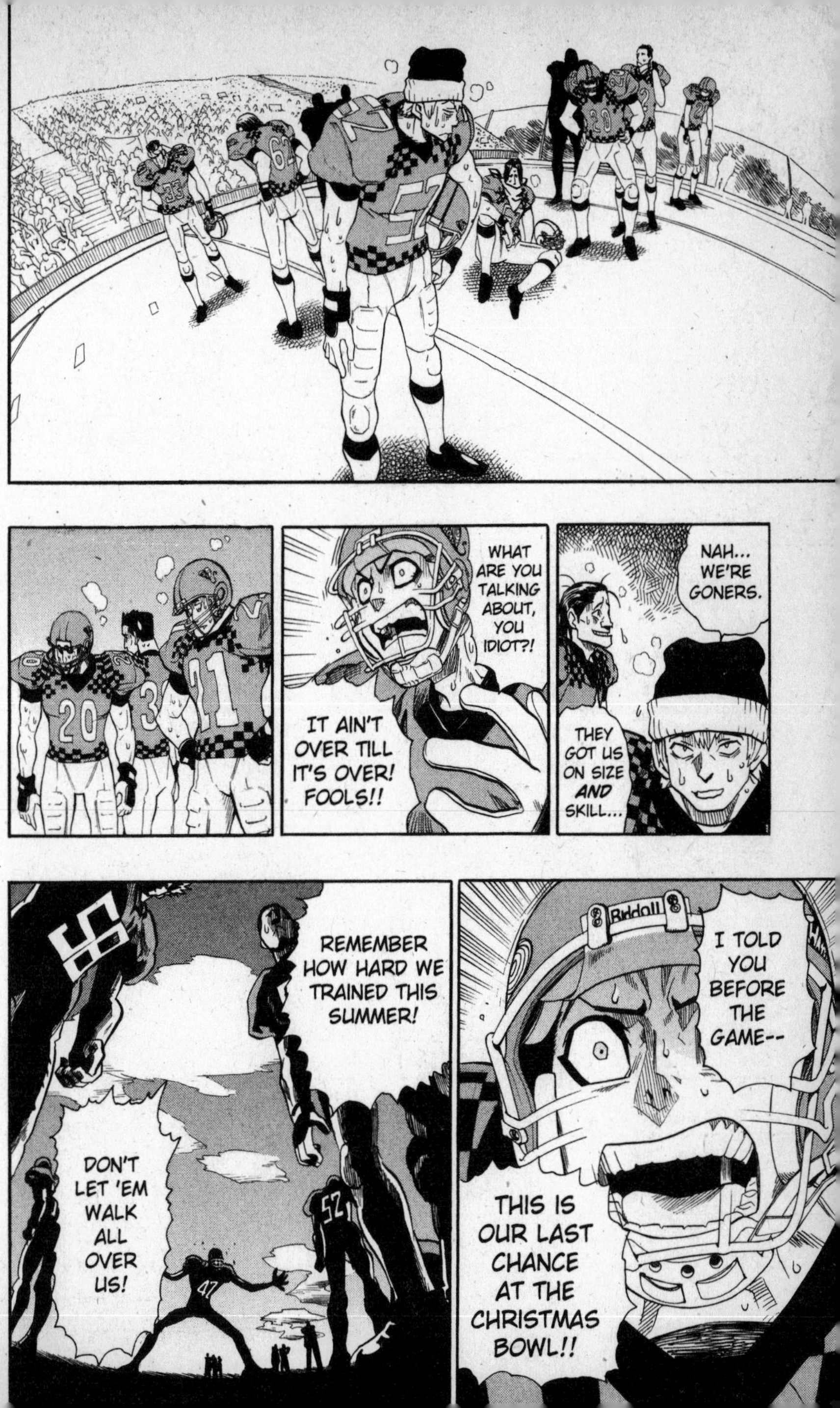
NAH... WE'RE GONERS.
THEY GOT US ON SIZE AND SKILL...
WHAT ARE YOU TALKING ABOUT, YOU IDIOT?!
IT AIN'T OVER TILL IT'S OVER! FOOLS!!
I TOLD YOU BEFORE THE GAME--
THIS IS OUR LAST CHANCE AT THE CHRISTMAS BOWL!!
REMEMBER HOW HARD WE TRAINED THIS SUMMER!
DON'T LET 'EM WALK ALL OVER US!

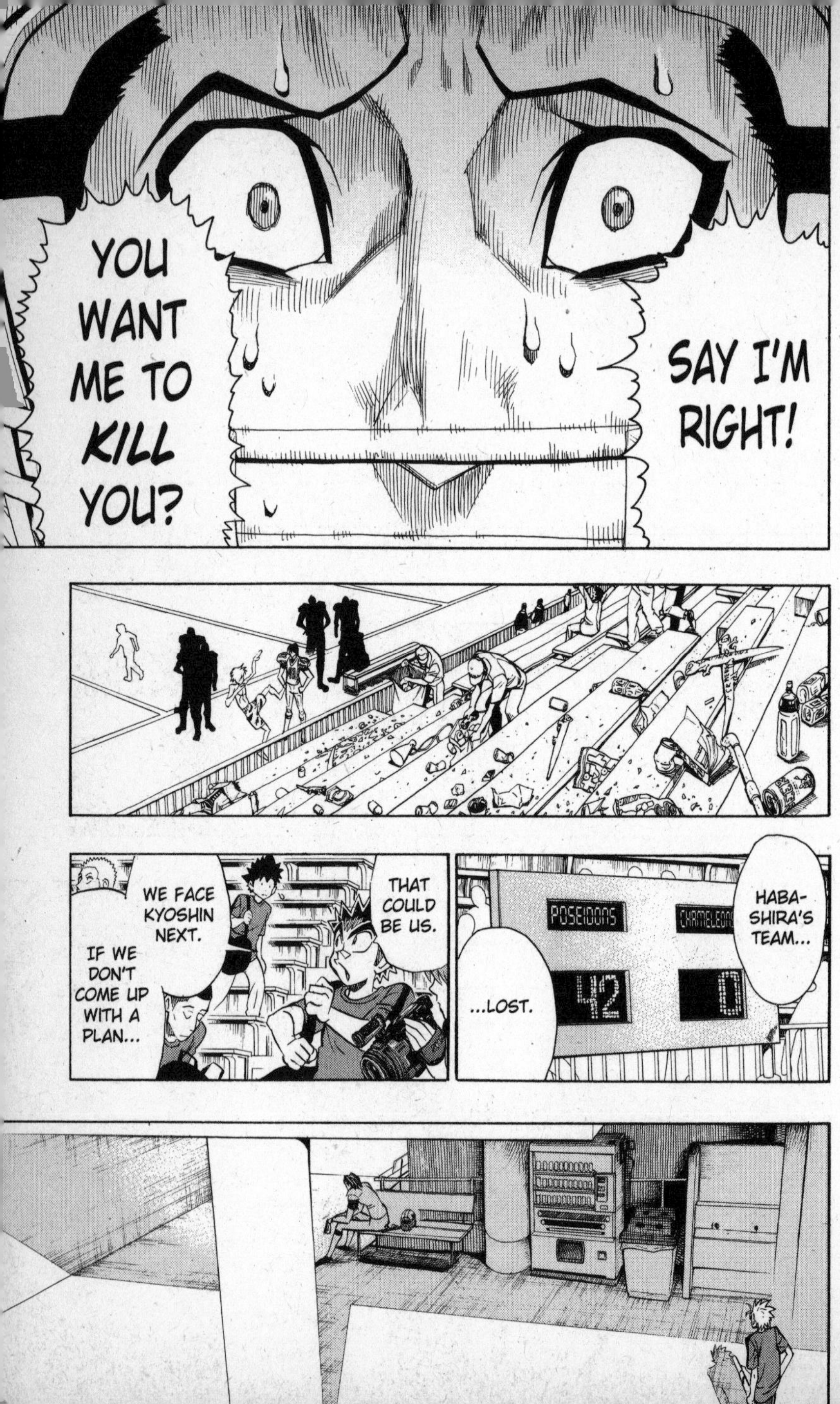
SAY I'M RIGHT!
YOU WANT ME TO KILL YOU?
HABA-SHIRA'S TEAM...
POSEIDONS
42
0
...LOST.
THAT COULD BE US.
WE FACE KYOSHIN NEXT.
IF WE DON'T COME UP WITH A PLAN...

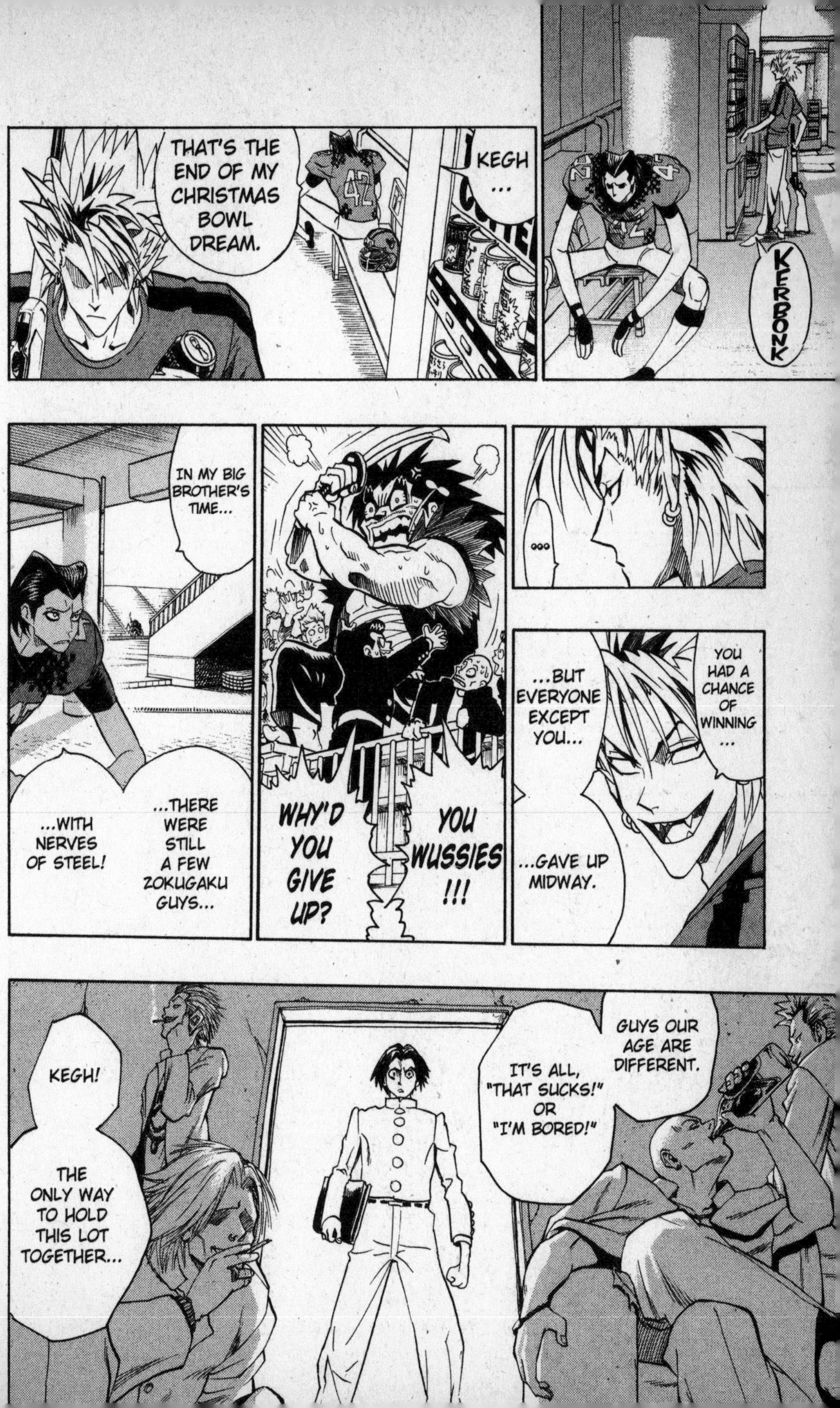
KERBONK
KEGH ...
THAT'S THE END OF MY CHRISTMAS BOWL DREAM.
...
YOU HAD A CHANCE OF WINNING ...
...BUT EVERYONE EXCEPT YOU...
...GAVE UP MIDWAY.
YOU WUSSIES !!!
WHY'D YOU GIVE UP?
IN MY BIG BROTHER'S TIME...
...THERE WERE STILL A FEW ZOKUGAKU GUYS...
...WITH NERVES OF STEEL!
GUYS OUR AGE ARE DIFFERENT.
IT'S ALL, "THAT SUCKS!" OR "I'M BORED!"
KEGH!
THE ONLY WAY TO HOLD THIS LOT TOGETHER...

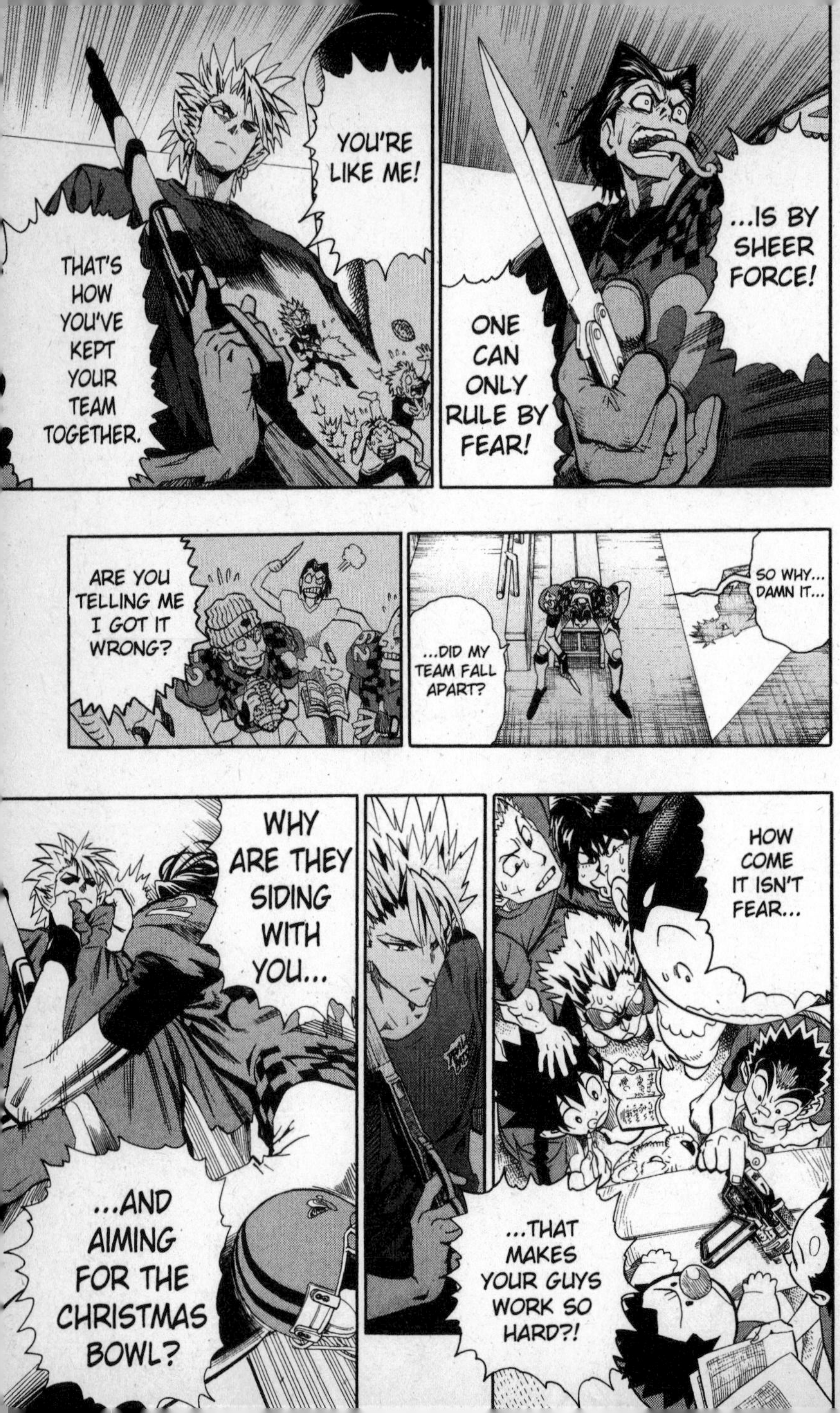
...IS BY SHEER FORCE!
ONE CAN ONLY RULE BY FEAR!
YOU'RE LIKE ME!
THAT'S HOW YOU'VE KEPT YOUR TEAM TOGETHER.
SO WHY... DAMN IT...
...DID MY TEAM FALL APART?
ARE YOU TELLING ME I GOT IT WRONG?
HOW COME IT ISN'T FEAR...
...THAT MAKES YOUR GUYS WORK SO HARD?!
WHY ARE THEY SIDING WITH YOU...
...AND AIMING FOR THE CHRISTMAS BOWL?

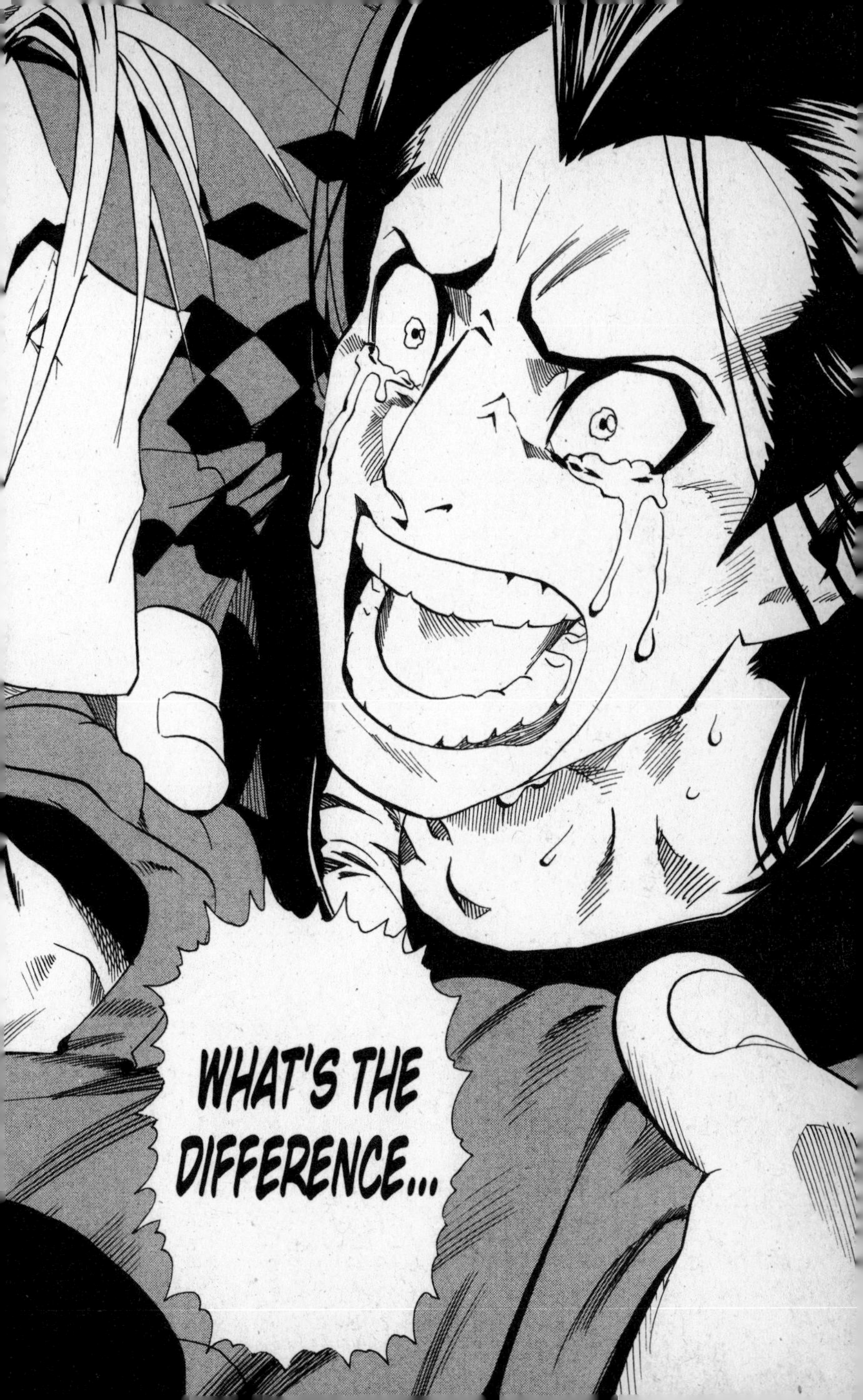
WHAT'S THE DIFFERENCE...

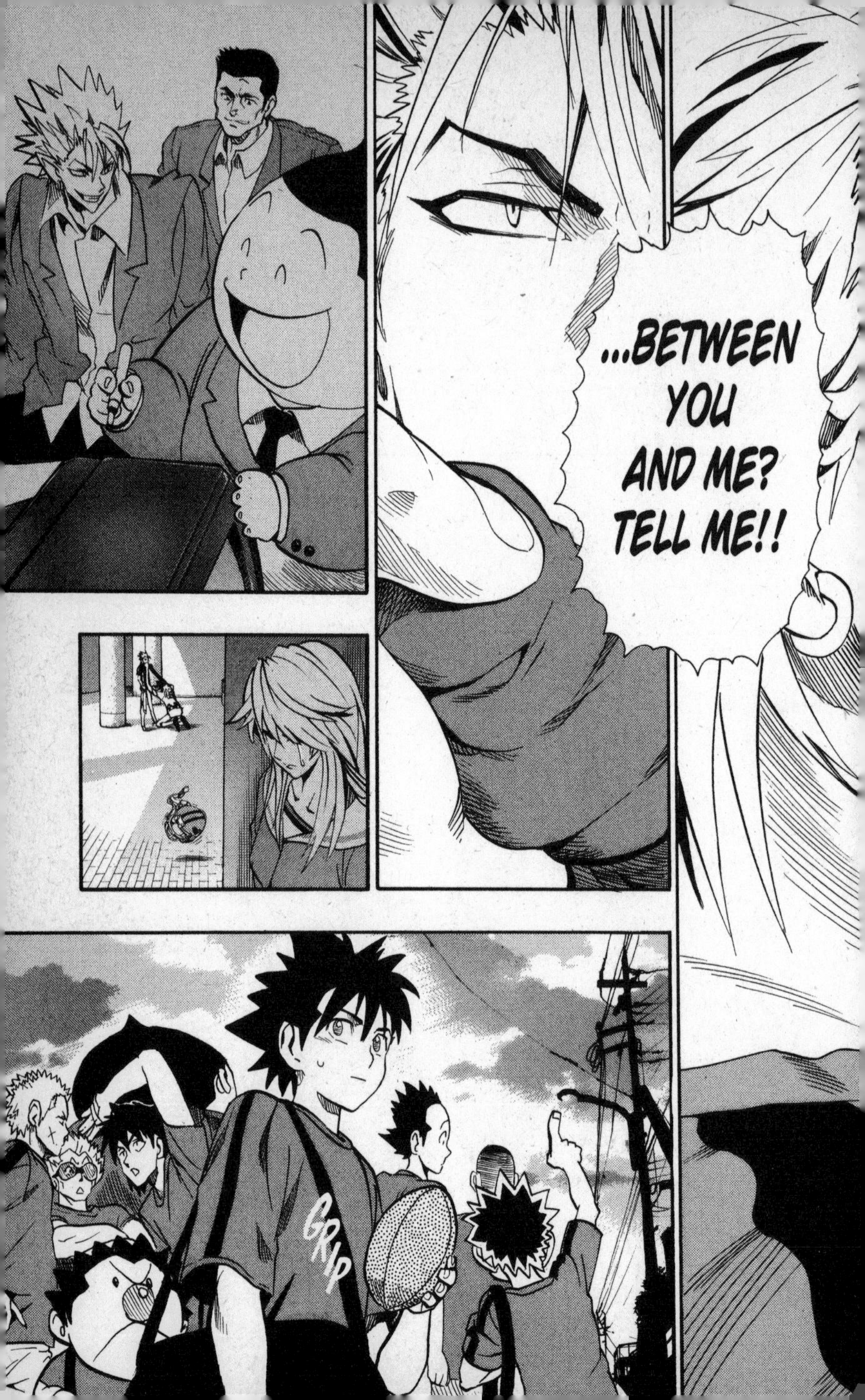
...BETWEEN YOU AND ME? TELL ME!!
GRIP

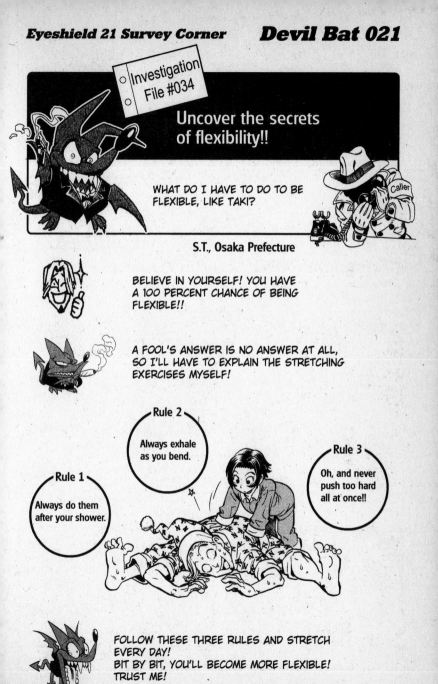

Investigation File #034

Uncover the secrets of flexibility!!

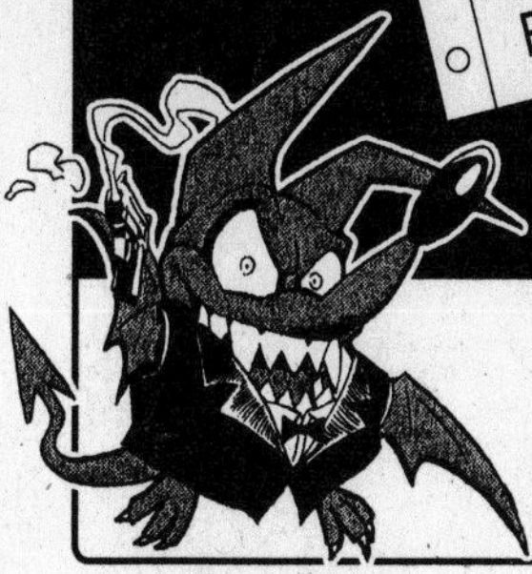

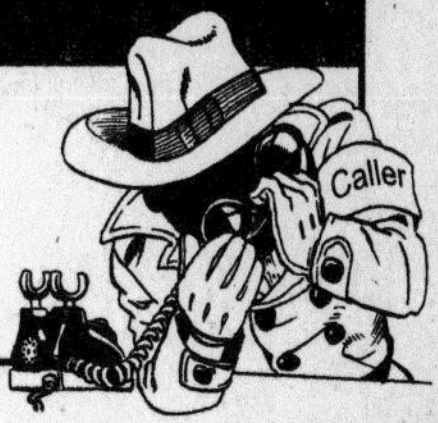
Caller

WHAT DO I HAVE TO DO TO BE FLEXIBLE, LIKE TAKI?

S.T., Osaka Prefecture

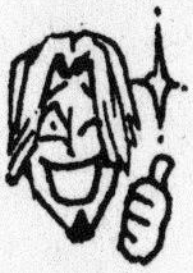

BELIEVE IN YOURSELF! YOU HAVE A 100 PERCENT CHANCE OF BEING FLEXIBLE!!

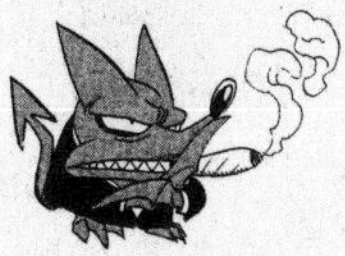

A FOOL'S ANSWER IS NO ANSWER AT ALL, SO I'LL HAVE TO EXPLAIN THE STRETCHING EXERCISES MYSELF!

Rule 1
Always do them after your shower.

Rule 2
Always exhale as you bend.

Rule 3
Oh, and never push too hard all at once!!

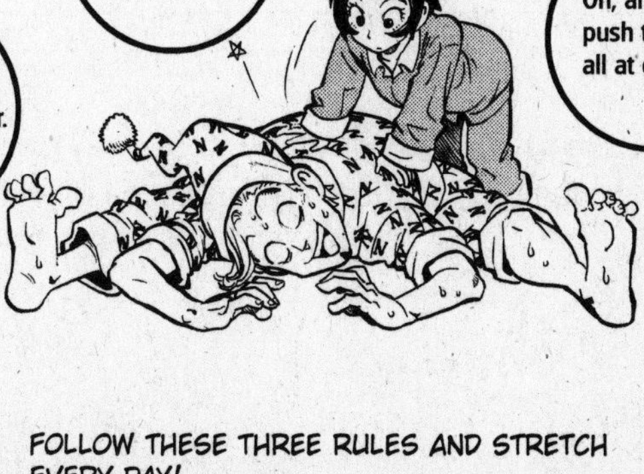

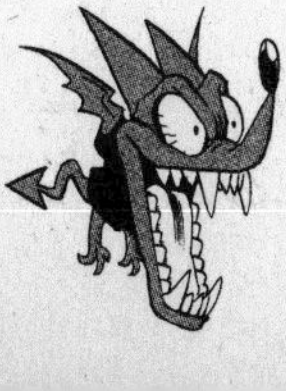

FOLLOW THESE THREE RULES AND STRETCH EVERY DAY!
BIT BY BIT, YOU'LL BECOME MORE FLEXIBLE!
TRUST ME!

Chapter 111 The Quarterfinals

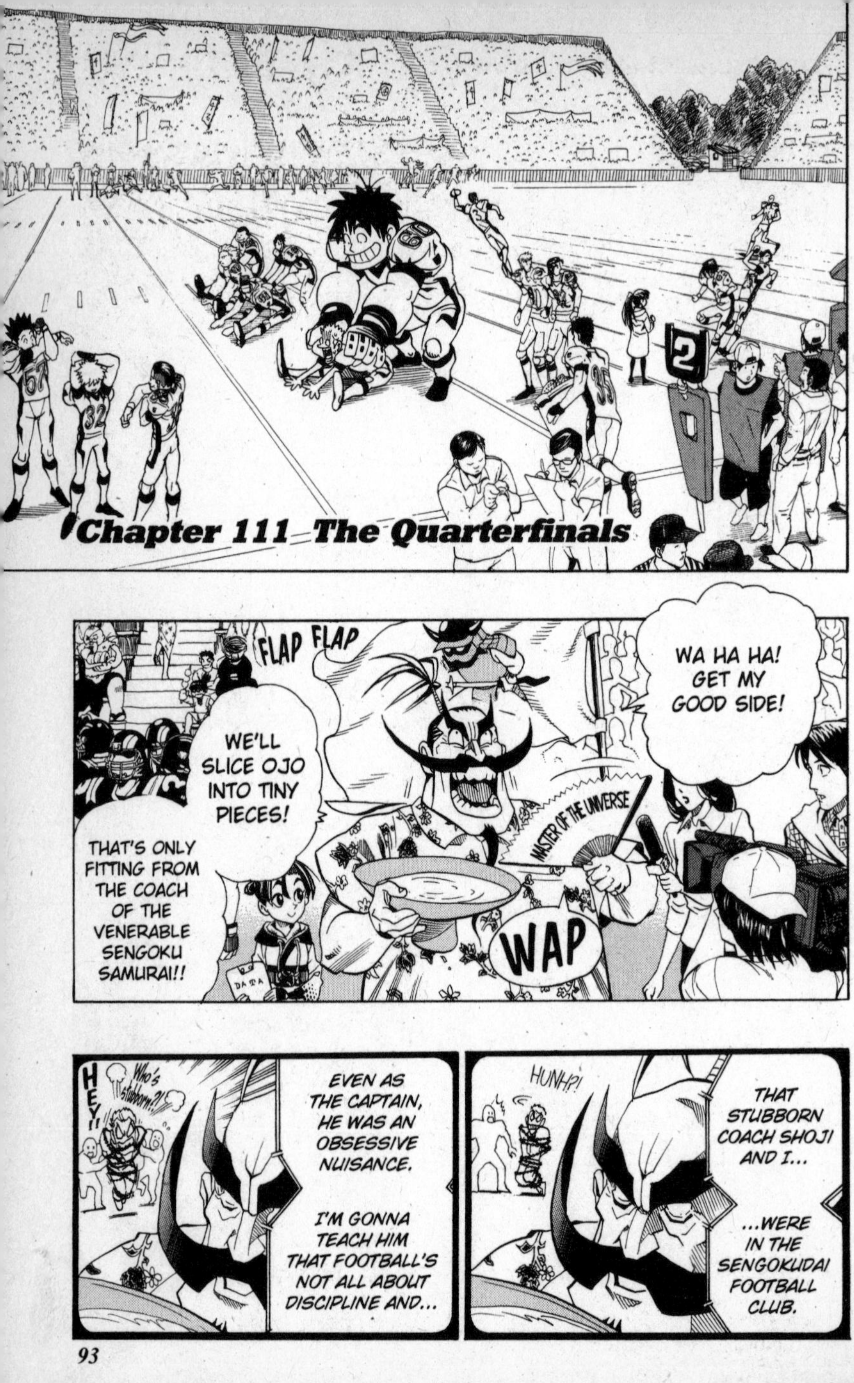

WA HA HA! GET MY GOOD SIDE!
FLAP FLAP
WE'LL SLICE OJO INTO TINY PIECES!
THAT'S ONLY FITTING FROM THE COACH OF THE VENERABLE SENGOKU SAMURAI!!
MASTER OF THE UNIVERSE
WAP
DATA
THAT STUBBORN COACH SHOJI AND I...
...WERE IN THE SENGOKUDAI FOOTBALL CLUB.
HUNH?!
EVEN AS THE CAPTAIN, HE WAS AN OBSESSIVE NUISANCE.
I'M GONNA TEACH HIM THAT FOOTBALL'S NOT ALL ABOUT DISCIPLINE AND...
HEY!!
Who's stubborn?!

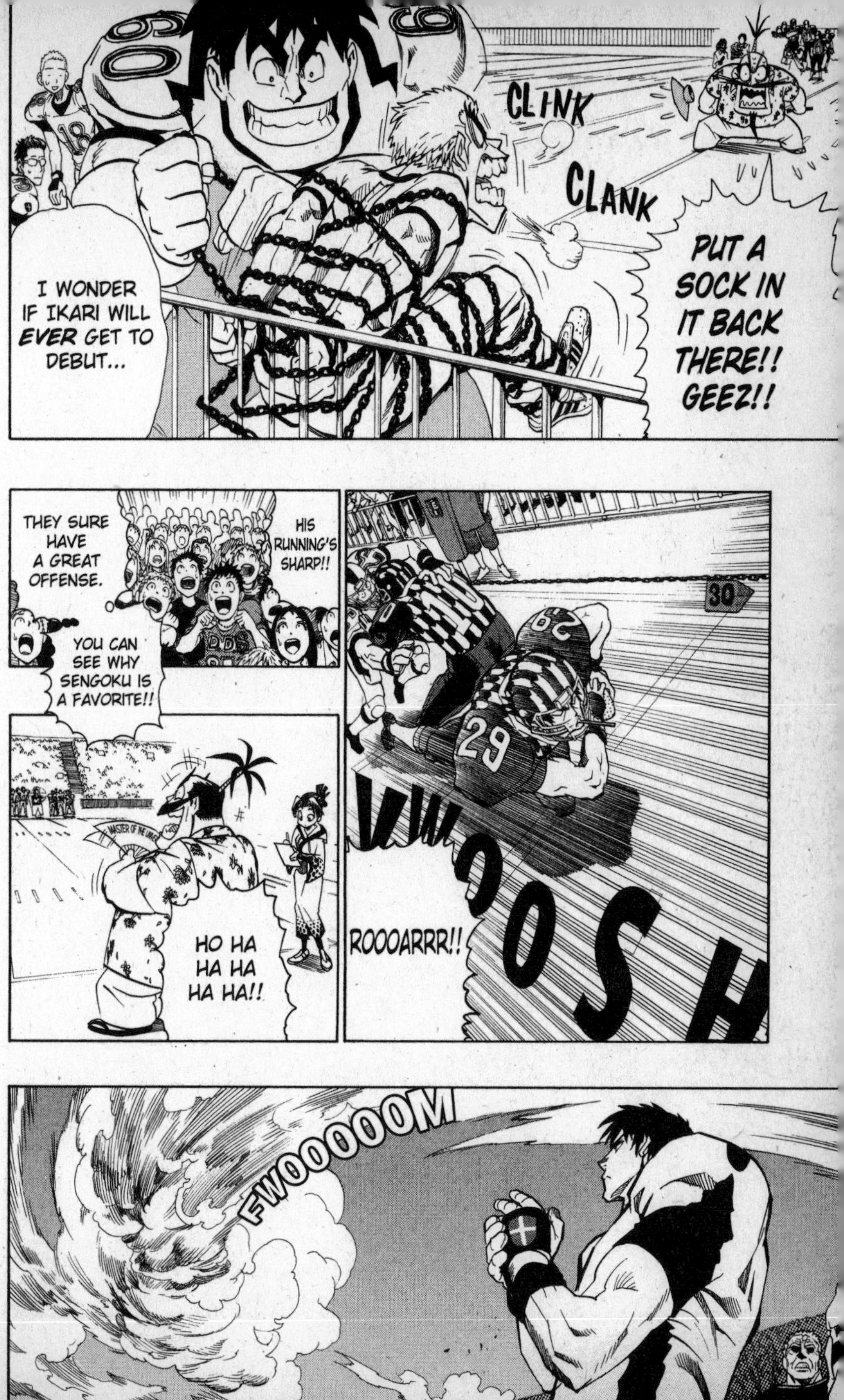
CLINK
CLANK
PUT A SOCK IN IT BACK THERE!! GEEZ!!
I WONDER IF IKARI WILL EVER GET TO DEBUT...
VWOOSH
ROOOARRR!!
HIS RUNNING'S SHARP!!
THEY SURE HAVE A GREAT OFFENSE.
YOU CAN SEE WHY SENGOKU IS A FAVORITE!!
HO HA HA HA HA HA!!
FWOOOOOM

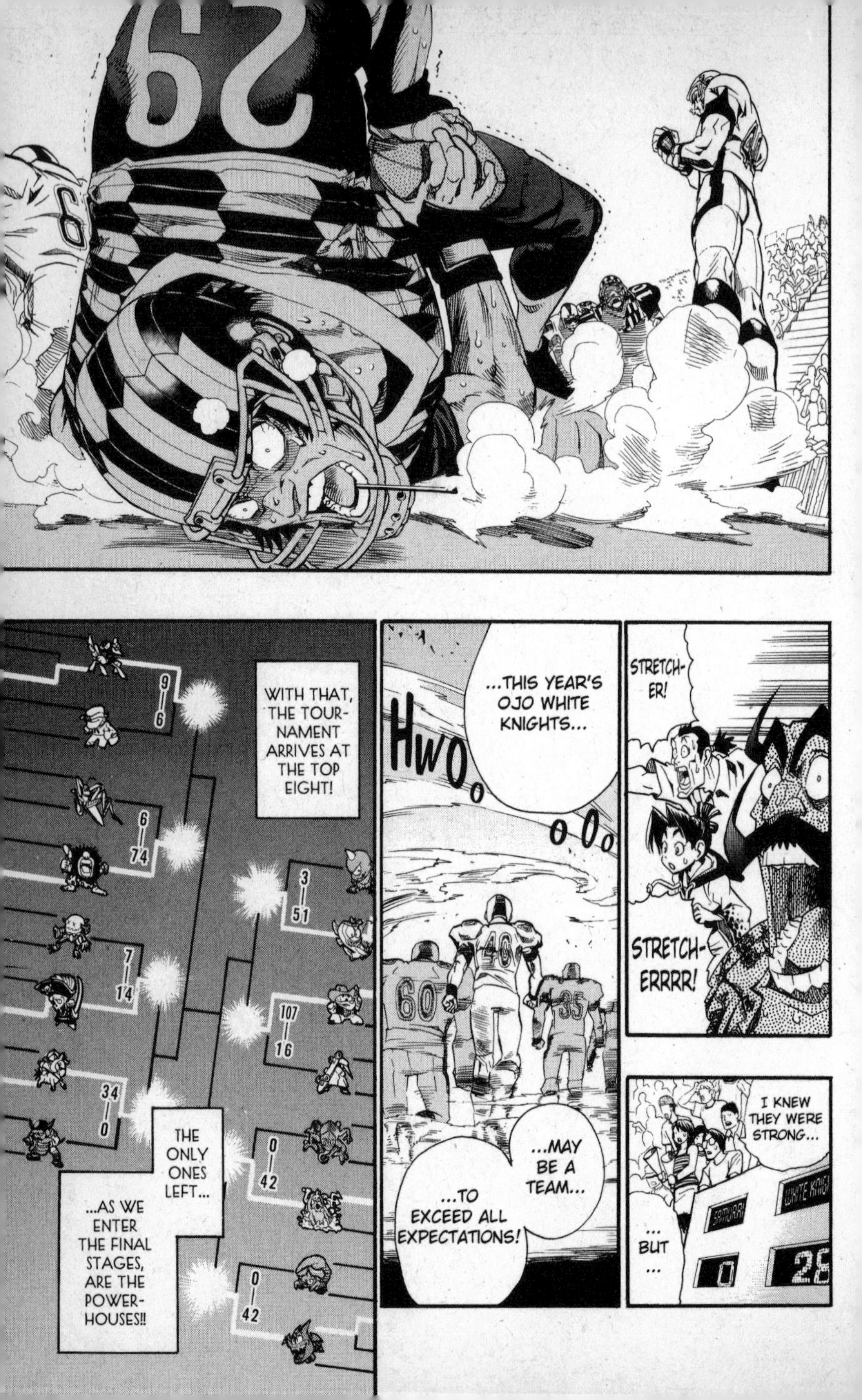
STRETCH-ER!
STRETCH-ERRRR!
I KNEW THEY WERE STRONG...
...BUT...
...THIS YEAR'S OJO WHITE KNIGHTS...
HWOoooOo
...MAY BE A TEAM...
...TO EXCEED ALL EXPECTATIONS!
WITH THAT, THE TOURNAMENT ARRIVES AT THE TOP EIGHT!
THE ONLY ONES LEFT...
...AS WE ENTER THE FINAL STAGES, ARE THE POWERHOUSES!!

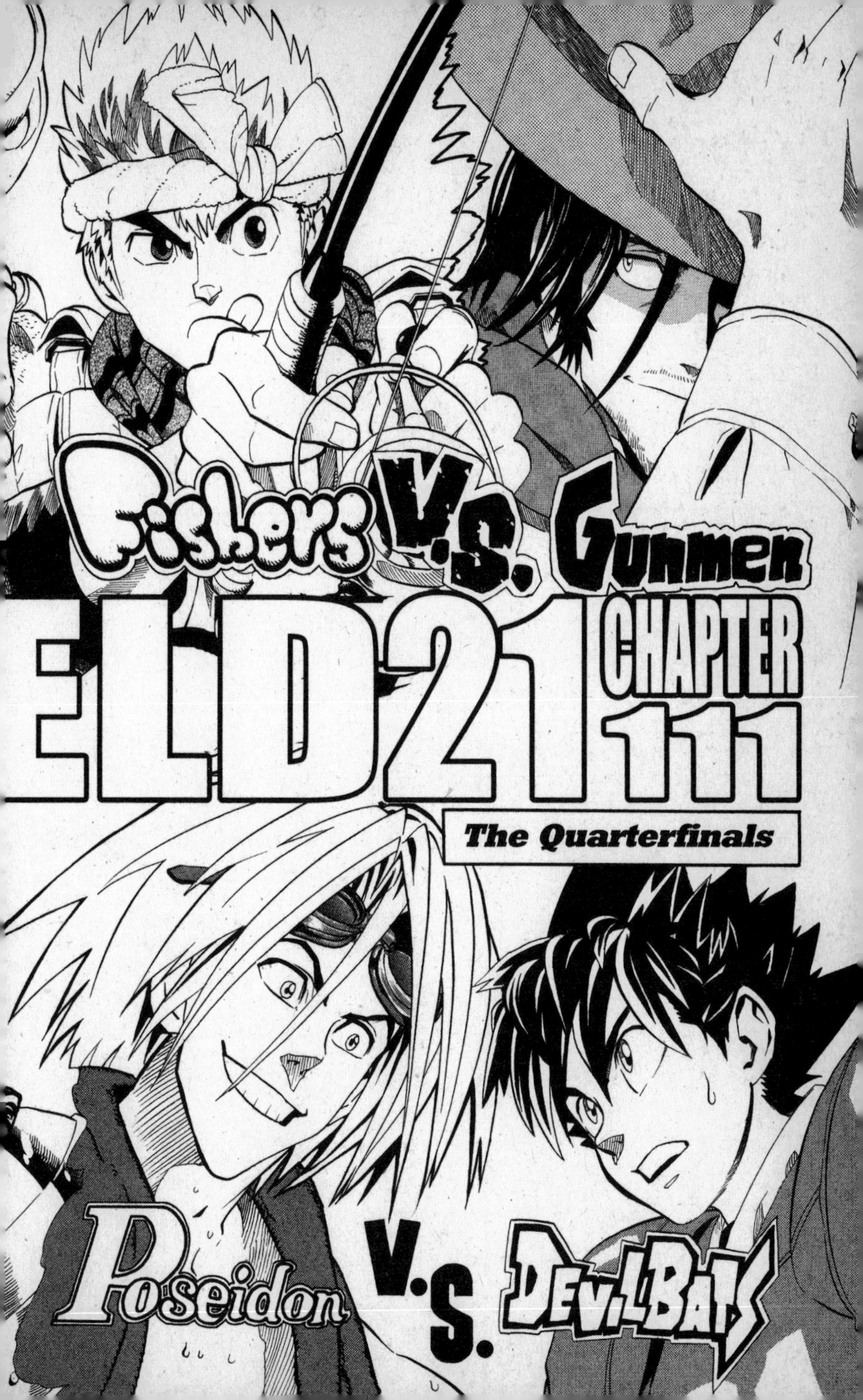
Fishers V.S. Gunmen
ELD21 CHAPTER 111
The Quarterfinals
Poseidon V.S. DevilBats

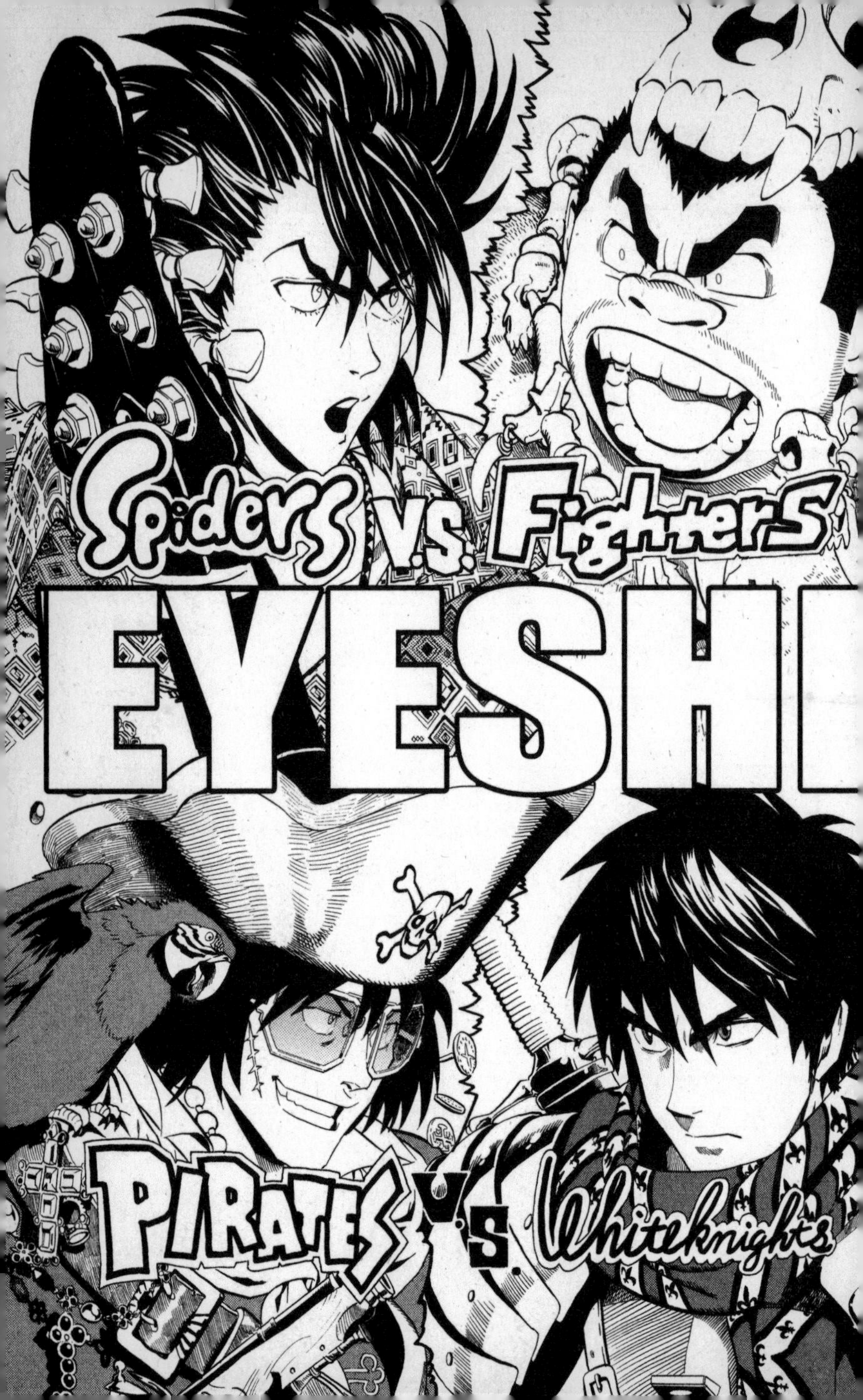

Spiders v.s. Fighters
EYESHI
PIRATES v.s Whiteknights

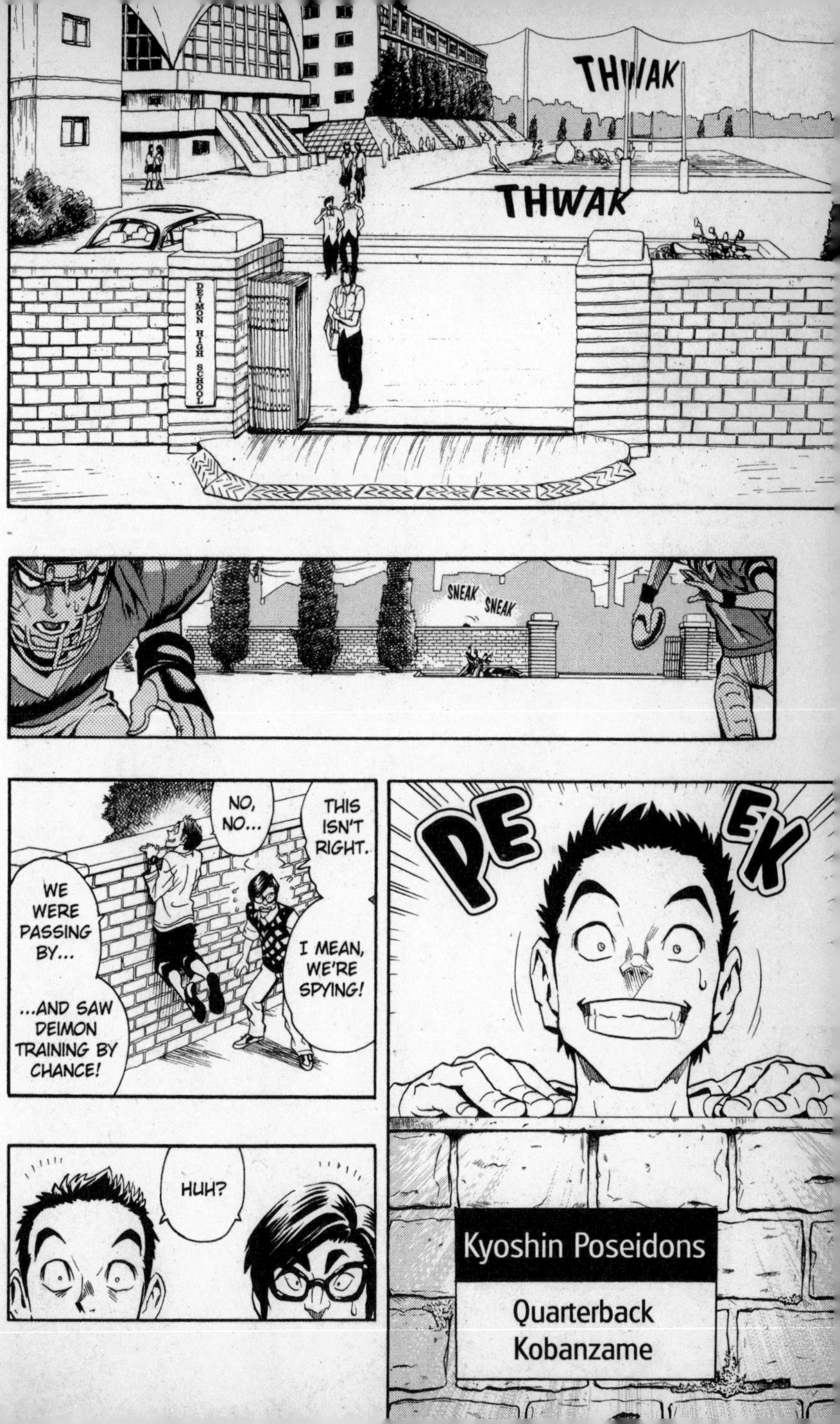
THWAK
THWAK
DEIMON HIGH SCHOOL
SNEAK SNEAK
PEEK
Kyoshin Poseidons
Quarterback Kobanzame
WE WERE PASSING BY...
...AND SAW DEIMON TRAINING BY CHANCE!
NO, NO...
THIS ISN'T RIGHT.
I MEAN, WE'RE SPYING!
HUH?

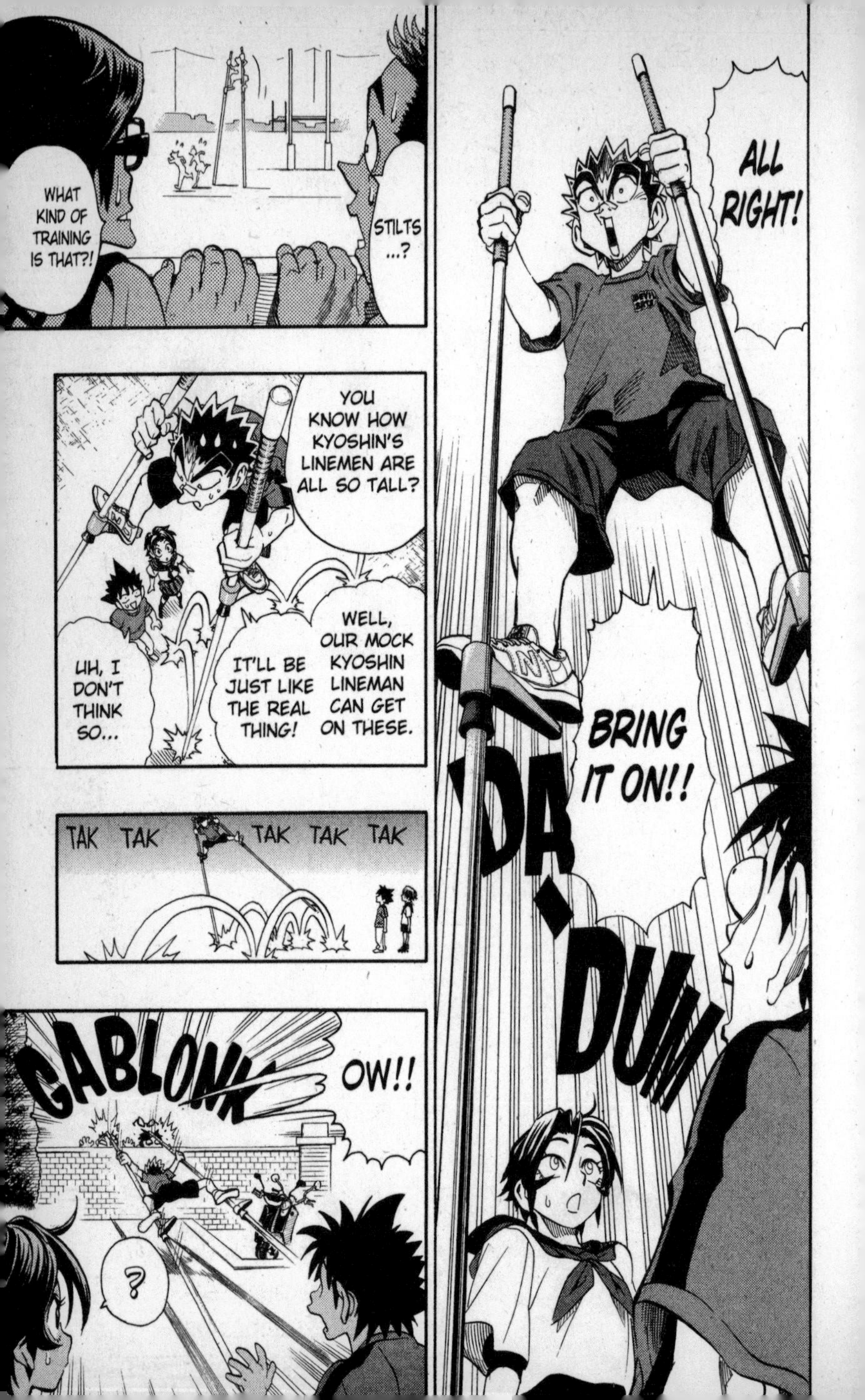
ALL RIGHT!
BRING IT ON!!
DA-DUM
STILTS ...?
WHAT KIND OF TRAINING IS THAT?!
YOU KNOW HOW KYOSHIN'S LINEMEN ARE ALL SO TALL?
WELL, OUR MOCK KYOSHIN LINEMAN CAN GET ON THESE.
IT'LL BE JUST LIKE THE REAL THING!
UH, I DON'T THINK SO...
TAK TAK TAK TAK TAK
OW!!
GABLONK
?

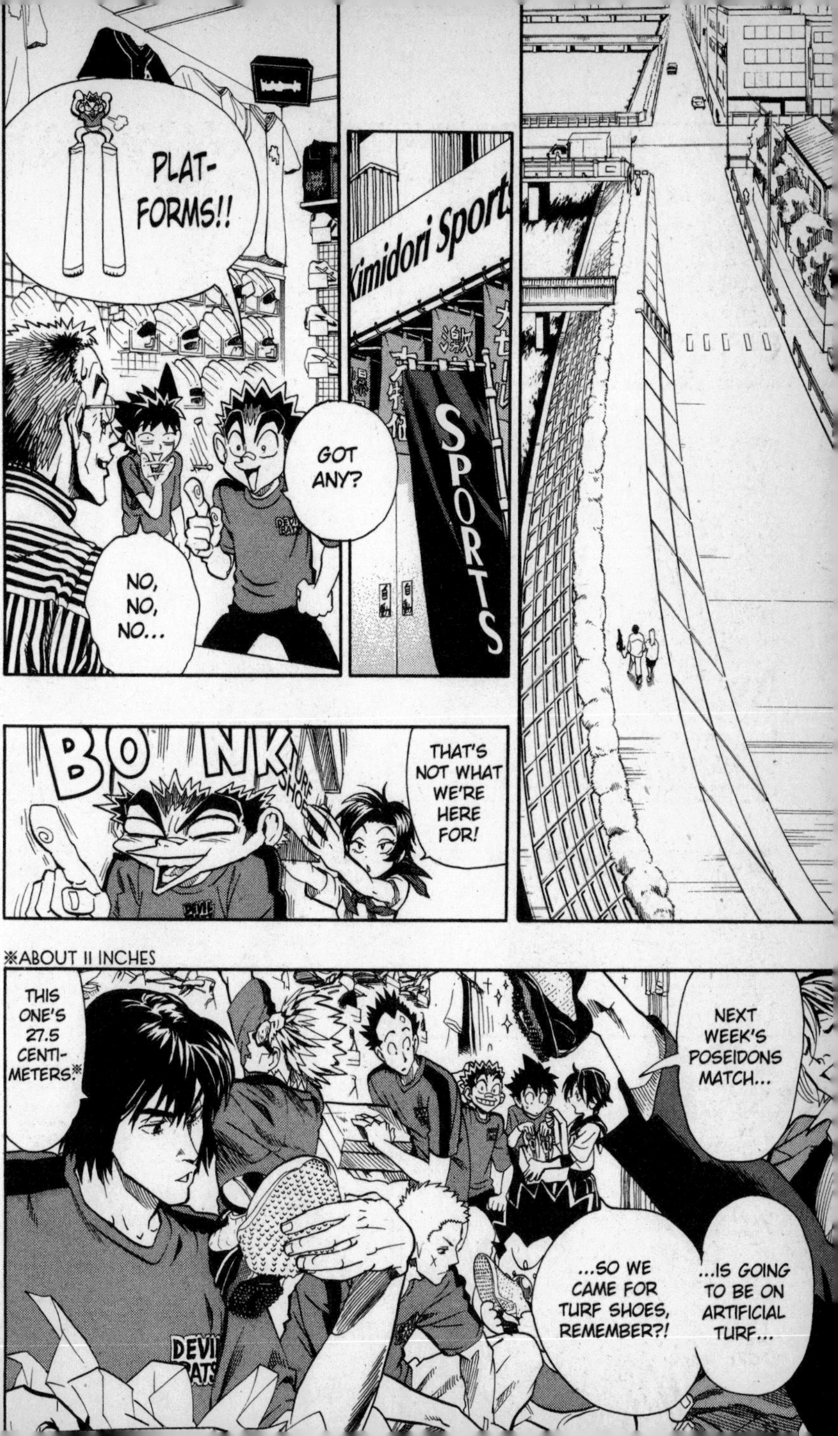
Kimidori Sports
SPORTS
PLAT-FORMS!!
GOT ANY?
NO, NO, NO...
BONK
TURF SHOES
THAT'S NOT WHAT WE'RE HERE FOR!
※ABOUT 11 INCHES
NEXT WEEK'S POSEIDONS MATCH...
...IS GOING TO BE ON ARTIFICIAL TURF...
...SO WE CAME FOR TURF SHOES, REMEMBER?!
THIS ONE'S 27.5 CENTIMETERS.※
DEVIL BATS

READ THIS WAY

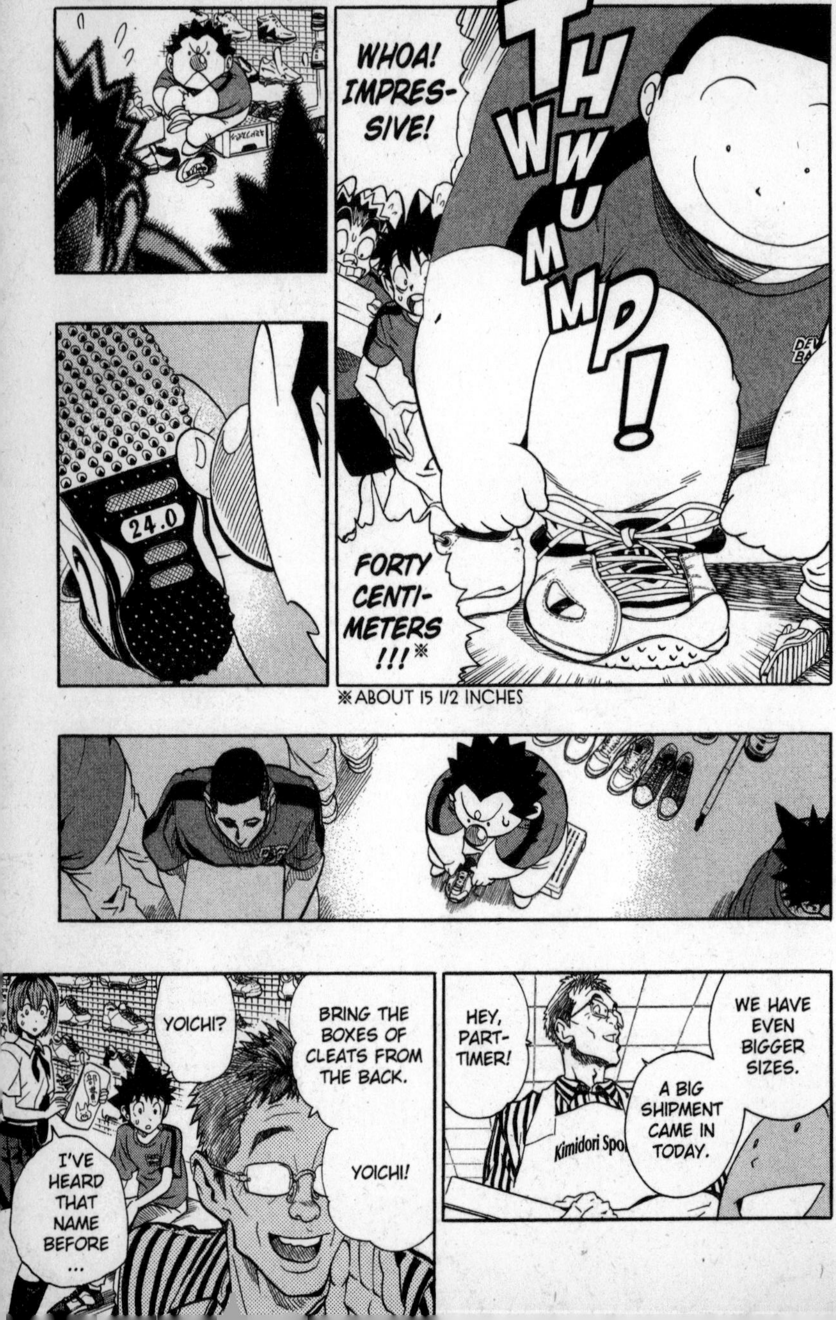
WHOA! IMPRESSIVE!
THWWUMMP!
FORTY CENTIMETERS!!!※
24.0
※ABOUT 15 1/2 INCHES
WE HAVE EVEN BIGGER SIZES.
A BIG SHIPMENT CAME IN TODAY.
HEY, PART-TIMER!
Kimidori Spo
BRING THE BOXES OF CLEATS FROM THE BACK.
YOICHI?
YOICHI!
I'VE HEARD THAT NAME BEFORE...

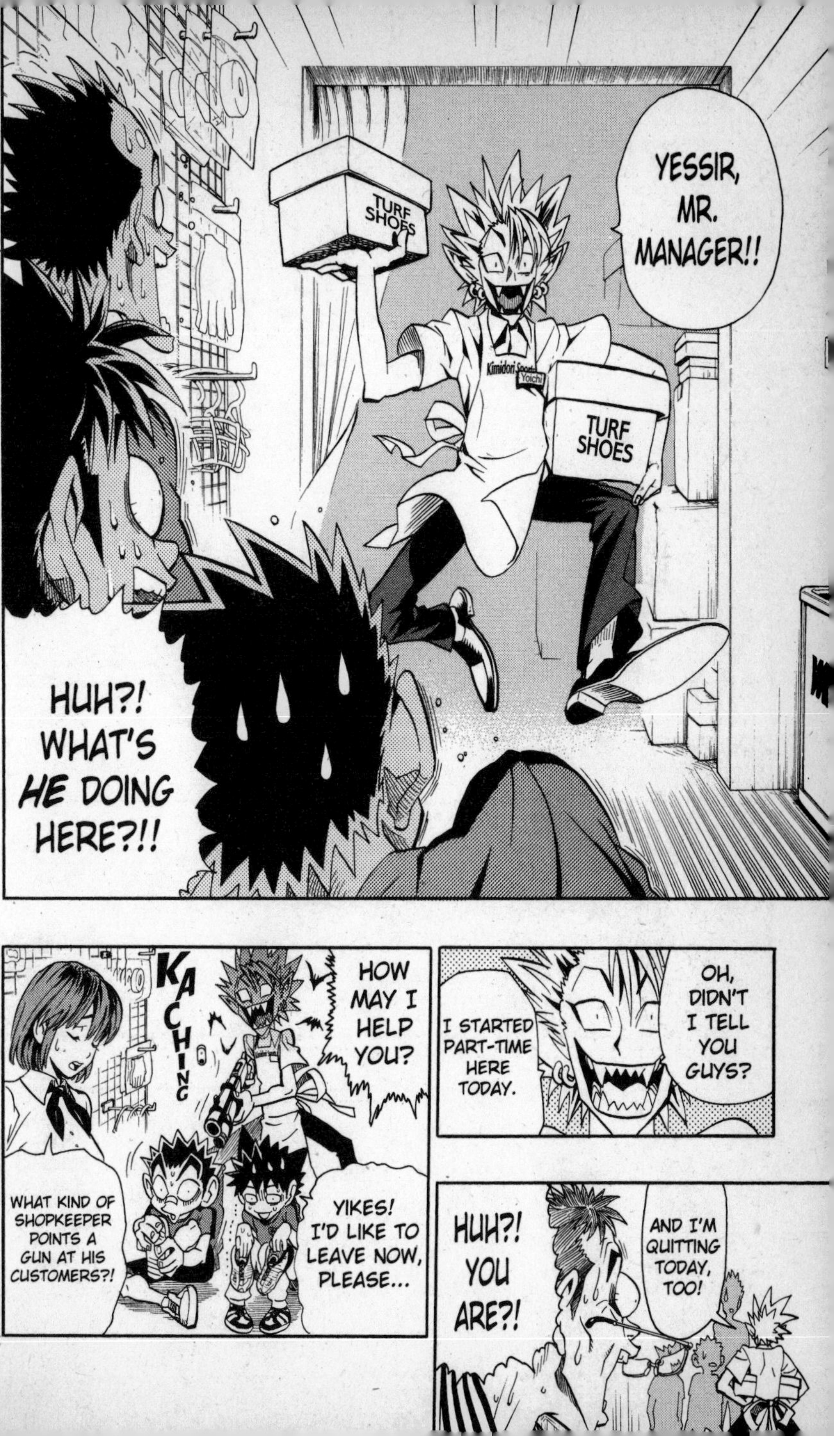
YESSIR, MR. MANAGER!!
TURF SHOES
TURF SHOES
HUH?! WHAT'S *HE* DOING HERE?!!
OH, DIDN'T I TELL YOU GUYS?
I STARTED PART-TIME HERE TODAY.
AND I'M QUITTING TODAY, TOO!
HUH?! YOU ARE?!
HOW MAY I HELP YOU?
KACHING
YIKES! I'D LIKE TO LEAVE NOW, PLEASE...
WHAT KIND OF SHOPKEEPER POINTS A GUN AT HIS CUSTOMERS?!

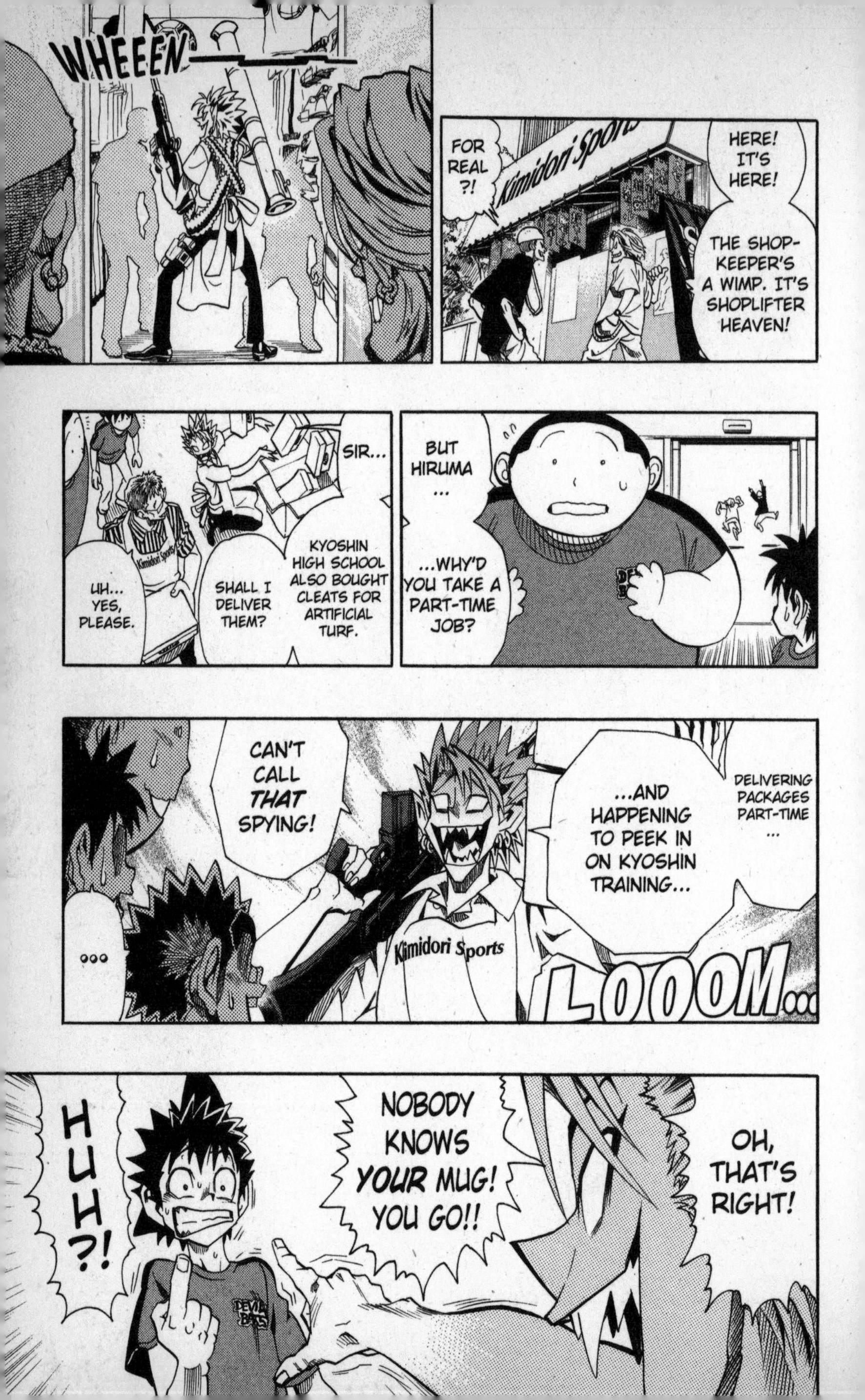
Kimidori Sports
HERE! IT'S HERE!
THE SHOP-KEEPER'S A WIMP. IT'S SHOPLIFTER HEAVEN!
FOR REAL?!
WHEEEN
BUT HIRUMA...
...WHY'D YOU TAKE A PART-TIME JOB?
SIR...
KYOSHIN HIGH SCHOOL ALSO BOUGHT CLEATS FOR ARTIFICIAL TURF.
SHALL I DELIVER THEM?
UH... YES, PLEASE.
Kimidori Sports
DELIVERING PACKAGES PART-TIME...
...AND HAPPENING TO PEEK IN ON KYOSHIN TRAINING...
CAN'T CALL *THAT* SPYING!
LOOOM...
Kimidori Sports
...
OH, THAT'S RIGHT!
NOBODY KNOWS *YOUR* MUG! YOU GO!!
HUH?!

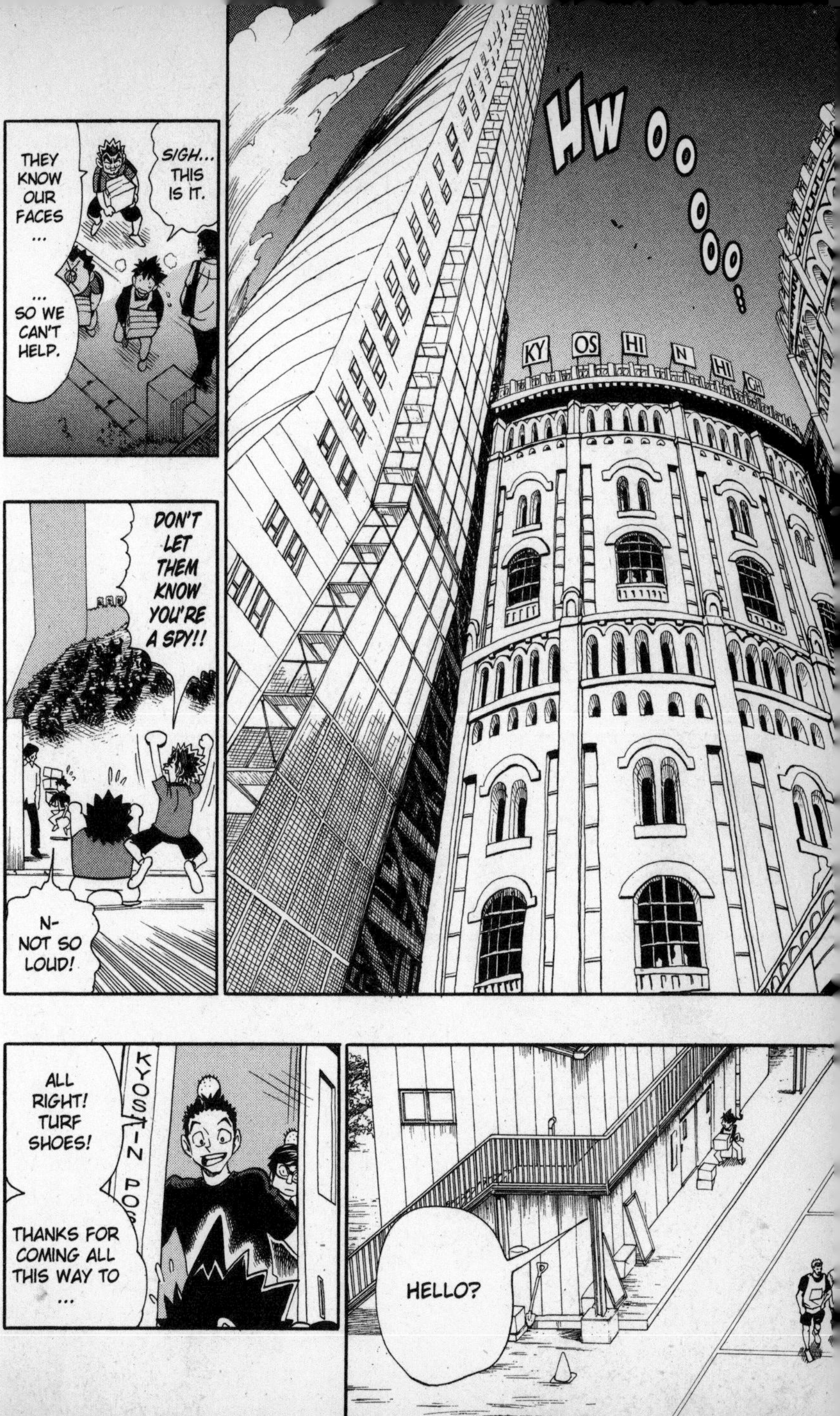
HWOOOOO..
KYOSHIN HIGH
SIGH... THIS IS IT.
THEY KNOW OUR FACES ...
... SO WE CAN'T HELP.
DON'T LET THEM KNOW YOU'RE A SPY!!
N- NOT SO LOUD!
HELLO?
ALL RIGHT! TURF SHOES!
KYOSHIN POS
THANKS FOR COMING ALL THIS WAY TO ...

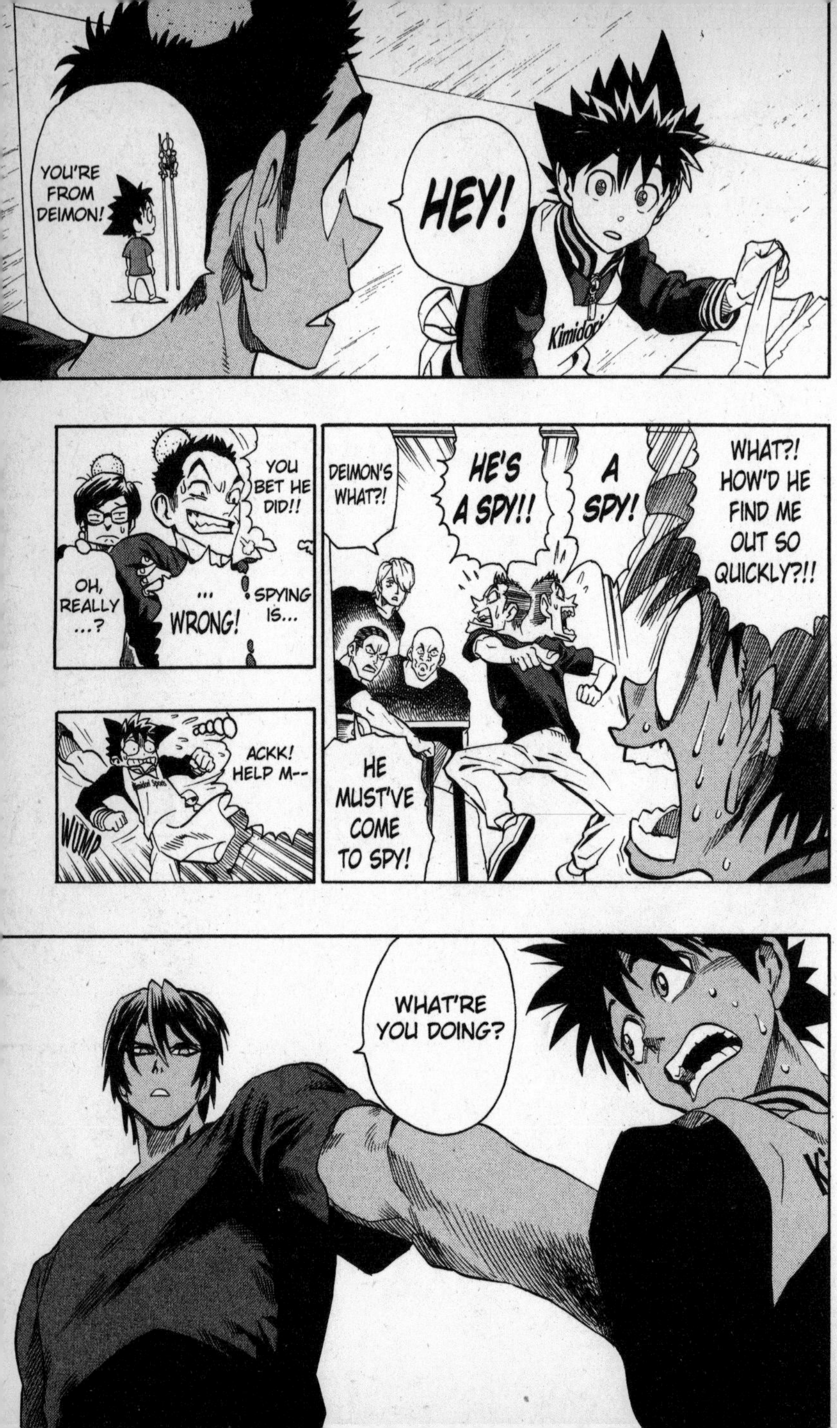
HEY!
YOU'RE FROM DEIMON!
Kimidori
WHAT?! HOW'D HE FIND ME OUT SO QUICKLY?!!
A SPY!
HE'S A SPY!!
DEIMON'S WHAT?!
HE MUST'VE COME TO SPY!
YOU BET HE DID!!
SPYING IS...
... WRONG!
OH, REALLY ...?
ACKK! HELP M--
WUMP
WHAT'RE YOU DOING?

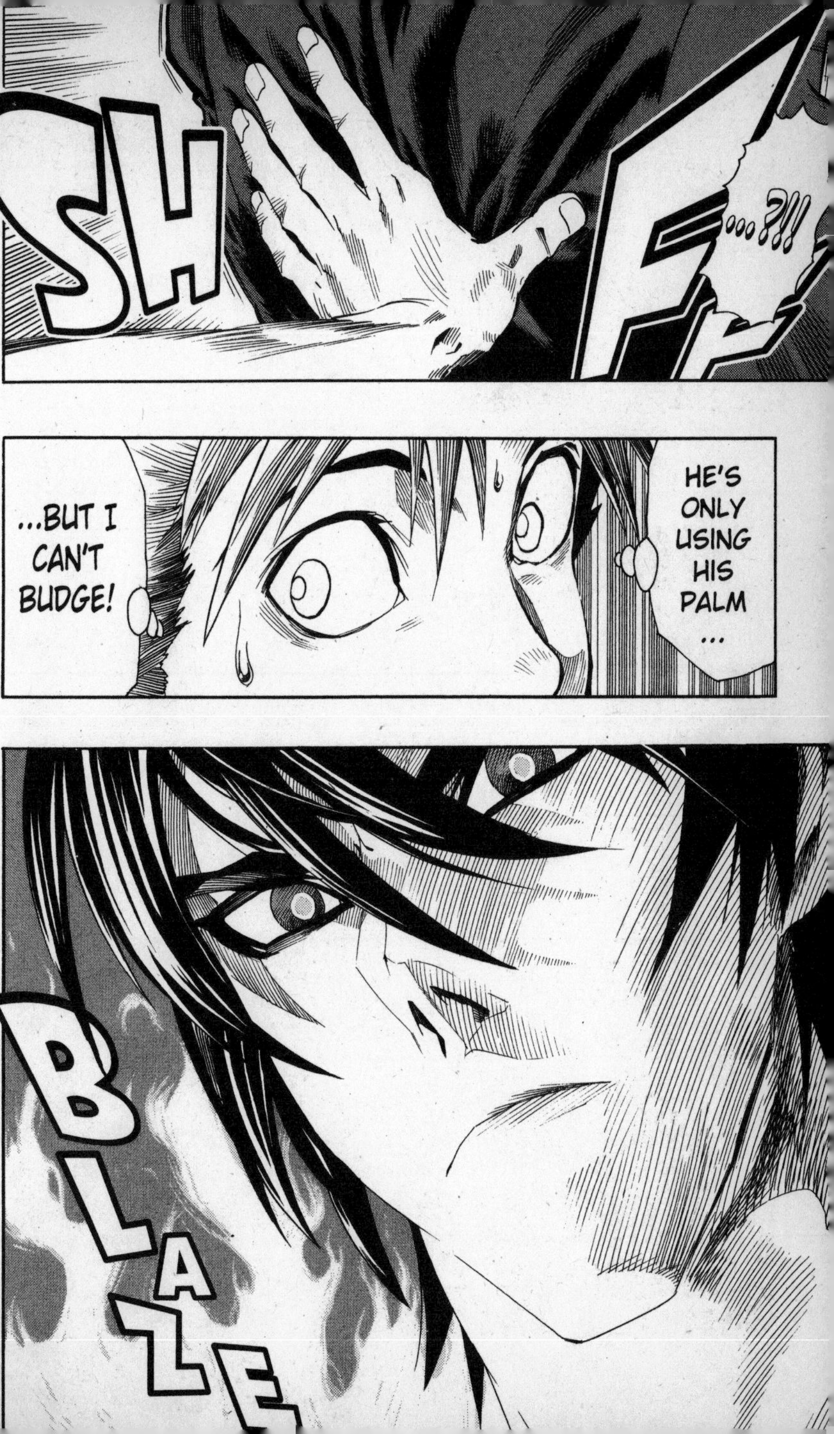
...?!!
SH
F
HE'S ONLY USING HIS PALM ...
...BUT I CAN'T BUDGE!
BLAZE

READ THIS WAY

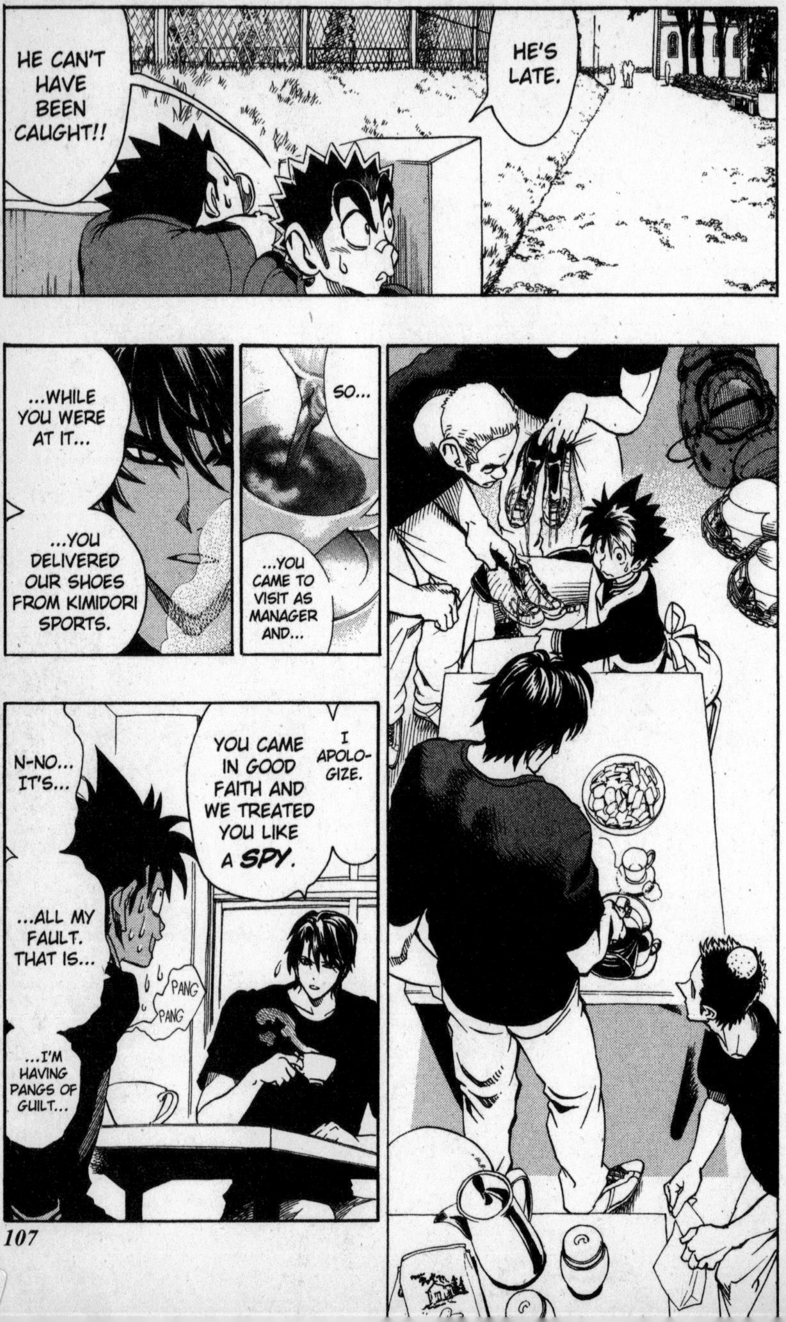
HE'S LATE.
HE CAN'T HAVE BEEN CAUGHT!!
SO...
...YOU CAME TO VISIT AS MANAGER AND...
...WHILE YOU WERE AT IT...
...YOU DELIVERED OUR SHOES FROM KIMIDORI SPORTS.
I APOLOGIZE.
YOU CAME IN GOOD FAITH AND WE TREATED YOU LIKE A SPY.
N-NO... IT'S...
...ALL MY FAULT. THAT IS...
PANG
PANG
...I'M HAVING PANGS OF GUILT...

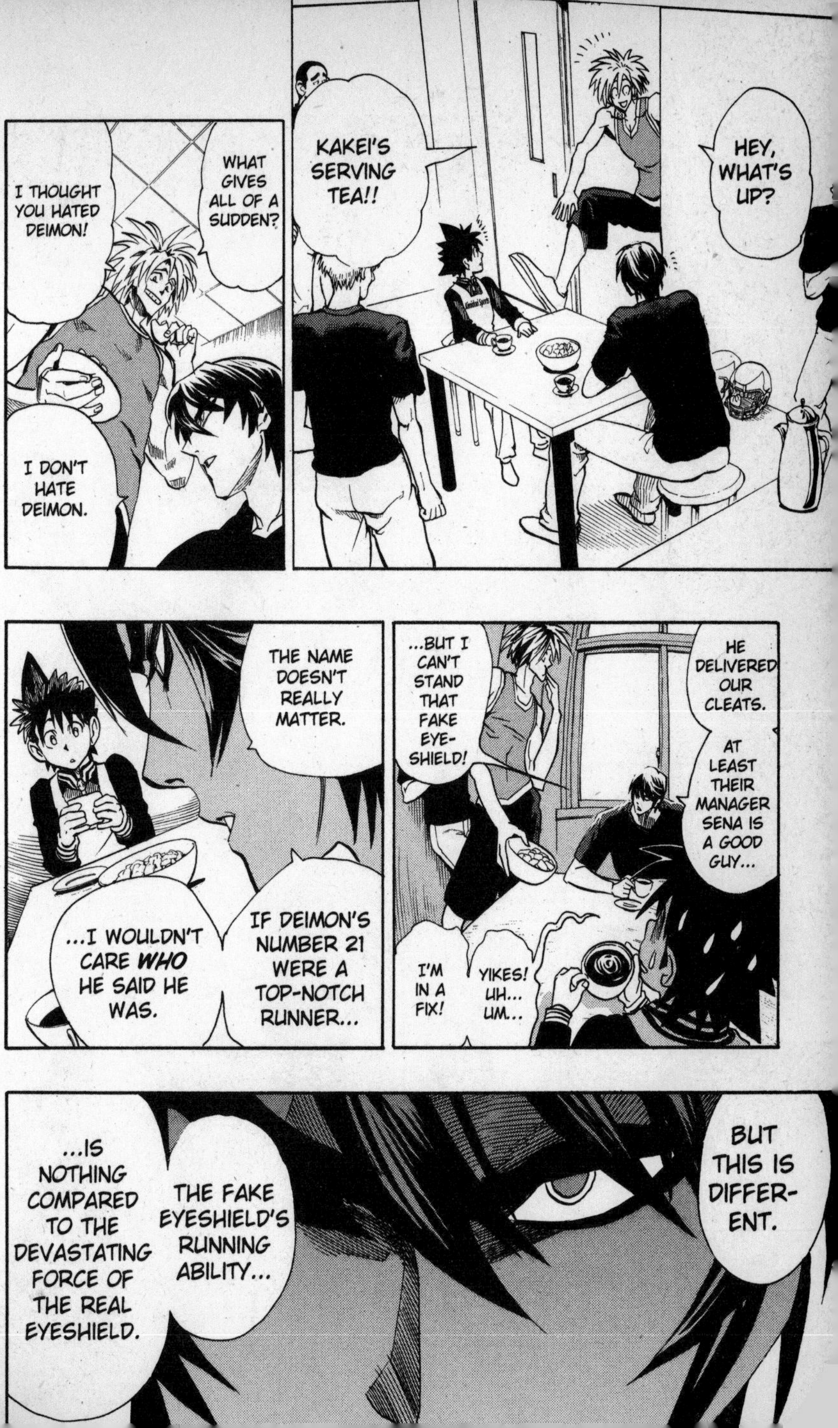
HEY, WHAT'S UP?
KAKEI'S SERVING TEA!!
WHAT GIVES ALL OF A SUDDEN?
I THOUGHT YOU HATED DEIMON!
I DON'T HATE DEIMON.
HE DELIVERED OUR CLEATS.
AT LEAST THEIR MANAGER SENA IS A GOOD GUY...
...BUT I CAN'T STAND THAT FAKE EYE-SHIELD!
YIKES! UH... UM...
I'M IN A FIX!
THE NAME DOESN'T REALLY MATTER.
IF DEIMON'S NUMBER 21 WERE A TOP-NOTCH RUNNER...
...I WOULDN'T CARE *WHO* HE SAID HE WAS.
BUT THIS IS DIFFER-ENT.
THE FAKE EYESHIELD'S RUNNING ABILITY...
...IS NOTHING COMPARED TO THE DEVASTATING FORCE OF THE REAL EYESHIELD.

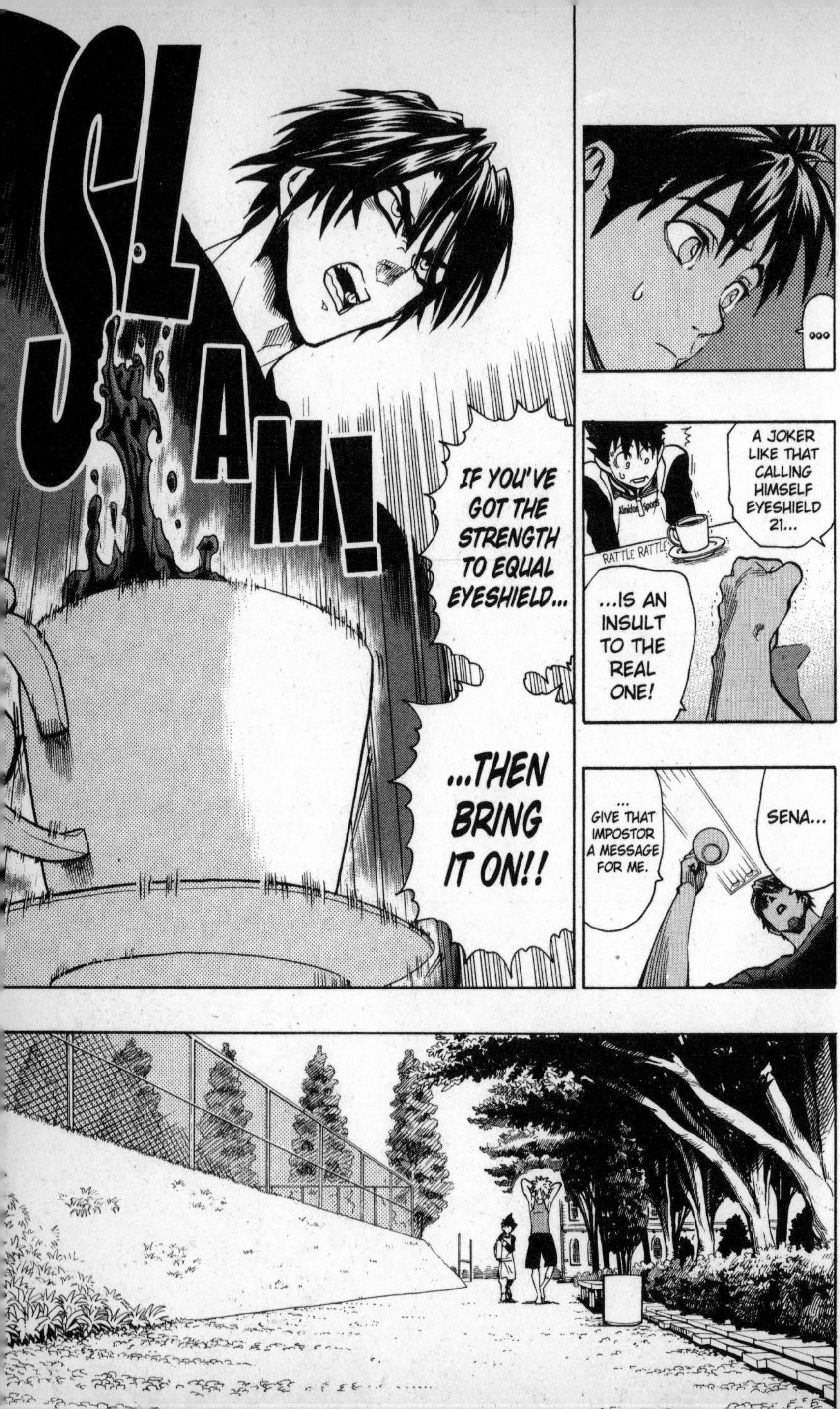
...
A JOKER LIKE THAT CALLING HIMSELF EYESHIELD 21...
RATTLE RATTLE
...IS AN INSULT TO THE REAL ONE!
SENA...
... GIVE THAT IMPOSTOR A MESSAGE FOR ME.
SLAM!
IF YOU'VE GOT THE STRENGTH TO EQUAL EYESHIELD...
...THEN BRING IT ON!!

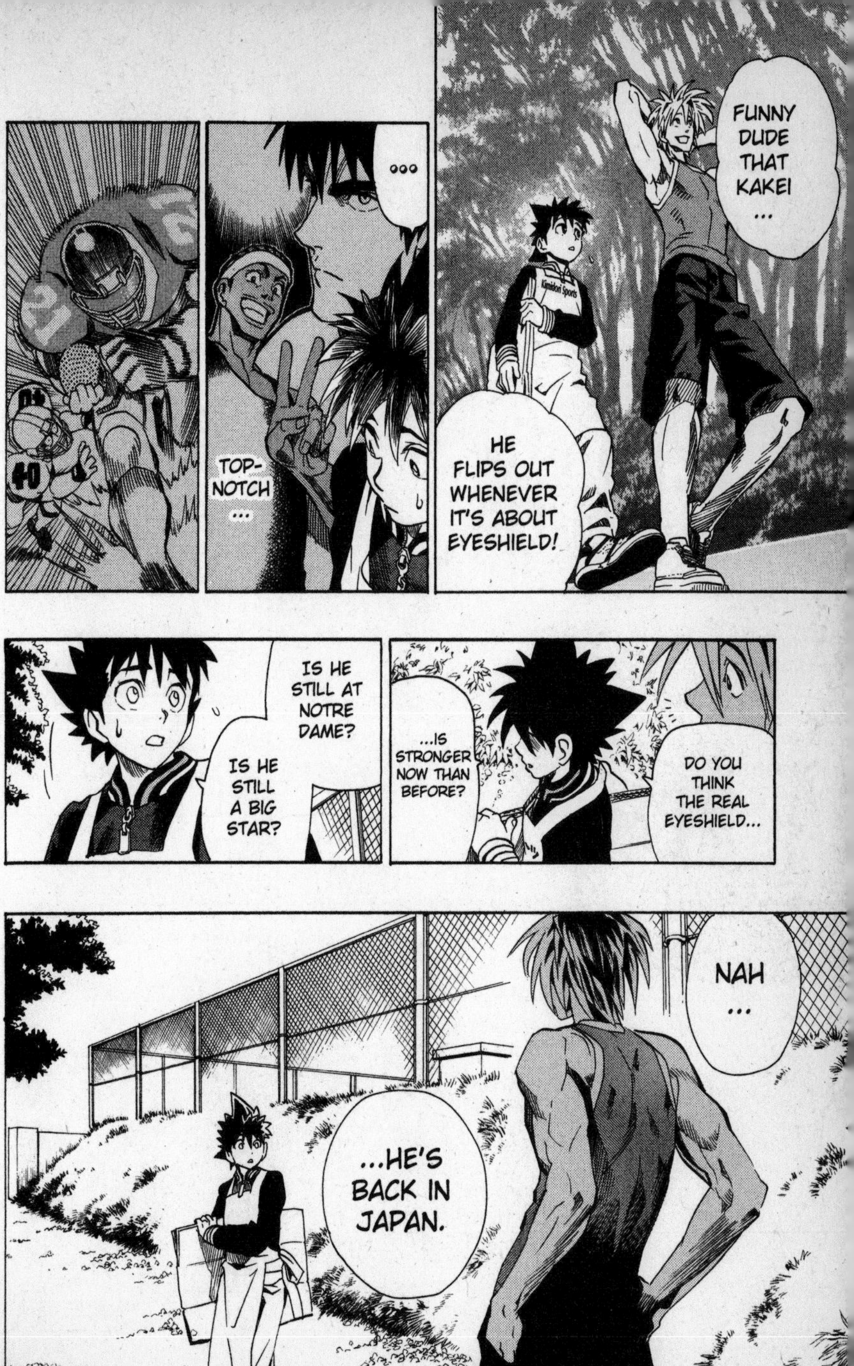
FUNNY DUDE THAT KAKEI ...
HE FLIPS OUT WHENEVER IT'S ABOUT EYESHIELD!
...
TOP-NOTCH ...
DO YOU THINK THE REAL EYESHIELD...
...IS STRONGER NOW THAN BEFORE?
IS HE STILL AT NOTRE DAME?
IS HE STILL A BIG STAR?
NAH ...
...HE'S BACK IN JAPAN.

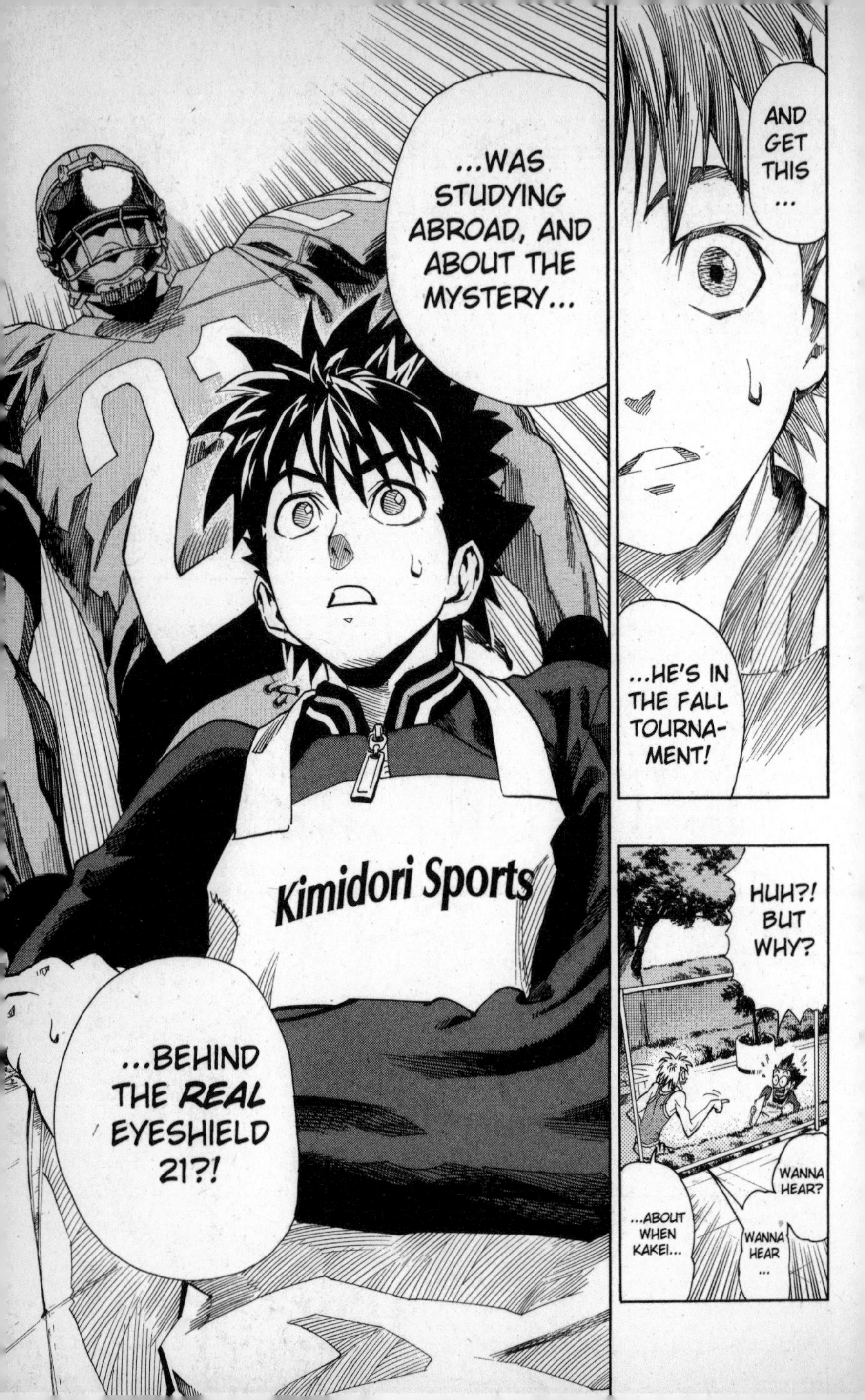
AND GET THIS ...
...HE'S IN THE FALL TOURNAMENT!
HUH?! BUT WHY?
WANNA HEAR?
WANNA HEAR ...
...ABOUT WHEN KAKEI...
...WAS STUDYING ABROAD, AND ABOUT THE MYSTERY...
Kimidori Sports
...BEHIND THE *REAL* EYESHIELD 21?!

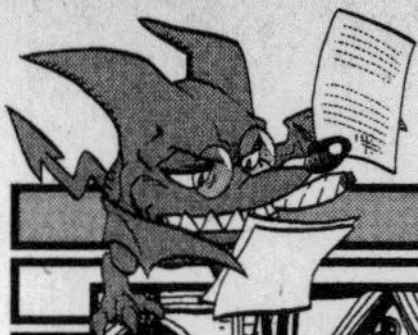

High School Selection Guidance for Prospective Applicants!

OJO HIGH SCHOOL

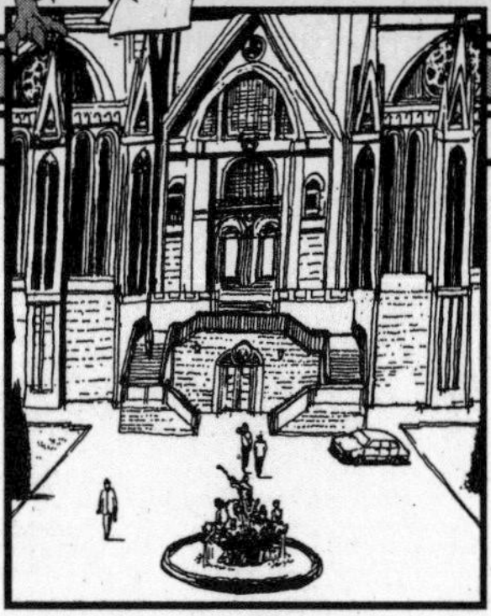

Student Body: 1,070

Special Campus Facilities: Throne Room

Major Career Options after Graduation

OJO UNIVERSITY

CORONATION

Offers continuous education from junior high through university. The academic entrance requirements are extremely difficult, but the door is open to jocks through sports scholarships. However, the recent acceptance of a certain Mr. O has led to suggestions that a written test of some kind be required of such applicants.

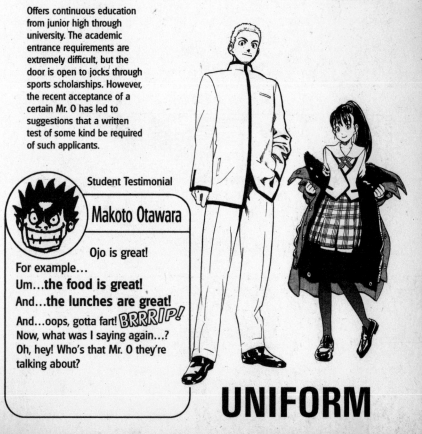

Student Testimonial

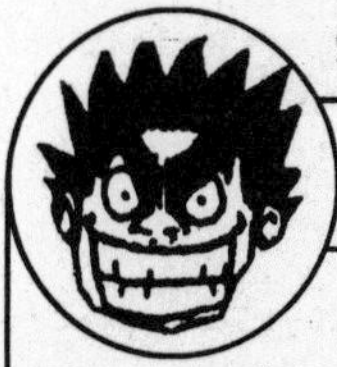

Makoto Otawara

Ojo is great!
For example...
Um...**the food is great!**
And...**the lunches are great!**
And...oops, gotta fart! BRRRIP!
Now, what was I saying again...?
Oh, hey! Who's that Mr. O they're talking about?

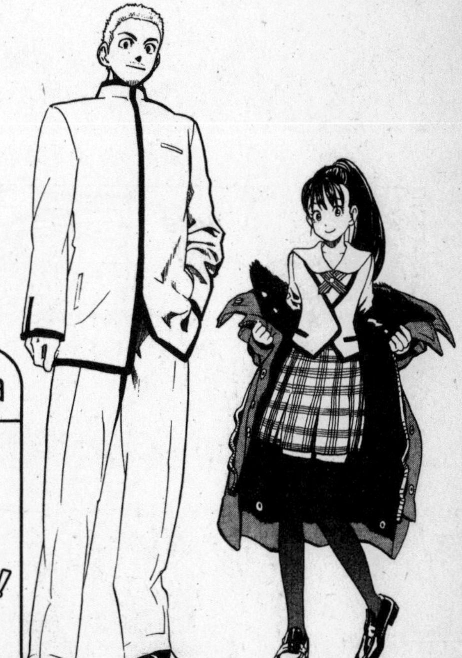

UNIFORM

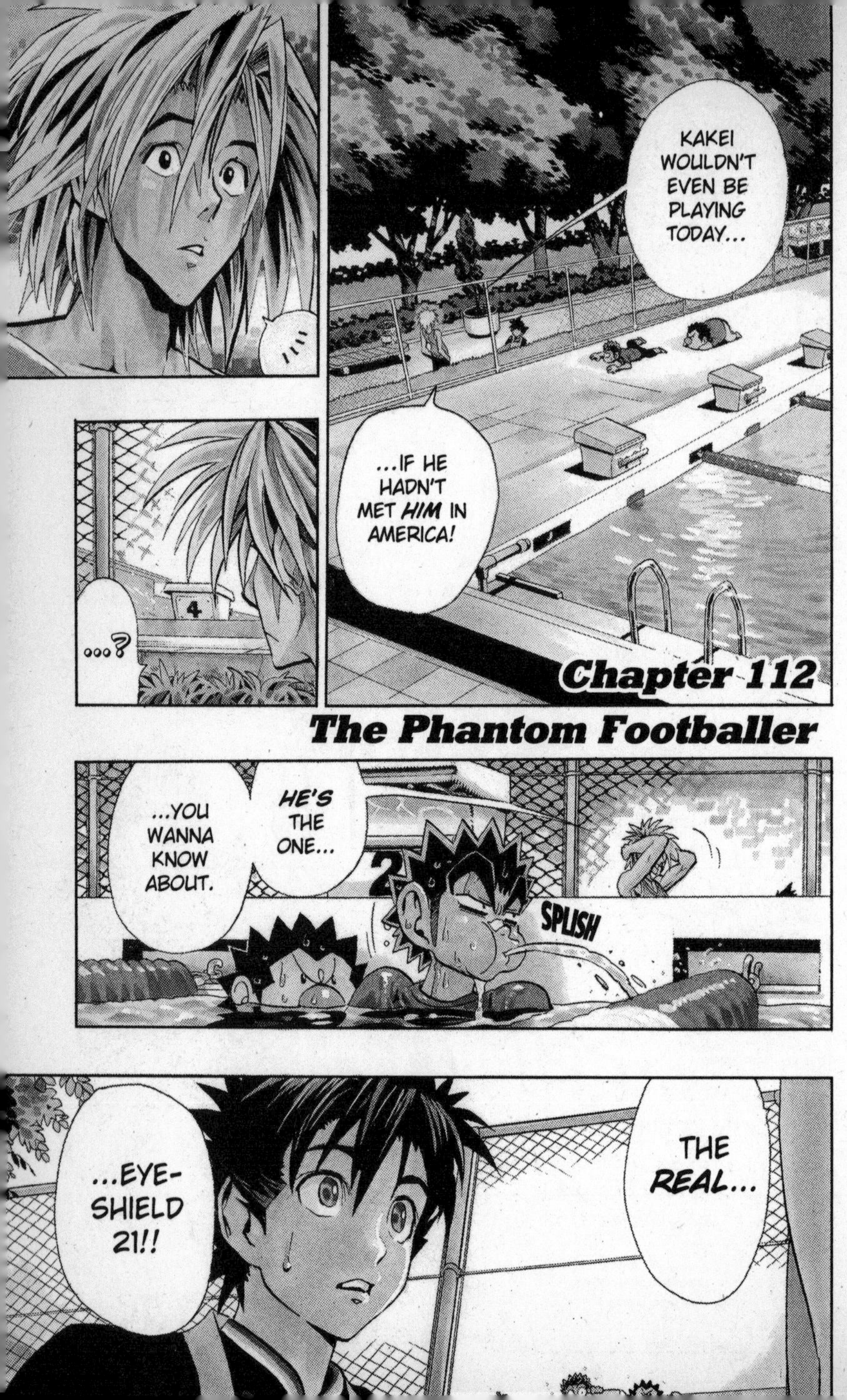
KAKEI WOULDN'T EVEN BE PLAYING TODAY...
...IF HE HADN'T MET *HIM* IN AMERICA!
...?
Chapter 112
The Phantom Footballer
HE'S THE ONE...
...YOU WANNA KNOW ABOUT.
SPLISH
THE *REAL*...
...EYE-SHIELD 21!!

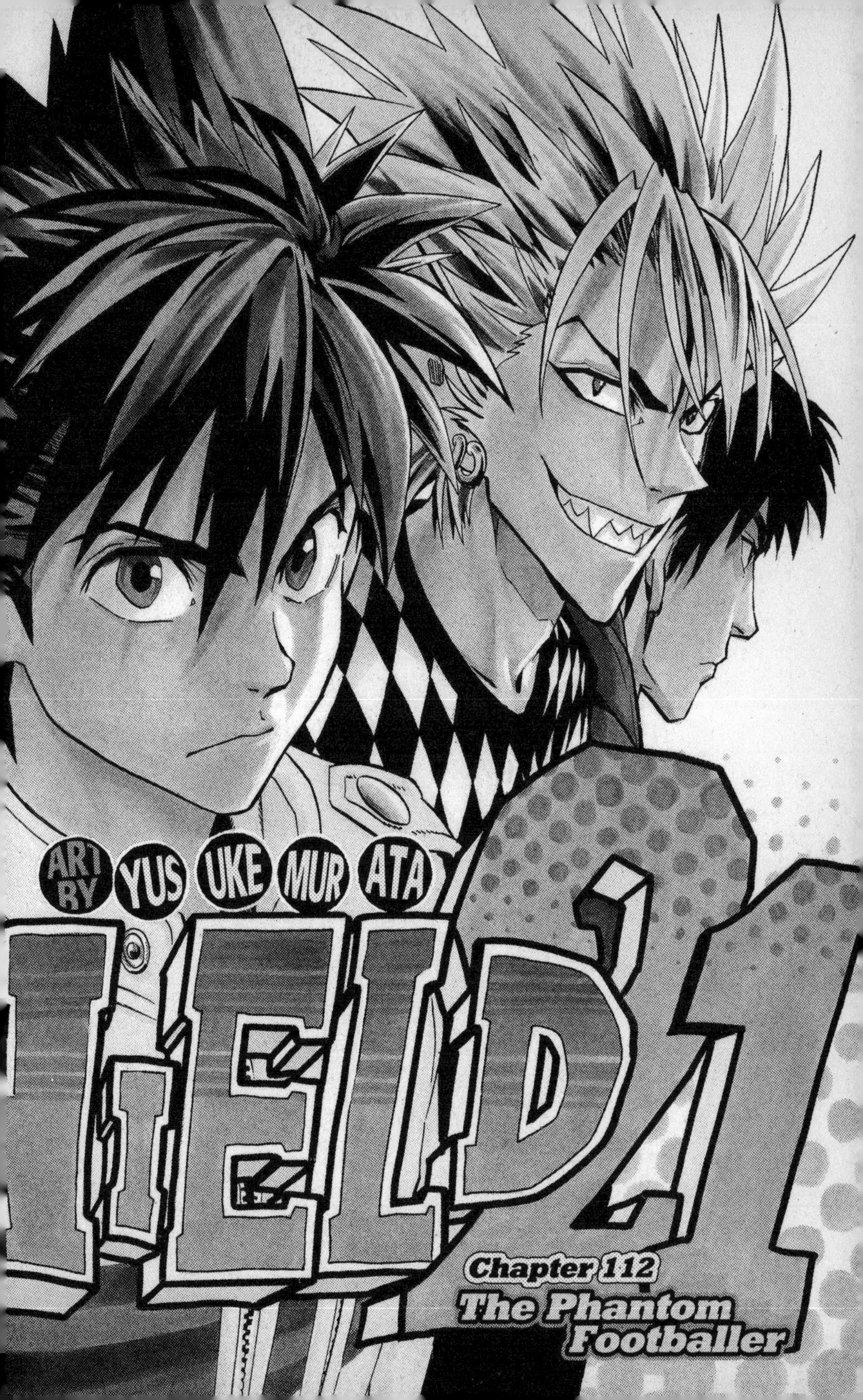
ART BY YUSUKE MURATA
Chapter 112
The Phantom Footballer

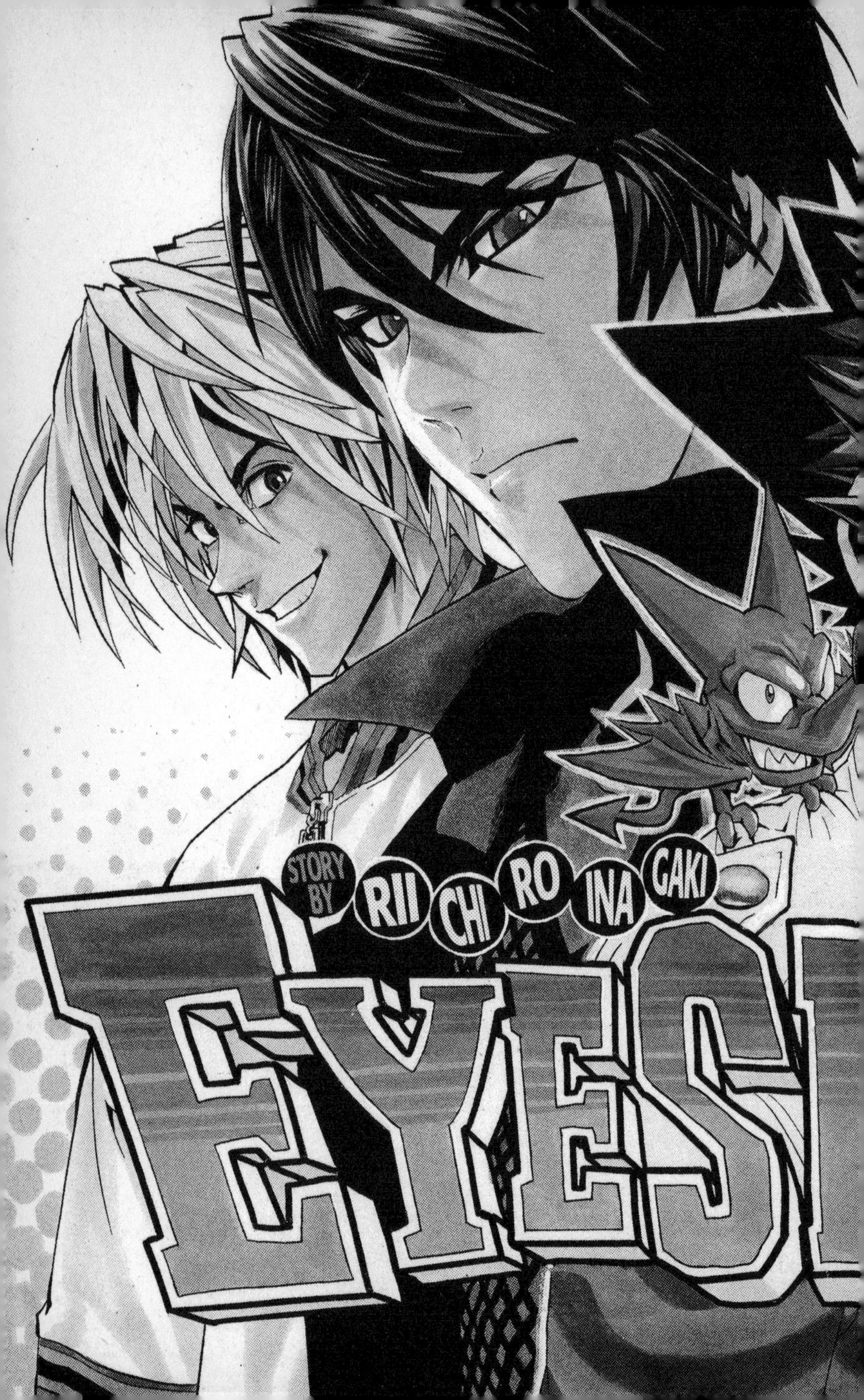
STORY BY RIICHIRO INAGAKI
EYES

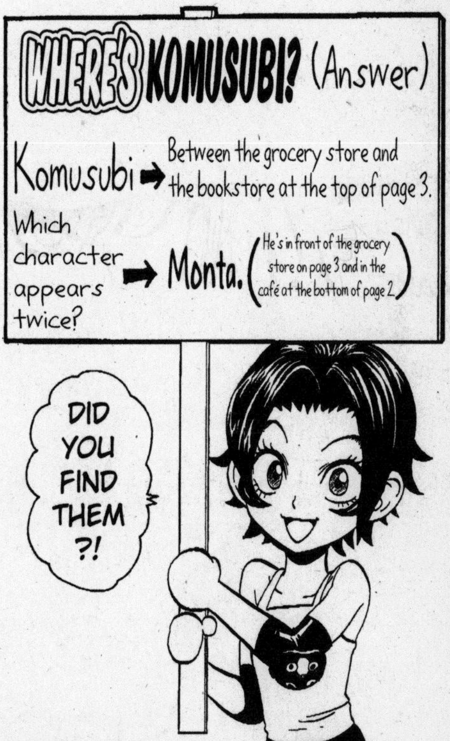
WHERE'S KOMUSUBI? (Answer)
Komusubi → Between the grocery store and the bookstore at the top of page 3.
Which character appears twice? → Monta. (He's in front of the grocery store on page 3 and in the café at the bottom of page 2.)
DID YOU FIND THEM ?!

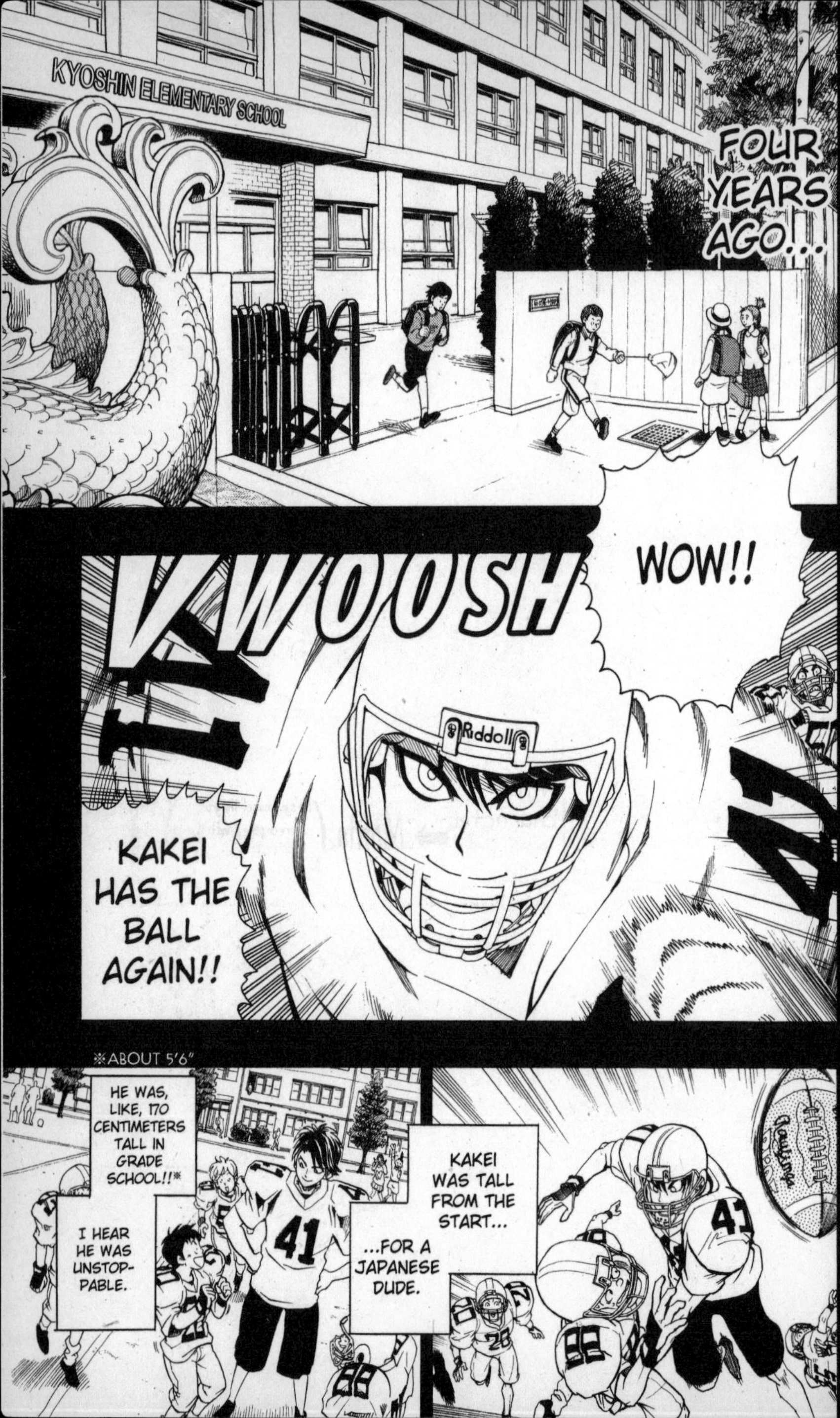
KYOSHIN ELEMENTARY SCHOOL
FOUR YEARS AGO!!!
WOW!!
VWOOSH
KAKEI HAS THE BALL AGAIN!!
Riddoll
KAKEI WAS TALL FROM THE START...
...FOR A JAPANESE DUDE.
41
HE WAS, LIKE, 170 CENTIMETERS TALL IN GRADE SCHOOL!!※
I HEAR HE WAS UNSTOP-PABLE.
41
※ABOUT 5'6"

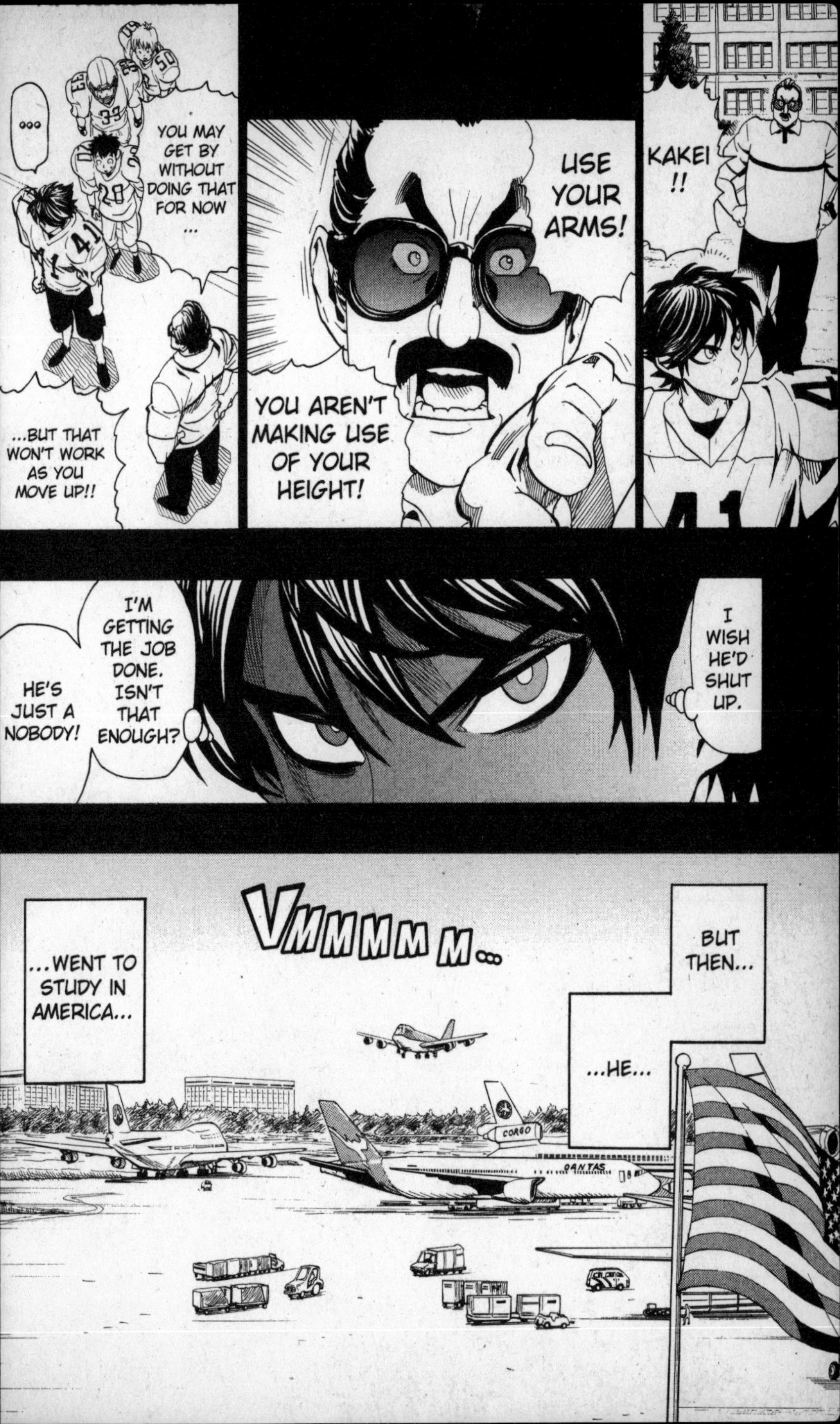
KAKEI !!
USE YOUR ARMS!
YOU AREN'T MAKING USE OF YOUR HEIGHT!
...
YOU MAY GET BY WITHOUT DOING THAT FOR NOW ...
...BUT THAT WON'T WORK AS YOU MOVE UP!!
I WISH HE'D SHUT UP.
I'M GETTING THE JOB DONE. ISN'T THAT ENOUGH?
HE'S JUST A NOBODY!
BUT THEN...
...HE...
VMMMMM M...
...WENT TO STUDY IN AMERICA...

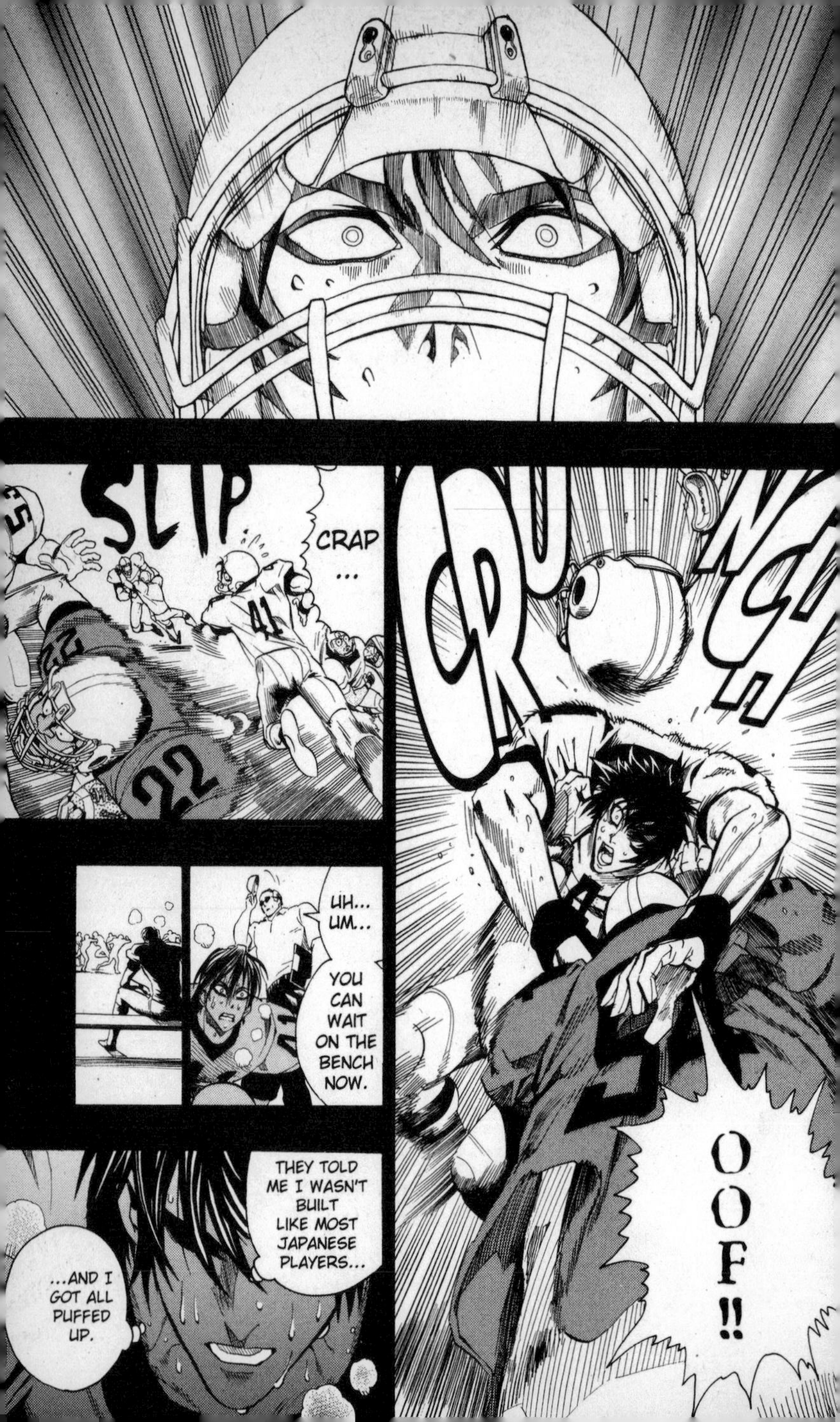
CRUNCH
OOF!!
SLIP
CRAP ...
UH... UM...
YOU CAN WAIT ON THE BENCH NOW.
THEY TOLD ME I WASN'T BUILT LIKE MOST JAPANESE PLAYERS...
...AND I GOT ALL PUFFED UP.

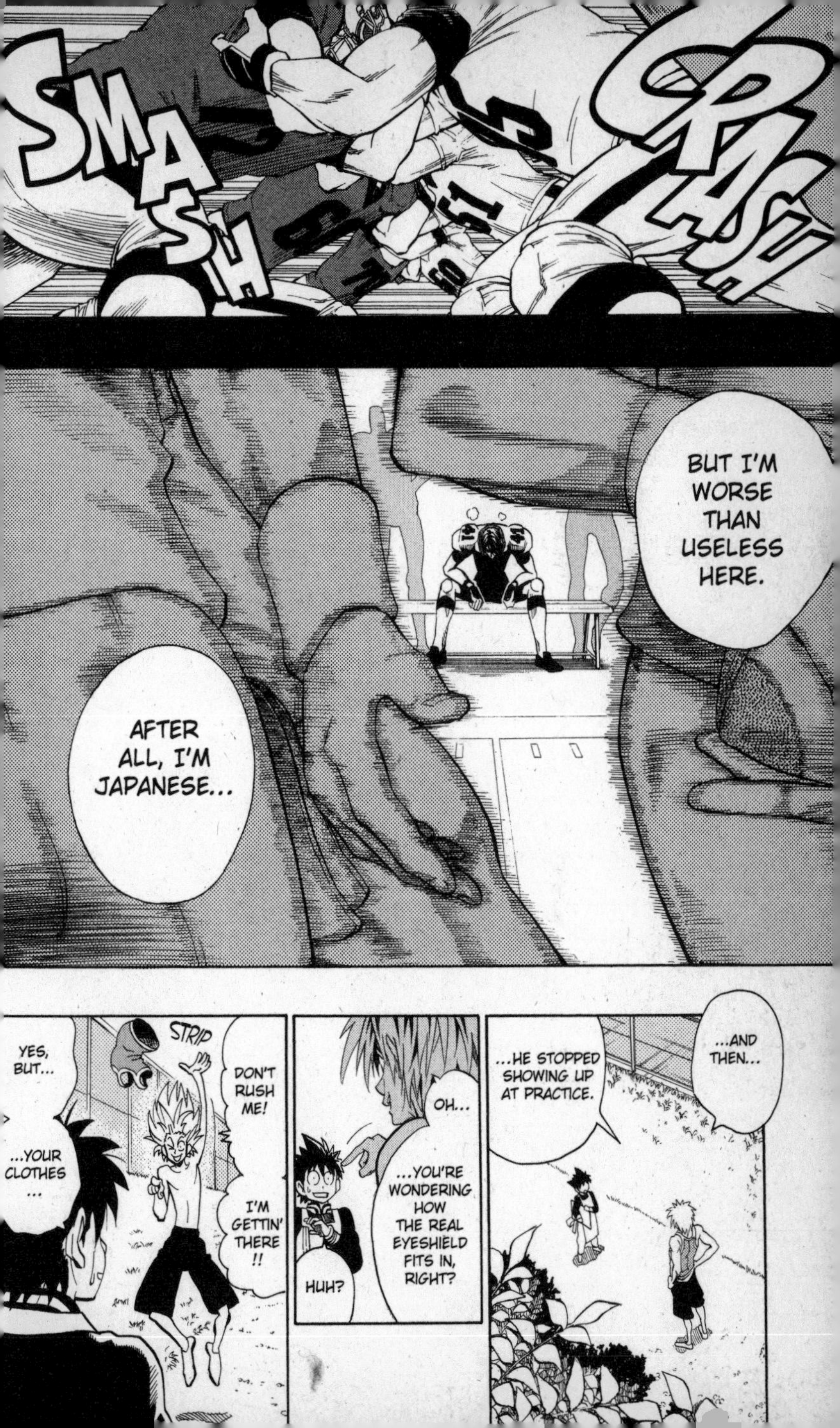
CRASH!!
SMASH
BUT I'M WORSE THAN USELESS HERE.
AFTER ALL, I'M JAPANESE...
...AND THEN...
...HE STOPPED SHOWING UP AT PRACTICE.
OH...
...YOU'RE WONDERING HOW THE REAL EYESHIELD FITS IN, RIGHT?
HUH?
DON'T RUSH ME!
STRIP
YES, BUT...
...YOUR CLOTHES ...
I'M GETTIN' THERE !!

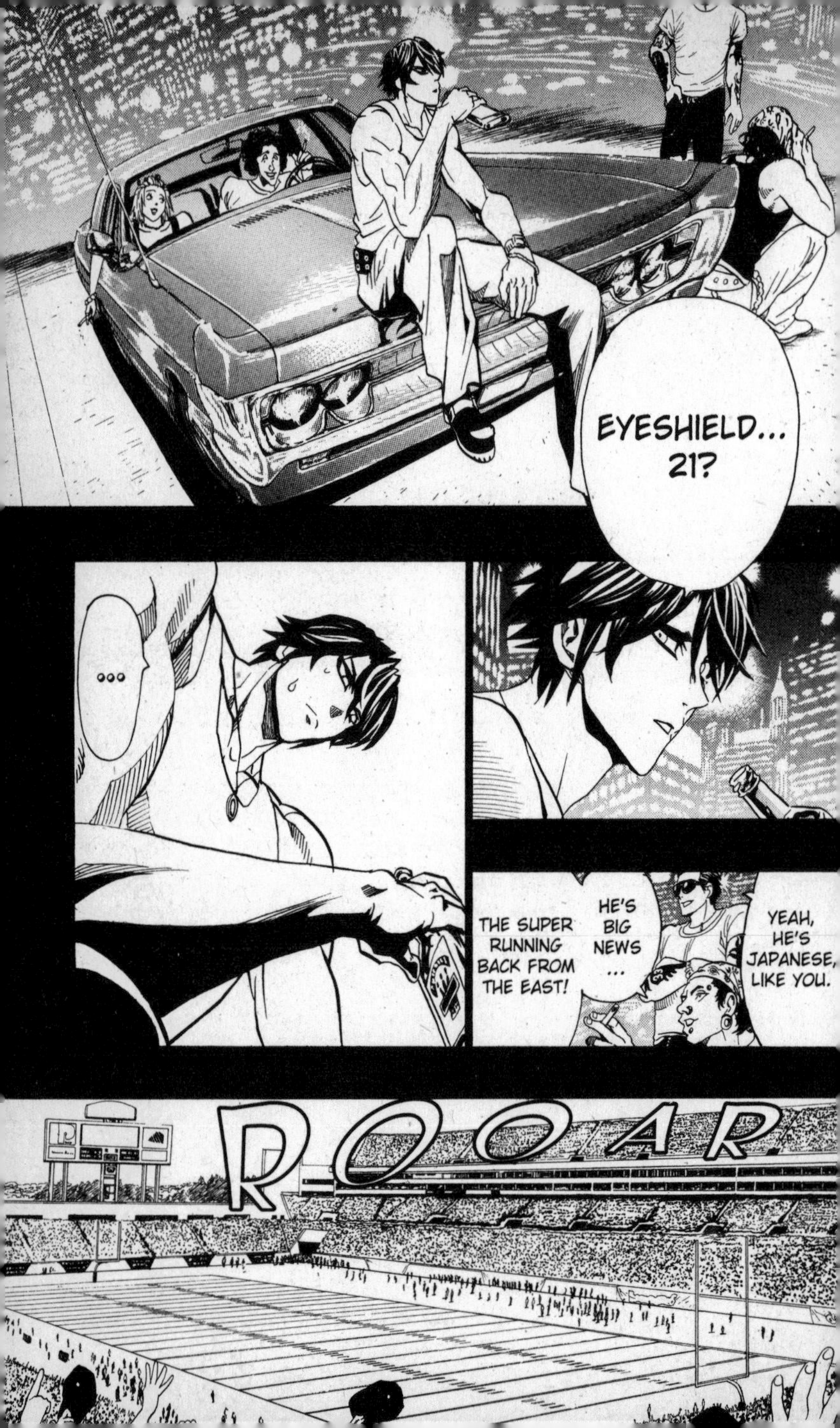

EYESHIELD... 21?
YEAH, HE'S JAPANESE, LIKE YOU.
HE'S BIG NEWS...
THE SUPER RUNNING BACK FROM THE EAST!
...
ROOOAR

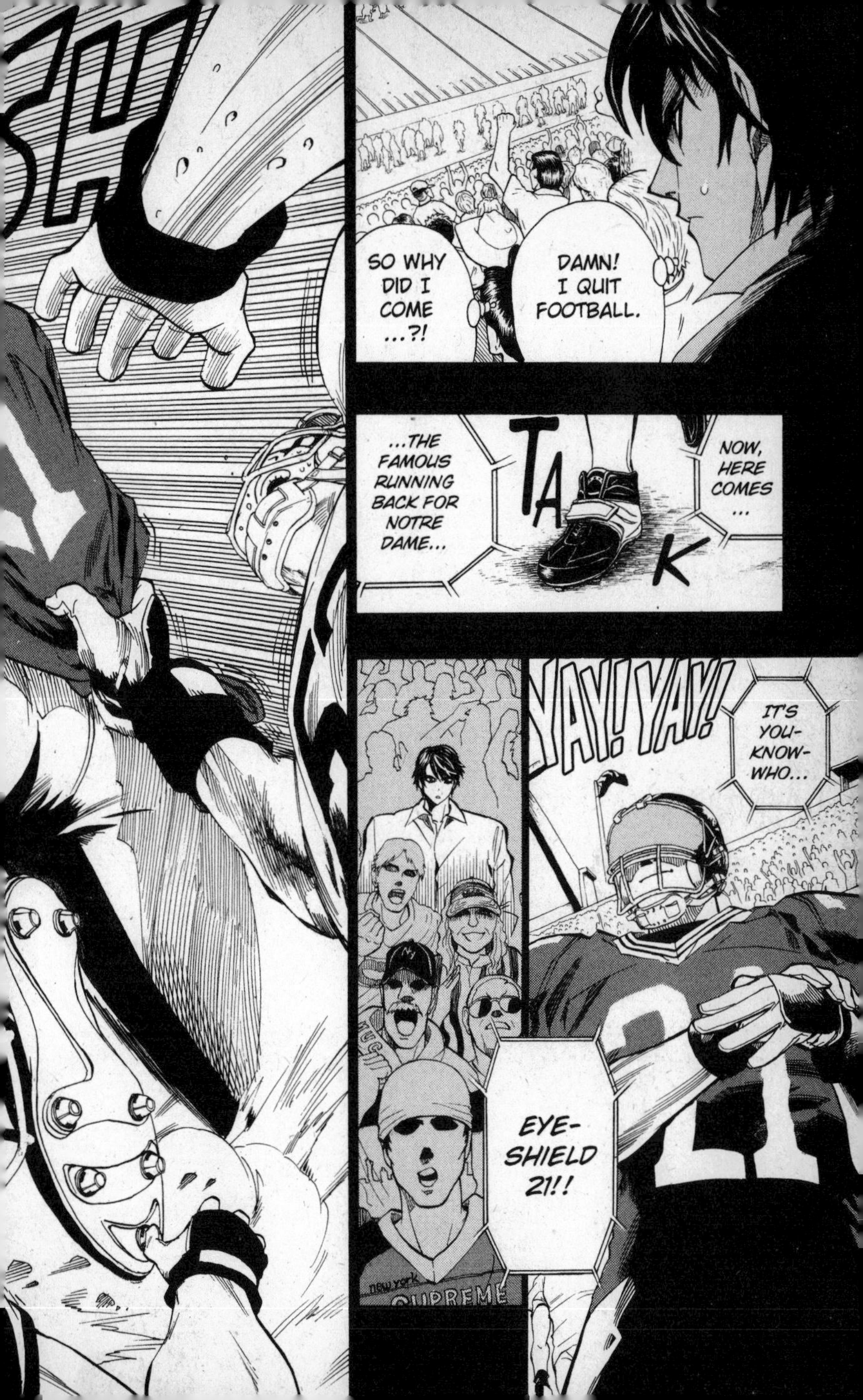
DAMN! I QUIT FOOTBALL.
SO WHY DID I COME ...?!
NOW, HERE COMES ...
TAK
...THE FAMOUS RUNNING BACK FOR NOTRE DAME...
YAY! YAY!
IT'S YOU-KNOW-WHO...
EYE-SHIELD 21!!

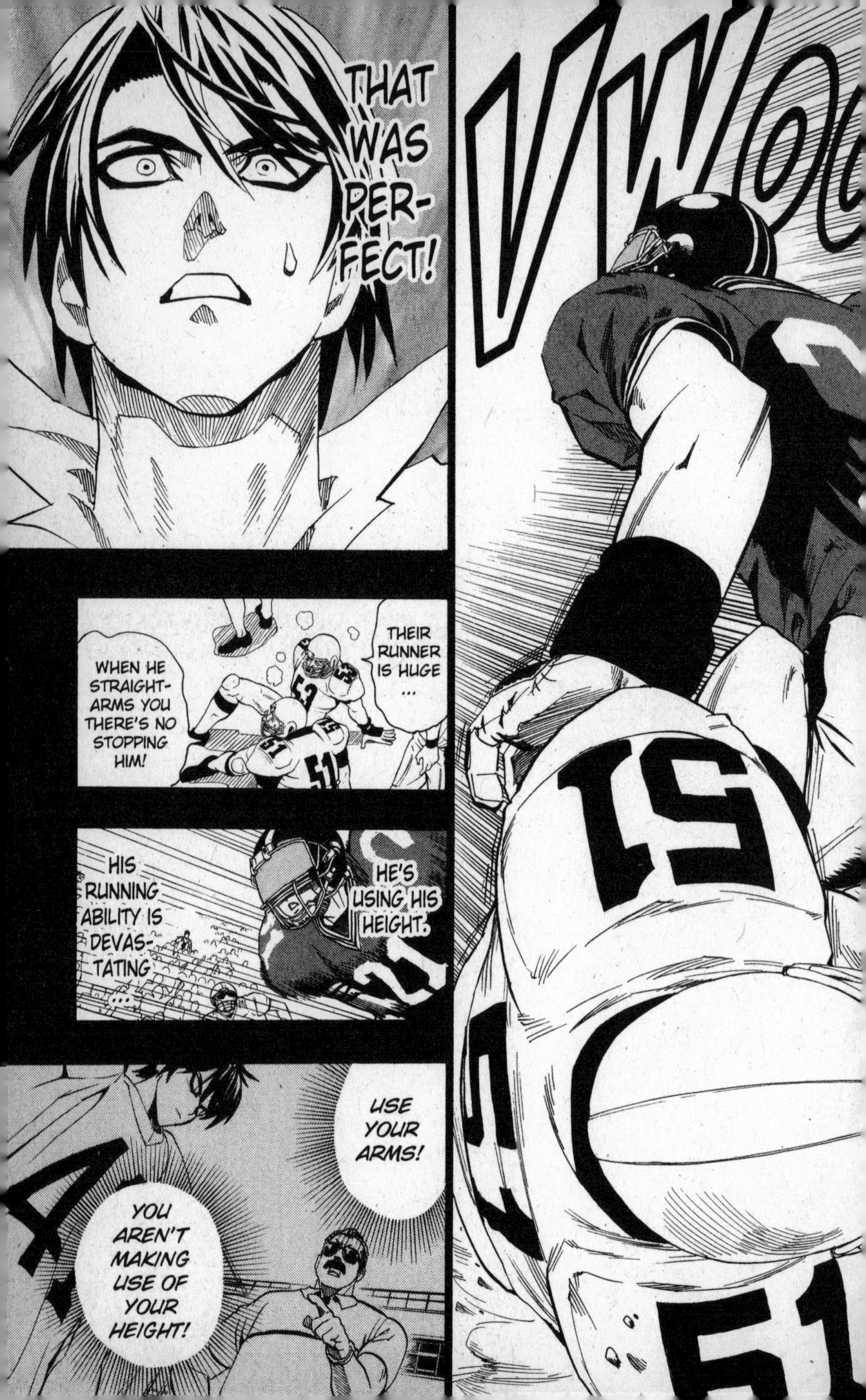
VWOO
THAT WAS PER-FECT!
THEIR RUNNER IS HUGE ...
WHEN HE STRAIGHT-ARMS YOU THERE'S NO STOPPING HIM!
HE'S USING HIS HEIGHT.
HIS RUNNING ABILITY IS DEVAS-TATING
...
USE YOUR ARMS!
YOU AREN'T MAKING USE OF YOUR HEIGHT!

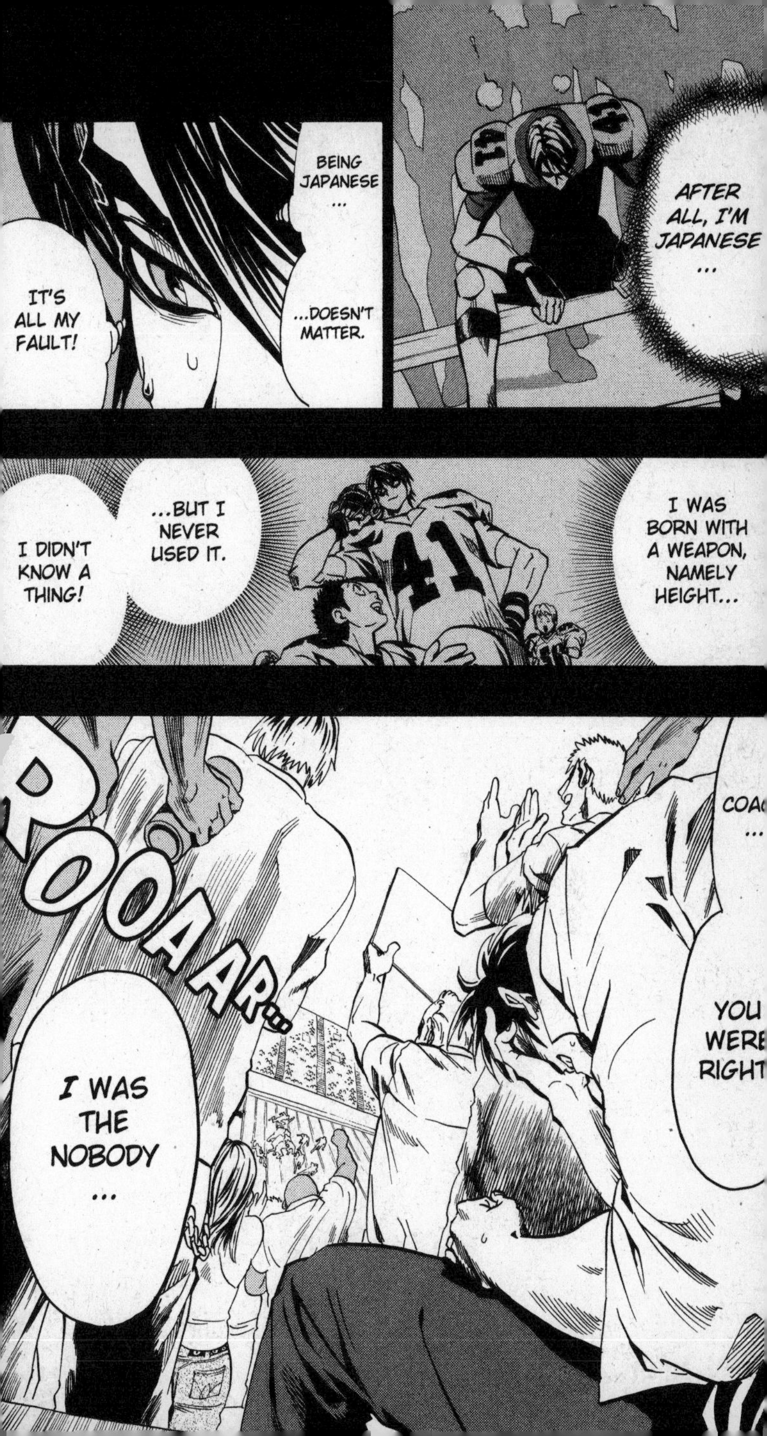
AFTER ALL, I'M JAPANESE ...
BEING JAPANESE ...
...DOESN'T MATTER.
IT'S ALL MY FAULT!
I WAS BORN WITH A WEAPON, NAMELY HEIGHT...
...BUT I NEVER USED IT.
I DIDN'T KNOW A THING!
COA ...
YOU WERE RIGHT
ROOOAAR...
I WAS THE NOBODY ...

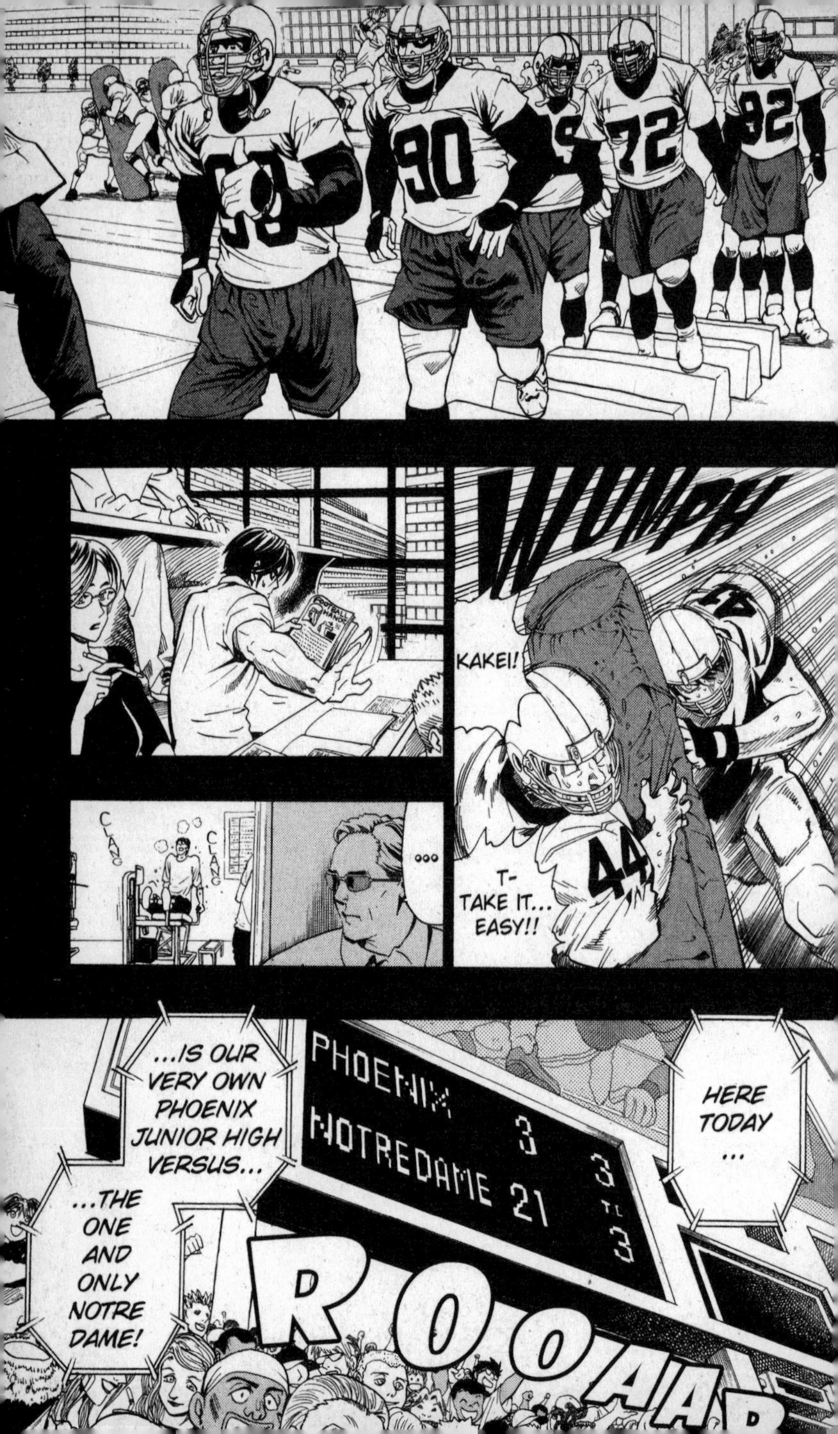
WUMPH
KAKEI!
T- TAKE IT... EASY!!
...
CLANG
CLANG
HERE TODAY...
...IS OUR VERY OWN PHOENIX JUNIOR HIGH VERSUS...
...THE ONE AND ONLY NOTRE DAME!
PHOENIX 3 3
NOTREDAME 21 3
TL 3
ROOAAR

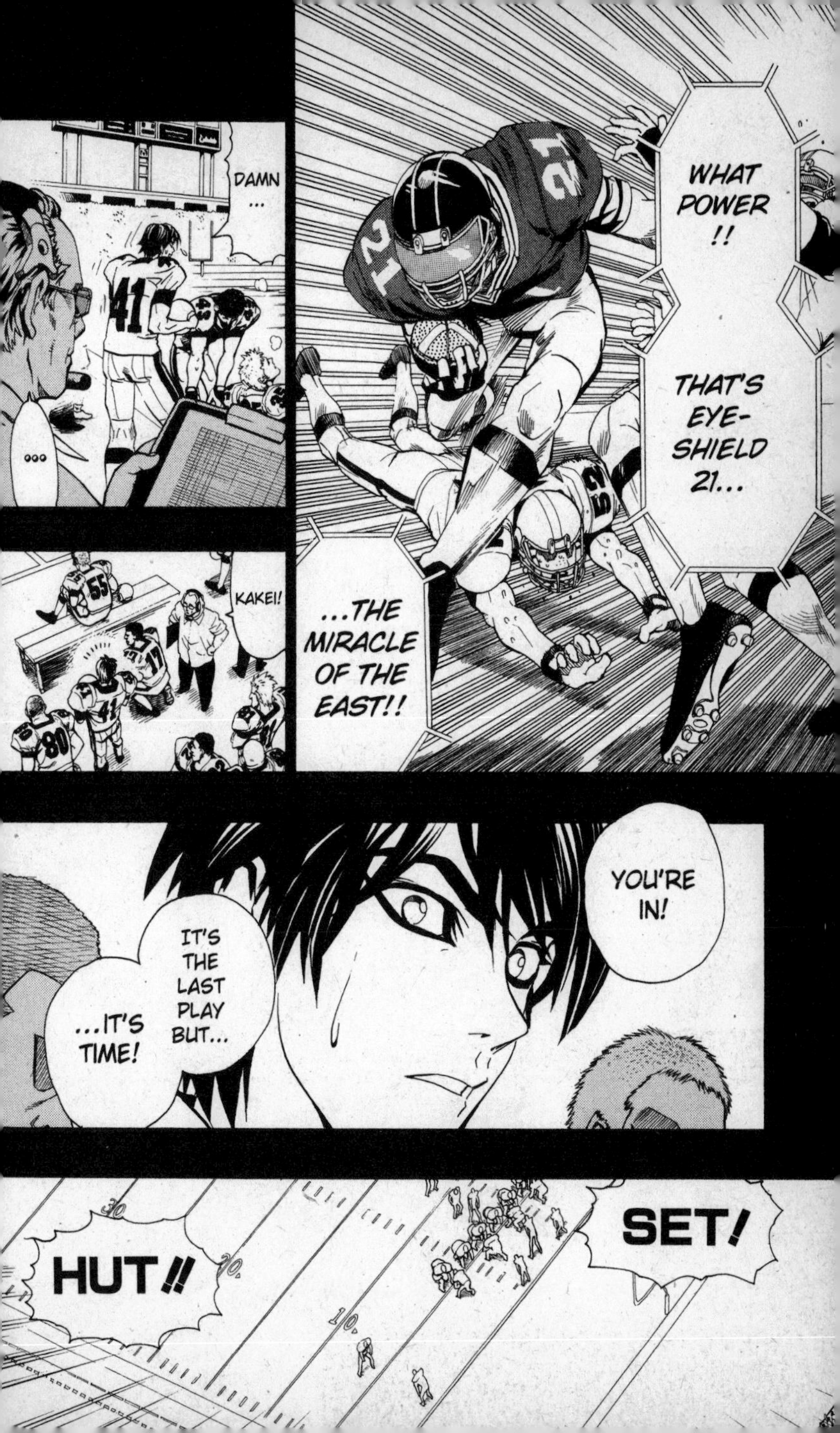
WHAT POWER!!
THAT'S EYE-SHIELD 21...
...THE MIRACLE OF THE EAST!!
DAMN...
...
KAKEI!
YOU'RE IN!
IT'S THE LAST PLAY BUT...
...IT'S TIME!
SET!
HUT!!

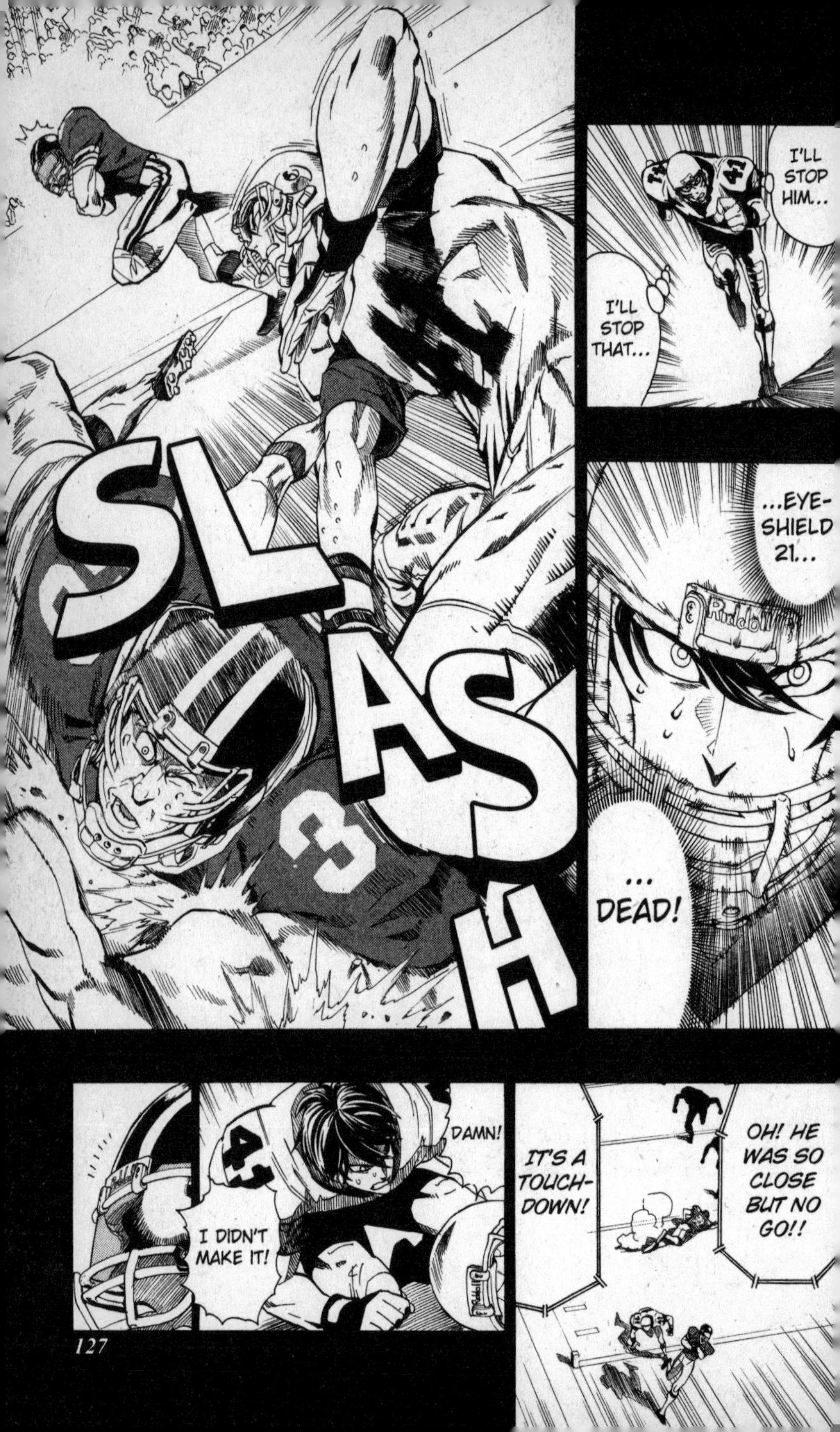
I'LL STOP HIM...
I'LL STOP THAT...
...EYE-SHIELD 21...
...DEAD!
SLASH
OH! HE WAS SO CLOSE BUT NO GO!!
IT'S A TOUCH-DOWN!
DAMN!
I DIDN'T MAKE IT!

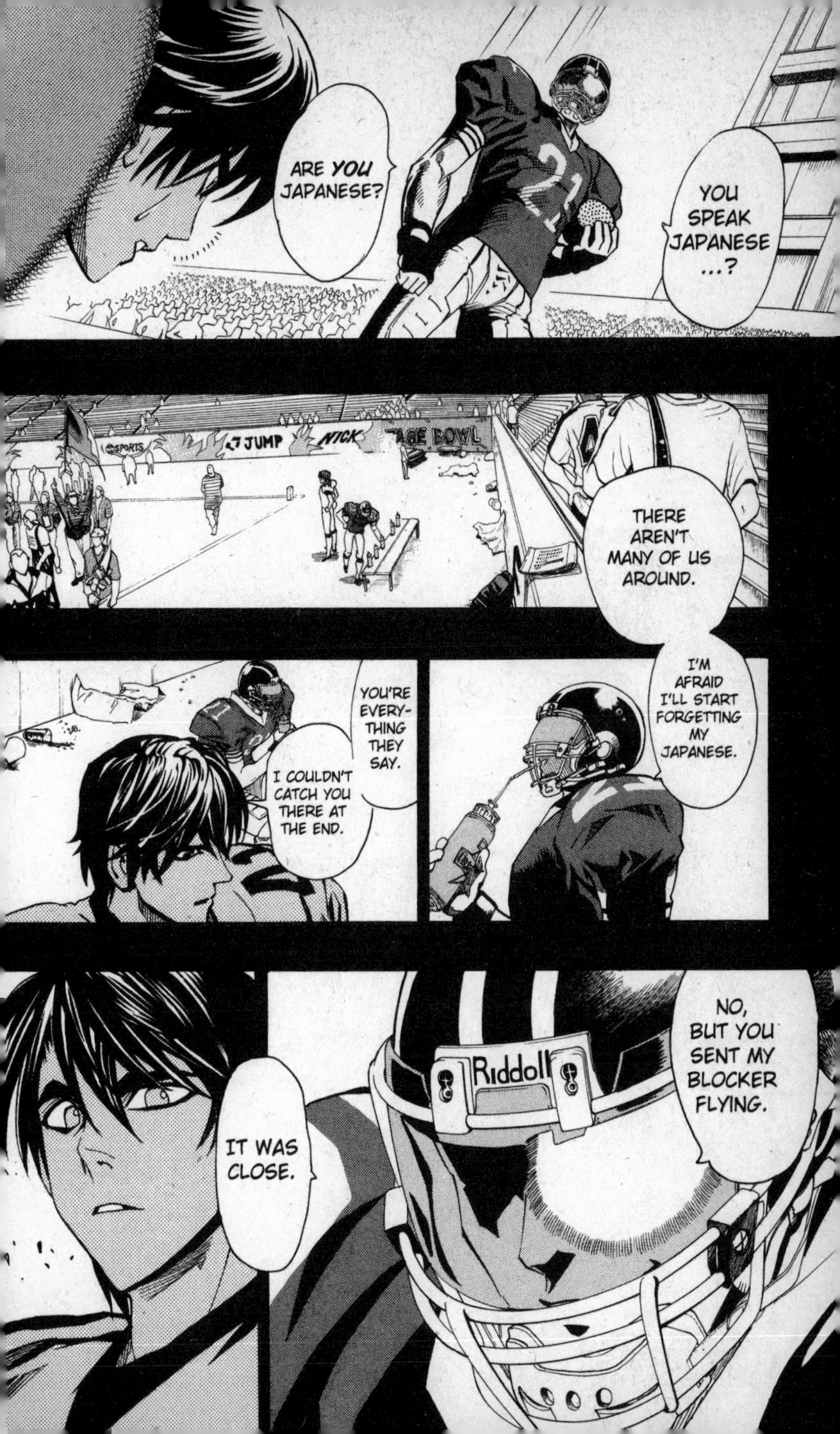
YOU SPEAK JAPANESE ...?
ARE YOU JAPANESE?
SPORTS
JUMP
NICK
THERE AREN'T MANY OF US AROUND.
I'M AFRAID I'LL START FORGETTING MY JAPANESE.
YOU'RE EVERY-THING THEY SAY.
I COULDN'T CATCH YOU THERE AT THE END.
NO, BUT YOU SENT MY BLOCKER FLYING.
Riddoll
IT WAS CLOSE.

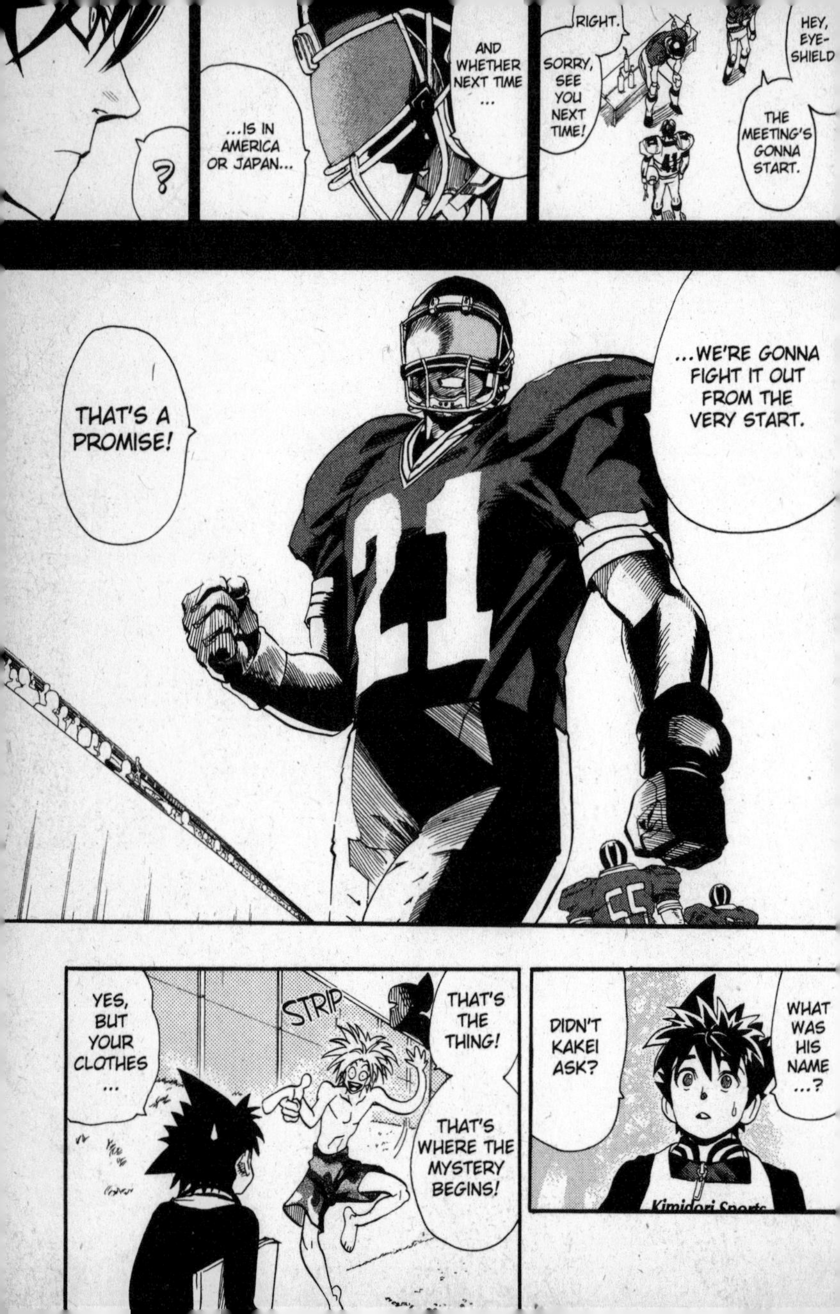
HEY, EYE-SHIELD
THE MEETING'S GONNA START.
RIGHT.
SORRY, SEE YOU NEXT TIME!
AND WHETHER NEXT TIME ...
...IS IN AMERICA OR JAPAN...
?
...WE'RE GONNA FIGHT IT OUT FROM THE VERY START.
THAT'S A PROMISE!
WHAT WAS HIS NAME ...?
DIDN'T KAKEI ASK?
Kimidori Sports
THAT'S THE THING!
THAT'S WHERE THE MYSTERY BEGINS!
STRIP
YES, BUT YOUR CLOTHES ...

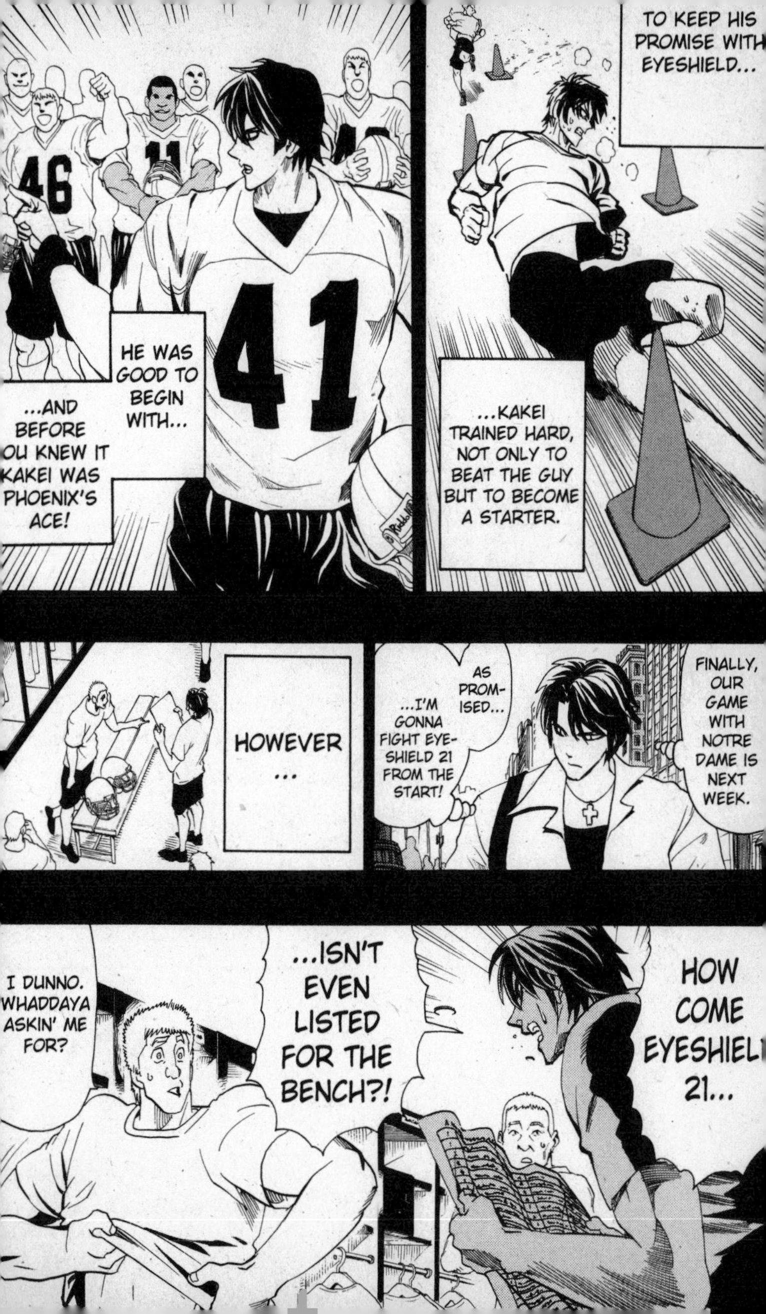
TO KEEP HIS PROMISE WITH EYESHIELD...
...KAKEI TRAINED HARD, NOT ONLY TO BEAT THE GUY BUT TO BECOME A STARTER.
HE WAS GOOD TO BEGIN WITH...
...AND BEFORE OU KNEW IT KAKEI WAS PHOENIX'S ACE!
FINALLY, OUR GAME WITH NOTRE DAME IS NEXT WEEK.
AS PROMISED...
...I'M GONNA FIGHT EYESHIELD 21 FROM THE START!
HOWEVER...
HOW COME EYESHIEL 21...
...ISN'T EVEN LISTED FOR THE BENCH?!
I DUNNO. WHADDAYA ASKIN' ME FOR?

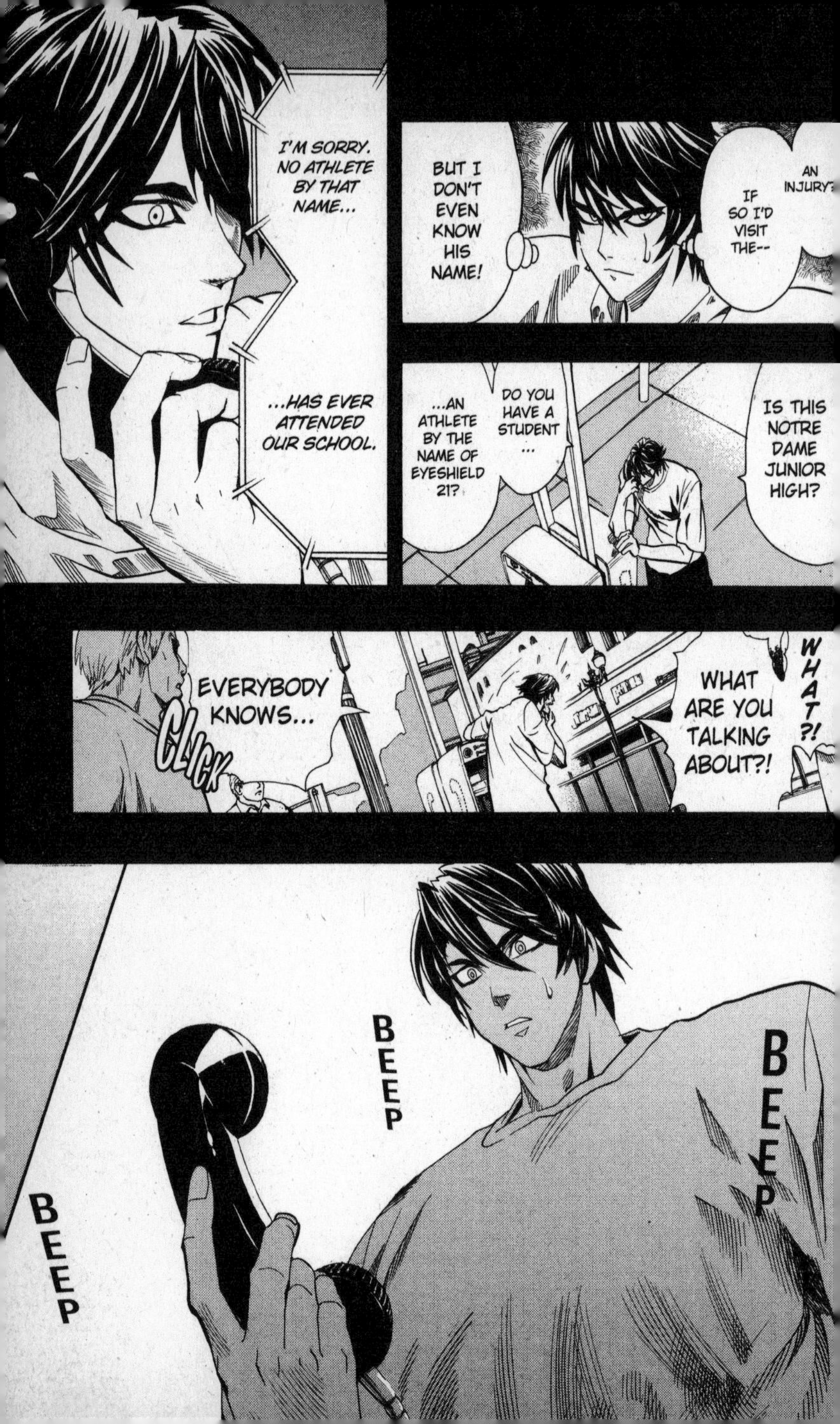
AN INJURY?
IF SO I'D VISIT THE--
BUT I DON'T EVEN KNOW HIS NAME!
IS THIS NOTRE DAME JUNIOR HIGH?
DO YOU HAVE A STUDENT...
...AN ATHLETE BY THE NAME OF EYESHIELD 21?
I'M SORRY. NO ATHLETE BY THAT NAME...
...HAS EVER ATTENDED OUR SCHOOL.
WHAT?!
WHAT ARE YOU TALKING ABOUT?!
EVERYBODY KNOWS...
CLICK
BEEP
BEEP
BEEP
BEEP

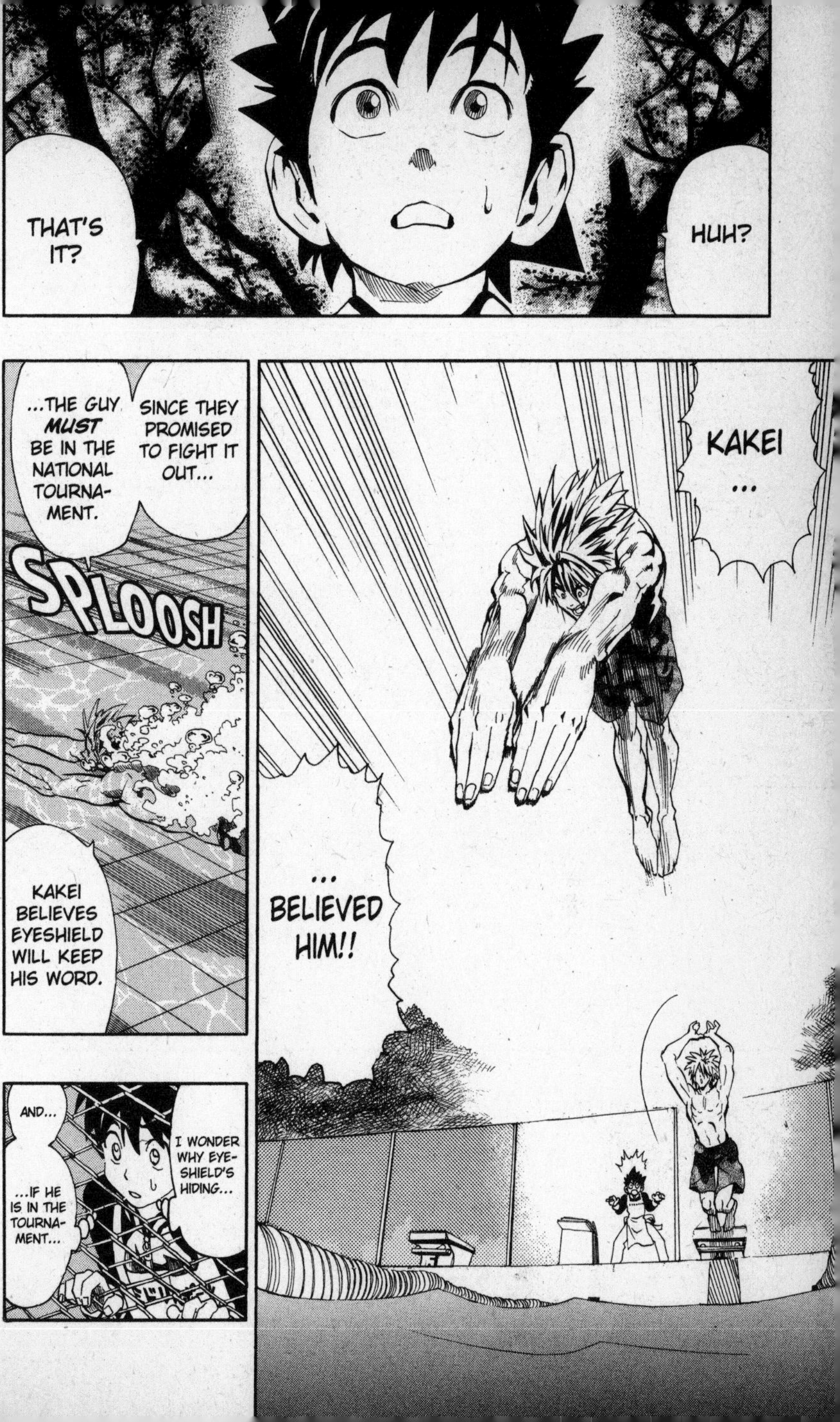
HUH?
THAT'S IT?
KAKEI ...
... BELIEVED HIM!!
SINCE THEY PROMISED TO FIGHT IT OUT...
...THE GUY *MUST* BE IN THE NATIONAL TOURNA-MENT.
SPLOOSH
KAKEI BELIEVES EYESHIELD WILL KEEP HIS WORD.
AND...
...IF HE IS IN THE TOURNA-MENT...
I WONDER WHY EYE-SHIELD'S HIDING...

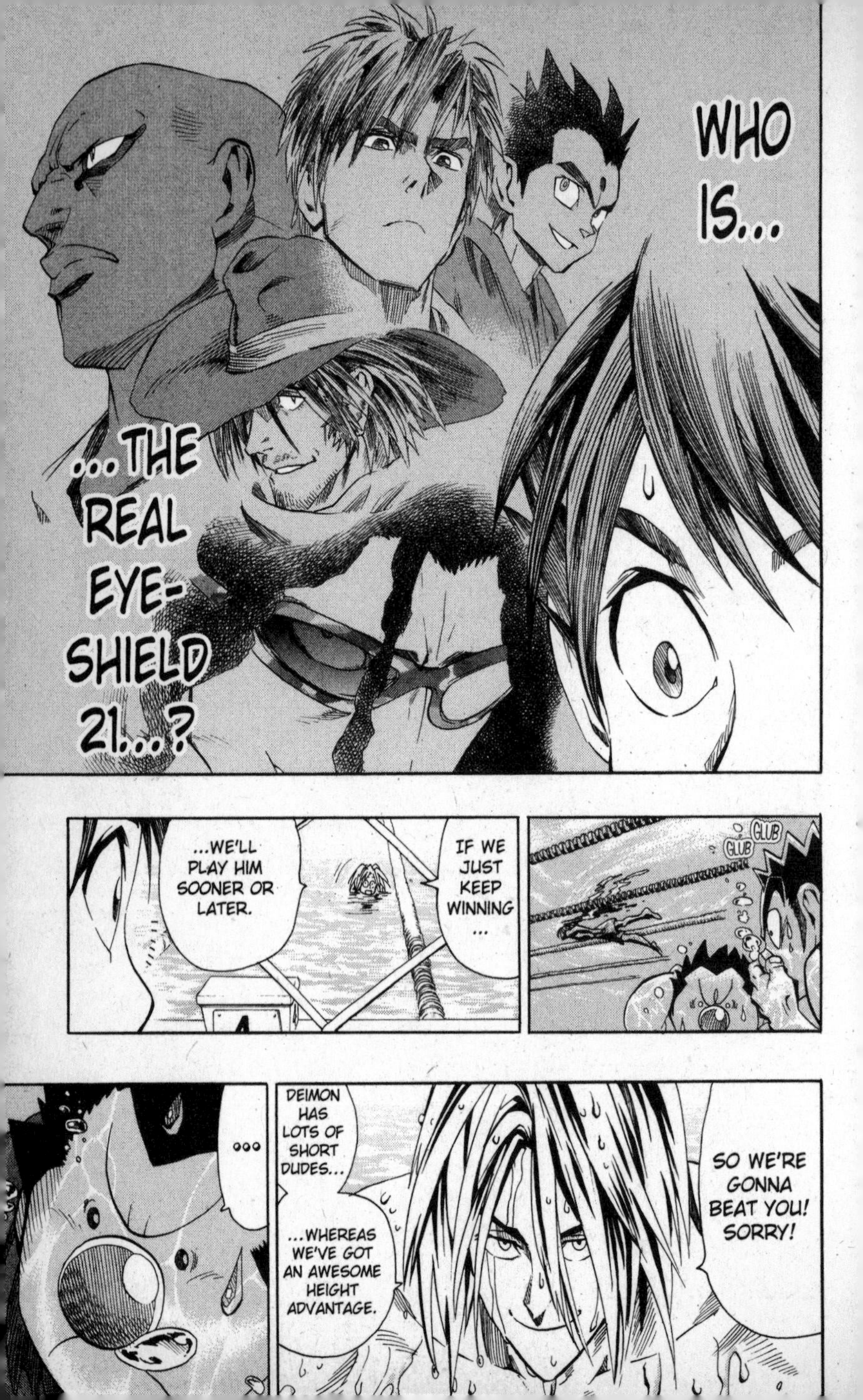
WHO IS...
...THE REAL EYE-SHIELD 21...?
GLUB GLUB
IF WE JUST KEEP WINNING...
...WE'LL PLAY HIM SOONER OR LATER.
DEIMON HAS LOTS OF SHORT DUDES...
...WHEREAS WE'VE GOT AN AWESOME HEIGHT ADVANTAGE.
SO WE'RE GONNA BEAT YOU! SORRY!
...

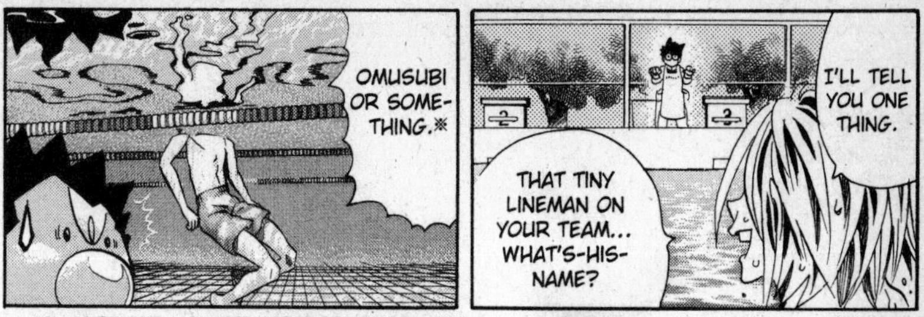
I'LL TELL YOU ONE THING.
THAT TINY LINEMAN ON YOUR TEAM... WHAT'S-HIS-NAME?
OMUSUBI OR SOME-THING.※

※A PLAY ON THE JAPANESE WORD FOR "RICE BALL"

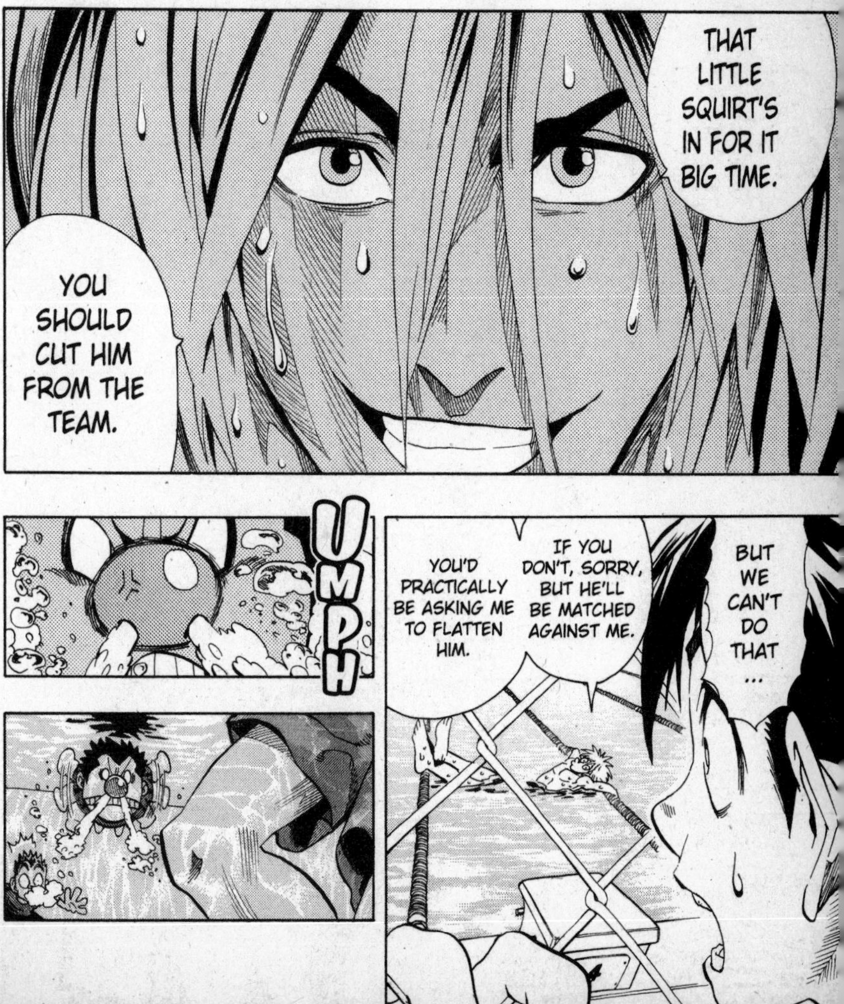
THAT LITTLE SQUIRT'S IN FOR IT BIG TIME.
YOU SHOULD CUT HIM FROM THE TEAM.
BUT WE CAN'T DO THAT...
IF YOU DON'T, SORRY, BUT HE'LL BE MATCHED AGAINST ME.
YOU'D PRACTICALLY BE ASKING ME TO FLATTEN HIM.
UMPH

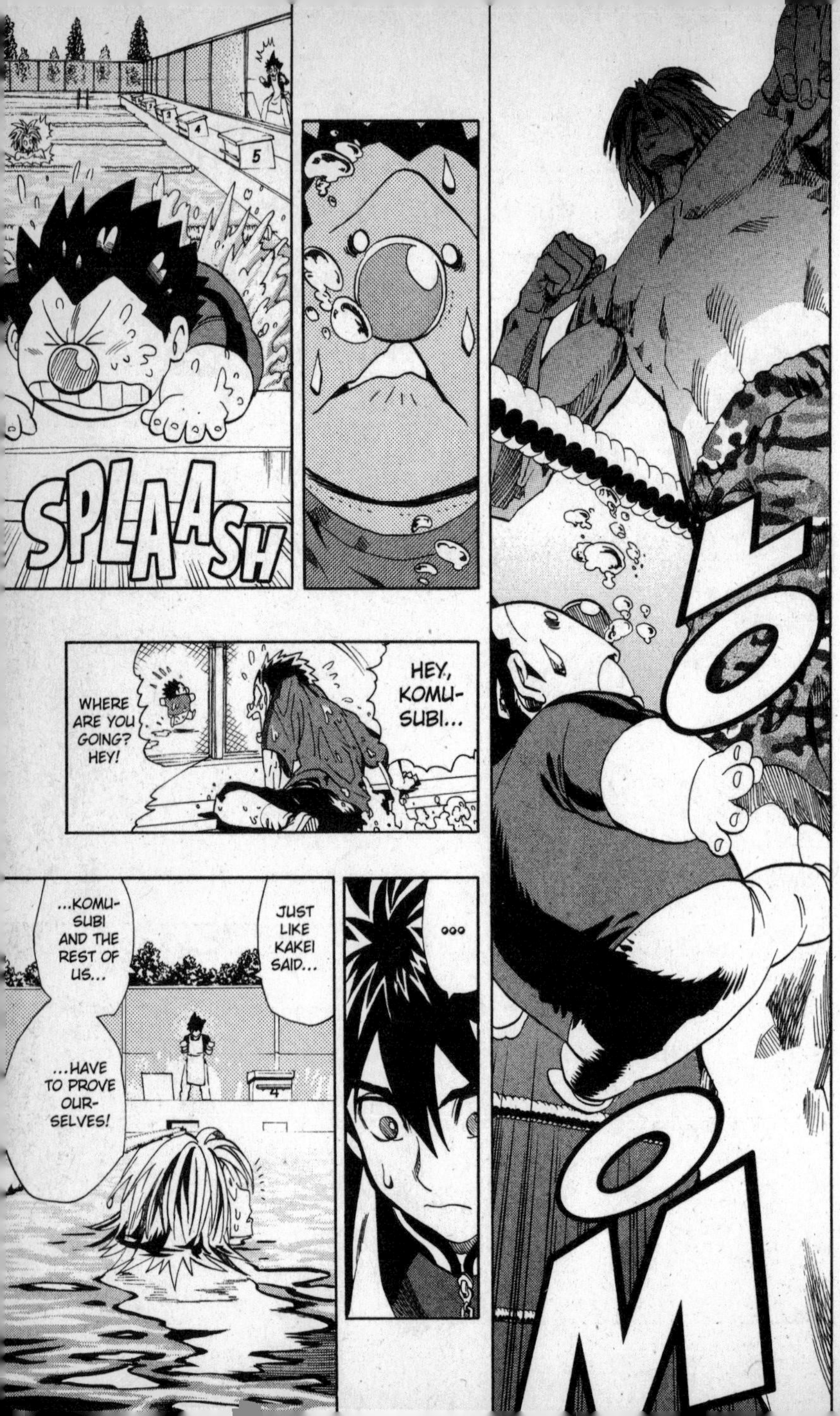
SPLAASH
HEY, KOMUSUBI...
WHERE ARE YOU GOING? HEY!
...
JUST LIKE KAKEI SAID...
...KOMUSUBI AND THE REST OF US...
...HAVE TO PROVE OURSELVES!

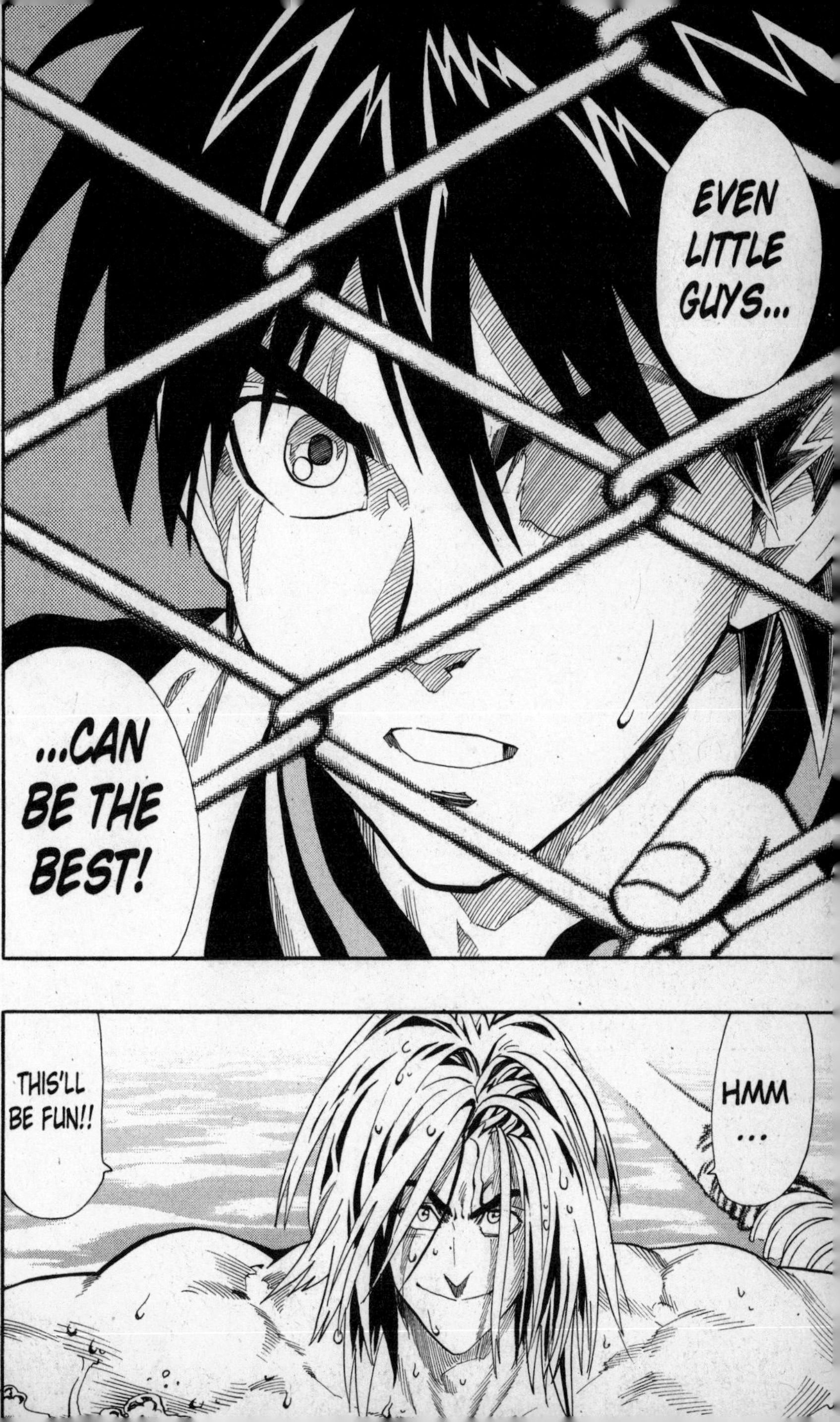
EVEN LITTLE GUYS...
...CAN BE THE BEST!
HMM ...
THIS'LL BE FUN!!

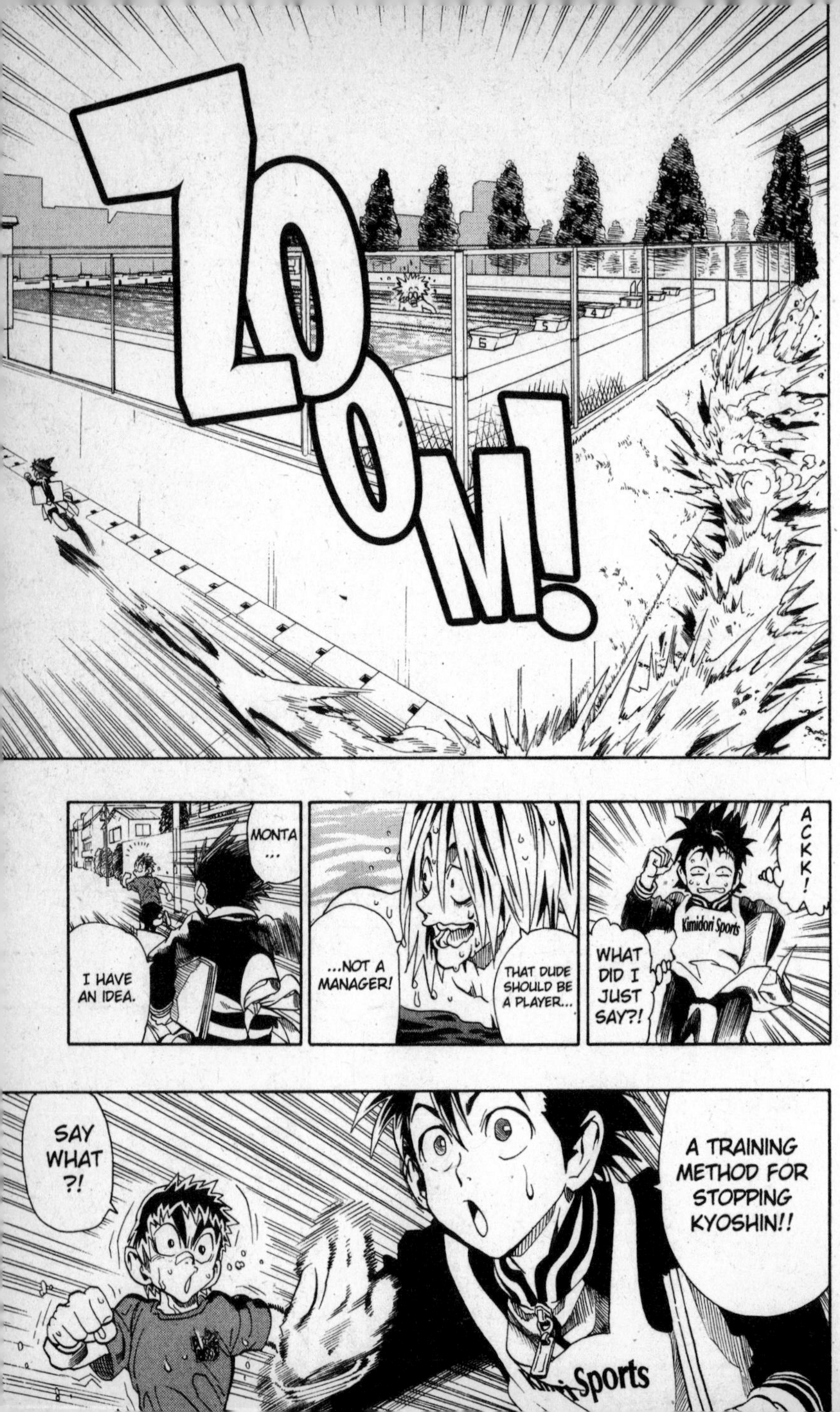
ZOOM!
ACKK!
Kimidori Sports
WHAT DID I JUST SAY?!
THAT DUDE SHOULD BE A PLAYER...
...NOT A MANAGER!
MONTA...
I HAVE AN IDEA.
A TRAINING METHOD FOR STOPPING KYOSHIN!!
SAY WHAT ?!

KYOSHIN HIGH SCHOOL

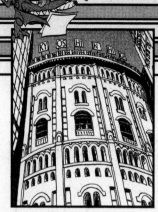

Student Body: 1,170

Special Campus Facilities: 10 Elevators

Major Career Options after Graduation

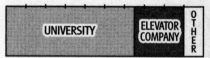

UNIVERSITY	ELEVATOR COMPANY	OTHER

This mammoth school sits on very narrow land so it was built unbelievably tall. Students have come to believe that elevators are mankind's greatest invention, and thus flood elevator companies with job applications upon graduation.

Student Testimonial

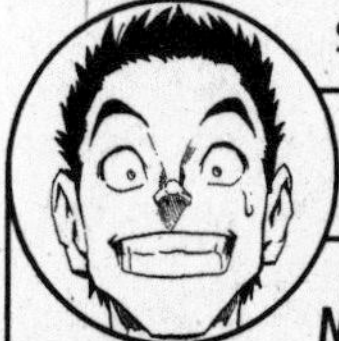

Osamu Kobanzame

My impression of Kyoshin? Hmm, I'd say...super tall! Tuper Sall!

Oh...not that kind of impression? The school atmosphere? Oh, yeah...yeah! I was going to tell you about that.

The freshmen are super tall! Tuper Sall!

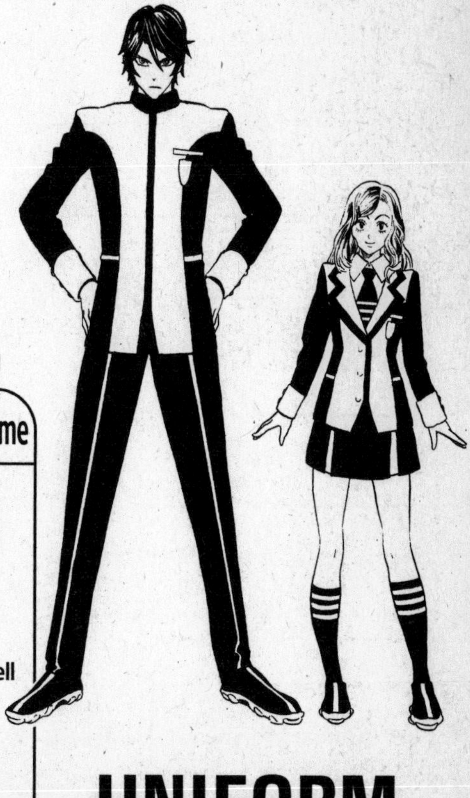

UNIFORM

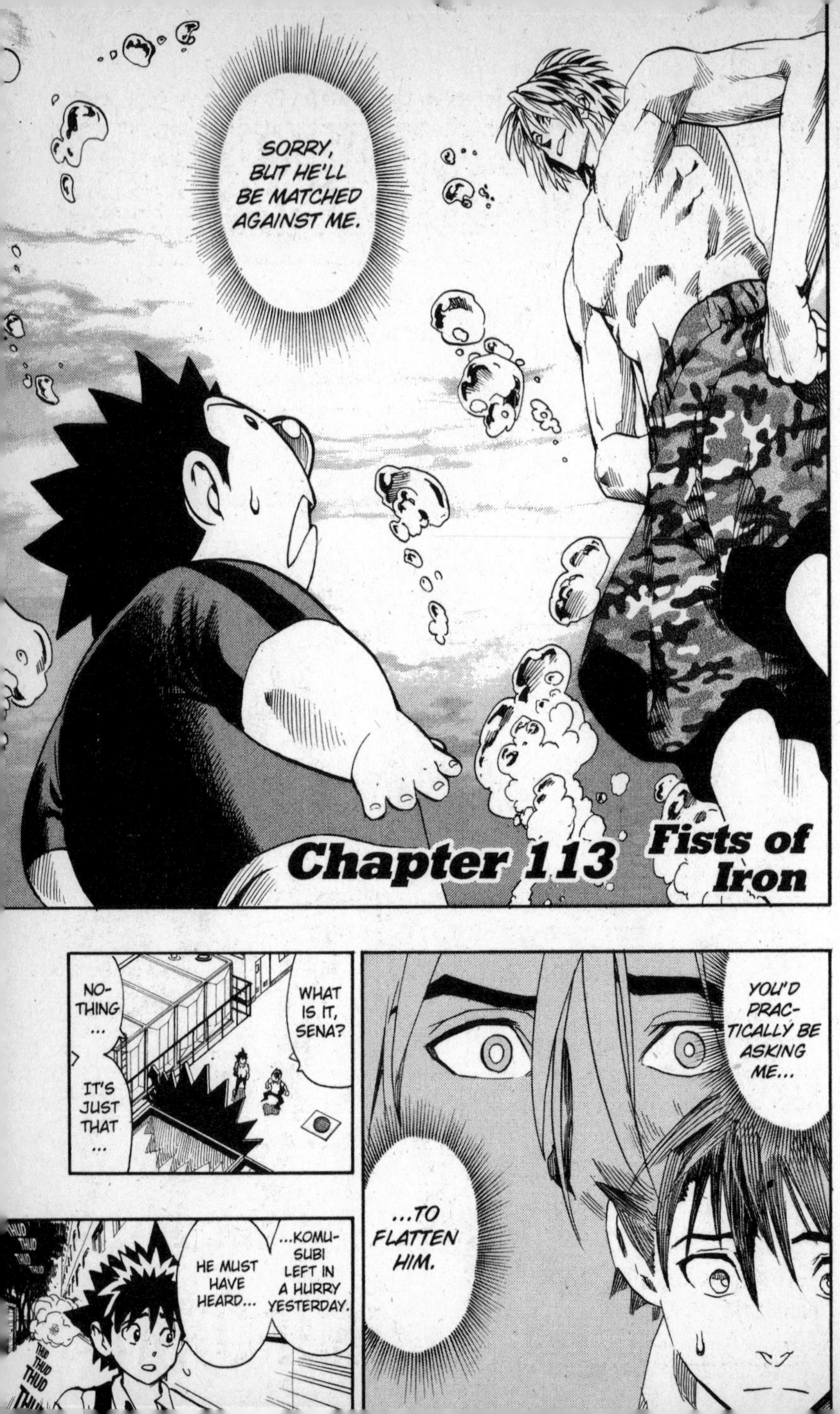
SORRY, BUT HE'LL BE MATCHED AGAINST ME.
Chapter 113 Fists of Iron
YOU'D PRACTICALLY BE ASKING ME...
...TO FLATTEN HIM.
WHAT IS IT, SENA?
NOTHING...
IT'S JUST THAT...
...KOMUSUBI LEFT IN A HURRY YESTERDAY.
HE MUST HAVE HEARD...
THUD THUD THUD THUD
THUD THUD THUD

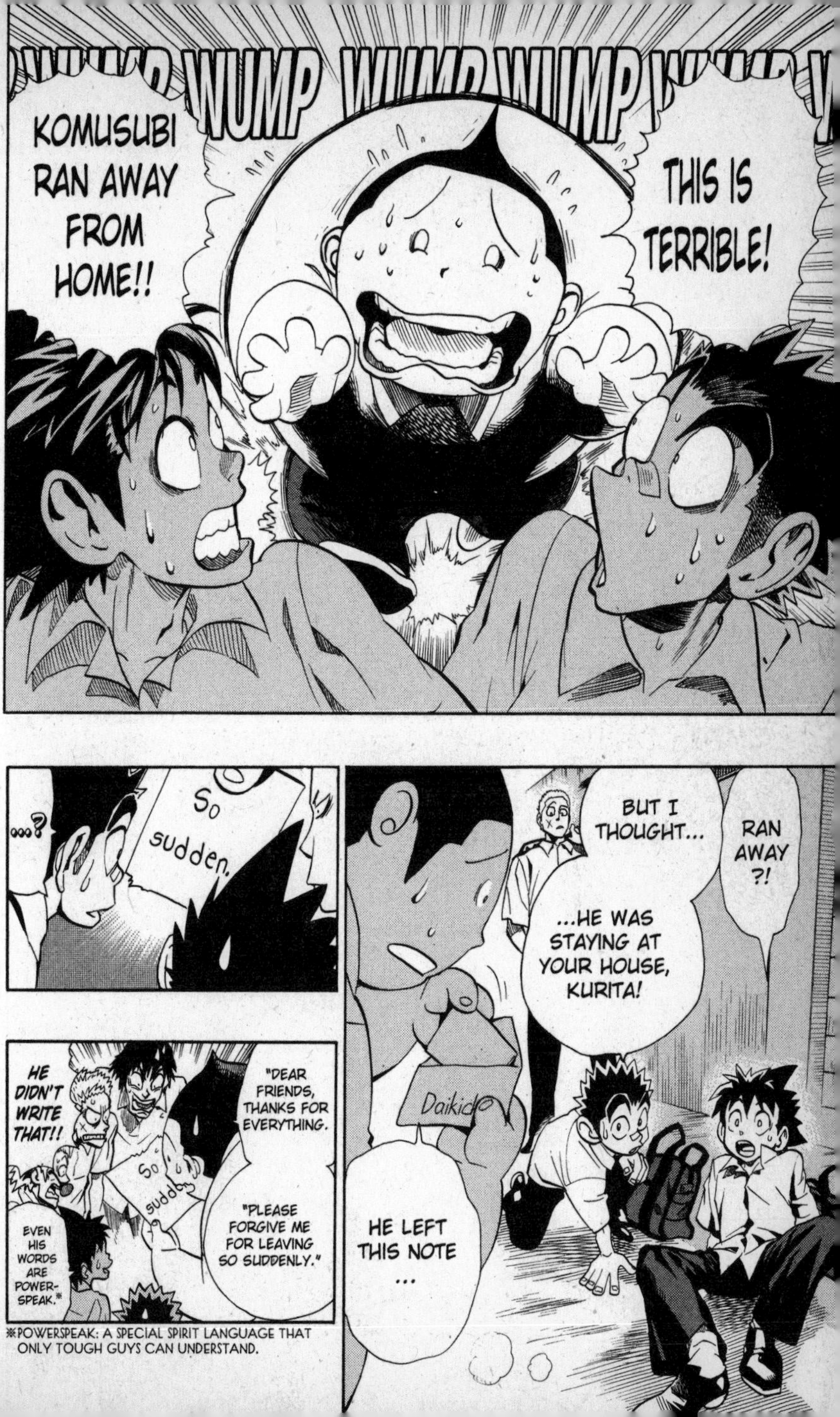
WUMP WUMP WUMP
THIS IS TERRIBLE!
KOMUSUBI RAN AWAY FROM HOME!!
RAN AWAY ?!
BUT I THOUGHT...
...HE WAS STAYING AT YOUR HOUSE, KURITA!
HE LEFT THIS NOTE ...
So sudden.
...?
"DEAR FRIENDS, THANKS FOR EVERYTHING.
"PLEASE FORGIVE ME FOR LEAVING SO SUDDENLY."
HE DIDN'T WRITE THAT!!
EVEN HIS WORDS ARE POWER-SPEAK.※

※POWERSPEAK: A SPECIAL SPIRIT LANGUAGE THAT ONLY TOUGH GUYS CAN UNDERSTAND.

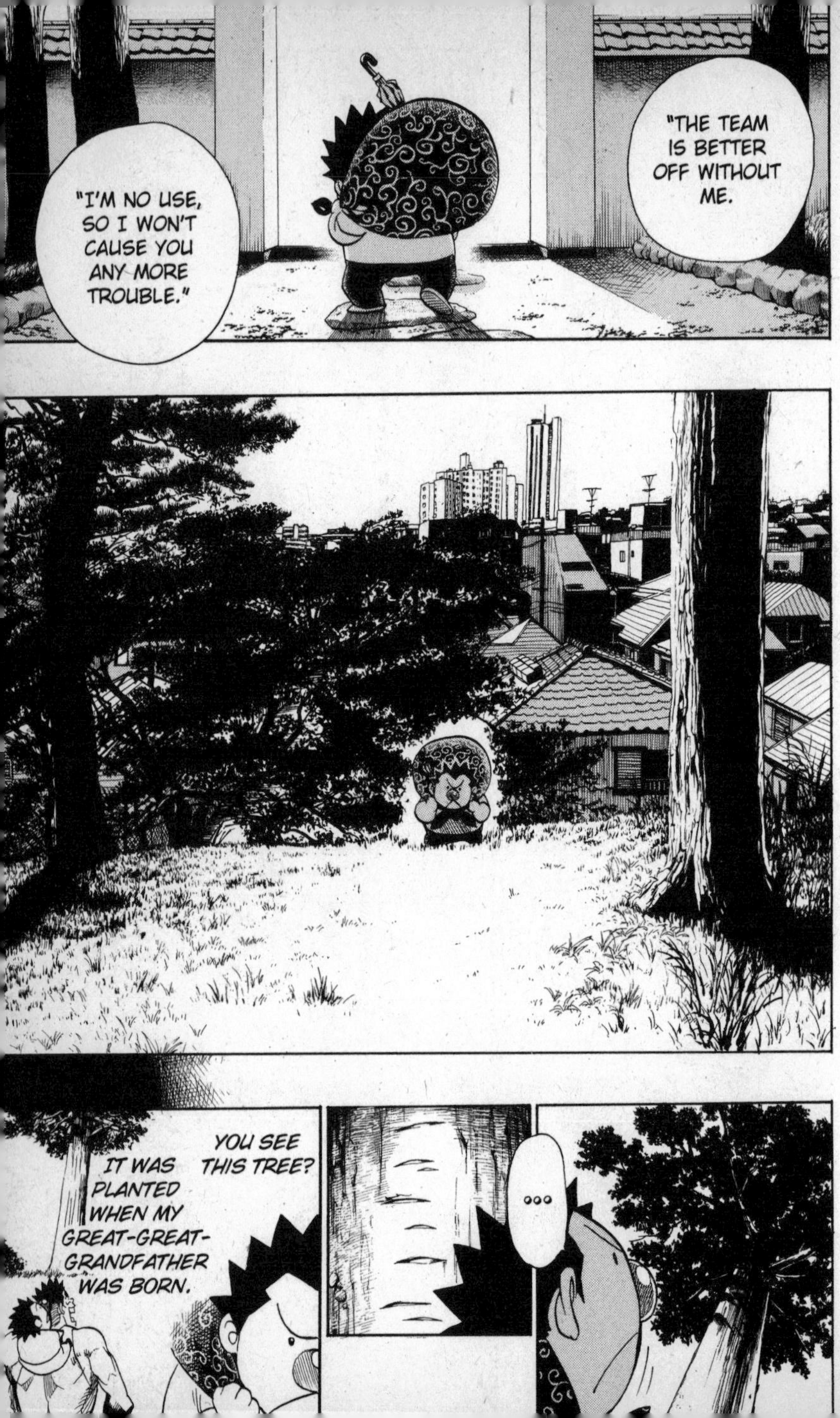
"THE TEAM IS BETTER OFF WITHOUT ME.
"I'M NO USE, SO I WON'T CAUSE YOU ANY MORE TROUBLE."
...
YOU SEE THIS TREE?
IT WAS PLANTED WHEN MY GREAT-GREAT-GRANDFATHER WAS BORN.

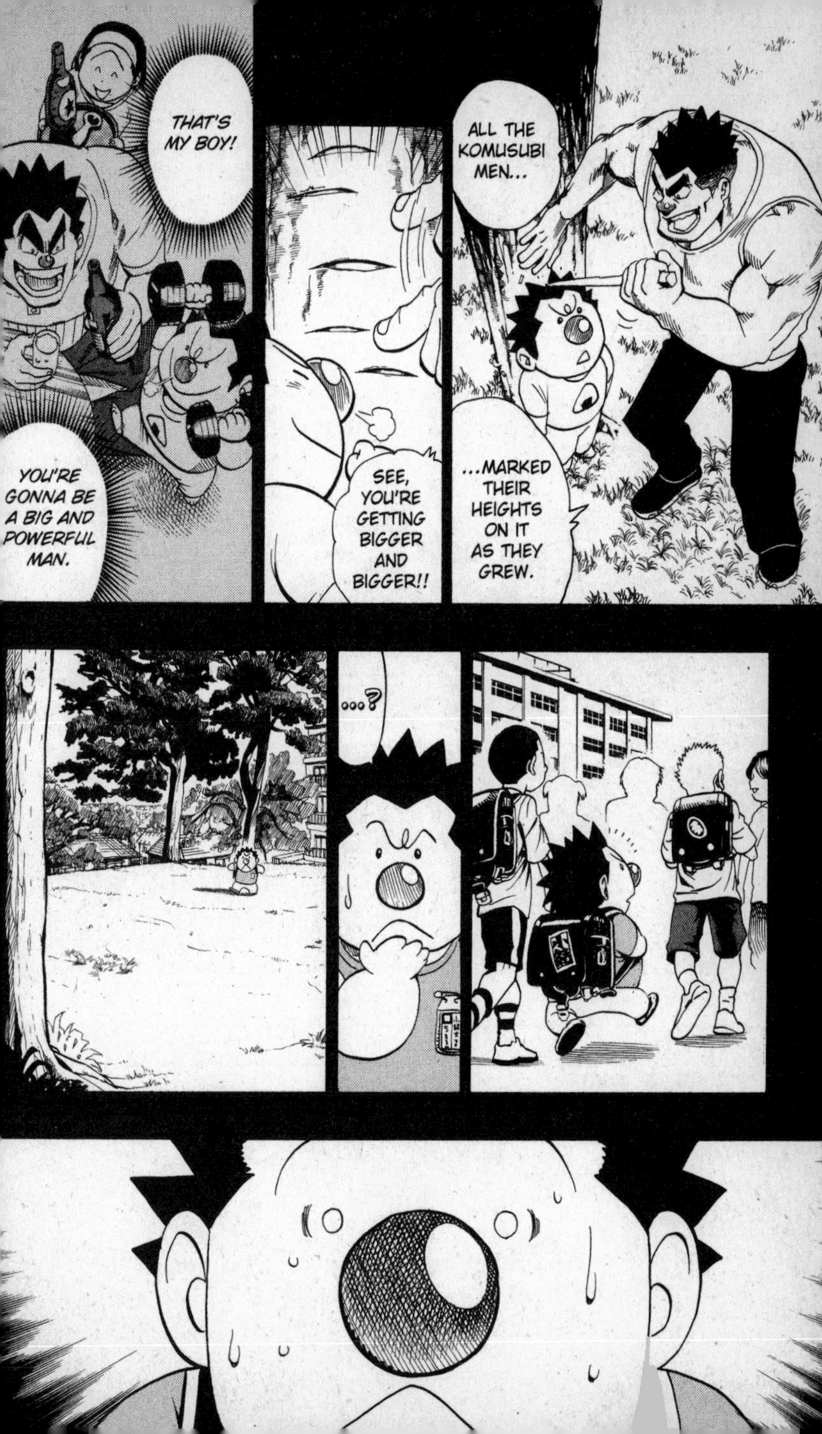
ALL THE KOMUSUBI MEN...
...MARKED THEIR HEIGHTS ON IT AS THEY GREW.
SEE, YOU'RE GETTING BIGGER AND BIGGER!!
THAT'S MY BOY!
YOU'RE GONNA BE A BIG AND POWERFUL MAN.
...?

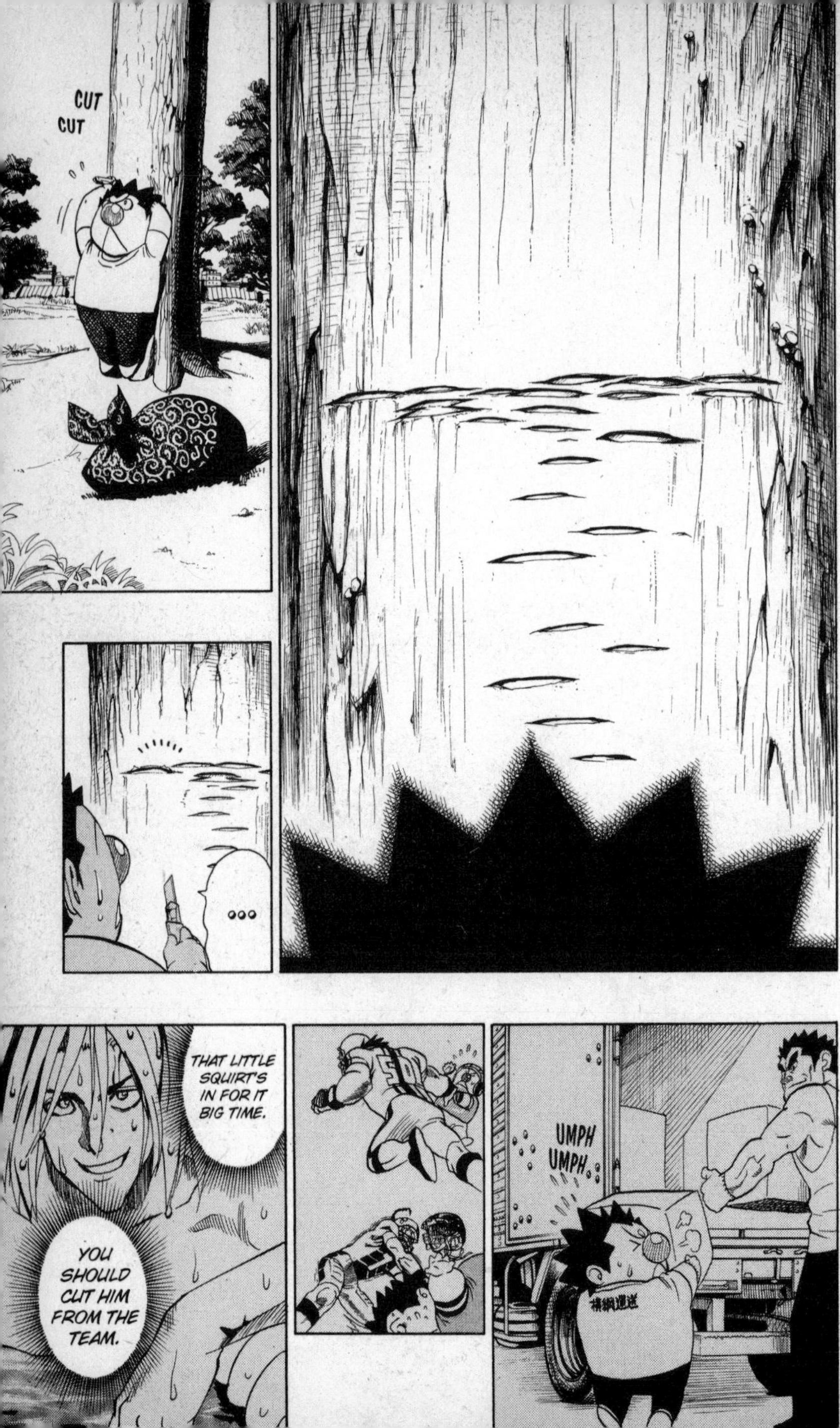
CUT
CUT
...
UMPH
UMPH
THAT LITTLE SQUIRT'S IN FOR IT BIG TIME.
YOU SHOULD CUT HIM FROM THE TEAM.

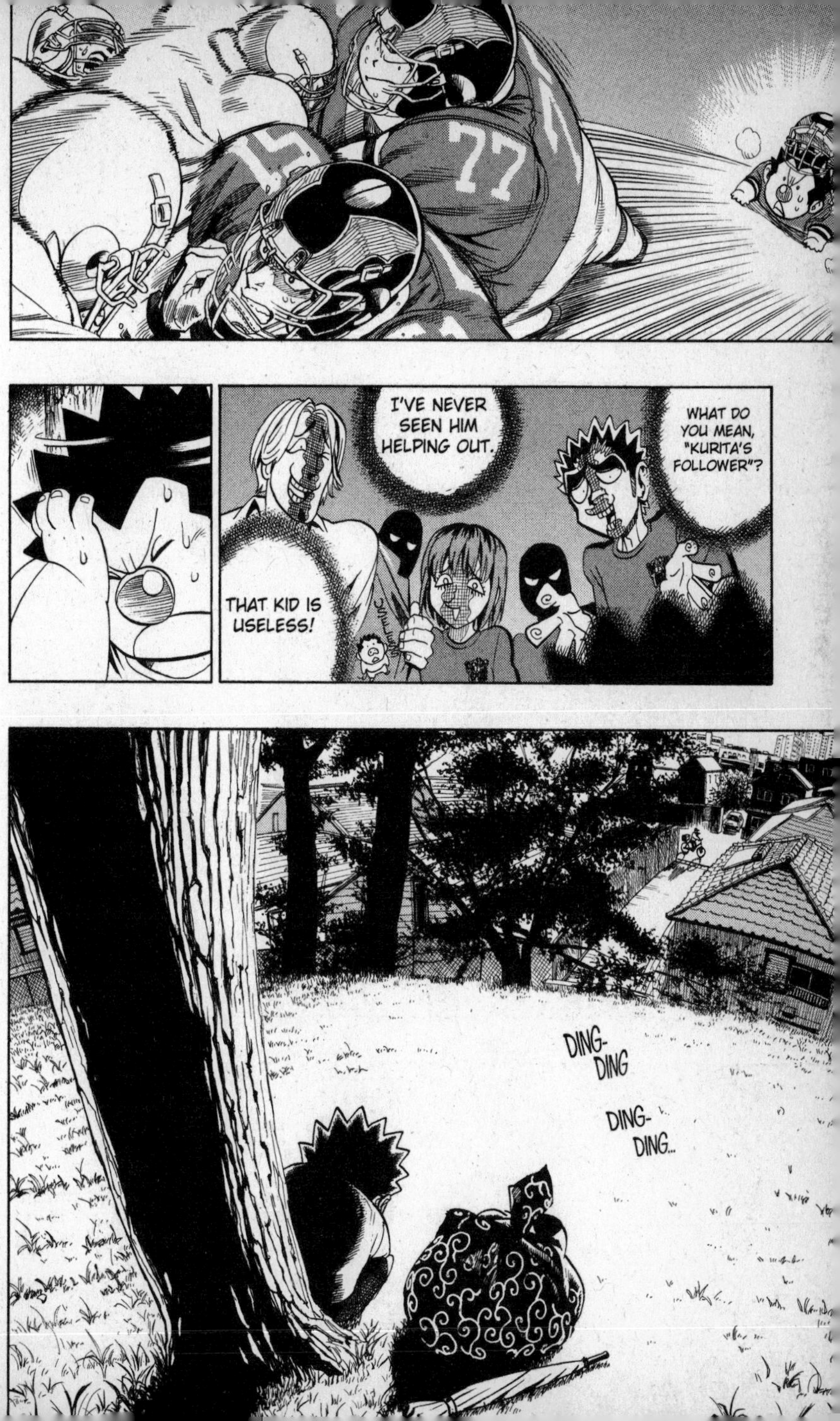
WHAT DO YOU MEAN, "KURITA'S FOLLOWER"?
I'VE NEVER SEEN HIM HELPING OUT.
THAT KID IS USELESS!
DING-DING
DING-DING...

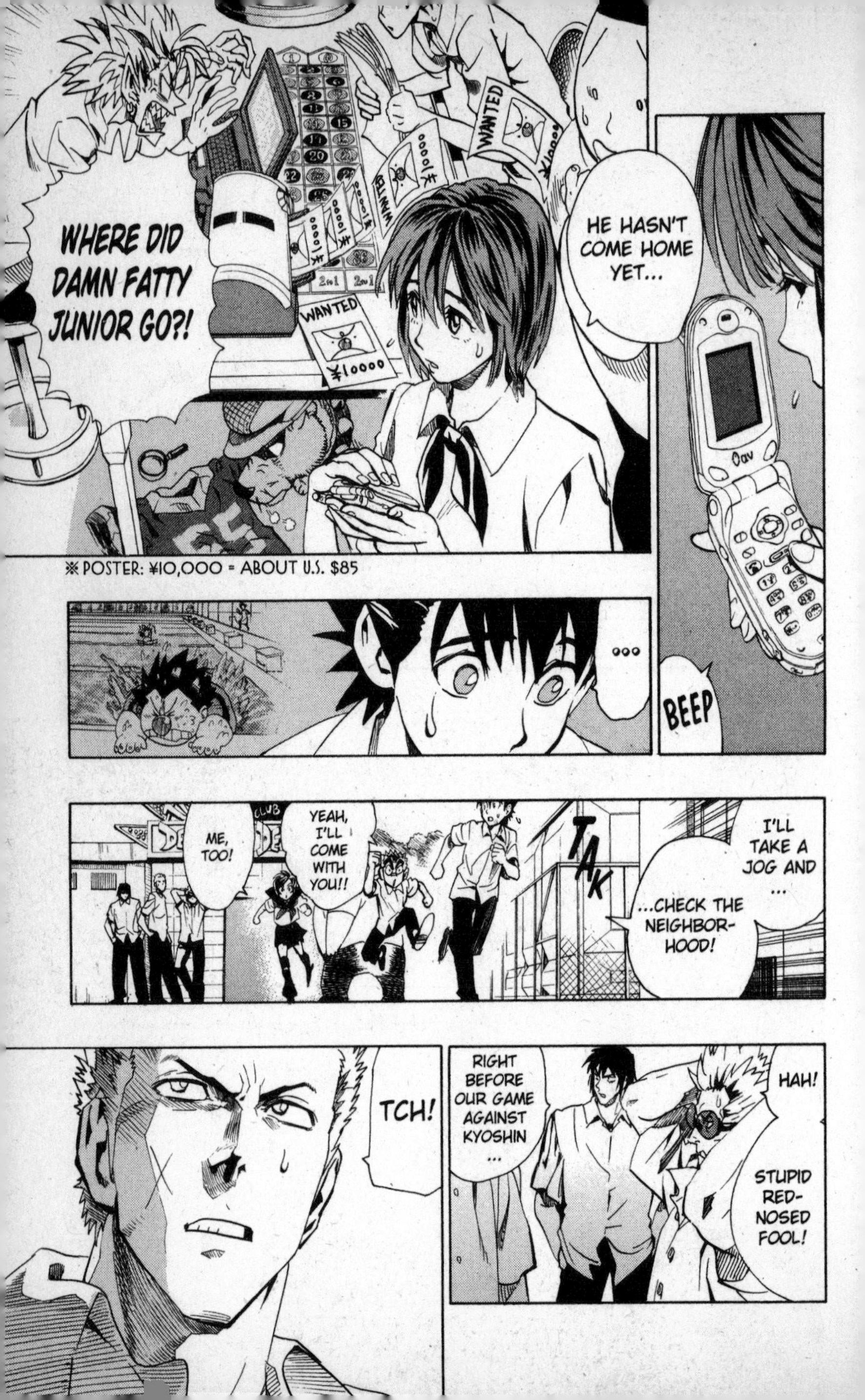
BEEP
HE HASN'T COME HOME YET...
WHERE DID DAMN FATTY JUNIOR GO?!
WANTED
¥10000
※ POSTER: ¥10,000 = ABOUT U.S. $85
...
I'LL TAKE A JOG AND ...
...CHECK THE NEIGHBOR-HOOD!
TAK
YEAH, I'LL COME WITH YOU!!
ME, TOO!
HAH!
STUPID RED-NOSED FOOL!
RIGHT BEFORE OUR GAME AGAINST KYOSHIN ...
TCH!

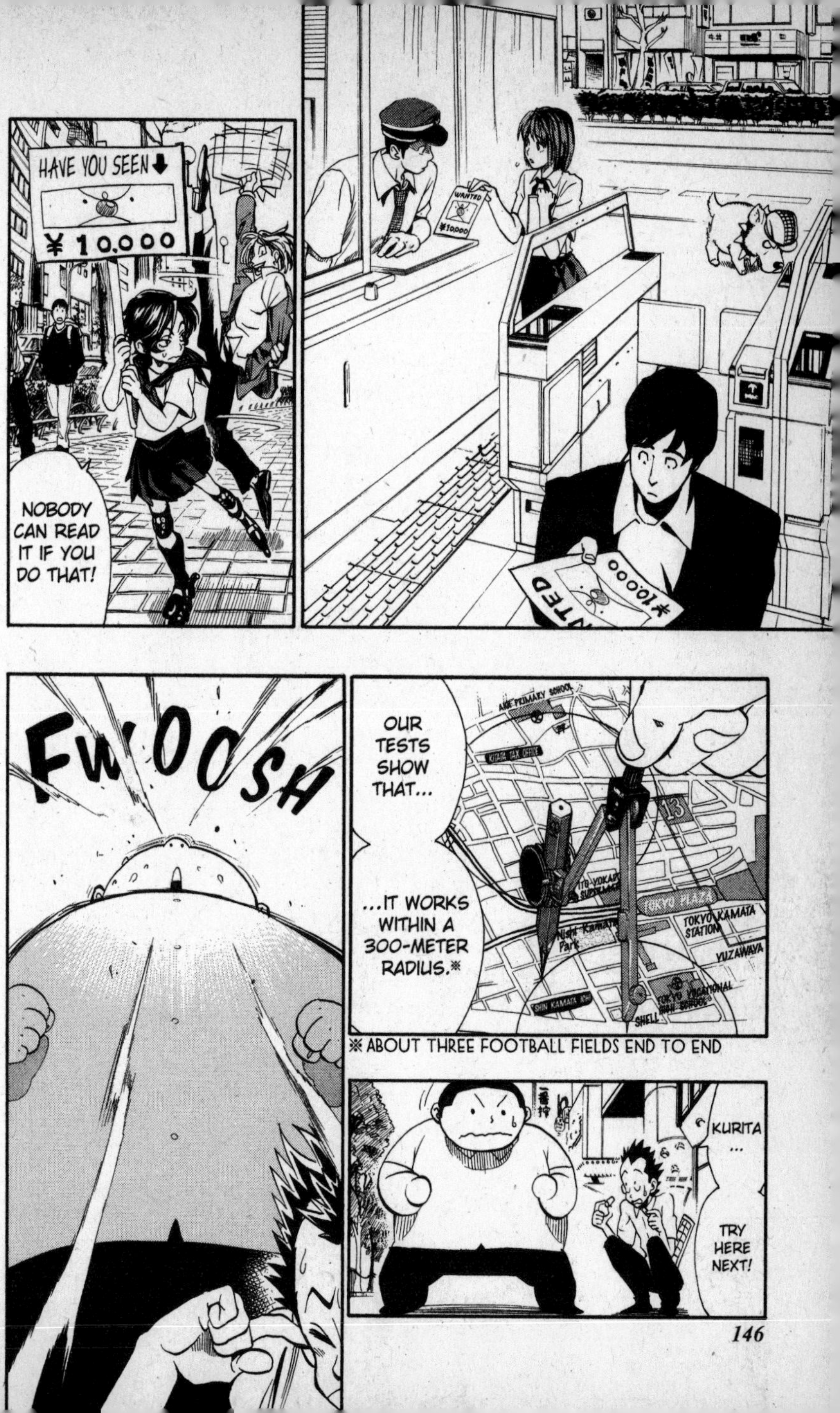
WANTED
¥10,000
HAVE YOU SEEN
¥10,000
NOBODY CAN READ IT IF YOU DO THAT!
OUR TESTS SHOW THAT...
...IT WORKS WITHIN A 300-METER RADIUS.※
TOKYO PLAZA
TOKYO KAMATA STATION
YUZAWAYA
SHELL
※ ABOUT THREE FOOTBALL FIELDS END TO END
KURITA ...
TRY HERE NEXT!
FWOOSH

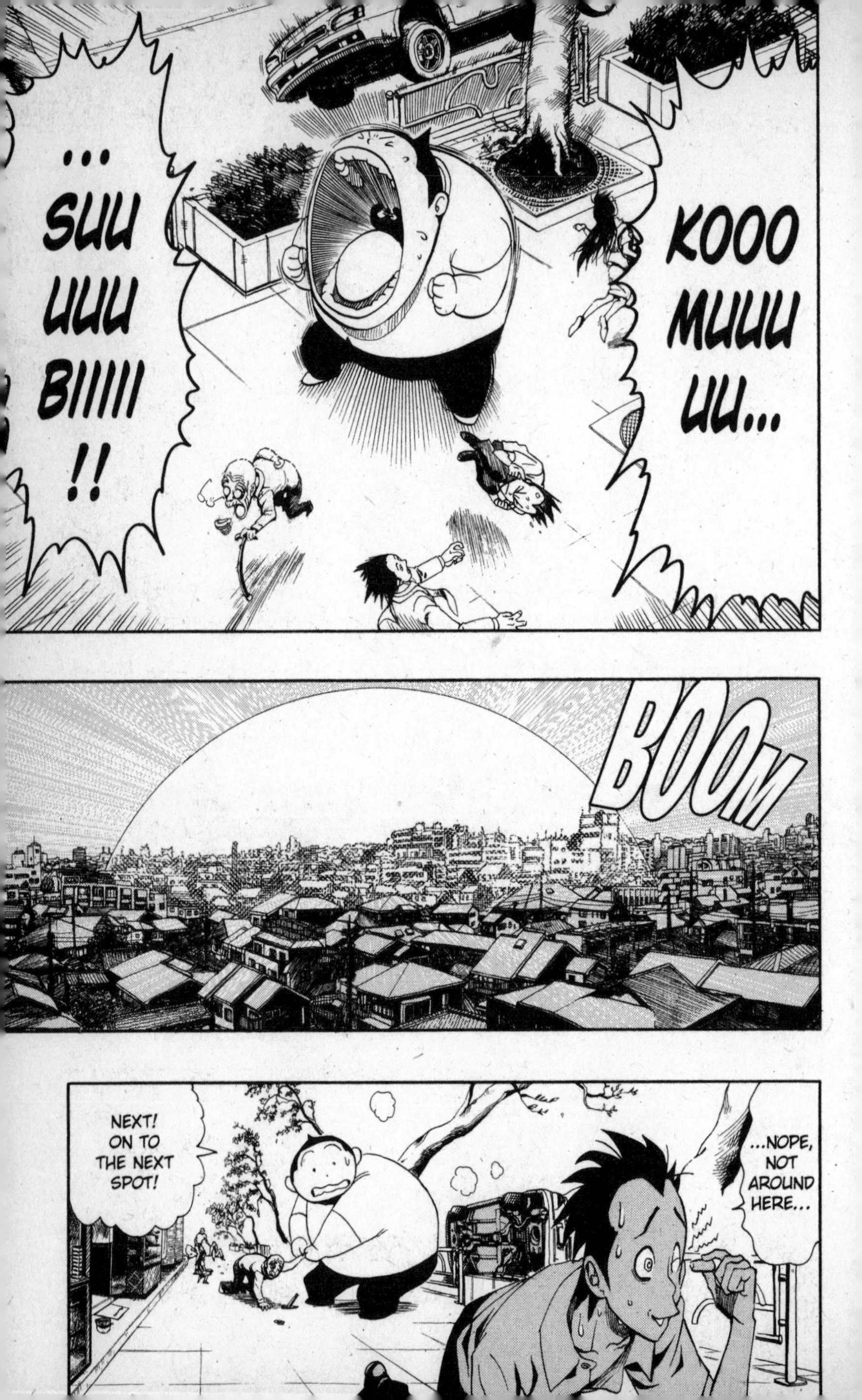
KOOO MUUUU UU...
...SUU UUU BIIIII !!
BOOM
...NOPE, NOT AROUND HERE...
NEXT! ON TO THE NEXT SPOT!

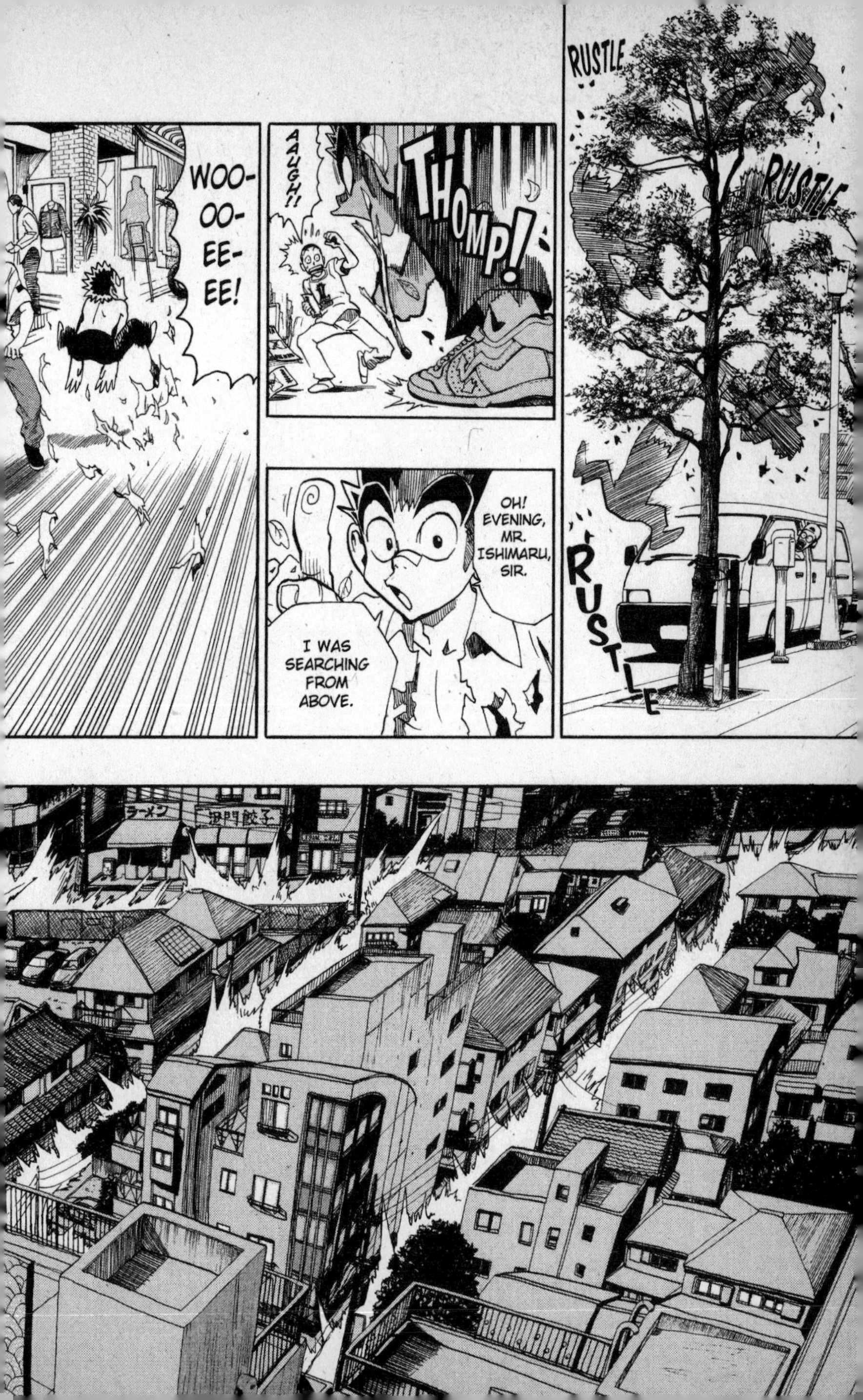
RUSTLE
RUSTLE
RUSTLE
AAUGH!!
THOMP!
OH! EVENING, MR. ISHIMARU, SIR.
I WAS SEARCHING FROM ABOVE.
WOO-OO-EE-EE!
ラーメン

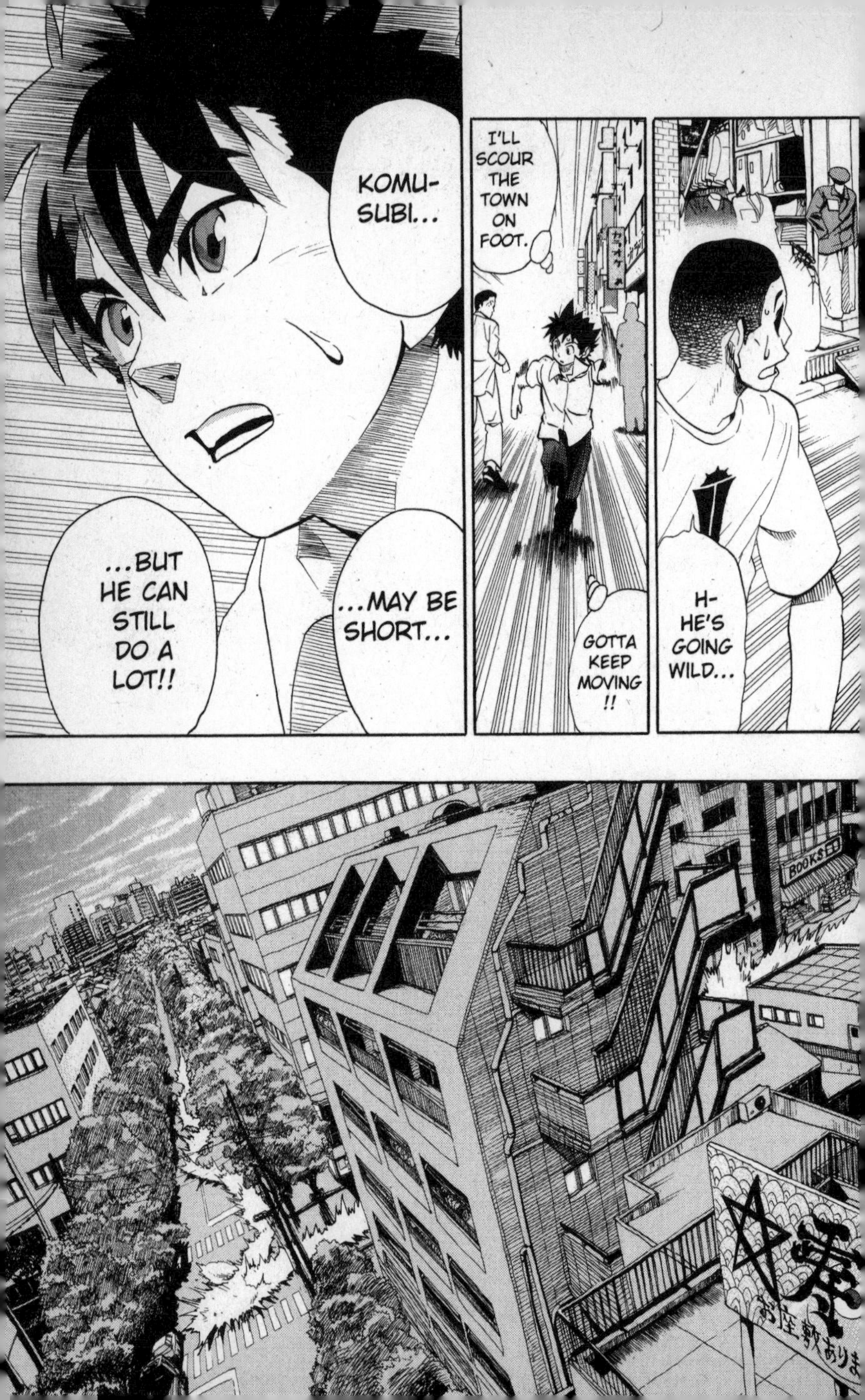
H-HE'S GOING WILD...
I'LL SCOUR THE TOWN ON FOOT.
GOTTA KEEP MOVING!!
KOMU-SUBI...
...MAY BE SHORT...
...BUT HE CAN STILL DO A LOT!!
BOOKS

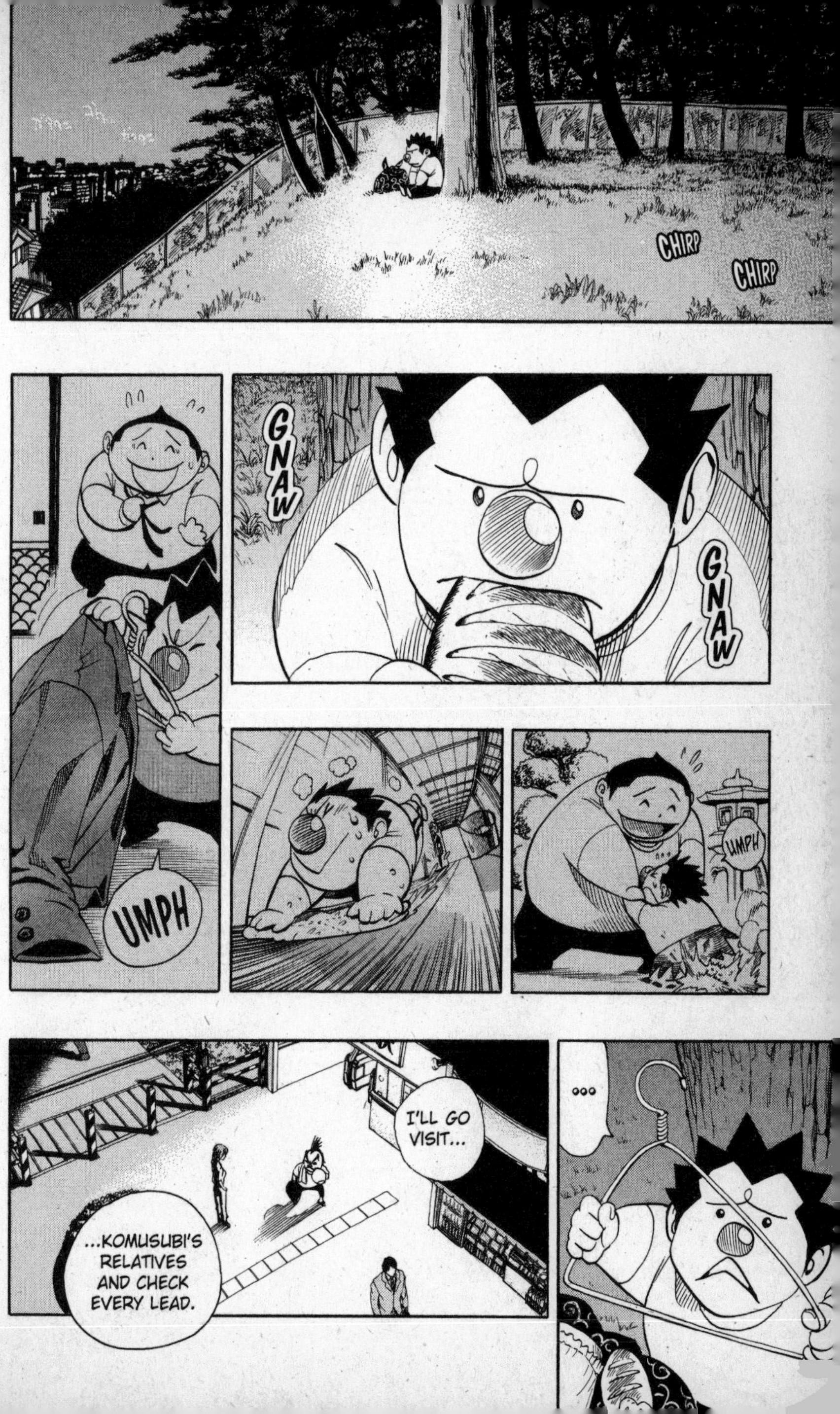
CHIRP
CHIRP
GNAW
GNAW
UMPH
UMPH
...
I'LL GO VISIT...
...KOMUSUBI'S RELATIVES AND CHECK EVERY LEAD.

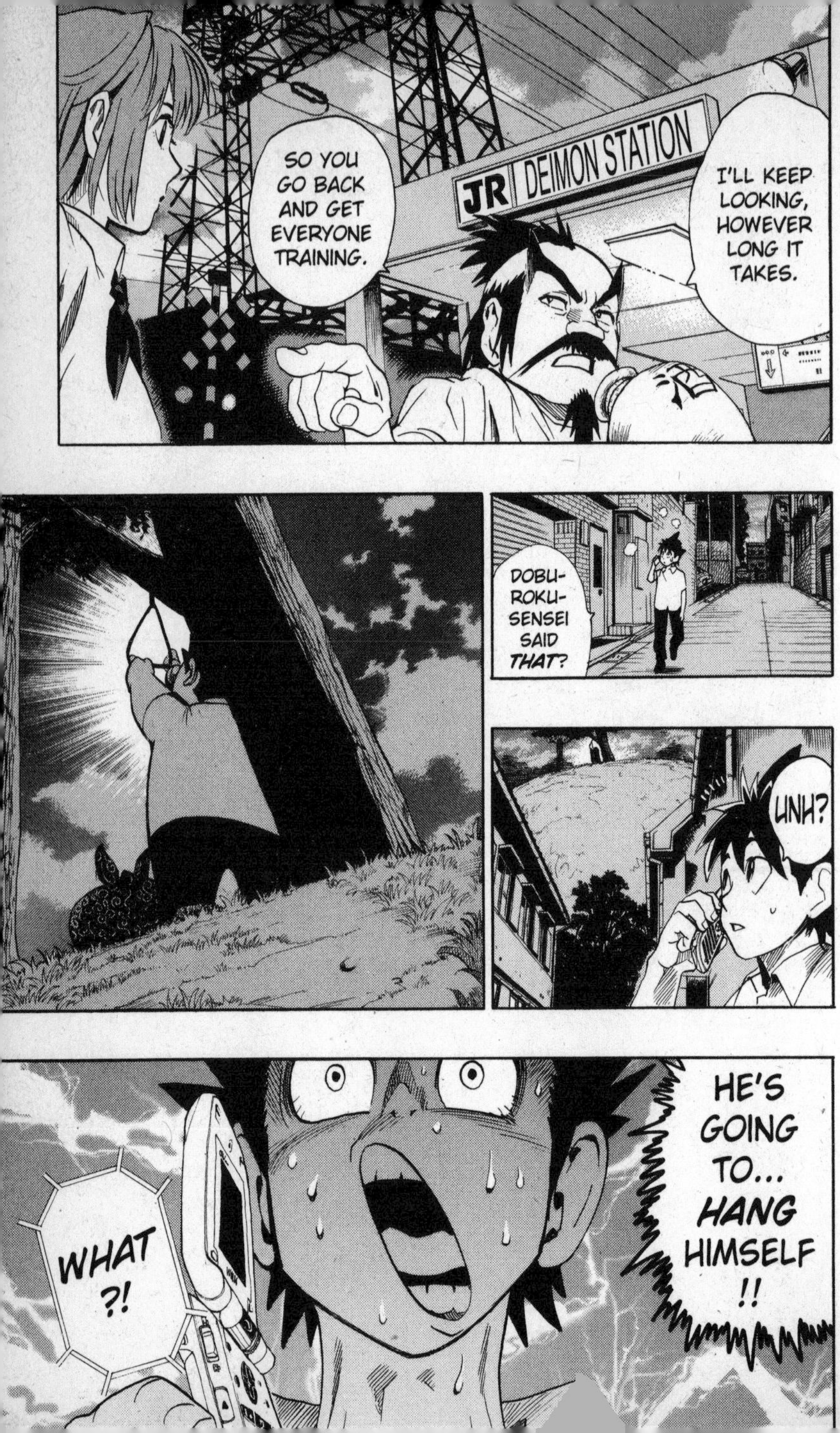
I'LL KEEP LOOKING, HOWEVER LONG IT TAKES.
JR DEIMON STATION
SO YOU GO BACK AND GET EVERYONE TRAINING.
DOBU-ROKU-SENSEI SAID *THAT*?
UNH?
HE'S GOING TO... *HANG* HIMSELF !!
WHAT ?!

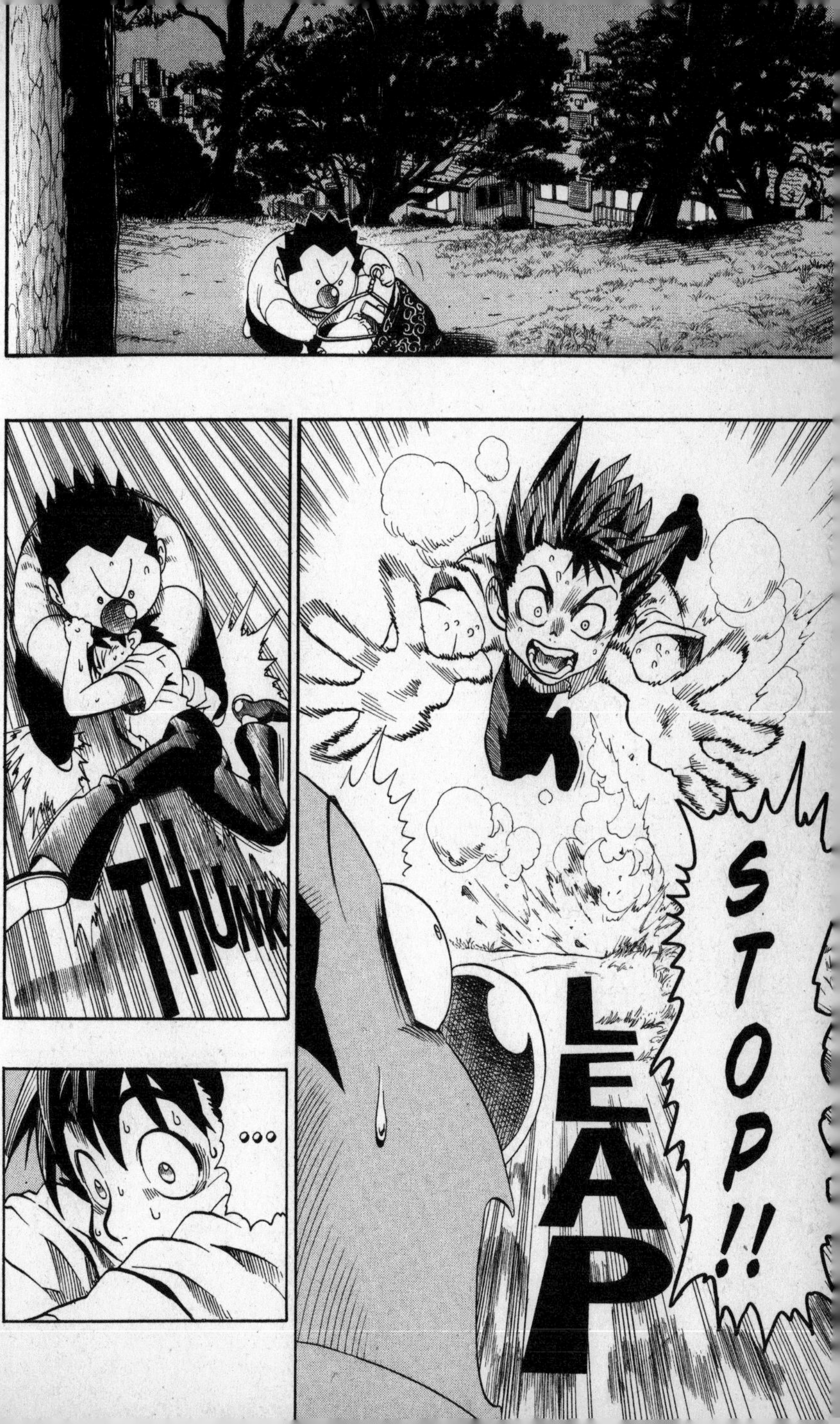
STOP!!
LEAP
THUNK
...

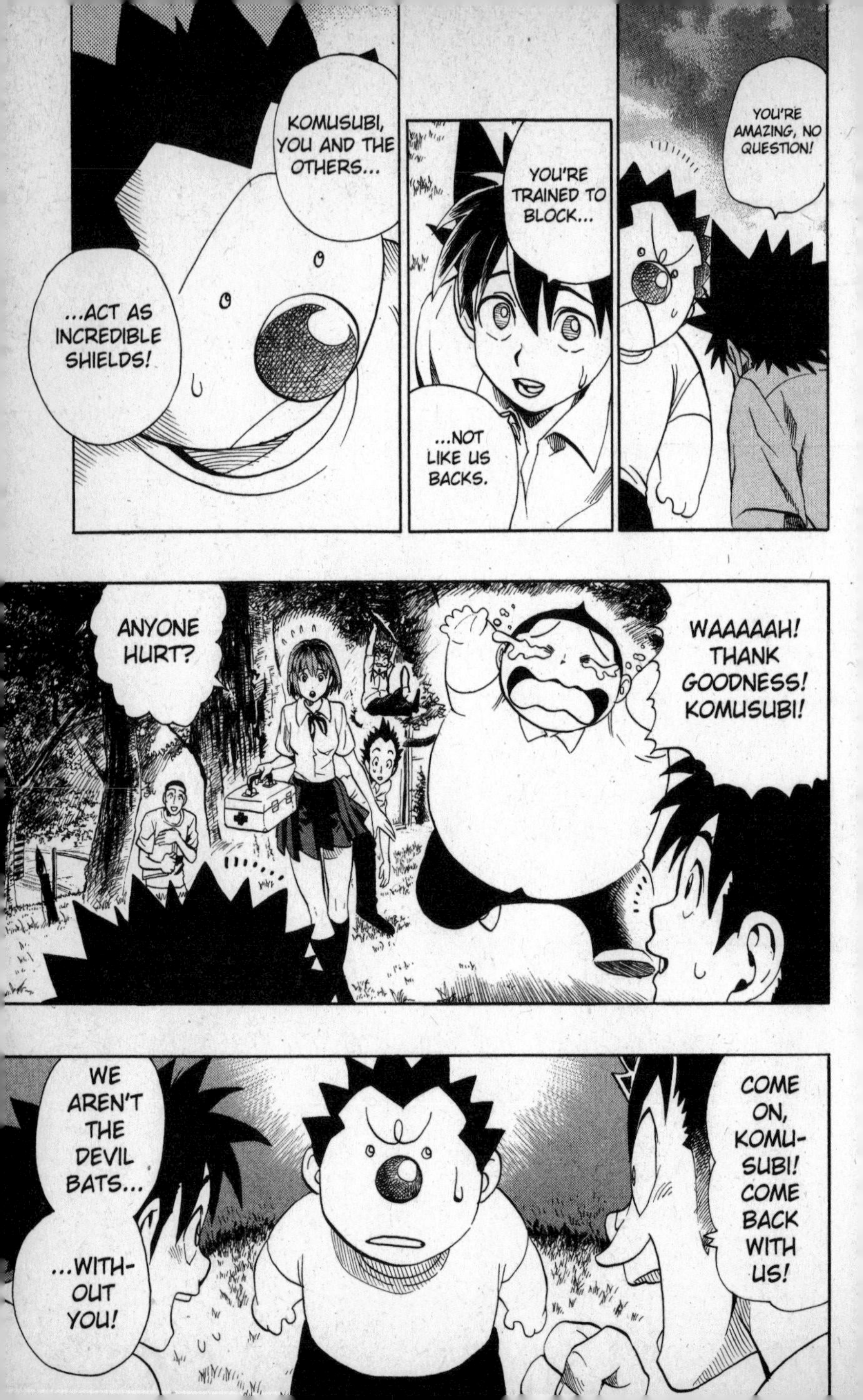
YOU'RE AMAZING, NO QUESTION!
YOU'RE TRAINED TO BLOCK...
...NOT LIKE US BACKS.
KOMUSUBI, YOU AND THE OTHERS...
...ACT AS INCREDIBLE SHIELDS!
WAAAAAH! THANK GOODNESS! KOMUSUBI!
ANYONE HURT?
COME ON, KOMU-SUBI! COME BACK WITH US!
WE AREN'T THE DEVIL BATS...
...WITH-OUT YOU!

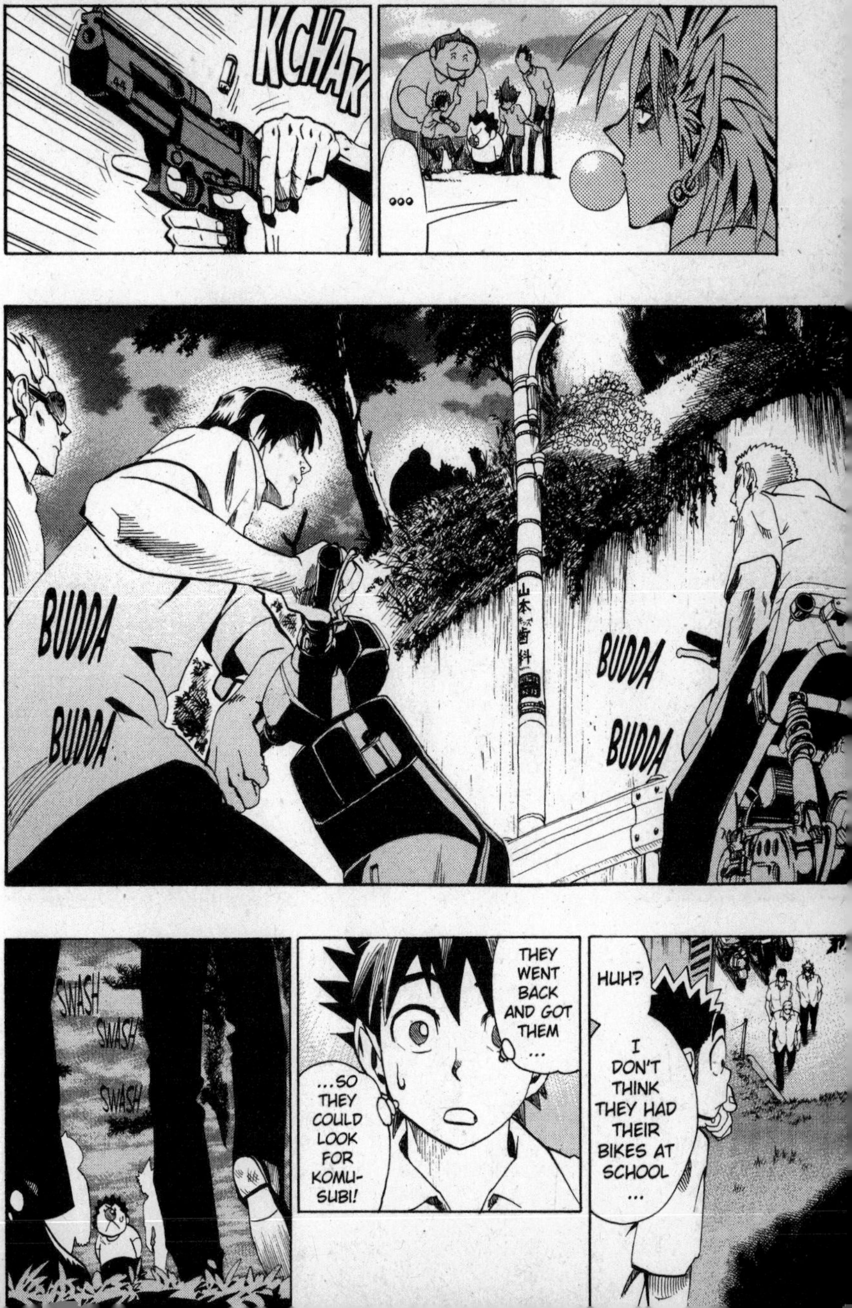
...
KCHAK
BUDDA BUDDA
BUDDA BUDDA
HUH?
I DON'T THINK THEY HAD THEIR BIKES AT SCHOOL ...
THEY WENT BACK AND GOT THEM ...
...SO THEY COULD LOOK FOR KOMU-SUBI!
SWASH SWASH SWASH

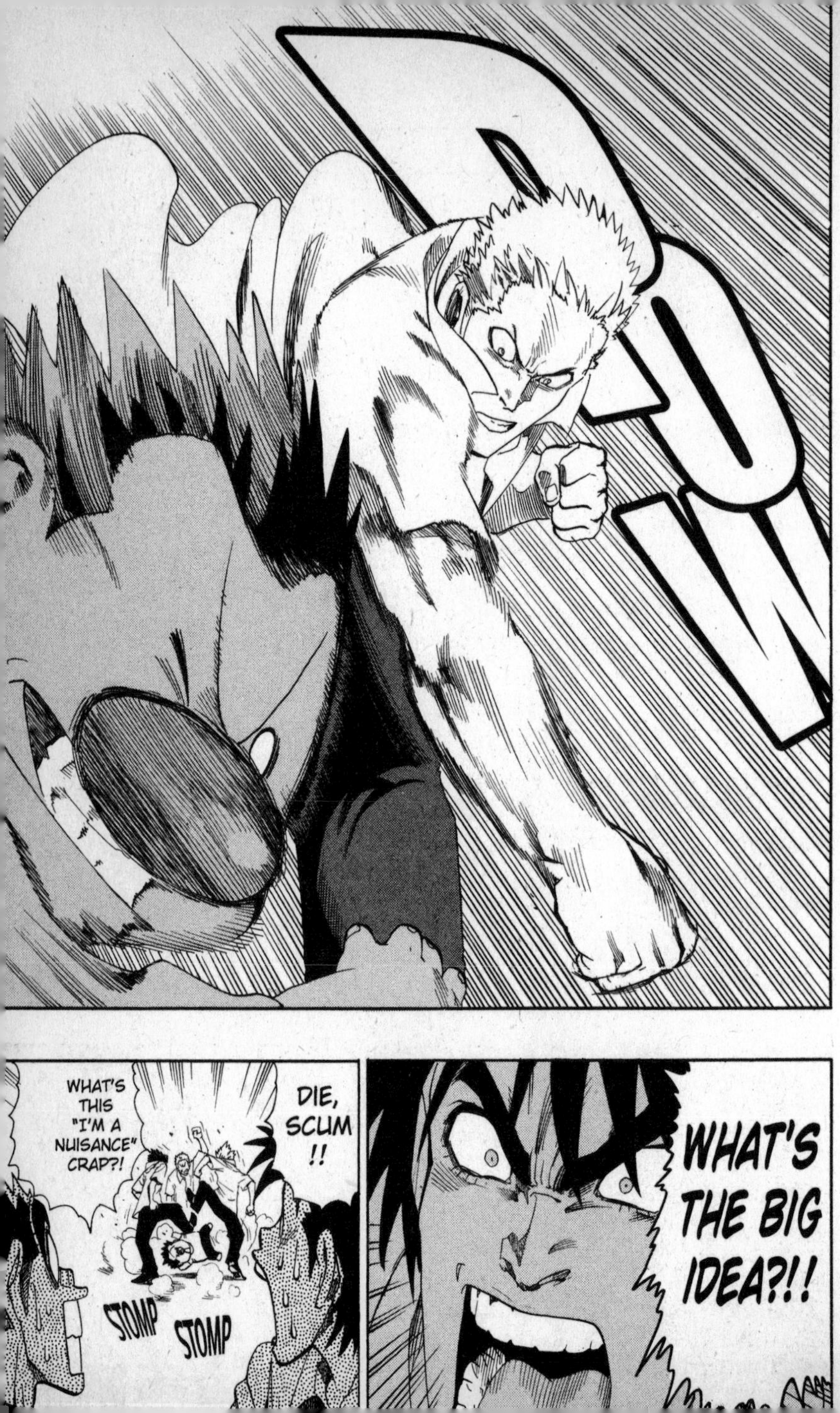
WHAT'S THE BIG IDEA?!!
DIE, SCUM !!
WHAT'S THIS "I'M A NUISANCE" CRAP?!
STOMP
STOMP

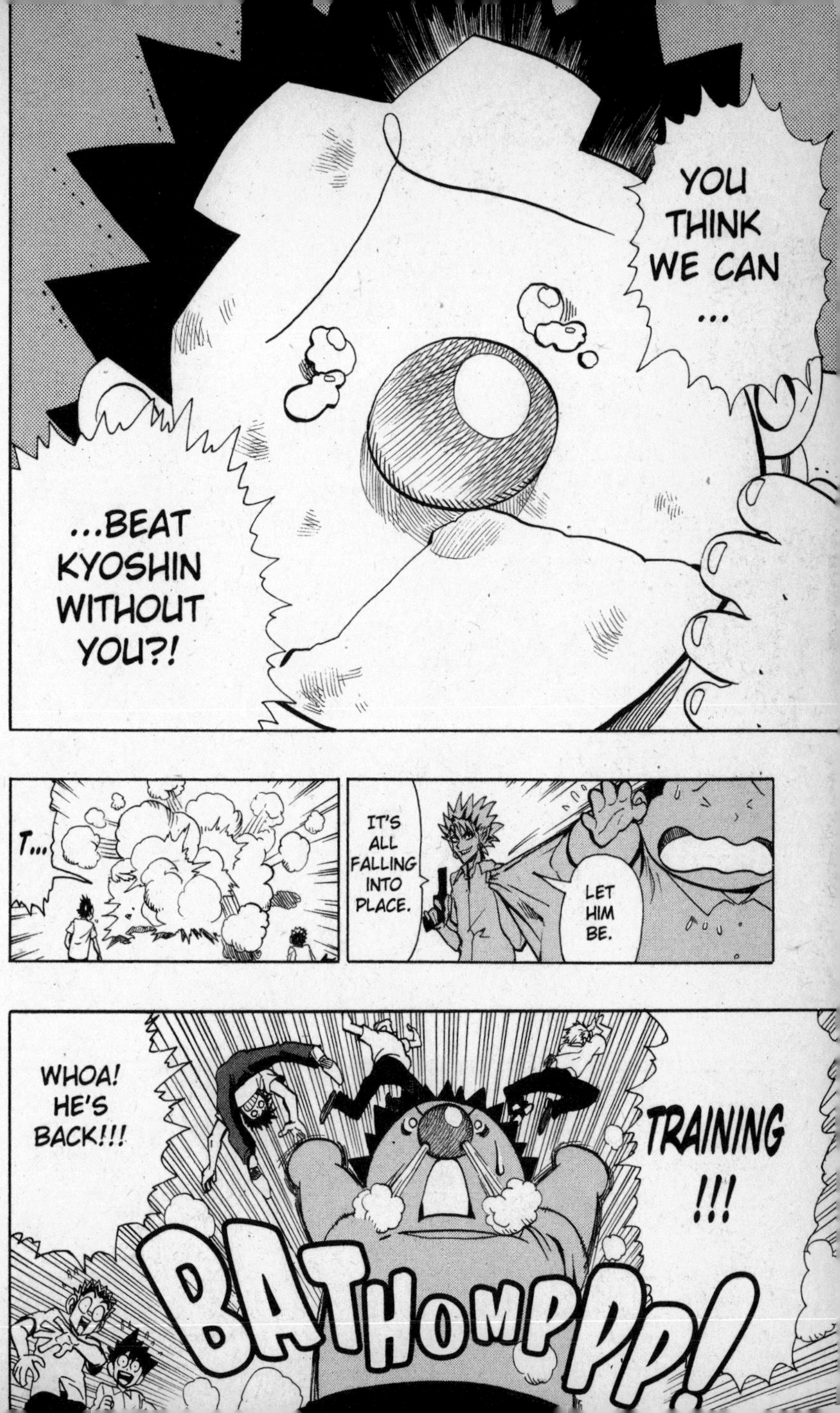
YOU THINK WE CAN ...
...BEAT KYOSHIN WITHOUT YOU?!
LET HIM BE.
IT'S ALL FALLING INTO PLACE.
T...
TRAINING !!!
WHOA! HE'S BACK!!!
BATHOMPPP!

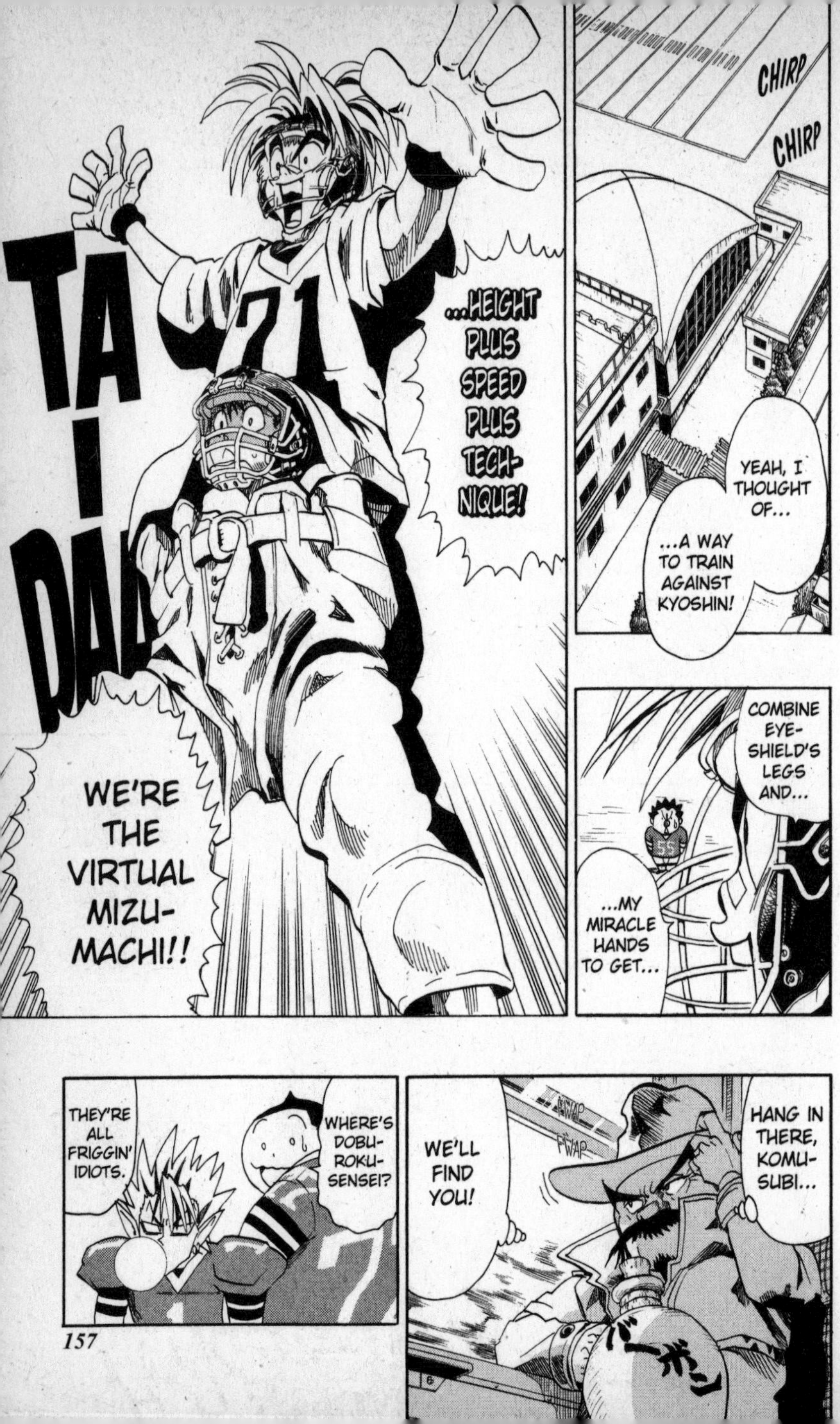
CHIRP
CHIRP
YEAH, I THOUGHT OF...
...A WAY TO TRAIN AGAINST KYOSHIN!
COMBINE EYE-SHIELD'S LEGS AND...
...MY MIRACLE HANDS TO GET...
...HEIGHT PLUS SPEED PLUS TECH-NIQUE!
TA I DAA
WE'RE THE VIRTUAL MIZU-MACHI!!
HANG IN THERE, KOMU-SUBI...
FWAP
FWAP
WE'LL FIND YOU!
WHERE'S DOBU-ROKU-SENSEI?
THEY'RE ALL FRIGGIN' IDIOTS.

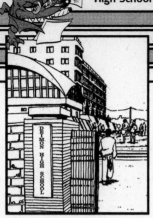

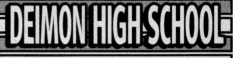

High School Selection Guidance for Prospective Applicants!

DEIMON HIGH SCHOOL

DEIMON HIGH SCHOOL

Student Body: 719

Special Campus Facilities: Several Armories

Major Career Options after Graduation

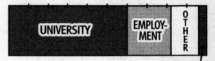

UNIVERSITY
EMPLOY-MENT
OTHER
Pawn for a certain Mr. H

The school values autonomy among its students and fosters a spirit of independence. At least that's how it turned out since no one could do anything about a certain Mr. H.

Despite this hands-off approach, there is hardly any trouble at the school. The students are actively involved in club activities and enjoy school life. Of course, it's impossible to act up under Mr. H's rule...but the result is that things seem to be going quite well.

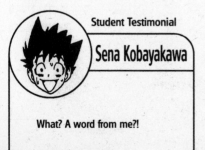

Student Testimonial

Sena Kobayakawa

What? A word from me?!

Um...well…hello…

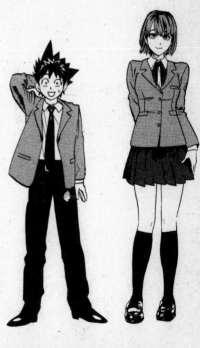

UNIFORM

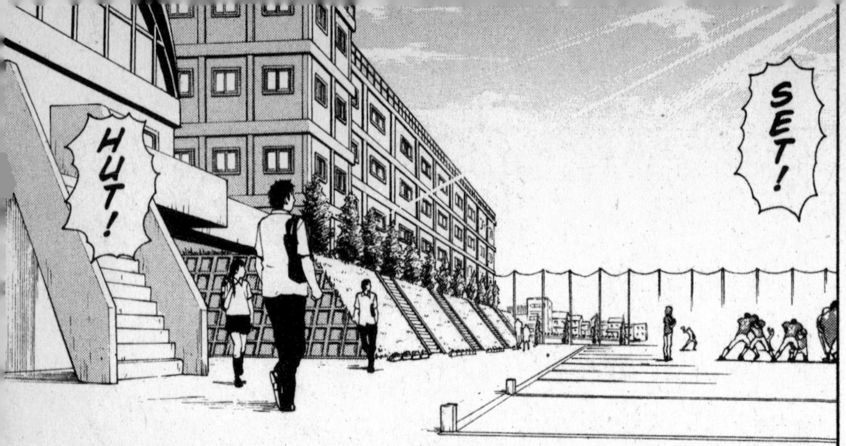
SET!
HUT!

Chapter 114 Komusubi's Last-Ditch Move

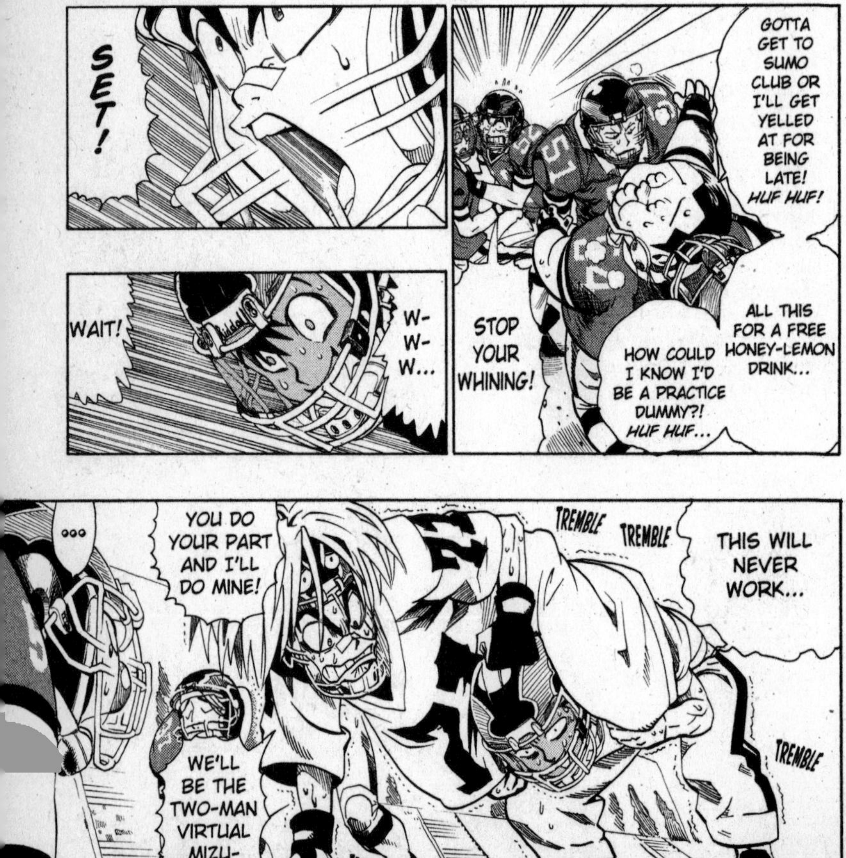
GOTTA GET TO SUMO CLUB OR I'LL GET YELLED AT FOR BEING LATE! HUF HUF!
ALL THIS FOR A FREE HONEY-LEMON DRINK...
HOW COULD I KNOW I'D BE A PRACTICE DUMMY?! HUF HUF...
STOP YOUR WHINING!
SET!
W-W-W...
WAIT!
THIS WILL NEVER WORK...
TREMBLE
TREMBLE
YOU DO YOUR PART AND I'LL DO MINE!
...
TREMBLE
WE'LL BE THE TWO-MAN VIRTUAL MIZU-MACHI!!
TREMBLE

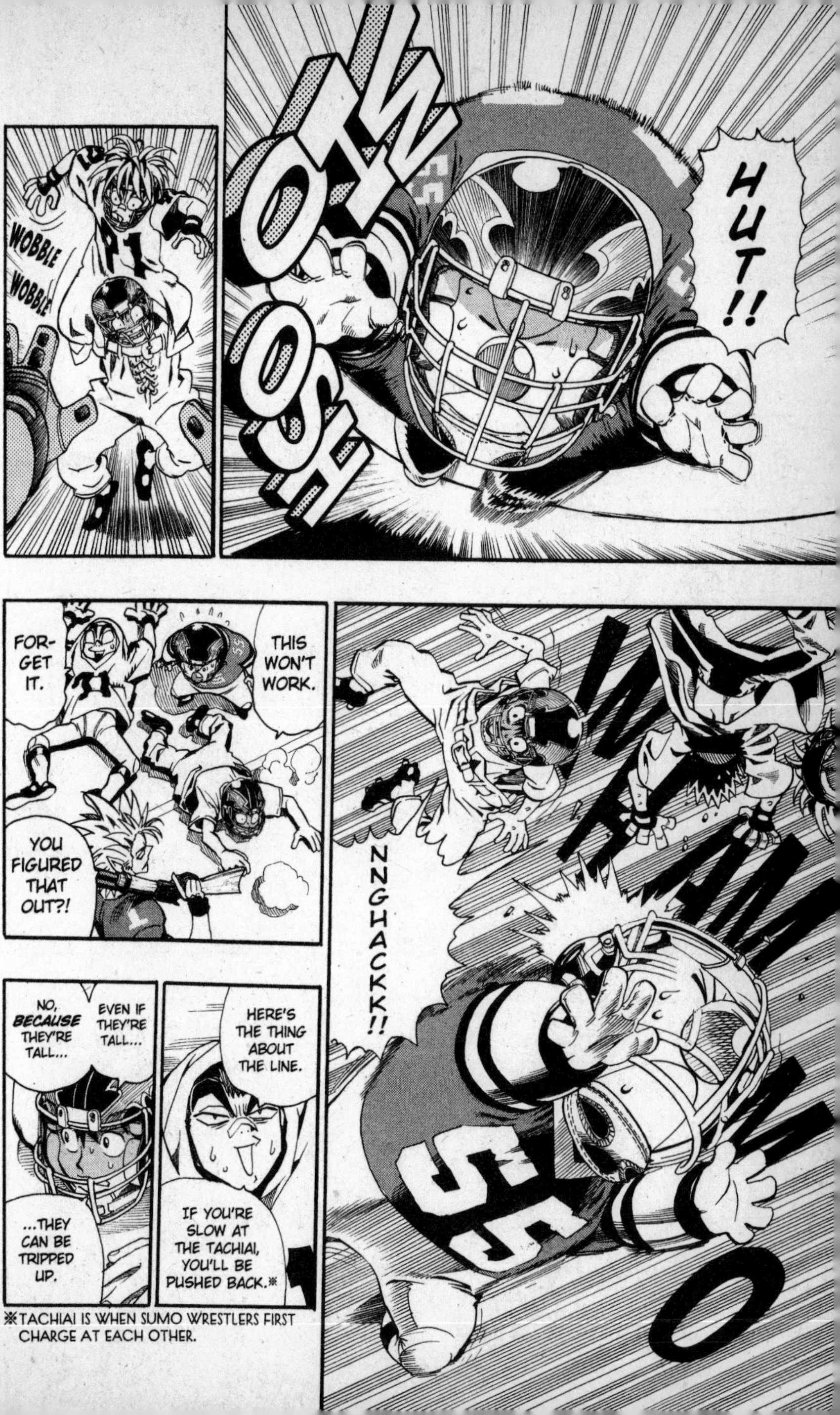
HUT!!
WHOOSH
WOBBLE
WOBBLE
WHAMMO
NNGHACKK!!
THIS WON'T WORK.
FOR-GET IT.
YOU FIGURED THAT OUT?!
HERE'S THE THING ABOUT THE LINE.
IF YOU'RE SLOW AT THE TACHIAI, YOU'LL BE PUSHED BACK.※
EVEN IF THEY'RE TALL...
NO, *BECAUSE* THEY'RE TALL...
...THEY CAN BE TRIPPED UP.

※TACHIAI IS WHEN SUMO WRESTLERS FIRST CHARGE AT EACH OTHER.

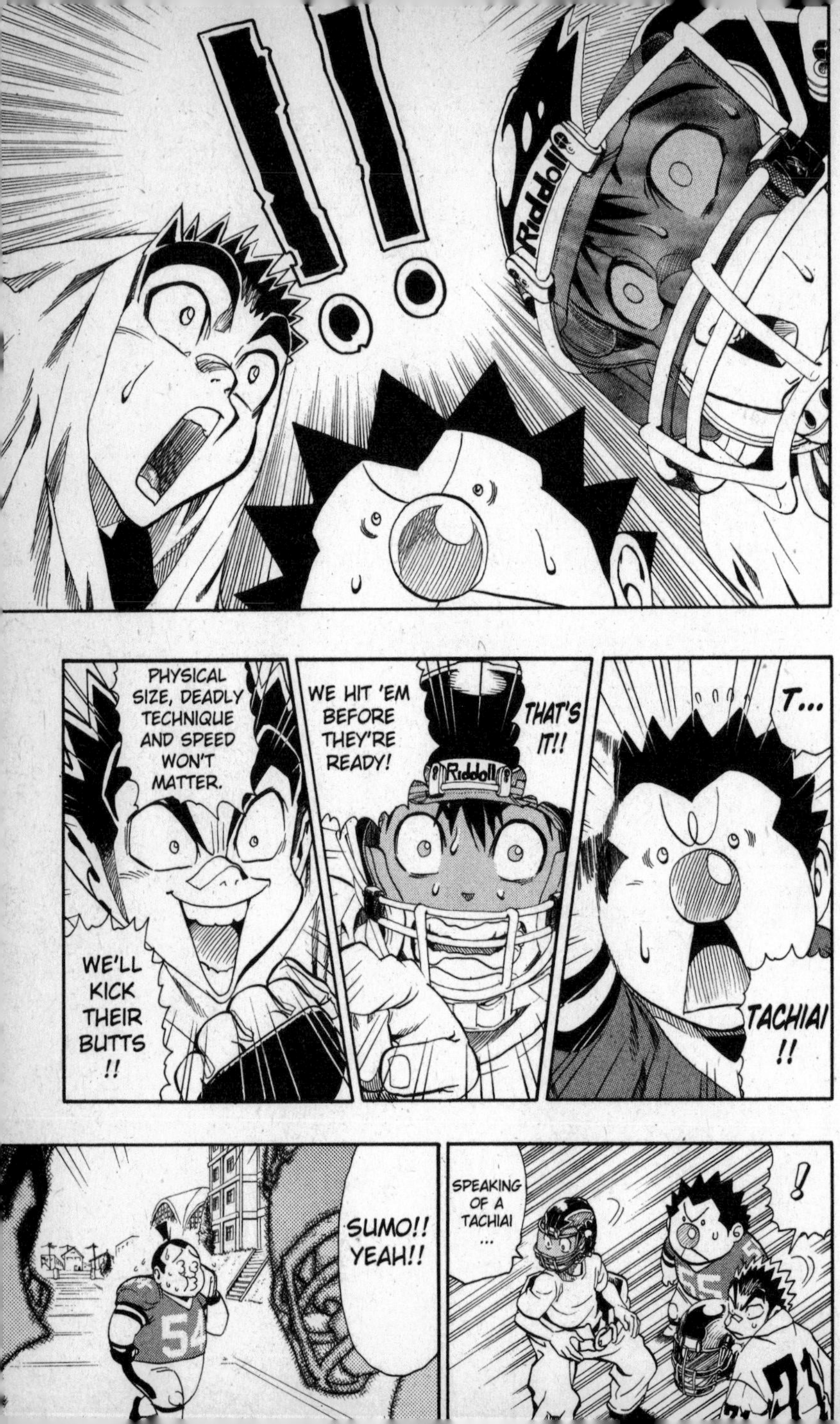
T...
TACHIAI !!
THAT'S IT!!
WE HIT 'EM BEFORE THEY'RE READY!
PHYSICAL SIZE, DEADLY TECHNIQUE AND SPEED WON'T MATTER.
WE'LL KICK THEIR BUTTS !!
!
SPEAKING OF A TACHIAI ...
SUMO!! YEAH!!

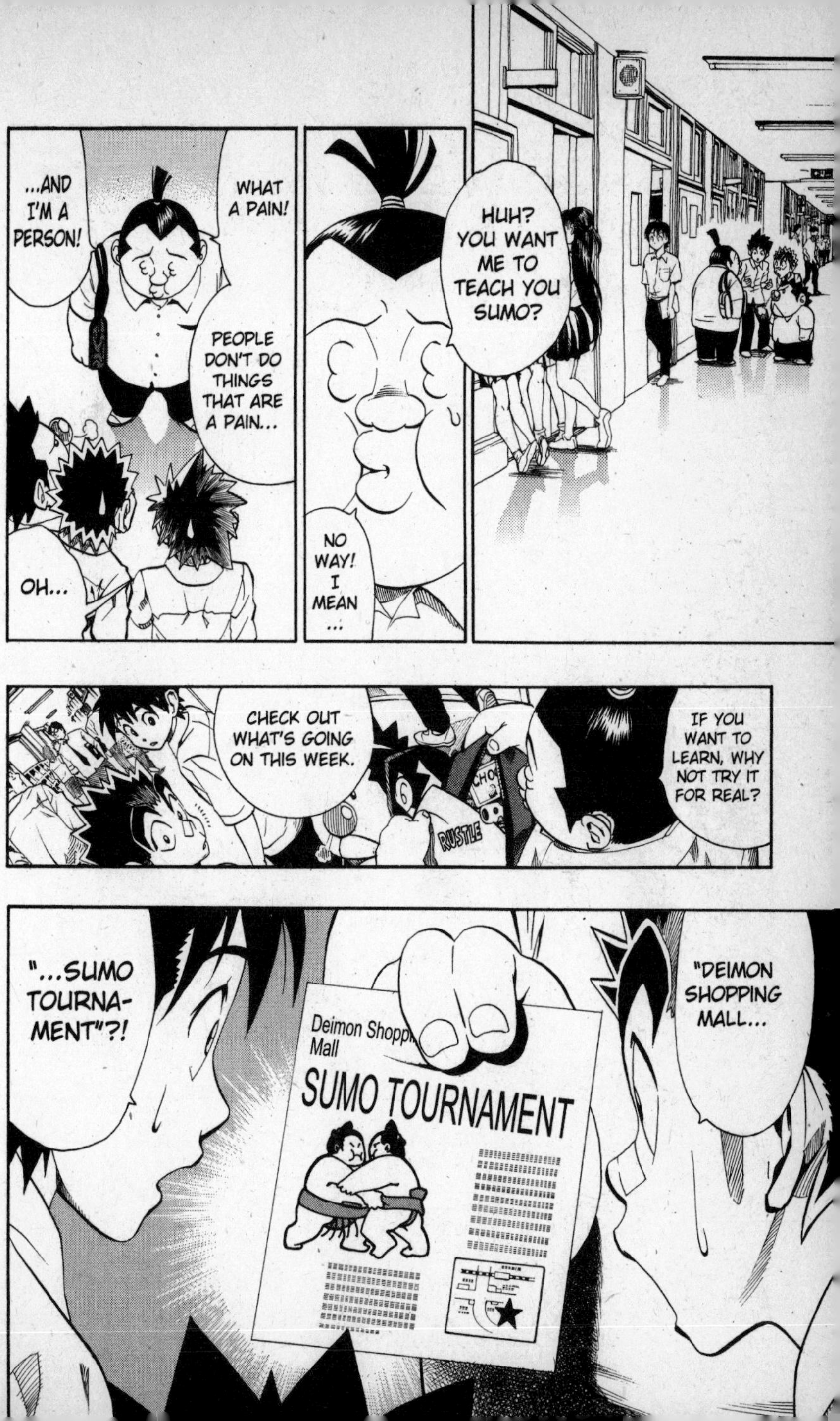
HUH? YOU WANT ME TO TEACH YOU SUMO?
NO WAY! I MEAN ...
WHAT A PAIN!
PEOPLE DON'T DO THINGS THAT ARE A PAIN...
...AND I'M A PERSON!
OH...
IF YOU WANT TO LEARN, WHY NOT TRY IT FOR REAL?
RUSTLE
CHECK OUT WHAT'S GOING ON THIS WEEK.
"DEIMON SHOPPING MALL...
Deimon Shoppi
Mall
SUMO TOURNAMENT
"...SUMO TOURNA-MENT"?!

Chapter 114

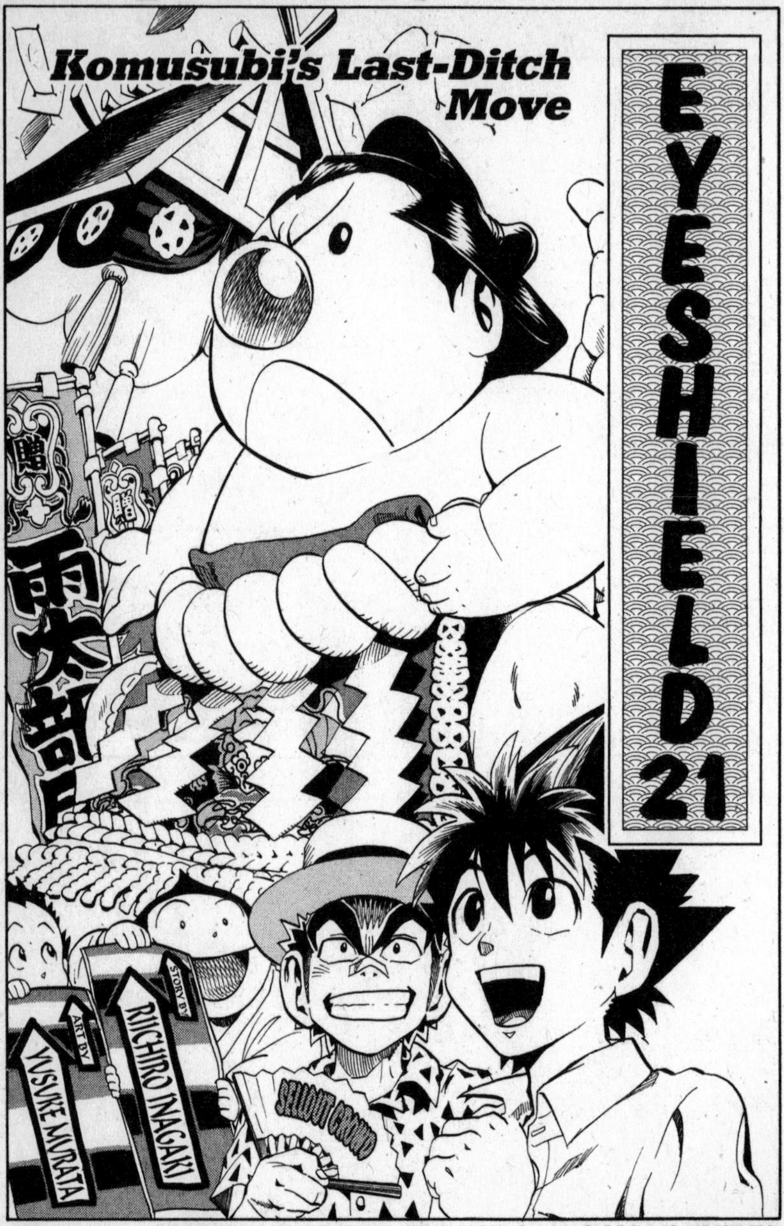
Komusubi's Last-Ditch Move
EYESHIELD 21
STORY BY
RIICHIRO INAGAKI
ART BY
YUSUKE MURATA
SHOUT CROWD

※BANNER: AMEFUTO STABLE ("STABLE" BEING A BAND OF SUMO WRESTLERS)

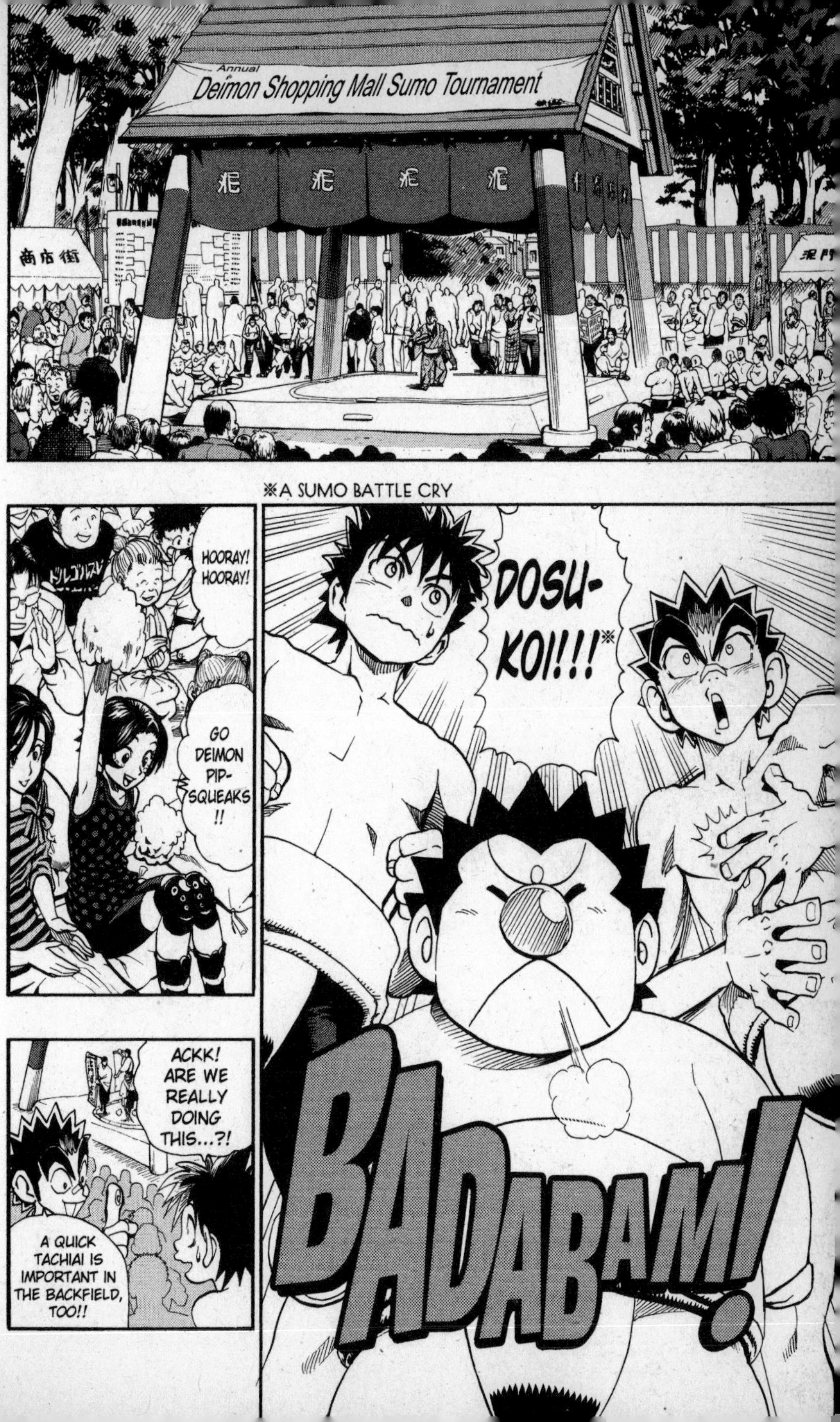
Annual
Deimon Shopping Mall Sumo Tournament
商店街
※A SUMO BATTLE CRY
DOSU-KOI!!!※
BADABAM!
HOORAY! HOORAY!
GO DEIMON PIP-SQUEAKS !!
ACKK! ARE WE REALLY DOING THIS...?!
A QUICK TACHIAI IS IMPORTANT IN THE BACKFIELD, TOO!!

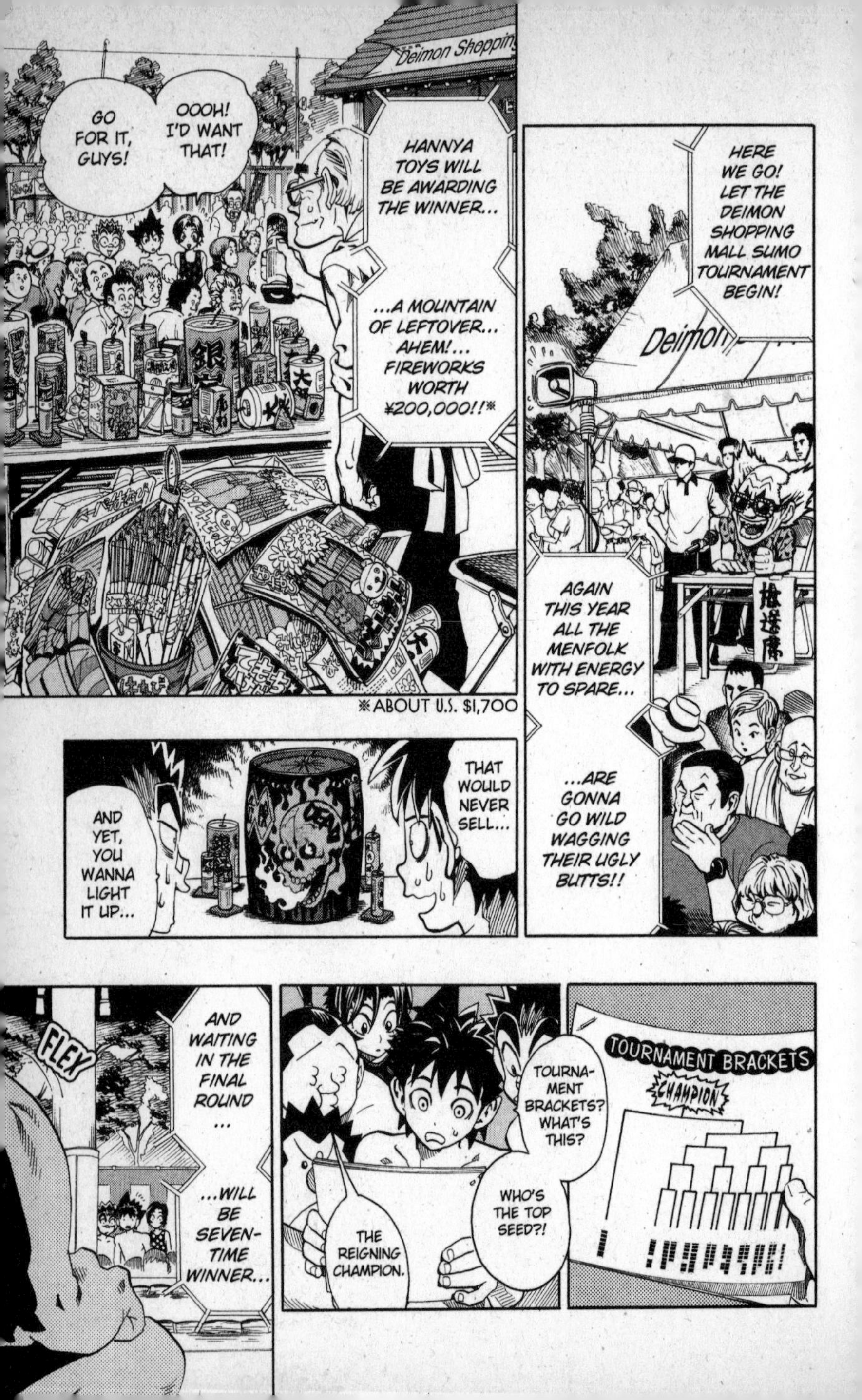
HERE WE GO! LET THE DEIMON SHOPPING MALL SUMO TOURNAMENT BEGIN!
AGAIN THIS YEAR ALL THE MENFOLK WITH ENERGY TO SPARE...
...ARE GONNA GO WILD WAGGING THEIR UGLY BUTTS!!
HANNYA TOYS WILL BE AWARDING THE WINNER...
...A MOUNTAIN OF LEFTOVER... AHEM!... FIREWORKS WORTH ¥200,000!!※
OOOH! I'D WANT THAT!
GO FOR IT, GUYS!
※ABOUT U.S. $1,700
THAT WOULD NEVER SELL...
AND YET, YOU WANNA LIGHT IT UP...
TOURNAMENT BRACKETS
CHAMPION
TOURNAMENT BRACKETS? WHAT'S THIS?
WHO'S THE TOP SEED?!
THE REIGNING CHAMPION.
AND WAITING IN THE FINAL ROUND...
...WILL BE SEVEN-TIME WINNER...
FLEX

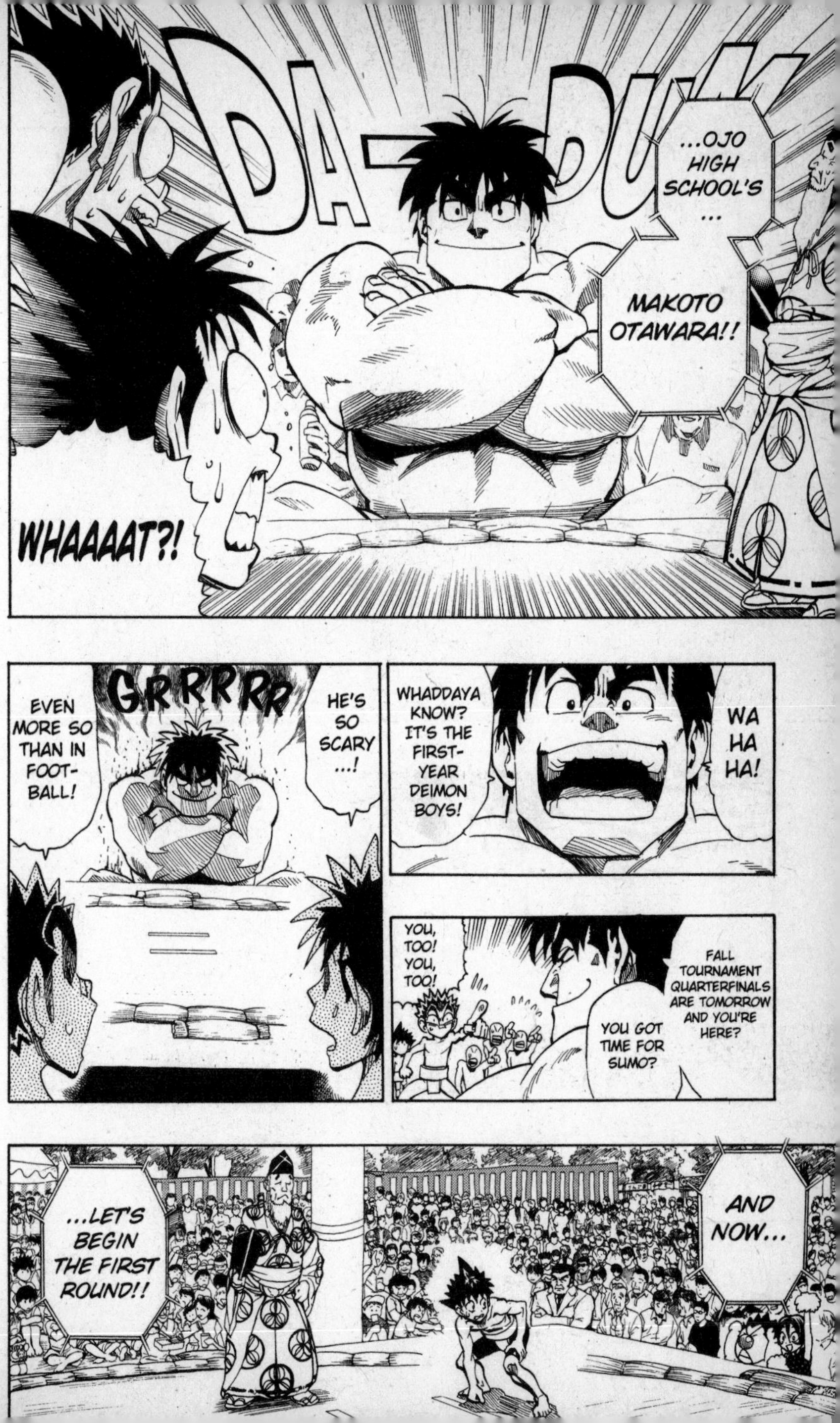
...OJO HIGH SCHOOL'S ...
MAKOTO OTAWARA!!
DA-DU
WHAAAAT?!
WA HA HA!
WHADDAYA KNOW? IT'S THE FIRST-YEAR DEIMON BOYS!
FALL TOURNAMENT QUARTERFINALS ARE TOMORROW AND YOU'RE HERE?
YOU GOT TIME FOR SUMO?
YOU, TOO! YOU, TOO!
GRRRRRR
HE'S SO SCARY ...!
EVEN MORE SO THAN IN FOOT-BALL!
AND NOW...
...LET'S BEGIN THE FIRST ROUND!!

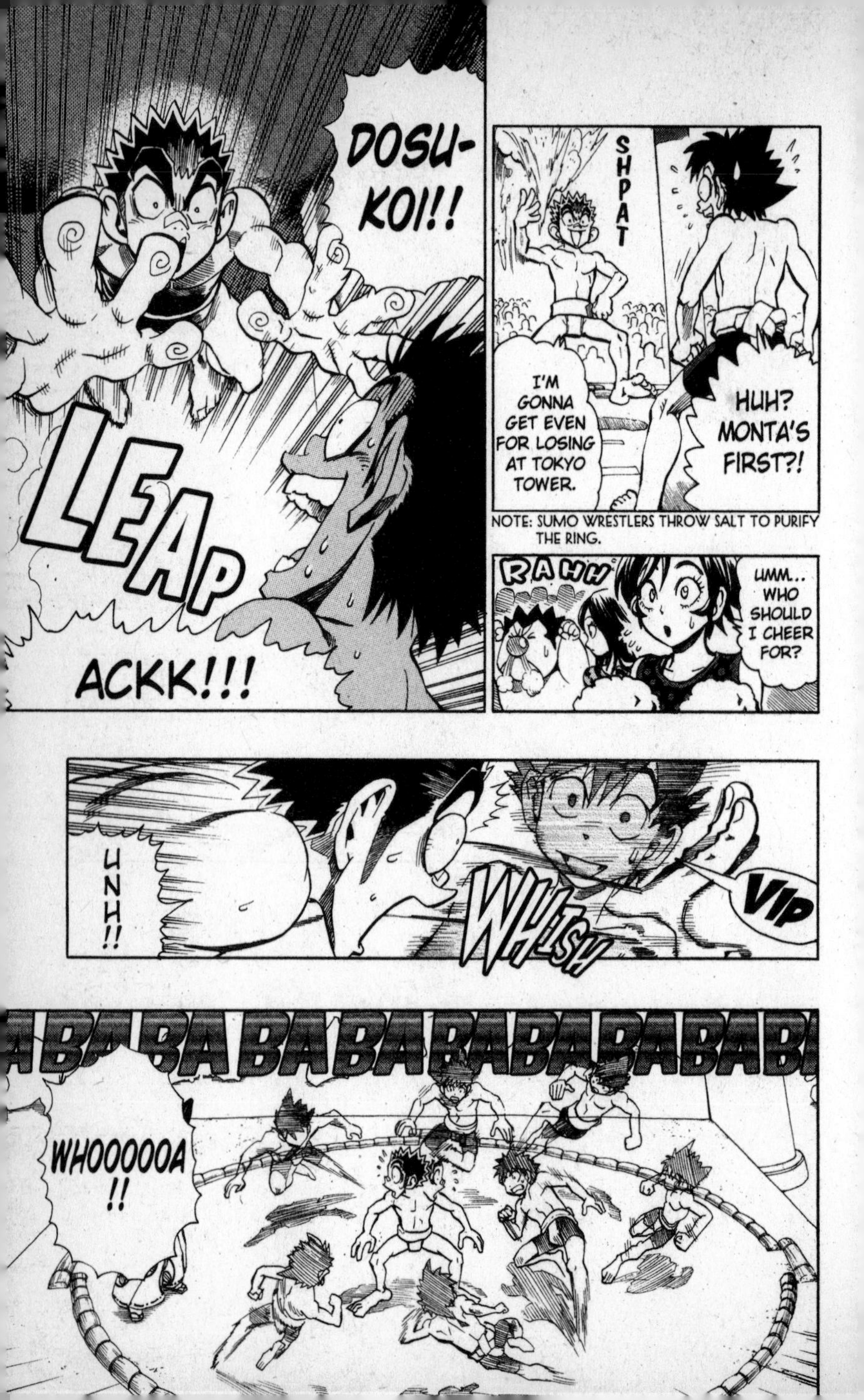
SHPAT
HUH? MONTA'S FIRST?!
I'M GONNA GET EVEN FOR LOSING AT TOKYO TOWER.
NOTE: SUMO WRESTLERS THROW SALT TO PURIFY THE RING.
UMM... WHO SHOULD I CHEER FOR?
RAHH
DOSU-KOI!!
LEAP
ACKK!!!
VIP
WHISH
UNH!!
BABABABABABABABAB
WHOOOOOA!!

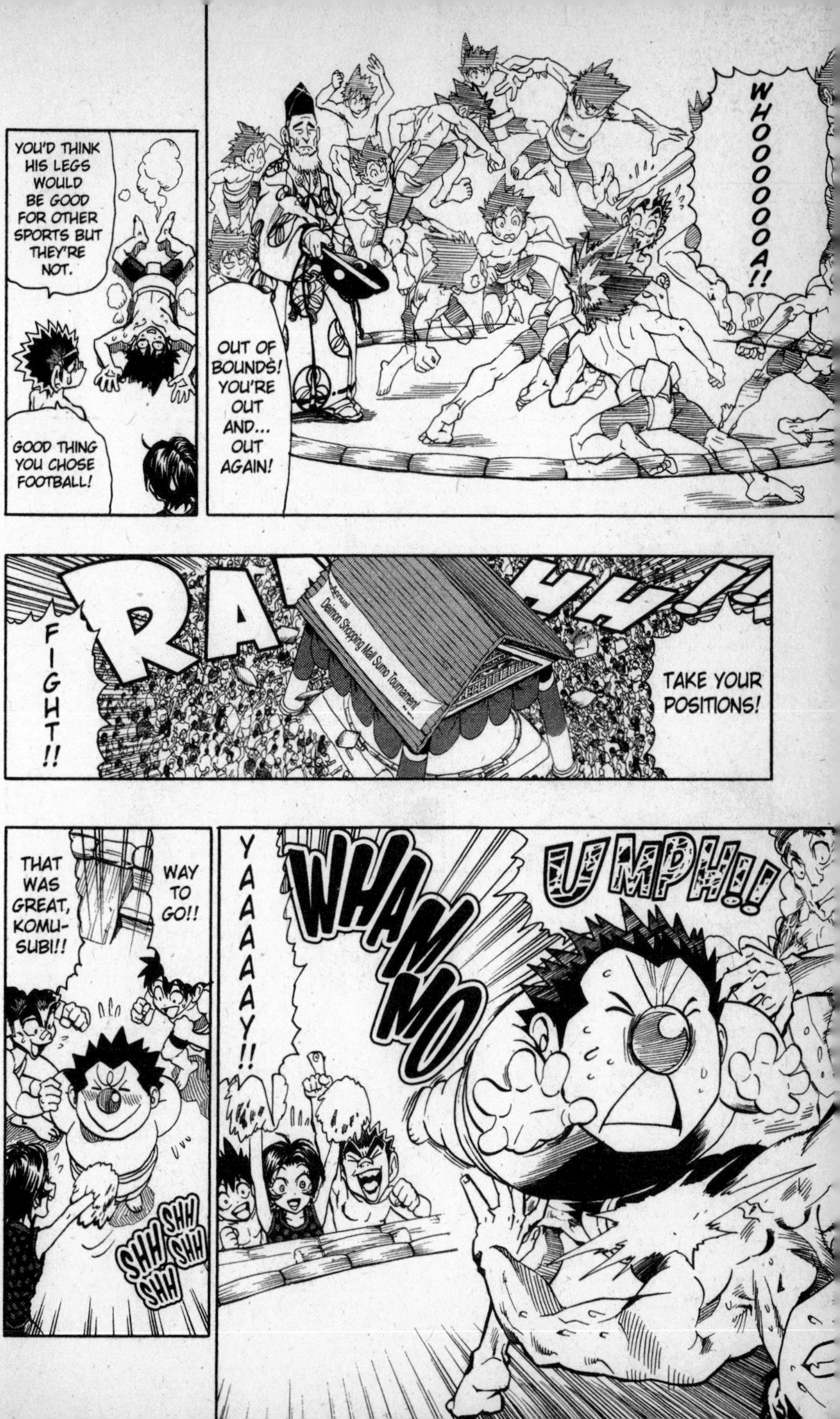
WHOOOOOOOA!!
OUT OF BOUNDS! YOU'RE OUT AND... OUT AGAIN!
YOU'D THINK HIS LEGS WOULD BE GOOD FOR OTHER SPORTS BUT THEY'RE NOT.
GOOD THING YOU CHOSE FOOTBALL!
TAKE YOUR POSITIONS!
Annual Daimon Shopping Mall Sumo Tournament
FIGHT!!
UMPH!!
WHAMMO
YAAAAAAY!!
WAY TO GO!!
THAT WAS GREAT, KOMUSUBI!!
SHH SHH SHH SHH

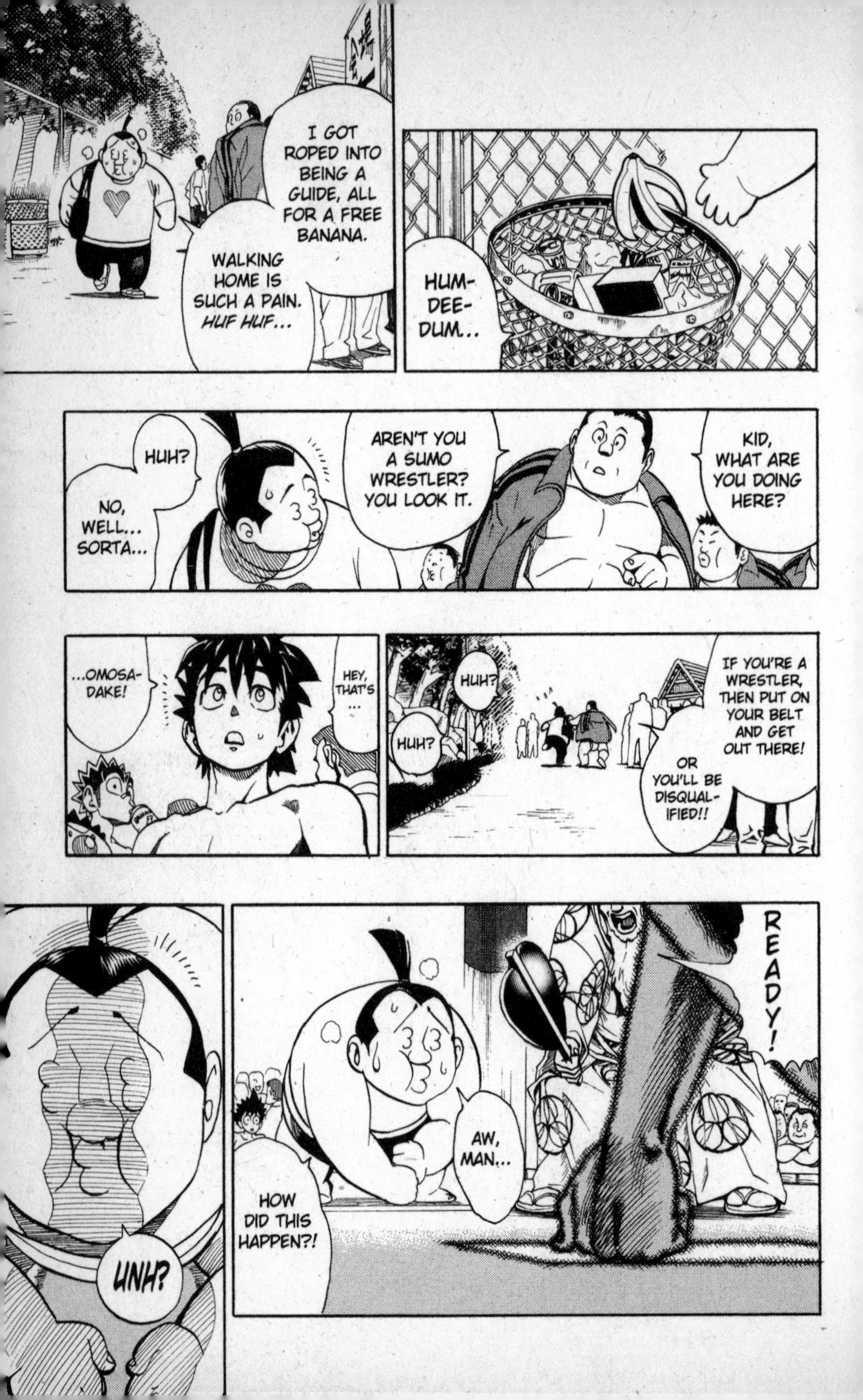
HUM-DEE-DUM...
I GOT ROPED INTO BEING A GUIDE, ALL FOR A FREE BANANA.
WALKING HOME IS SUCH A PAIN. HUF HUF...
KID, WHAT ARE YOU DOING HERE?
AREN'T YOU A SUMO WRESTLER? YOU LOOK IT.
HUH?
NO, WELL... SORTA...
IF YOU'RE A WRESTLER, THEN PUT ON YOUR BELT AND GET OUT THERE!
OR YOU'LL BE DISQUAL-IFIED!!
HUH?
HUH?
HEY, THAT'S ...
...OMOSA-DAKE!
READY!
AW, MAN...
HOW DID THIS HAPPEN?!
UNH?

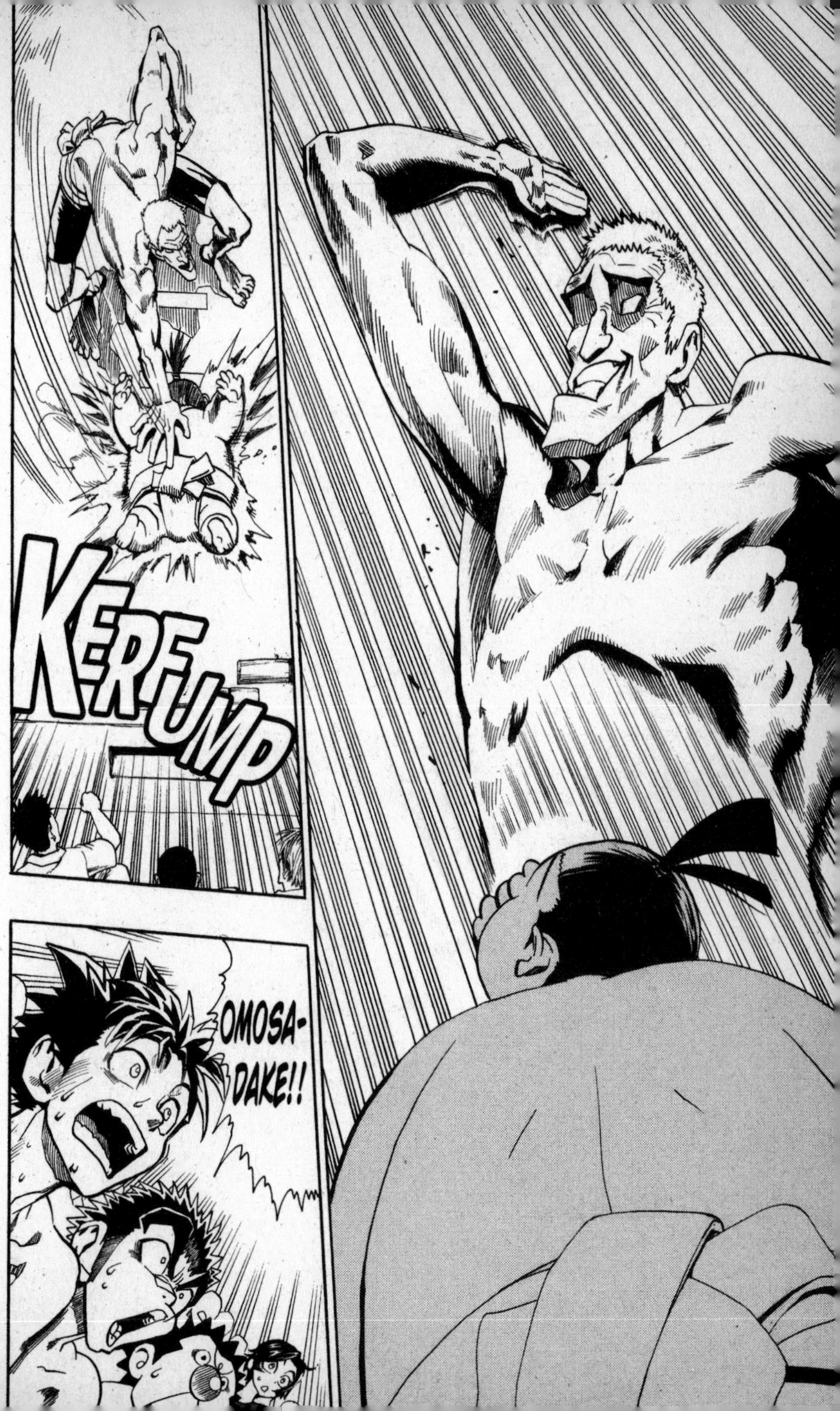
KERFUMP
OMOSA-DAKE!!

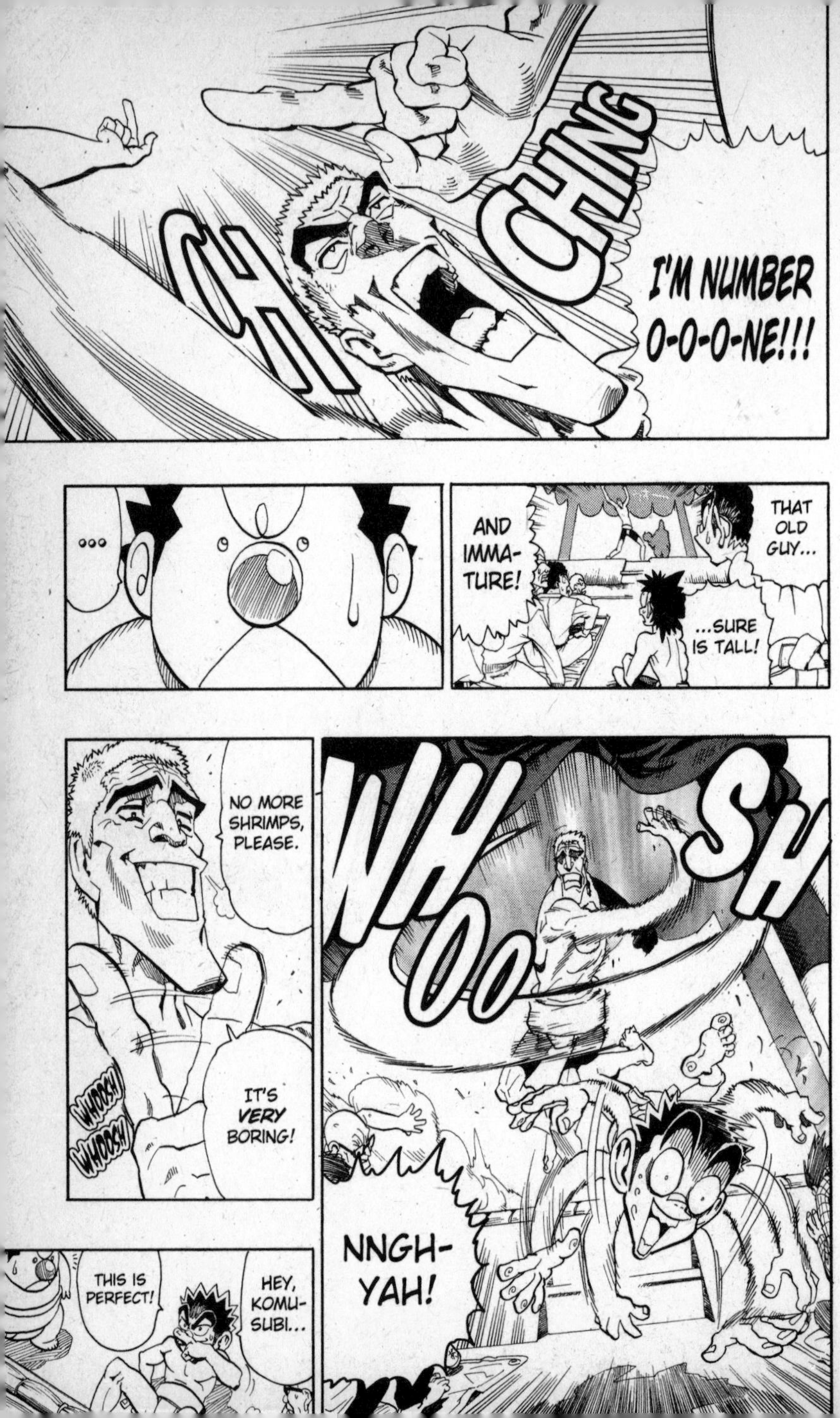
CHI
CHING
I'M NUMBER O-O-O-NE!!!
THAT OLD GUY...
...SURE IS TALL!
AND IMMA-TURE!
...
WHOOSH
NNGH-YAH!
NO MORE SHRIMPS, PLEASE.
IT'S *VERY* BORING!
WHOOSH WHOOSH
HEY, KOMU-SUBI...
THIS IS PERFECT!

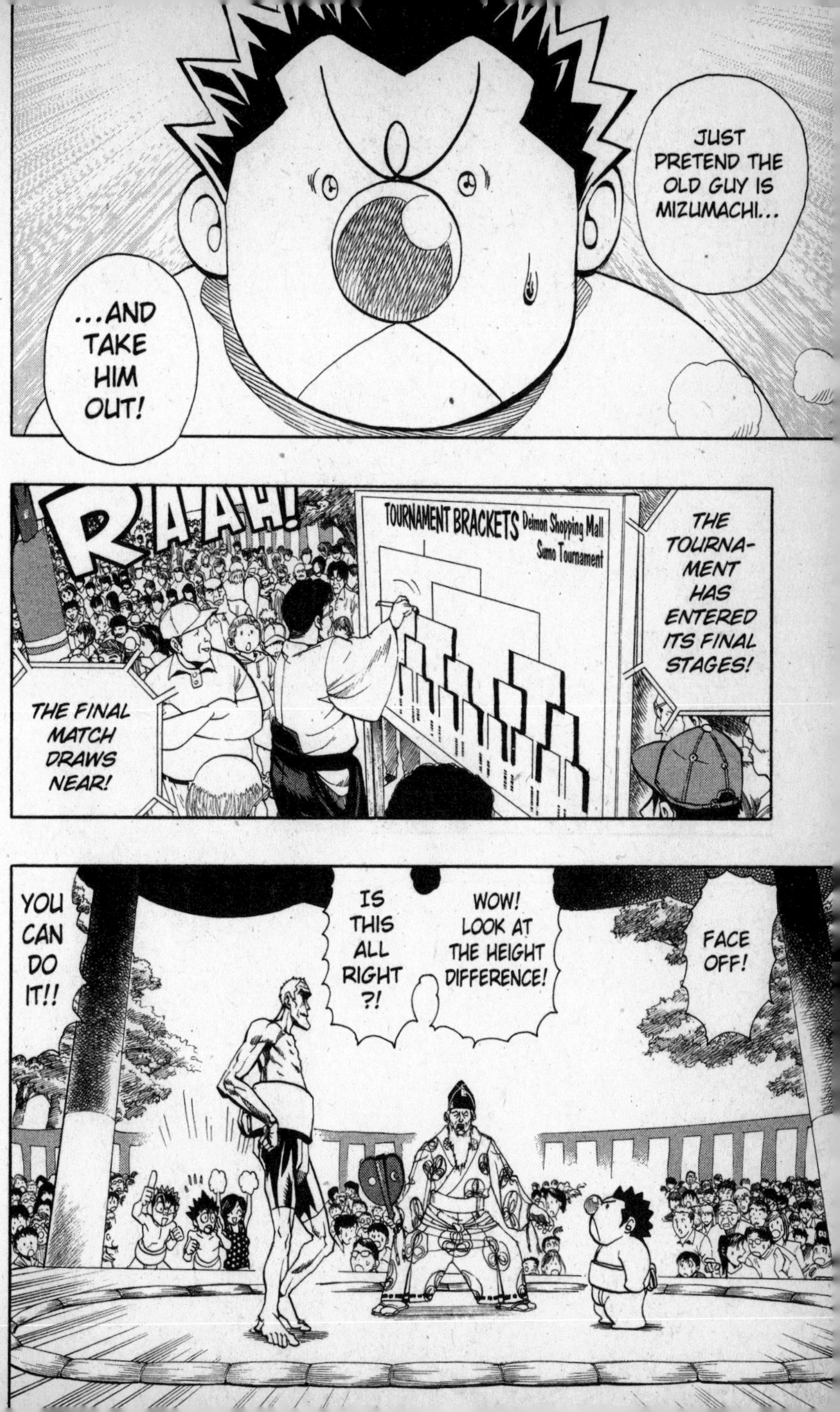
JUST PRETEND THE OLD GUY IS MIZUMACHI...
...AND TAKE HIM OUT!
THE TOURNAMENT HAS ENTERED ITS FINAL STAGES!
TOURNAMENT BRACKETS Deimon Shopping Mall Sumo Tournament
RAAH!
THE FINAL MATCH DRAWS NEAR!
FACE OFF!
WOW! LOOK AT THE HEIGHT DIFFERENCE!
IS THIS ALL RIGHT?!
YOU CAN DO IT!!

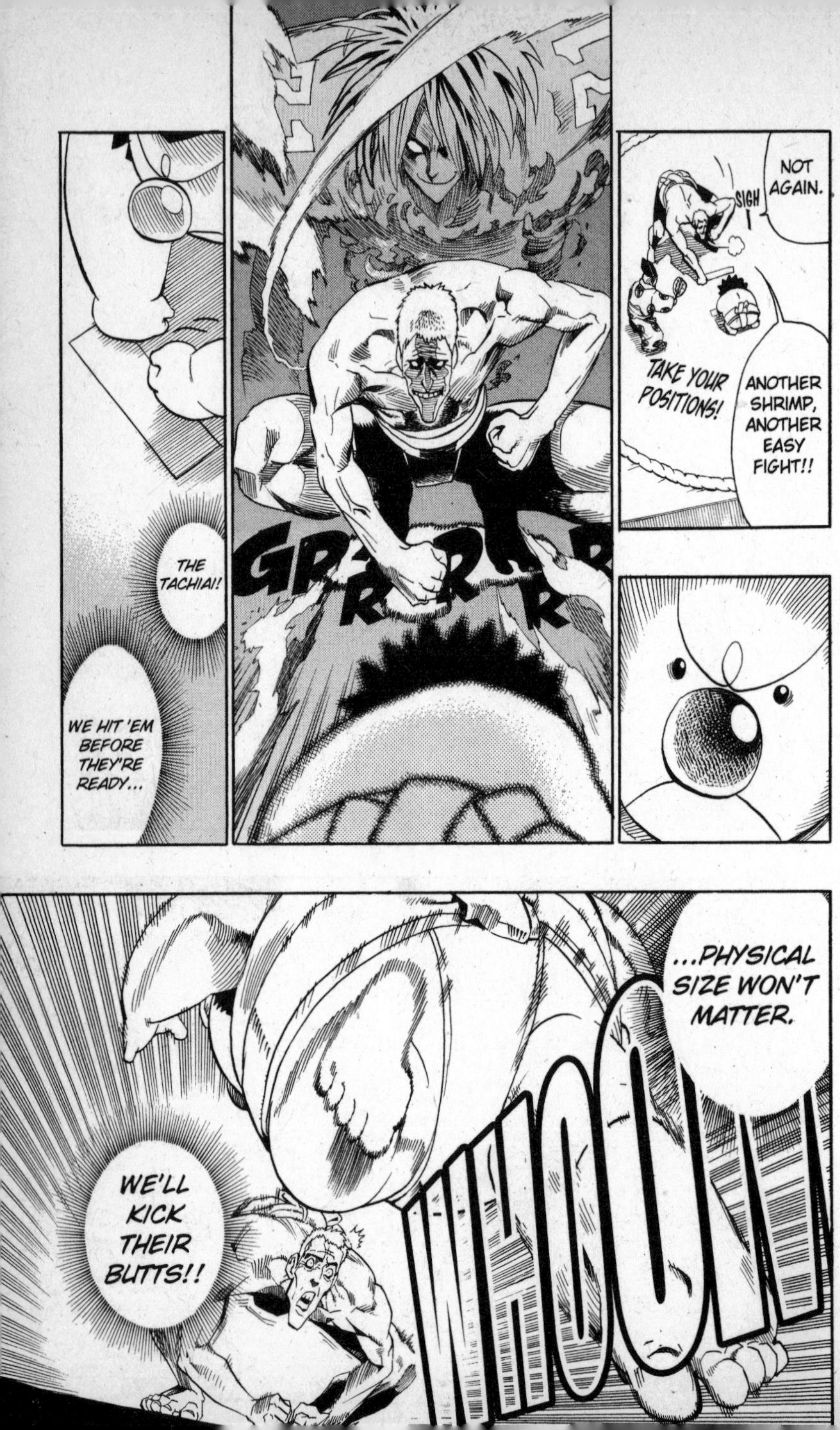
NOT AGAIN.
SIGH
ANOTHER SHRIMP, ANOTHER EASY FIGHT!!
TAKE YOUR POSITIONS!
GRRRRRR
THE TACHIAI!
WE HIT 'EM BEFORE THEY'RE READY...
...PHYSICAL SIZE WON'T MATTER.
WHOOM
WE'LL KICK THEIR BUTTS!!

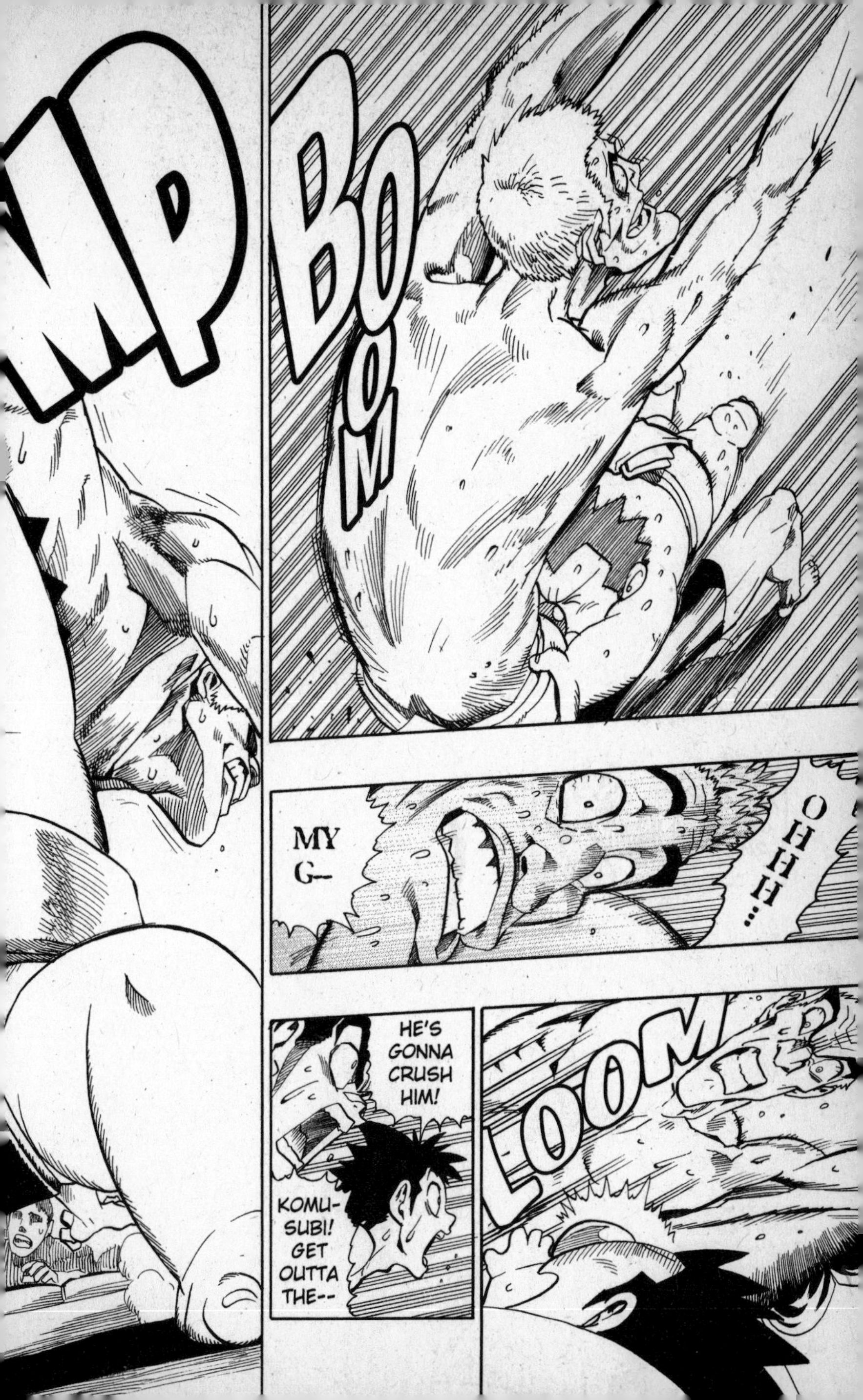
BOOM
OHHH...
MY G--
LOOM
HE'S GONNA CRUSH HIM!
KOMU-SUBI! GET OUTTA THE--
MP

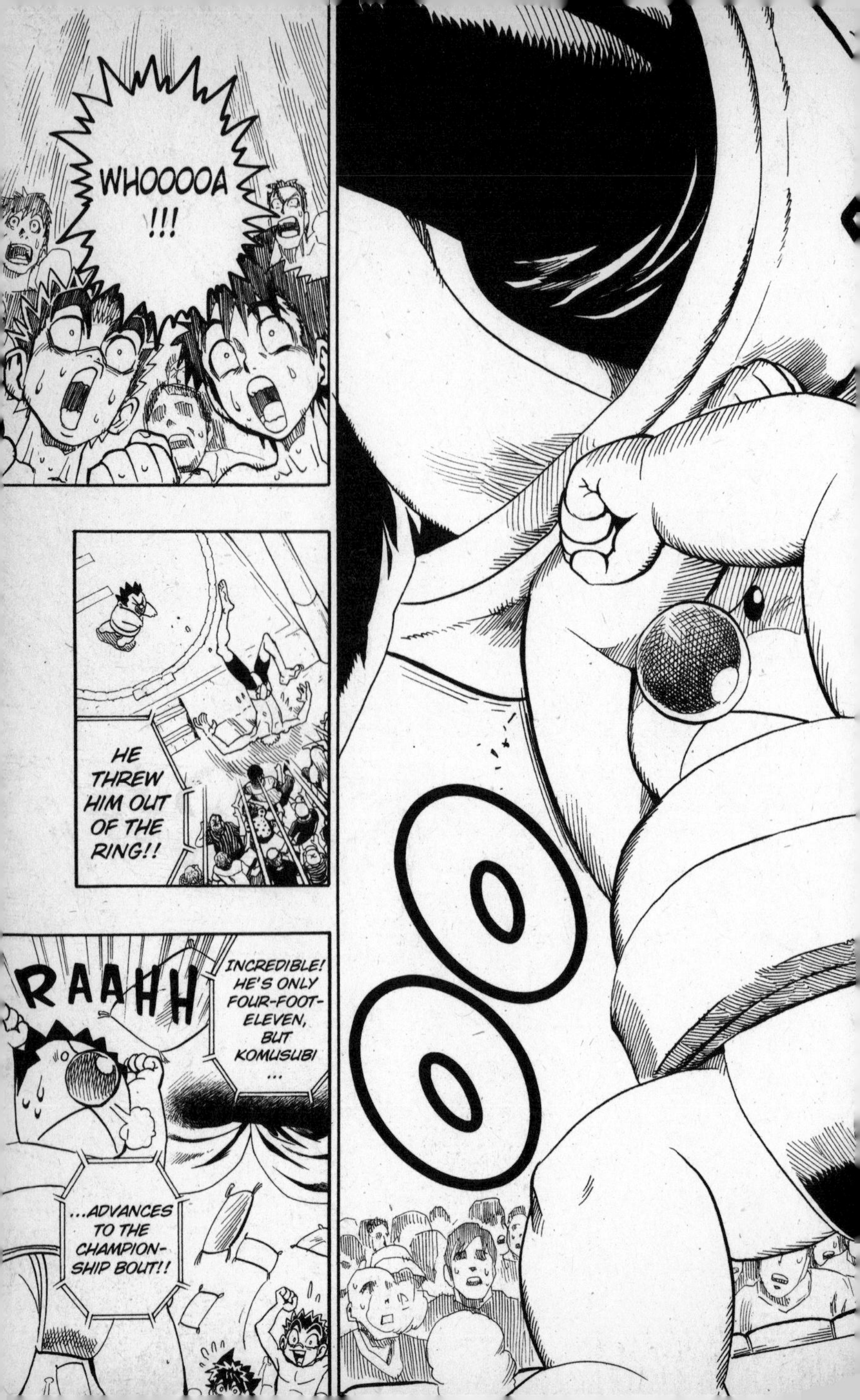
OO
WHOOOOA!!!
HE THREW HIM OUT OF THE RING!!
INCREDIBLE! HE'S ONLY FOUR-FOOT-ELEVEN, BUT KOMUSUBI ...
RAAHH
...ADVANCES TO THE CHAMPIONSHIP BOUT!!

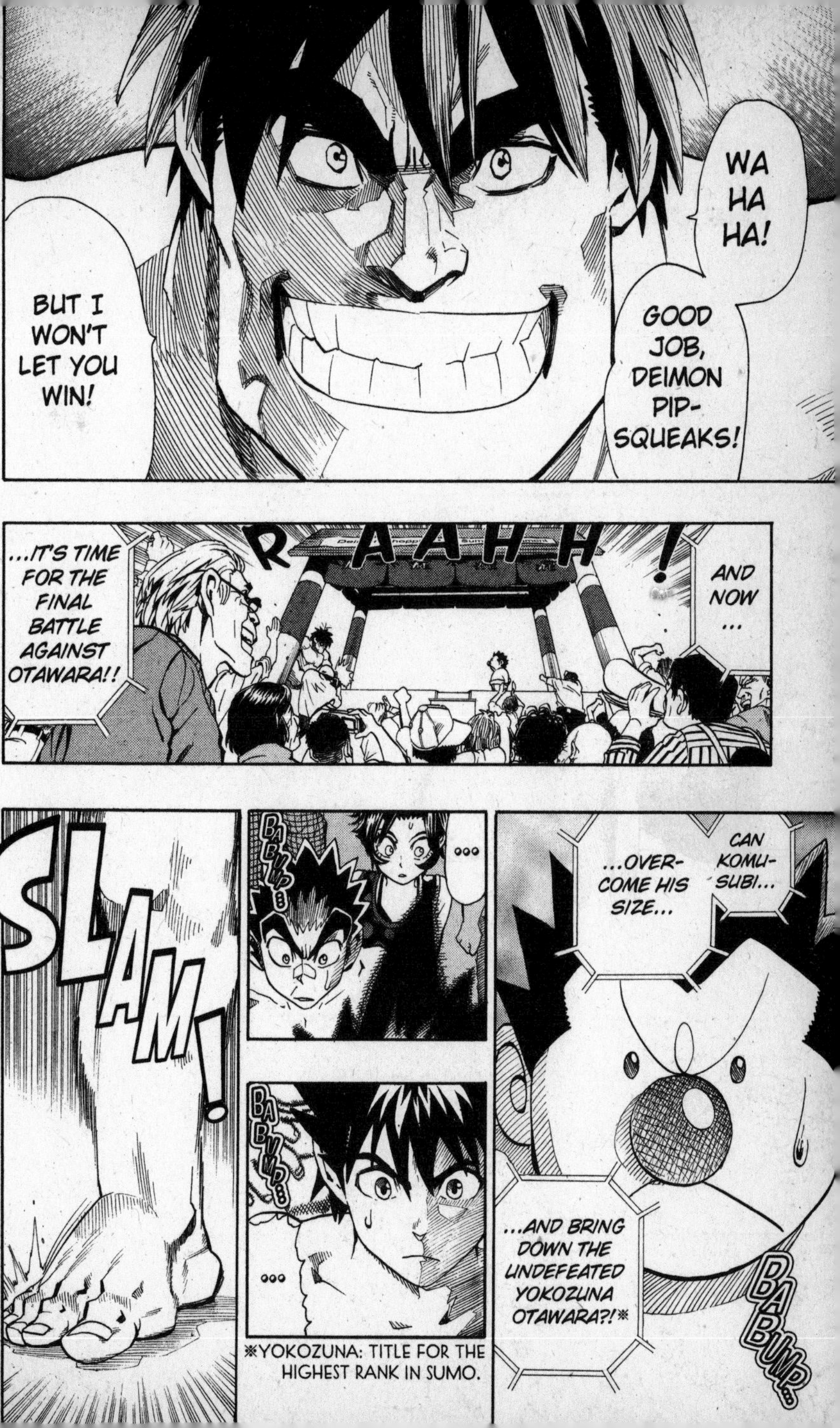
WA HA HA!
GOOD JOB, DEIMON PIP-SQUEAKS!
BUT I WON'T LET YOU WIN!
AND NOW...
RAAHH!
...IT'S TIME FOR THE FINAL BATTLE AGAINST OTAWARA!!
CAN KOMU-SUBI...
...OVER-COME HIS SIZE...
...AND BRING DOWN THE UNDEFEATED YOKOZUNA OTAWARA?!※
BA BUMP
...
BA BUMP
BA BUMP
...
SLAM!
※YOKOZUNA: TITLE FOR THE HIGHEST RANK IN SUMO.

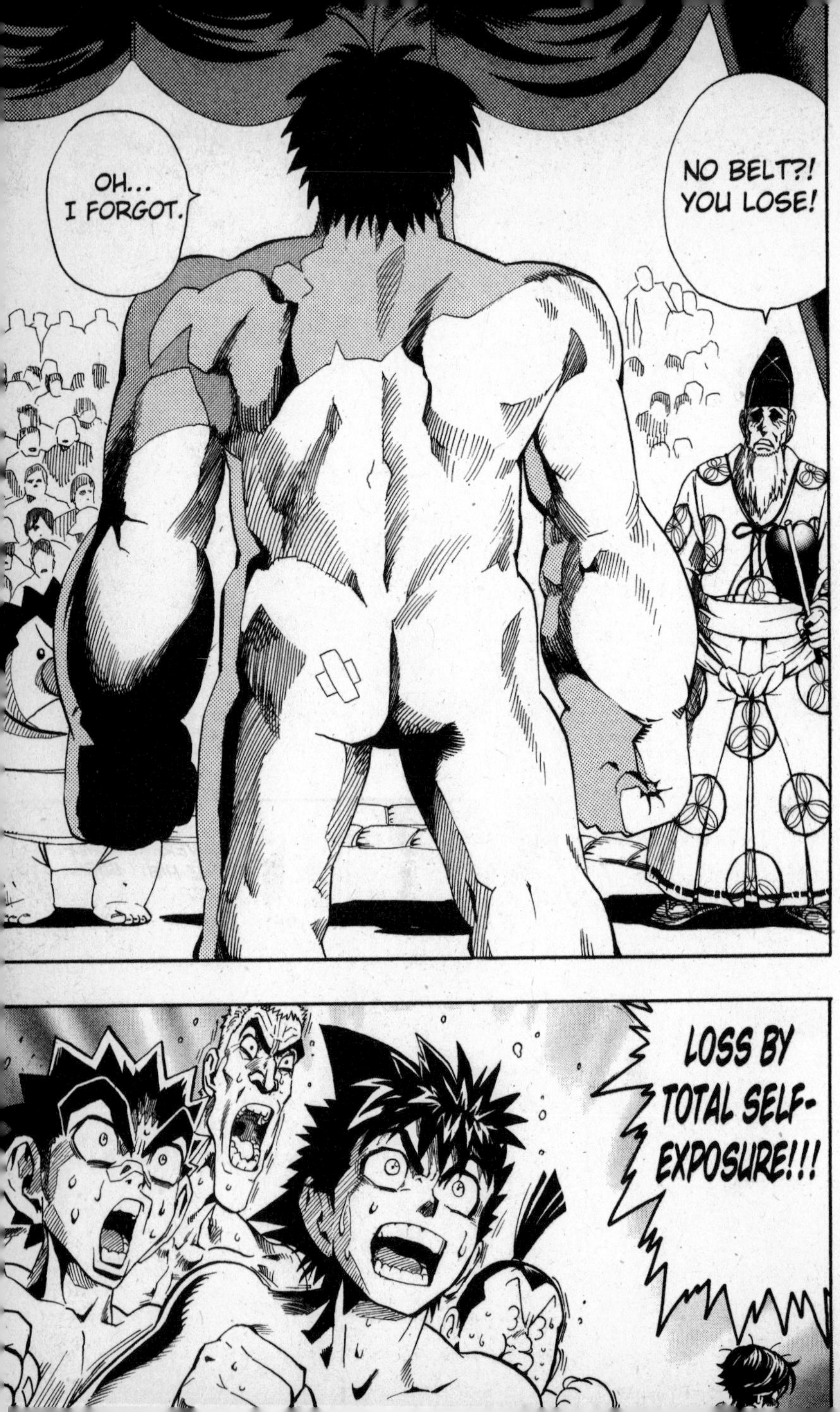
NO BELT?! YOU LOSE!
OH... I FORGOT.
LOSS BY TOTAL SELF-EXPOSURE!!!

Eyeshield 21 Survey Corner **Devil Bat 021**

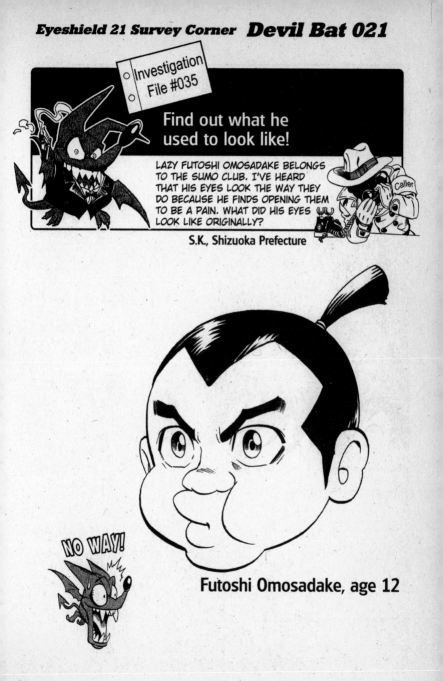

Investigation File #035

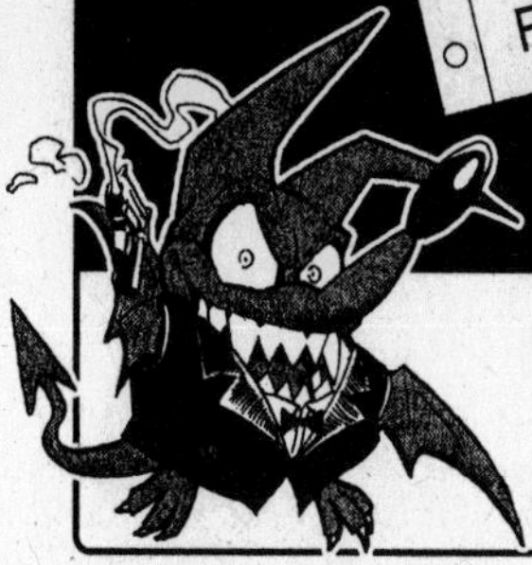

Find out what he used to look like!

LAZY FUTOSHI OMOSADAKE BELONGS TO THE SUMO CLUB. I'VE HEARD THAT HIS EYES LOOK THE WAY THEY DO BECAUSE HE FINDS OPENING THEM TO BE A PAIN. WHAT DID HIS EYES LOOK LIKE ORIGINALLY?

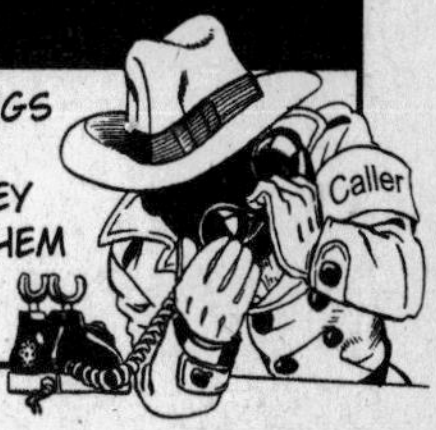
Caller

S.K., Shizuoka Prefecture

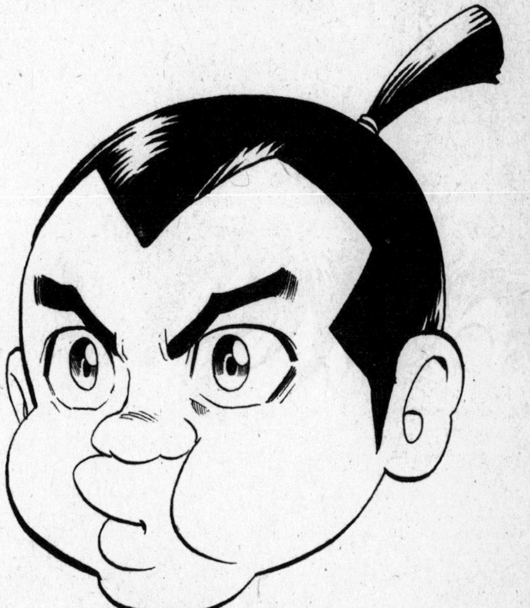

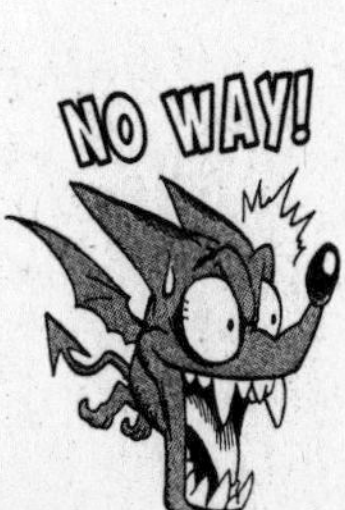
NO WAY!

Futoshi Omosadake, age 12

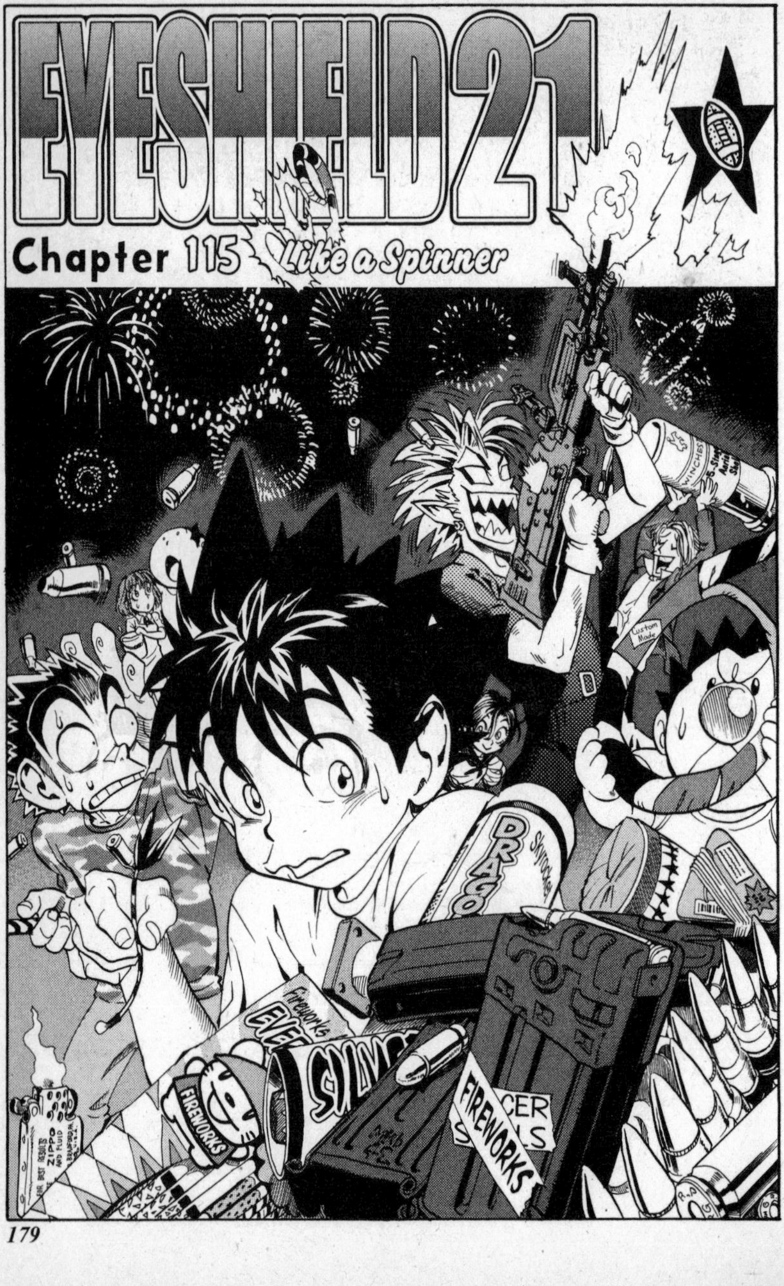
EYESHIELD 21
Chapter 115 Like a Spinner
Custom Made
DRAGO
Skyrocket
Fireworks
FIREWORKS
ZIPPO
FIREWORKS
FIREWORKS

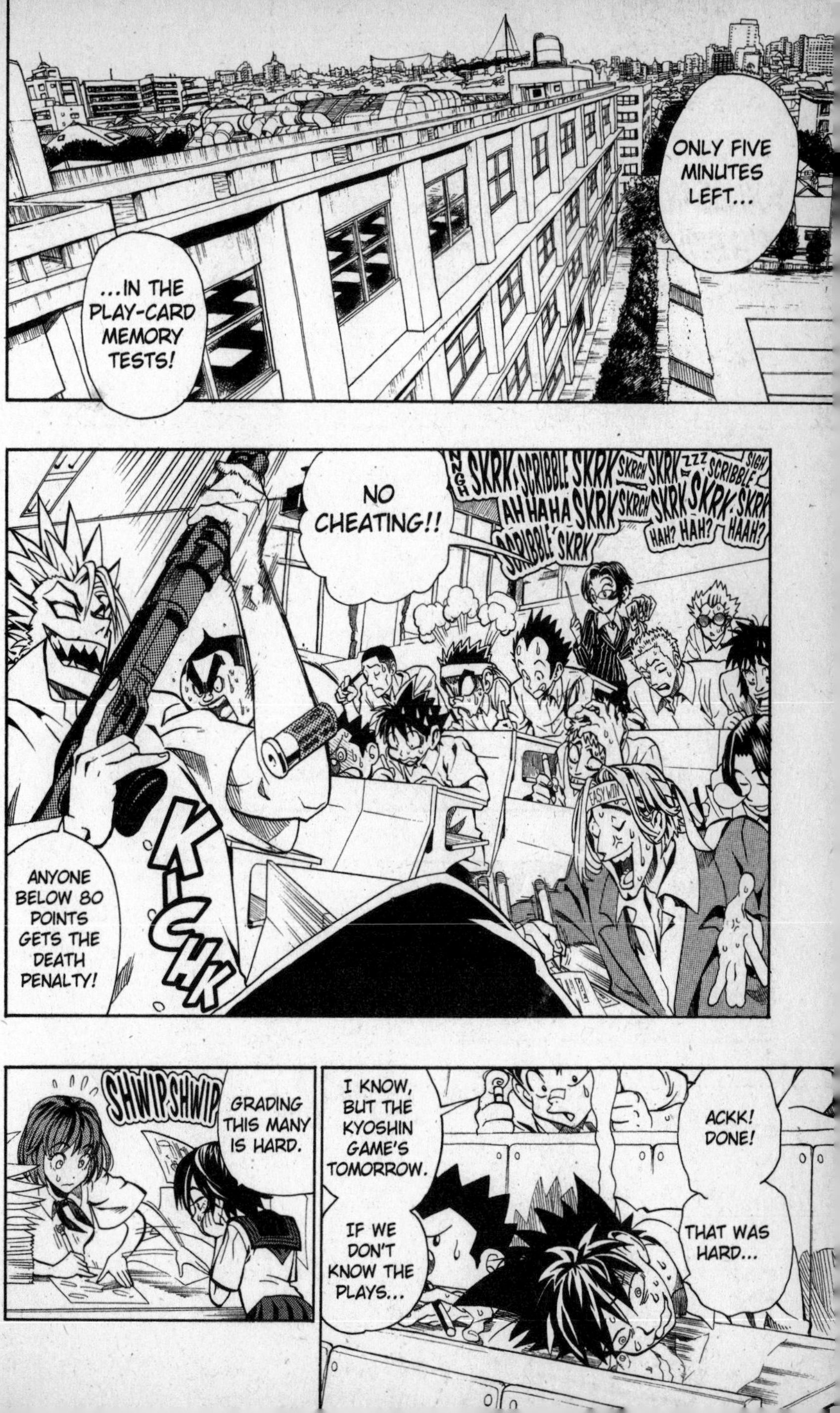
ONLY FIVE MINUTES LEFT...
...IN THE PLAY-CARD MEMORY TESTS!
SIGH
ZZZ
SCRIBBLE
SKRK
SKRK
SKRK
HAAH?
HAH?
HAH?
SKRCH
SKRCH
SKRK
SCRIBBLE
SKRK
AH HA HA
SCRIBBLE
SKRK
NO CHEATING!!
EASY WIN
K-CHK
ANYONE BELOW 80 POINTS GETS THE DEATH PENALTY!
ACKK! DONE!
THAT WAS HARD...
I KNOW, BUT THE KYOSHIN GAME'S TOMORROW.
IF WE DON'T KNOW THE PLAYS...
GRADING THIS MANY IS HARD.
SHWIP SHWIP

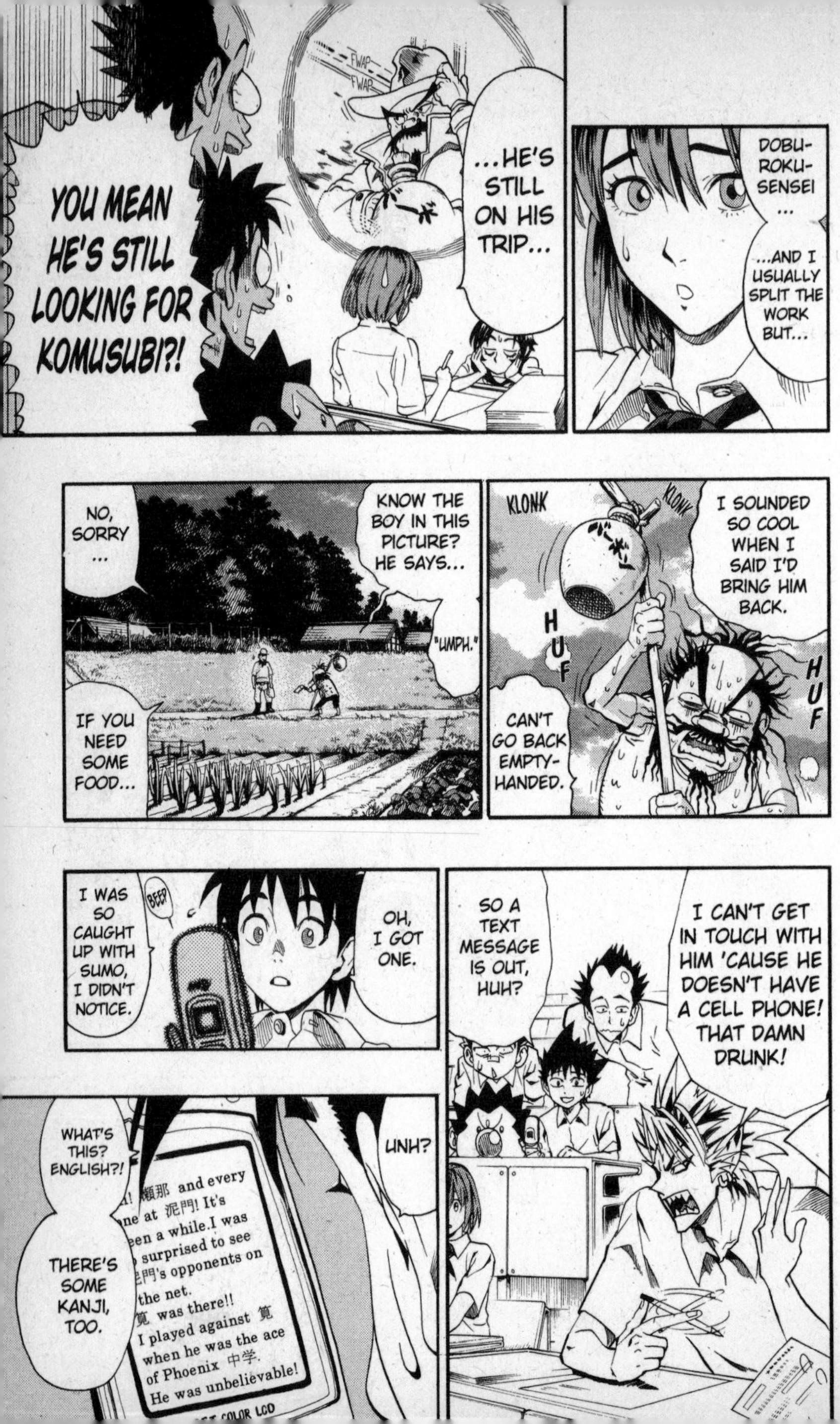
DOBU-ROKU-SENSEI ...
...AND I USUALLY SPLIT THE WORK BUT...
...HE'S STILL ON HIS TRIP...
FWAP
FWAP
YOU MEAN HE'S STILL LOOKING FOR KOMUSUBI?!
KLONK
KLONK
I SOUNDED SO COOL WHEN I SAID I'D BRING HIM BACK.
HUF
HUF
CAN'T GO BACK EMPTY-HANDED.
KNOW THE BOY IN THIS PICTURE? HE SAYS...
NO, SORRY ...
"UMPH."
IF YOU NEED SOME FOOD...
I CAN'T GET IN TOUCH WITH HIM 'CAUSE HE DOESN'T HAVE A CELL PHONE! THAT DAMN DRUNK!
SO A TEXT MESSAGE IS OUT, HUH?
OH, I GOT ONE.
BEEP
I WAS SO CAUGHT UP WITH SUMO, I DIDN'T NOTICE.
UNH?
WHAT'S THIS? ENGLISH?!
瀬那 and every
泥門! It's
een a while. I was
surprised to see
泥門's opponents on
the net.
筧 was there!!
I played against 筧
when he was the ace
of Phoenix 中学.
He was unbelievable!
THERE'S SOME KANJI, TOO.

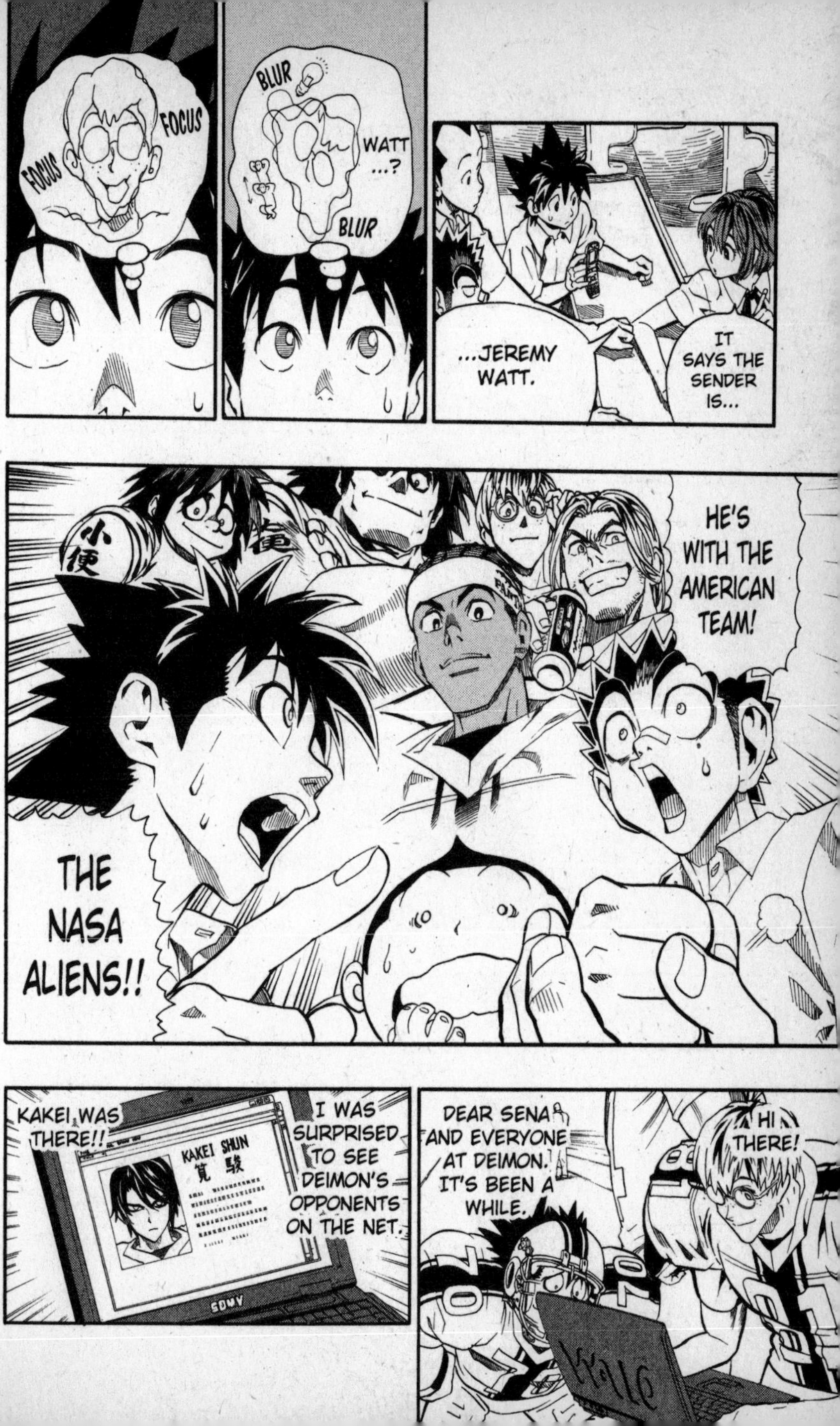
IT SAYS THE SENDER IS...
...JEREMY WATT.
BLUR
WATT ...?
BLUR
FOCUS
FOCUS
HE'S WITH THE AMERICAN TEAM!
小便
THE NASA ALIENS!!
HI THERE!
DEAR SENA AND EVERYONE AT DEIMON. IT'S BEEN A WHILE.
I WAS SURPRISED TO SEE DEIMON'S OPPONENTS ON THE NET.
KAKEI WAS THERE!!
KAKEI SHUN
筧 駿
SONY

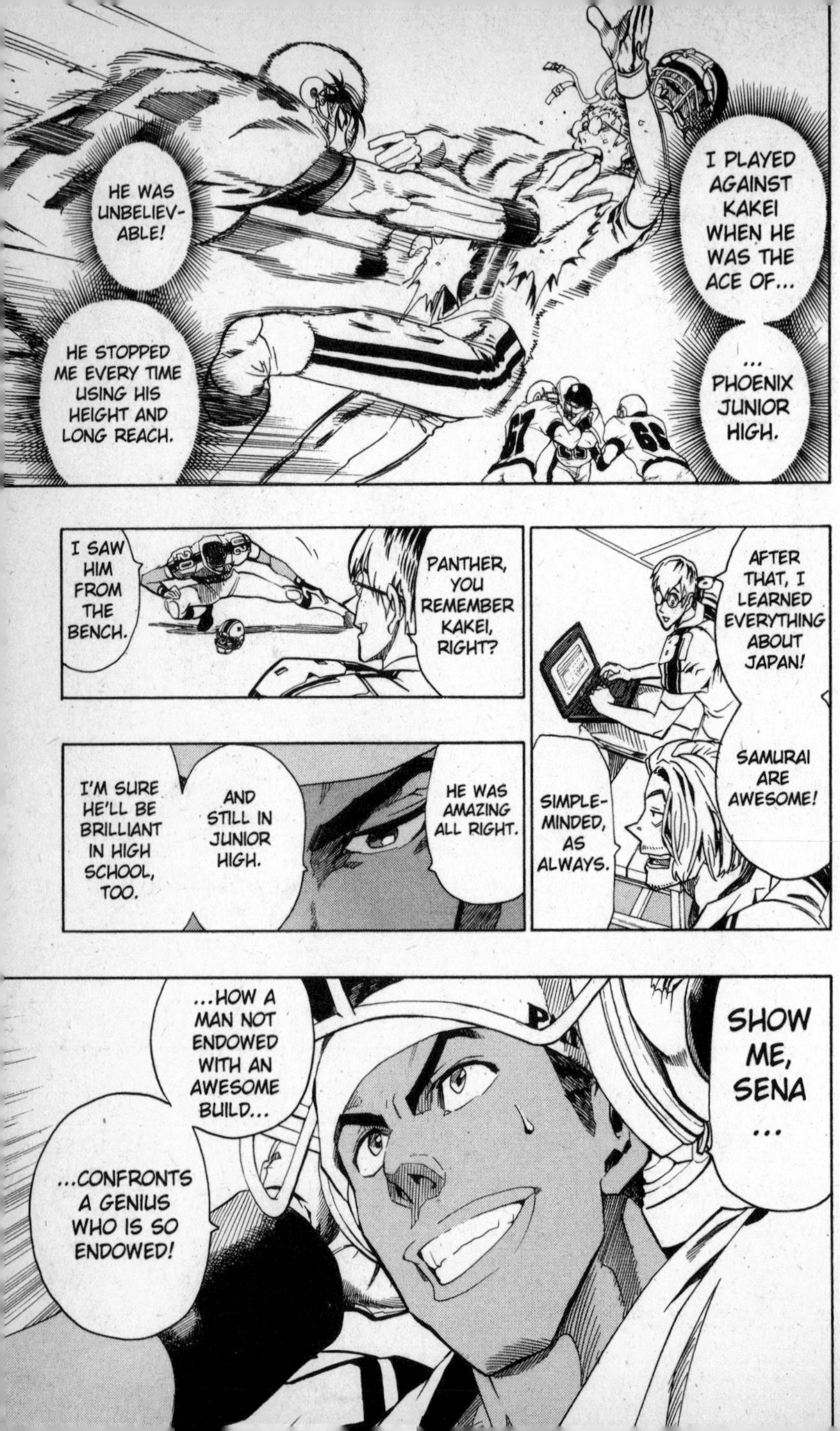
I PLAYED AGAINST KAKEI WHEN HE WAS THE ACE OF...
...PHOENIX JUNIOR HIGH.
HE WAS UNBELIEV-ABLE!
HE STOPPED ME EVERY TIME USING HIS HEIGHT AND LONG REACH.
AFTER THAT, I LEARNED EVERYTHING ABOUT JAPAN!
SAMURAI ARE AWESOME!
SIMPLE-MINDED, AS ALWAYS.
PANTHER, YOU REMEMBER KAKEI, RIGHT?
I SAW HIM FROM THE BENCH.
HE WAS AMAZING ALL RIGHT.
AND STILL IN JUNIOR HIGH.
I'M SURE HE'LL BE BRILLIANT IN HIGH SCHOOL, TOO.
SHOW ME, SENA...
...HOW A MAN NOT ENDOWED WITH AN AWESOME BUILD...
...CONFRONTS A GENIUS WHO IS SO ENDOWED!

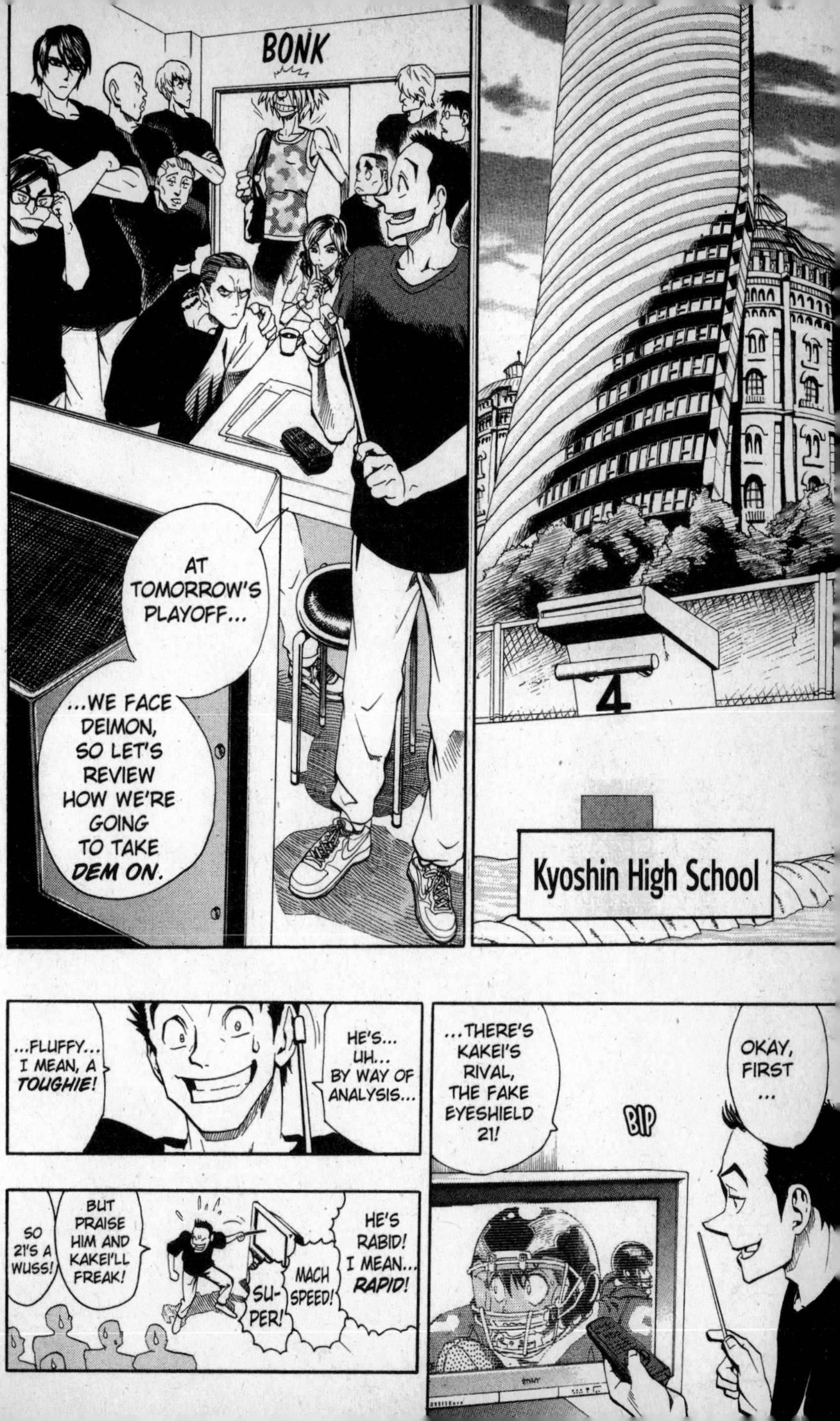
4
Kyoshin High School
BONK
AT TOMORROW'S PLAYOFF...
...WE FACE DEIMON, SO LET'S REVIEW HOW WE'RE GOING TO TAKE *DEM ON*.
OKAY, FIRST...
BIP
...THERE'S KAKEI'S RIVAL, THE FAKE EYESHIELD 21!
HE'S... UH... BY WAY OF ANALYSIS...
...FLUFFY... I MEAN, A *TOUGHIE*!
HE'S RABID! I MEAN... *RAPID*!
MACH SPEED!
SU-PER!
BUT PRAISE HIM AND KAKEI'LL FREAK!
SO 21'S A WUSS!

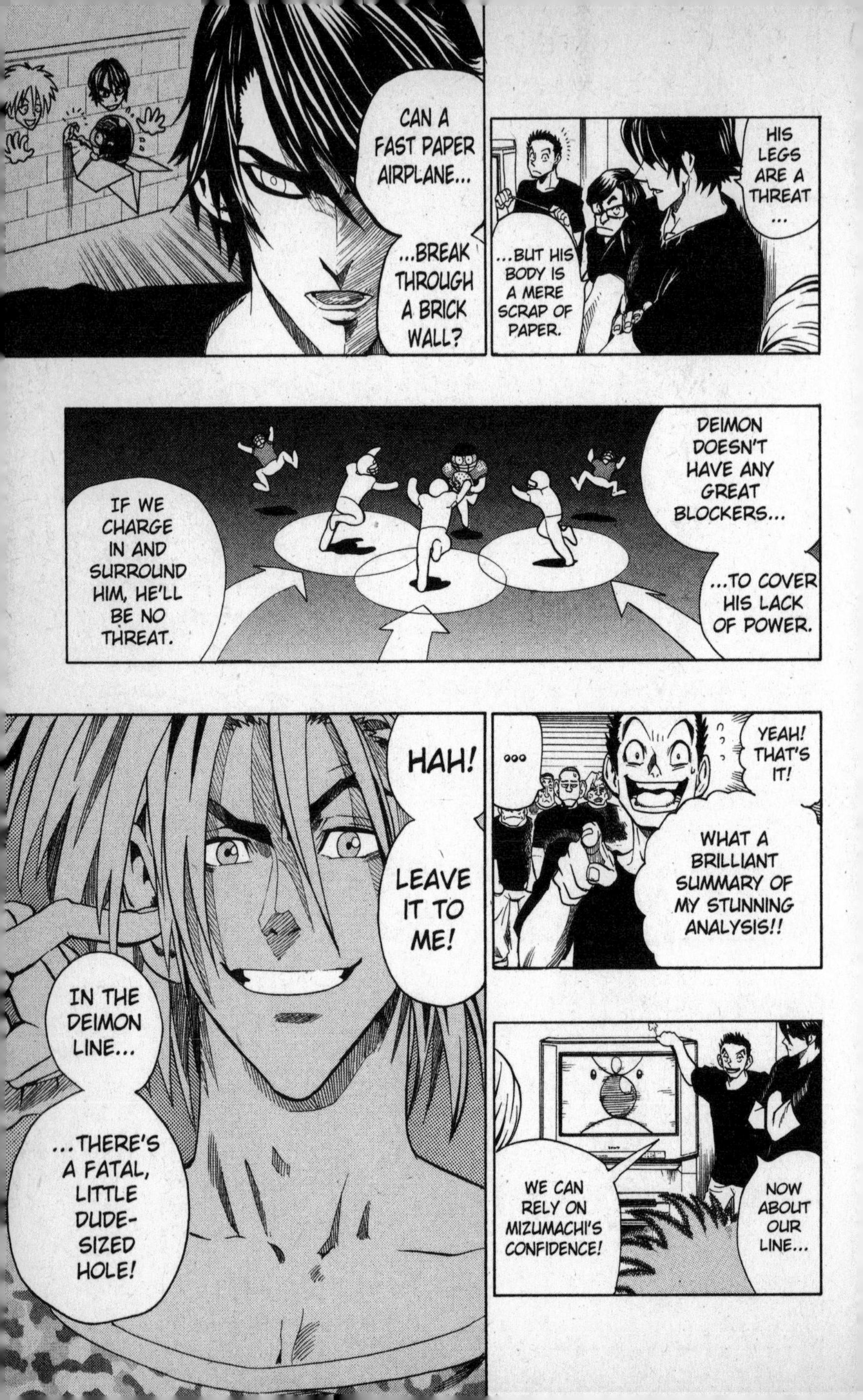
HIS LEGS ARE A THREAT...
...BUT HIS BODY IS A MERE SCRAP OF PAPER.
CAN A FAST PAPER AIRPLANE...
...BREAK THROUGH A BRICK WALL?
DEIMON DOESN'T HAVE ANY GREAT BLOCKERS...
...TO COVER HIS LACK OF POWER.
IF WE CHARGE IN AND SURROUND HIM, HE'LL BE NO THREAT.
YEAH! THAT'S IT!
WHAT A BRILLIANT SUMMARY OF MY STUNNING ANALYSIS!!
...
NOW ABOUT OUR LINE...
WE CAN RELY ON MIZUMACHI'S CONFIDENCE!
HAH!
LEAVE IT TO ME!
IN THE DEIMON LINE...
...THERE'S A FATAL, LITTLE DUDE-SIZED HOLE!

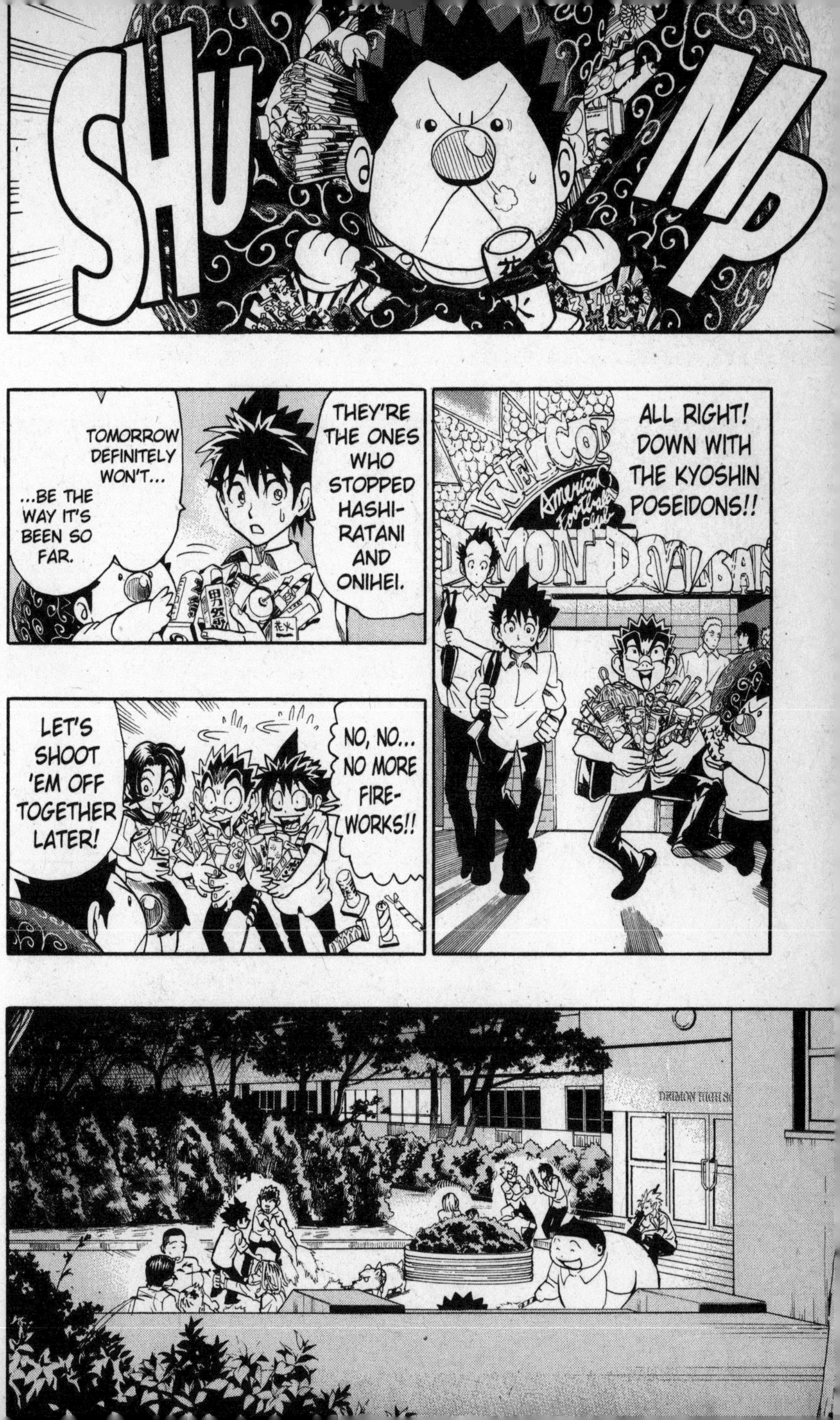
SHUMP
ALL RIGHT! DOWN WITH THE KYOSHIN POSEIDONS!!
THEY'RE THE ONES WHO STOPPED HASHI-RATANI AND ONIHEI.
TOMORROW DEFINITELY WON'T...
...BE THE WAY IT'S BEEN SO FAR.
NO, NO... NO MORE FIRE-WORKS!!
LET'S SHOOT 'EM OFF TOGETHER LATER!

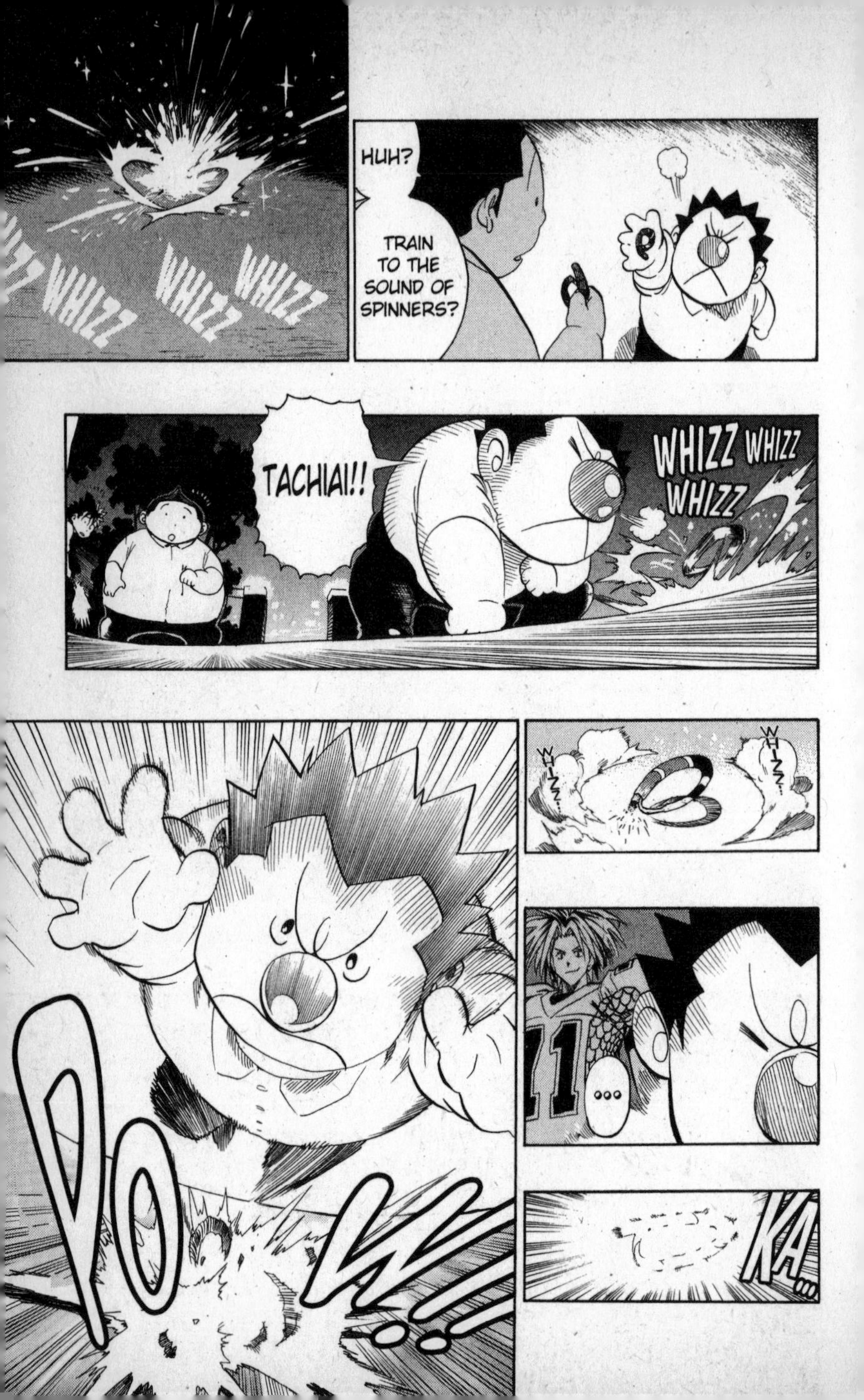
HUH?
TRAIN TO THE SOUND OF SPINNERS?
WHIZZ WHIZZ WHIZZ
WHIZZ WHIZZ WHIZZ
TACHIAI!!
WHIZZ...
WHIZZ...
...
KA...
POW!!...

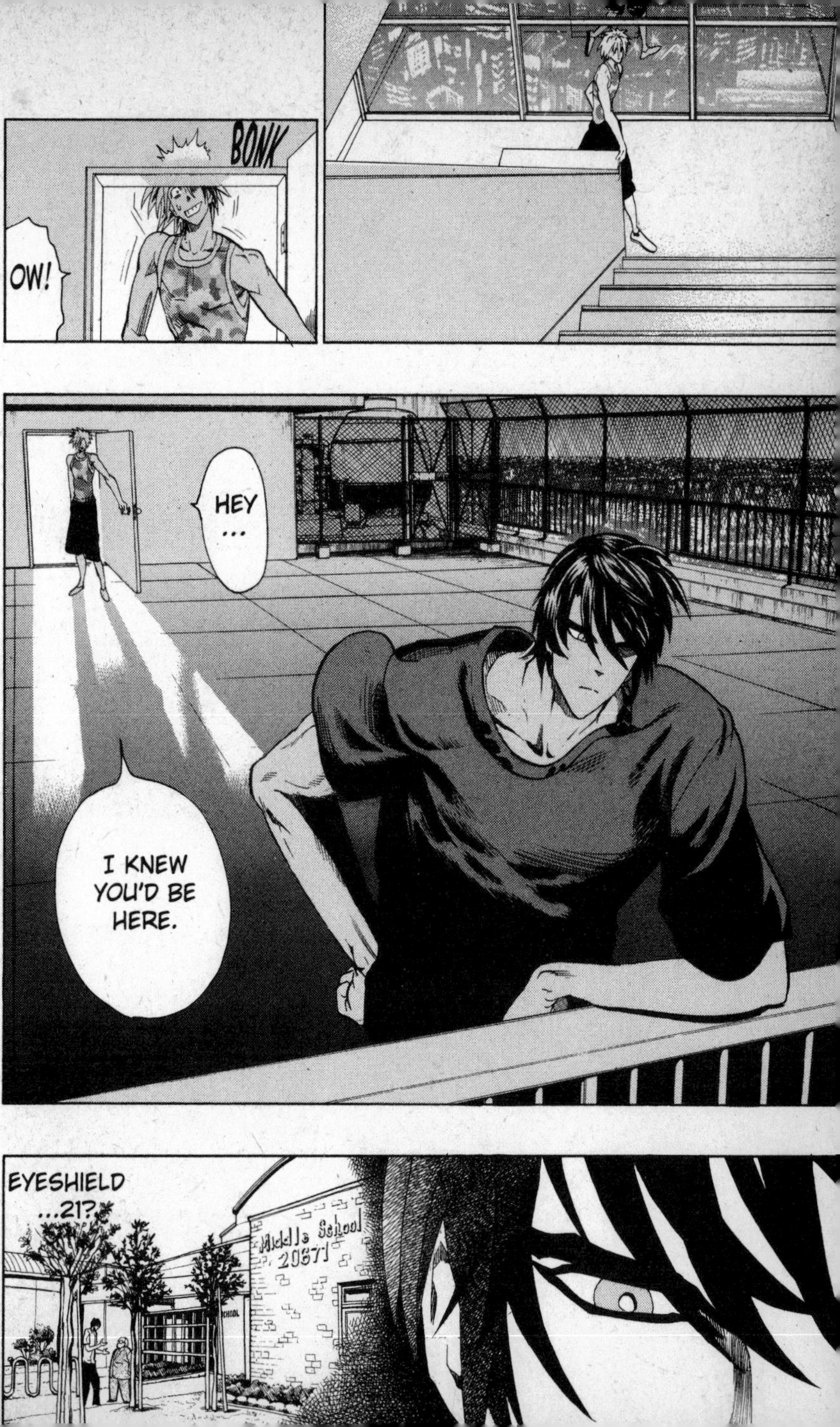
BONK
OW!
HEY ...
I KNEW YOU'D BE HERE.
EYESHIELD ...21?
Middle School 20671

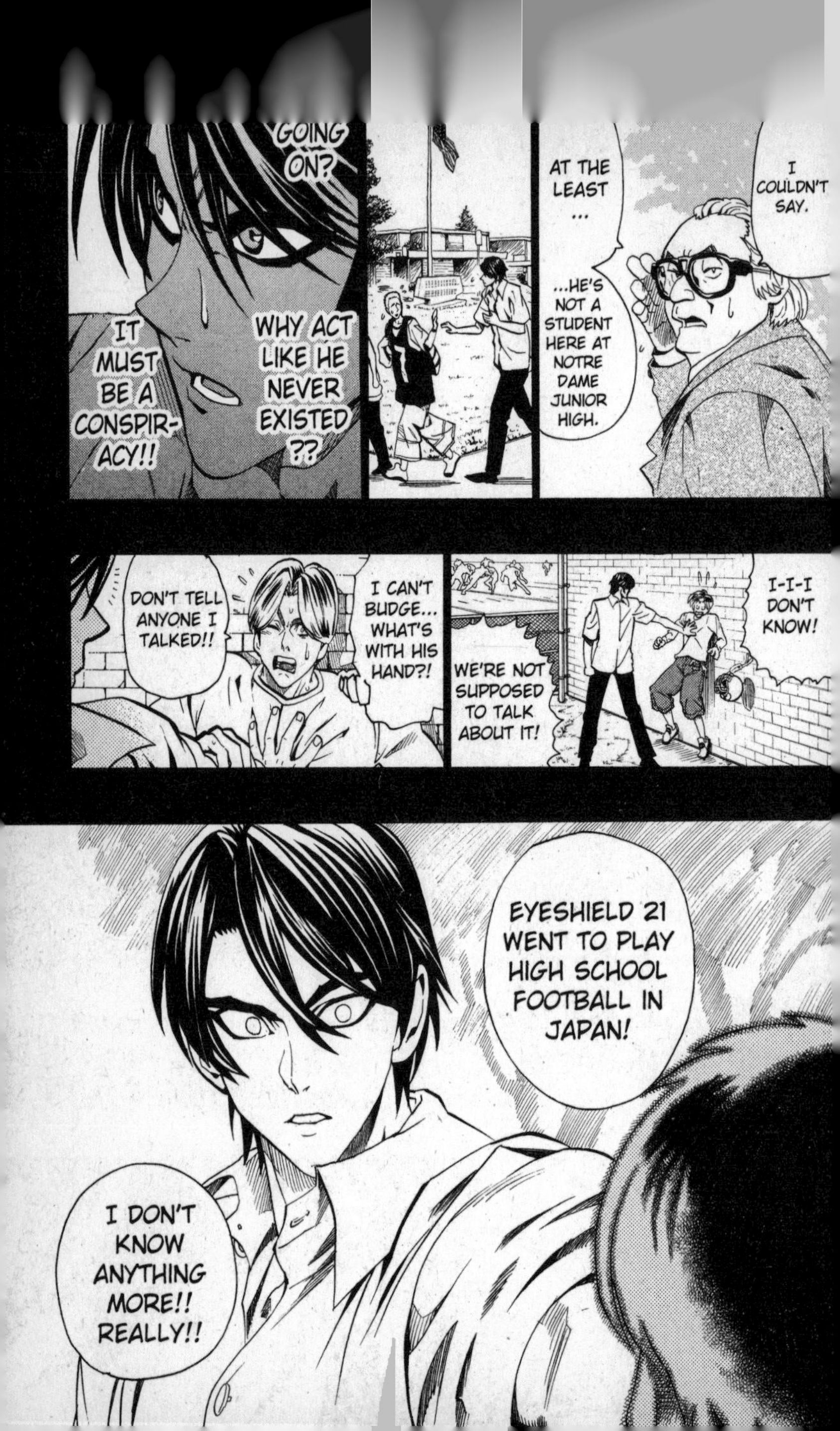
I COULDN'T SAY.
AT THE LEAST ...
...HE'S NOT A STUDENT HERE AT NOTRE DAME JUNIOR HIGH.
GOING ON?
WHY ACT LIKE HE NEVER EXISTED??
IT MUST BE A CONSPIR-ACY!!
I-I-I DON'T KNOW!
WE'RE NOT SUPPOSED TO TALK ABOUT IT!
I CAN'T BUDGE... WHAT'S WITH HIS HAND?!
DON'T TELL ANYONE I TALKED!!
EYESHIELD 21 WENT TO PLAY HIGH SCHOOL FOOTBALL IN JAPAN!
I DON'T KNOW ANYTHING MORE!! REALLY!!

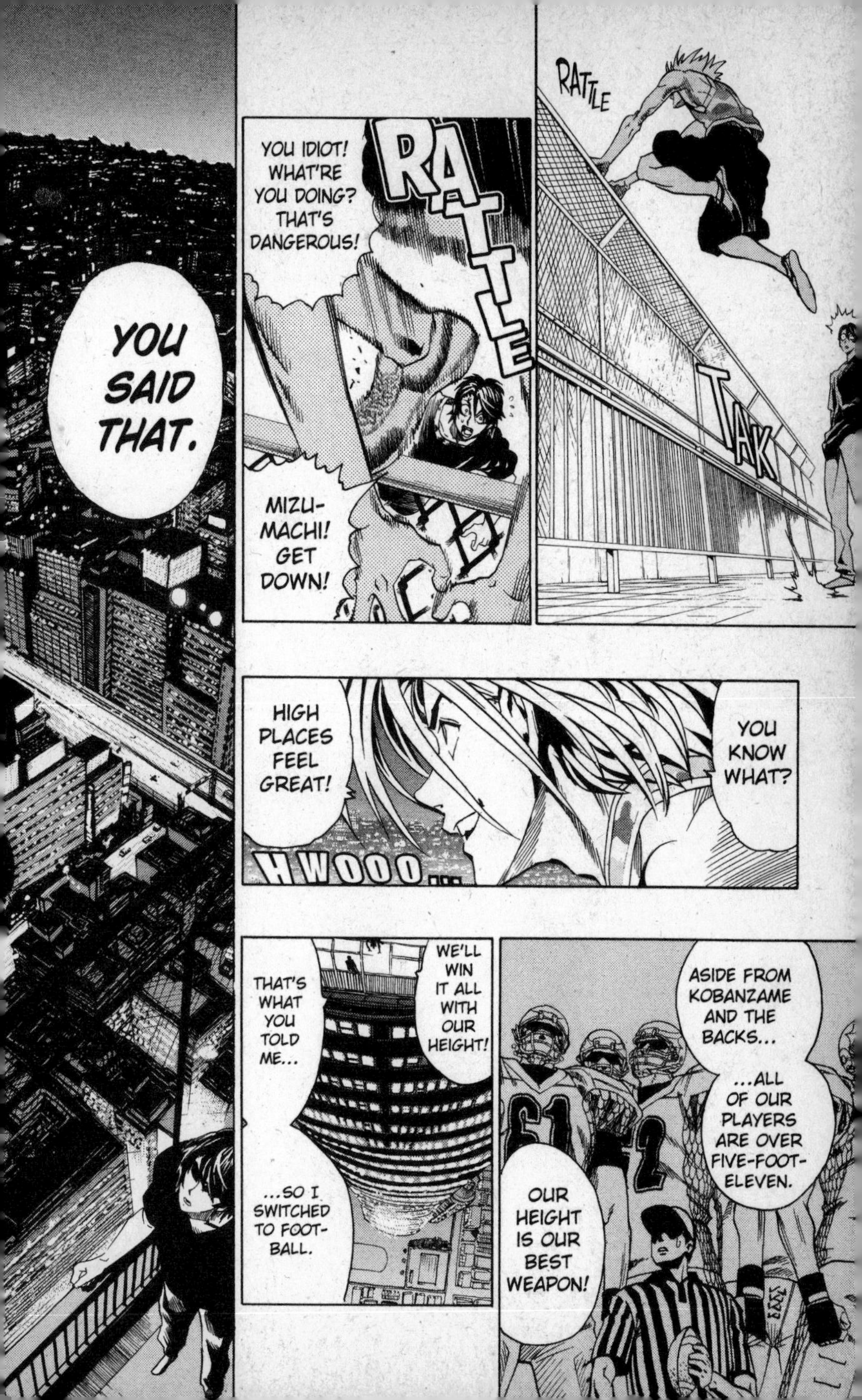
RATTLE
TAK
RATTLE
YOU IDIOT! WHAT'RE YOU DOING? THAT'S DANGEROUS!
MIZU-MACHI! GET DOWN!
YOU KNOW WHAT?
HIGH PLACES FEEL GREAT!
HWOOO...
ASIDE FROM KOBANZAME AND THE BACKS...
...ALL OF OUR PLAYERS ARE OVER FIVE-FOOT-ELEVEN.
OUR HEIGHT IS OUR BEST WEAPON!
WE'LL WIN IT ALL WITH OUR HEIGHT!
THAT'S WHAT YOU TOLD ME...
...SO I SWITCHED TO FOOT-BALL.
YOU SAID THAT.

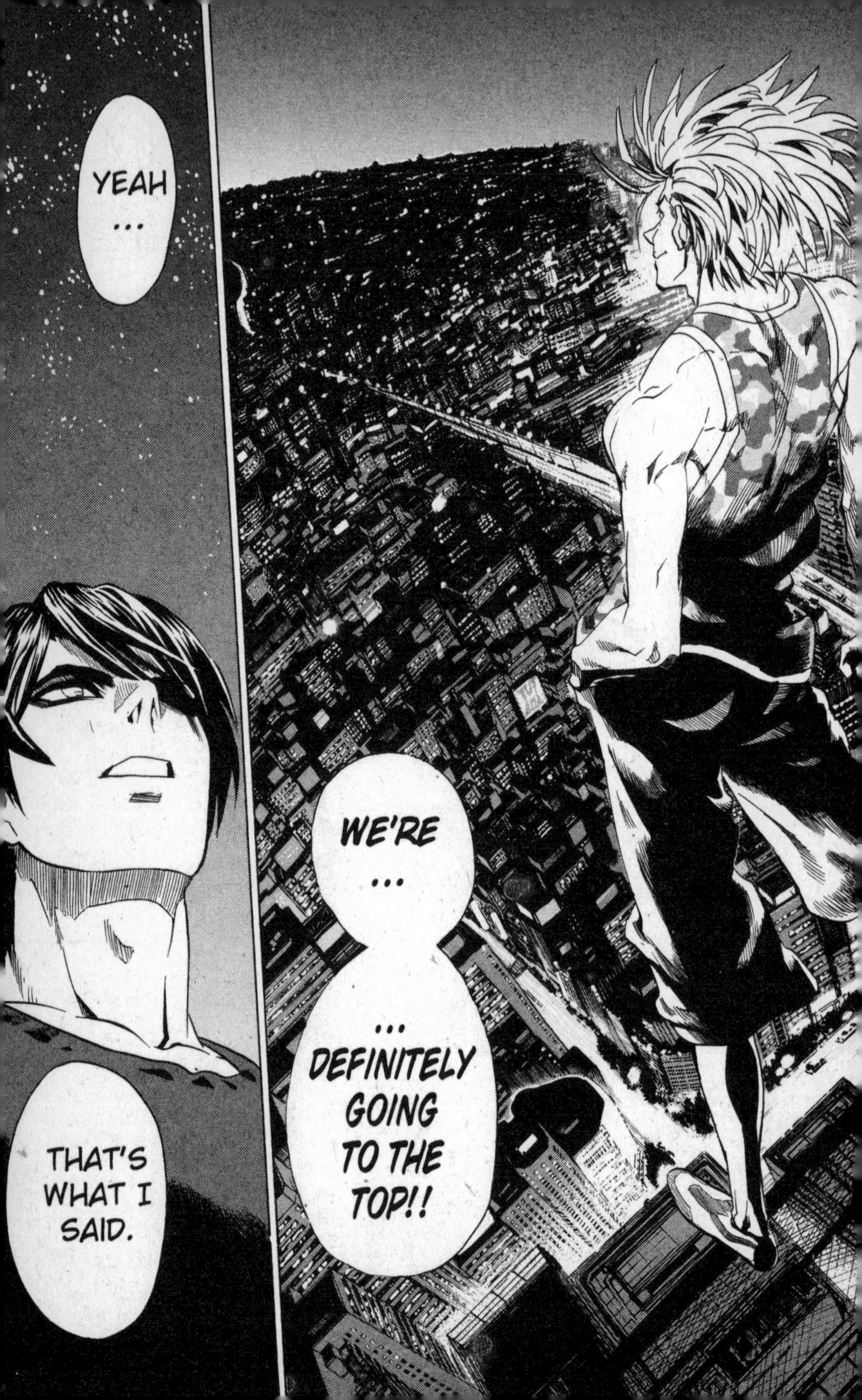
WE'RE ...
... DEFINITELY GOING TO THE TOP!!
YEAH ...
THAT'S WHAT I SAID.

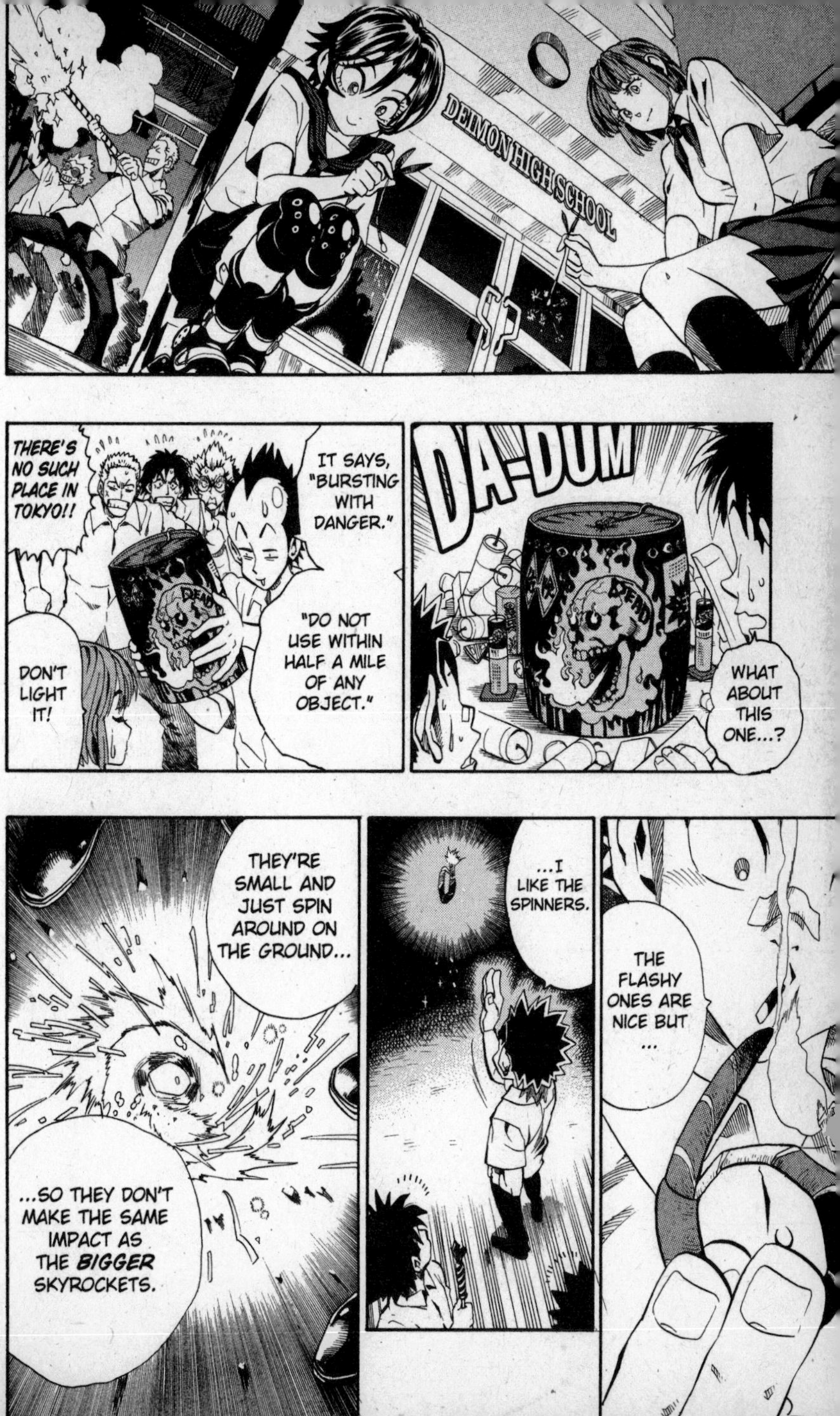
DEIMON HIGH SCHOOL
DA-DUM
WHAT ABOUT THIS ONE...?
IT SAYS, "BURSTING WITH DANGER."
THERE'S NO SUCH PLACE IN TOKYO!!
"DO NOT USE WITHIN HALF A MILE OF ANY OBJECT."
DON'T LIGHT IT!
THE FLASHY ONES ARE NICE BUT ...
...I LIKE THE SPINNERS.
THEY'RE SMALL AND JUST SPIN AROUND ON THE GROUND...
...SO THEY DON'T MAKE THE SAME IMPACT AS THE *BIGGER* SKYROCKETS.

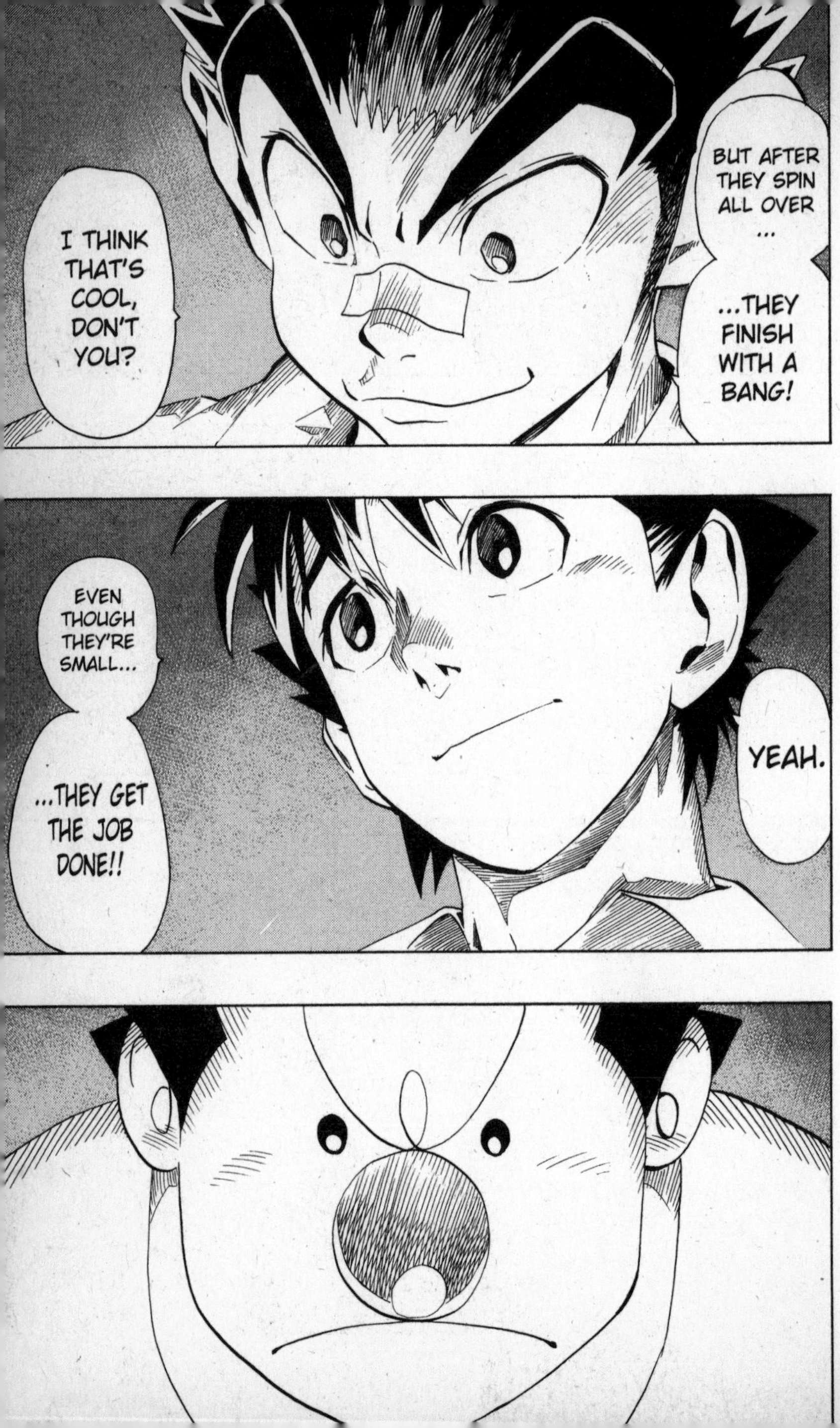
BUT AFTER THEY SPIN ALL OVER ...
...THEY FINISH WITH A BANG!
I THINK THAT'S COOL, DON'T YOU?
EVEN THOUGH THEY'RE SMALL...
...THEY GET THE JOB DONE!!
YEAH.

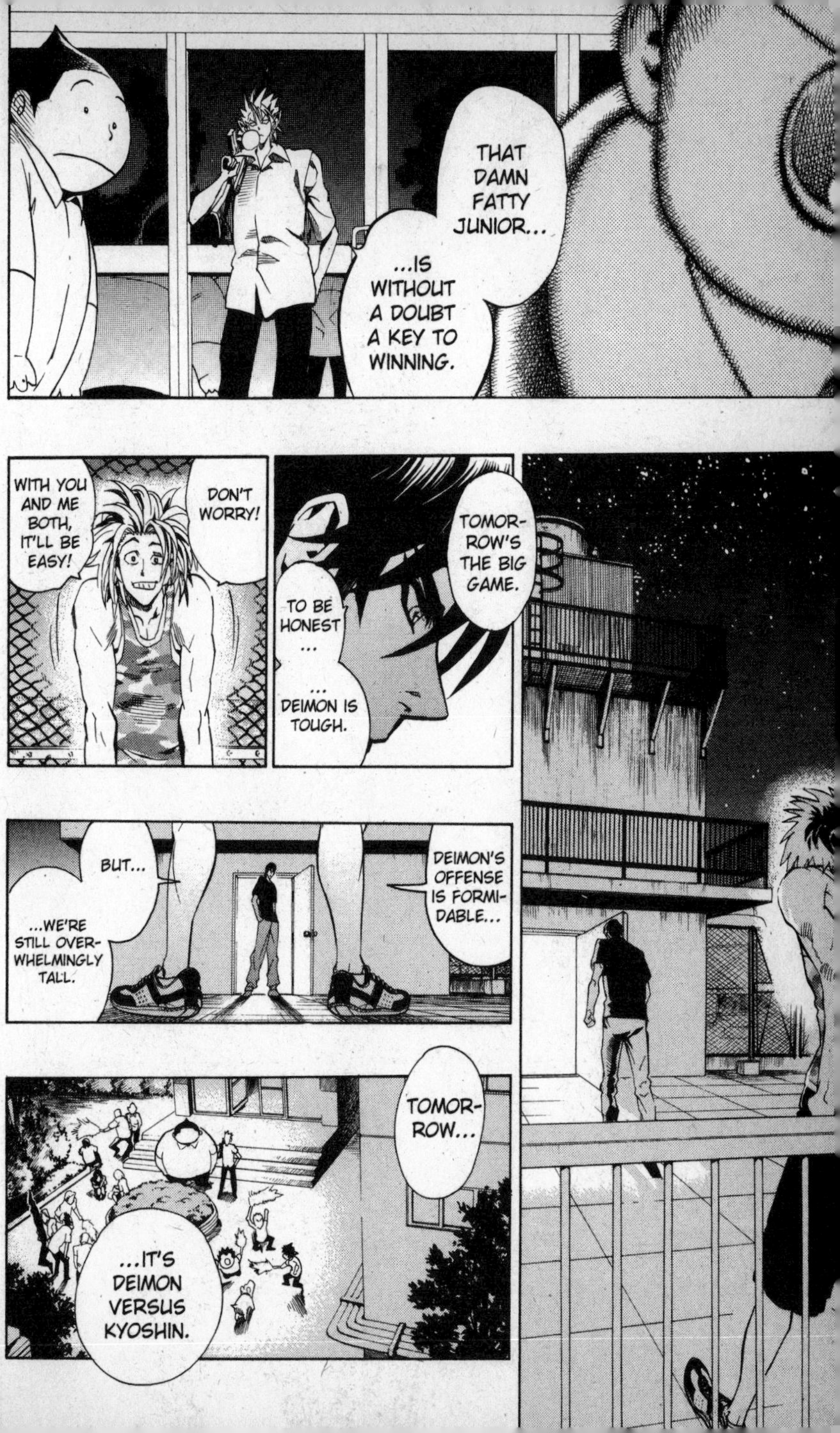
THAT DAMN FATTY JUNIOR...
...IS WITHOUT A DOUBT A KEY TO WINNING.
TOMORROW'S THE BIG GAME.
TO BE HONEST...
...DEIMON IS TOUGH.
DON'T WORRY!
WITH YOU AND ME BOTH, IT'LL BE EASY!
DEIMON'S OFFENSE IS FORMIDABLE...
BUT...
...WE'RE STILL OVERWHELMINGLY TALL.
TOMORROW...
...IT'S DEIMON VERSUS KYOSHIN.

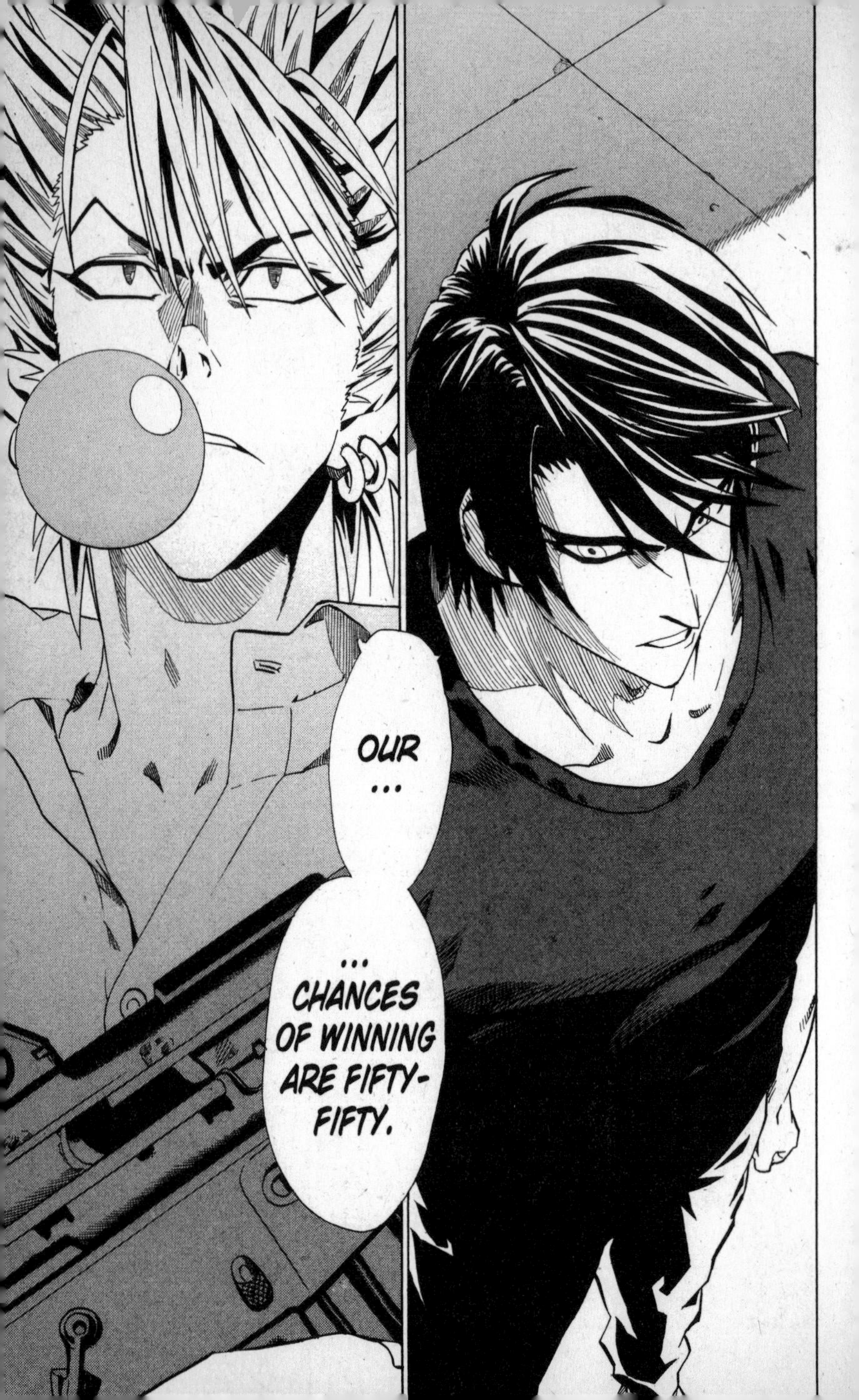
OUR ...
... CHANCES OF WINNING ARE FIFTY-FIFTY.

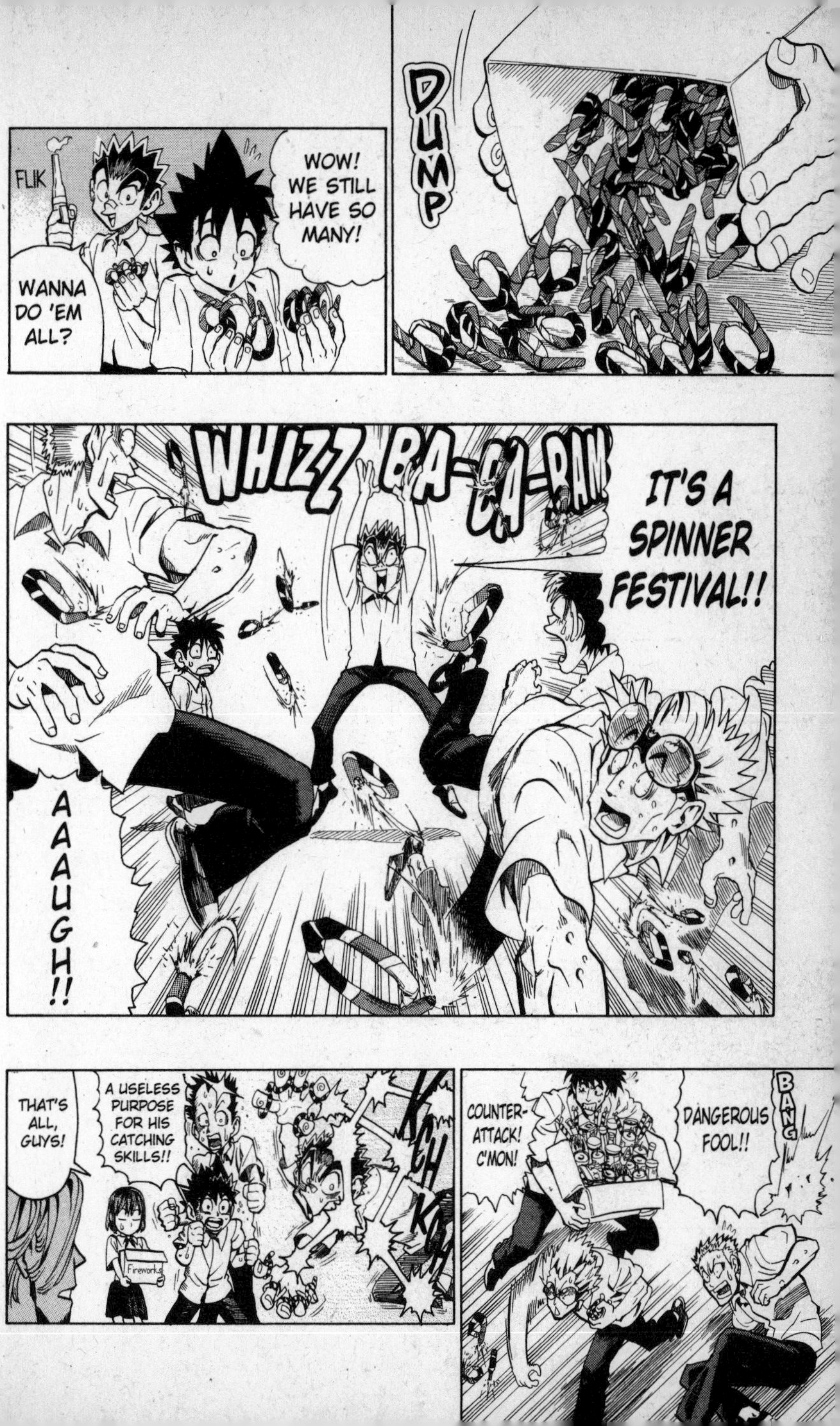
DUMP
WOW! WE STILL HAVE SO MANY!
FLIK
WANNA DO 'EM ALL?
WHIZZ BA-BA-BAM
IT'S A SPINNER FESTIVAL!!
AAAAUGH!!
BANG
DANGEROUS FOOL!!
COUNTER-ATTACK! C'MON!
A USELESS PURPOSE FOR HIS CATCHING SKILLS!!
THAT'S ALL, GUYS!
Fireworks

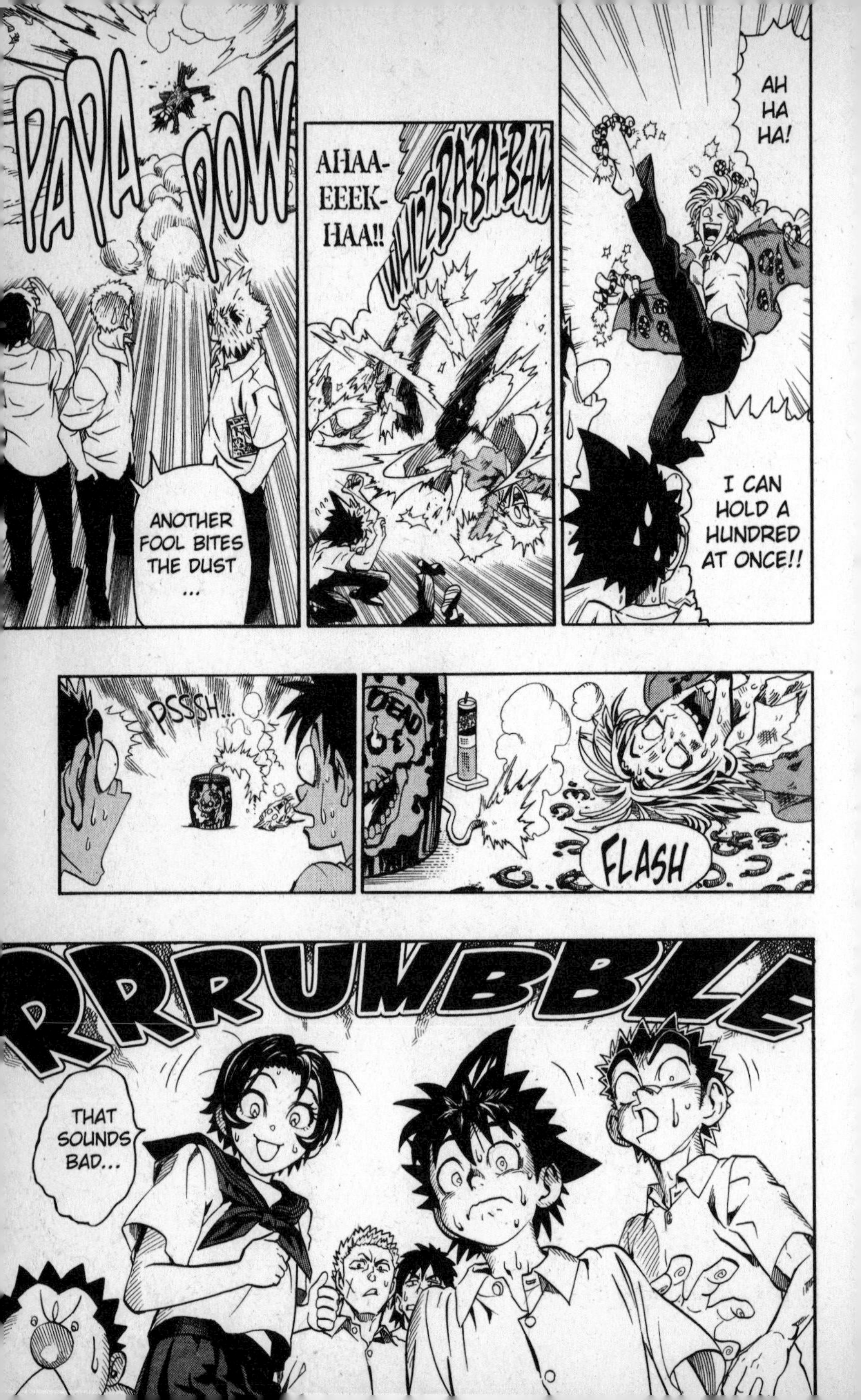
AH HA HA!
I CAN HOLD A HUNDRED AT ONCE!!
WHIZ BA-BA-BAM
AHAA-EEEK-HAA!!
POW
PAPA
ANOTHER FOOL BITES THE DUST ...
DEAD
FLASH
PSSSH...
RRRUMBLE
THAT SOUNDS BAD...

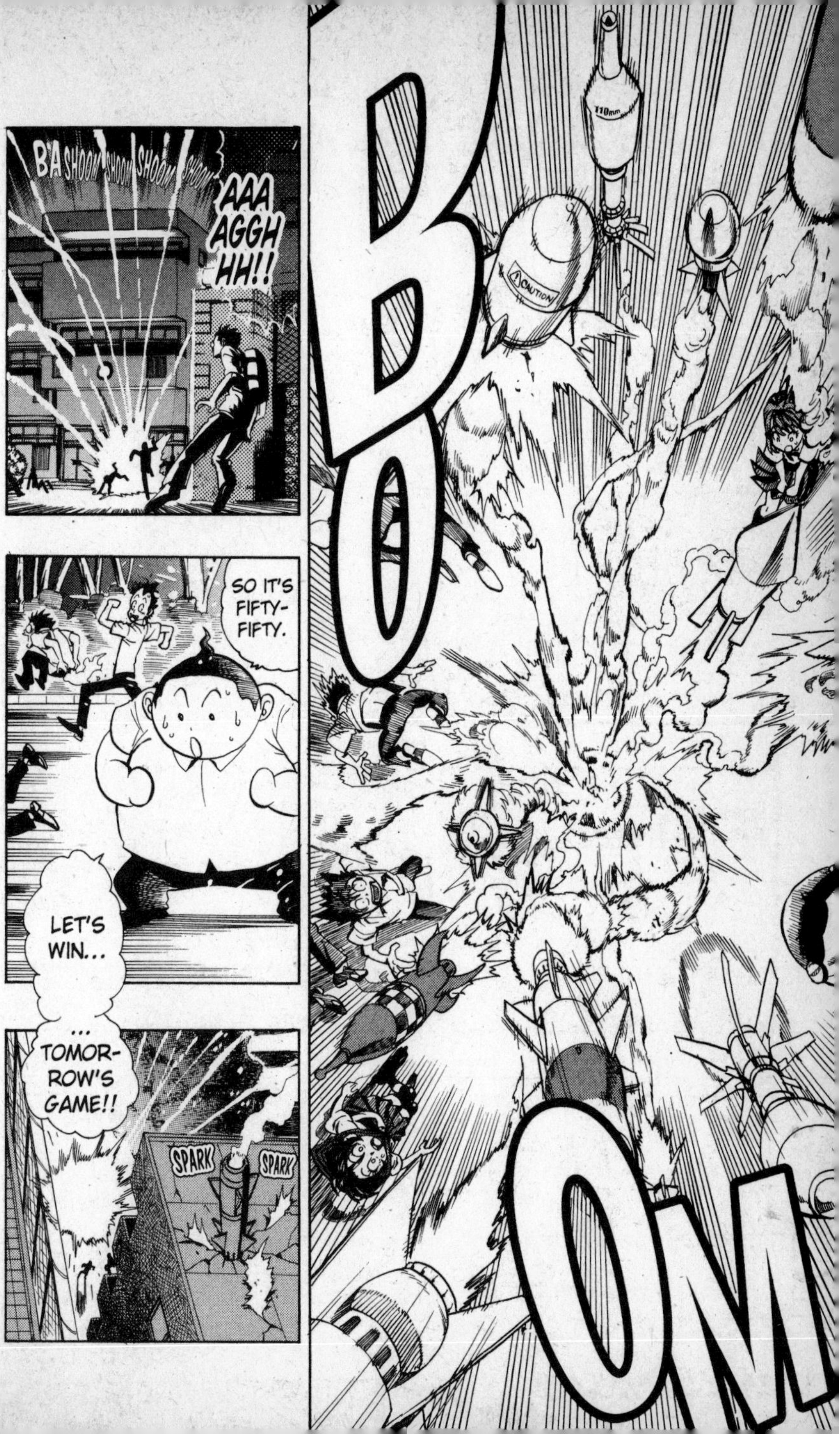
B
O
OM
110mm
CAUTION
BA SHOOM SHOOM SHOOM SHOOM
AAAAGGHHH!!
SO IT'S FIFTY-FIFTY.
LET'S WIN...
...TOMORROW'S GAME!!
SPARK
SPARK

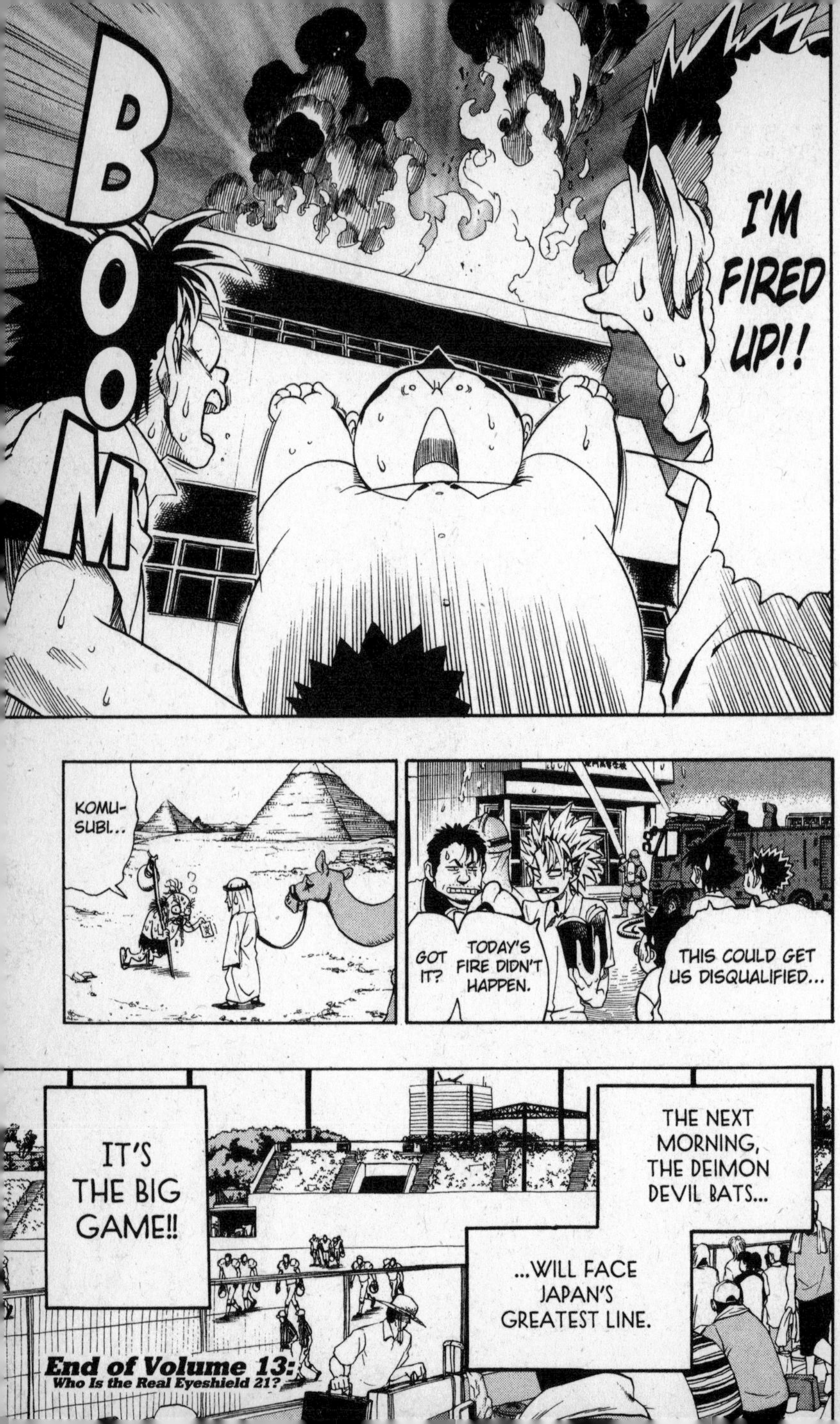
I'M FIRED UP!!
BOOM
THIS COULD GET US DISQUALIFIED...
TODAY'S FIRE DIDN'T HAPPEN.
GOT IT?
KOMUSUBI...
THE NEXT MORNING, THE DEIMON DEVIL BATS...
...WILL FACE JAPAN'S GREATEST LINE.
IT'S THE BIG GAME!!
End of Volume 13: Who Is the Real Eyeshield 21?

Eyeshield 21 Survey Corner **Devil Bat 021**

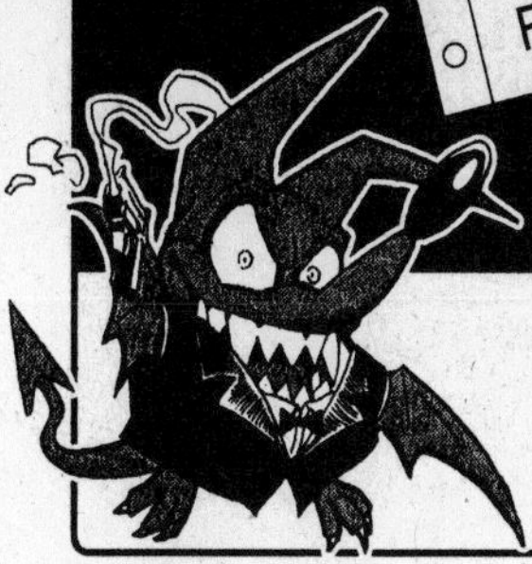

Investigation File #036

Get your hands on a manga by Togano!!

I KNOW TOGANO LOVES MANGA, AND I SAW HIM DRAWING ONE ON THE "COMIC STRIP HALFTIME" PAGES IN VOLUME 12. I WANT TO READ HIS WORK!!

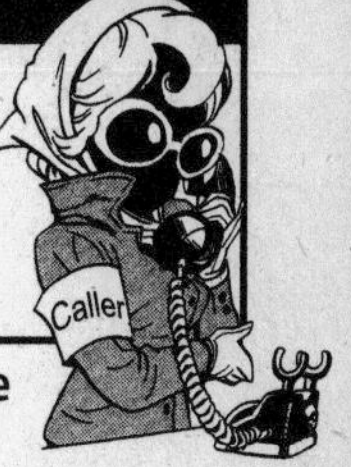
Caller

K.G., Yamaguchi Prefecture

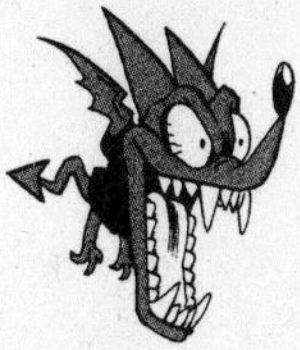

I STOLE AN UNFINISHED MANGA FROM HIM!

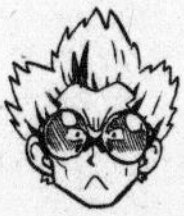

Summary of Togano's Manga

The main character, Shozo, dreams of becoming a master of kenpo, the Chinese version of boxing. He can stretch his arms like rubber and control his ki. He has psychic powers and can also use ninjutsu, which makes him incredibly powerful. He excels at tennis, baseball and basketball, and his slamdunks are forceful. On top of that, he has recently improved his skills as a lineman in football.

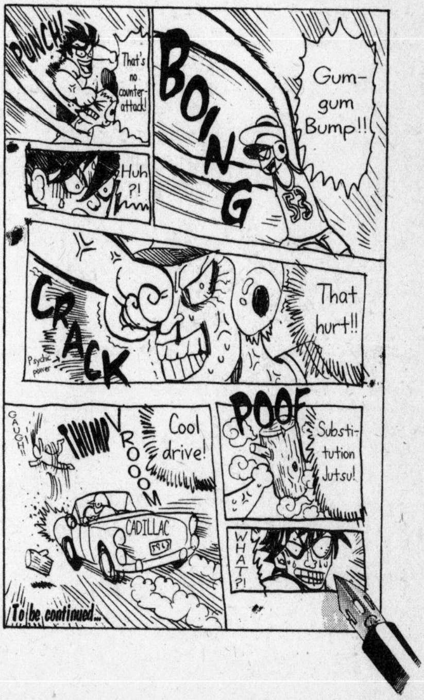
BOING
Gum-gum Bump!!
PUNCH!
That's no counter-attack!
Huh ?!
CRACK
That hurt!!
Psychic power
POOF
Substi-tution Jutsu!
WHAT?!
Cool drive!
VROOOOM
THUMP
GAUGH!!
CADILLAC
To be continued...

Eyeshield 21 Survey Corner **Devil Bat 021**

Investigation File #037

Investigate what Deimon's players like in a girl!

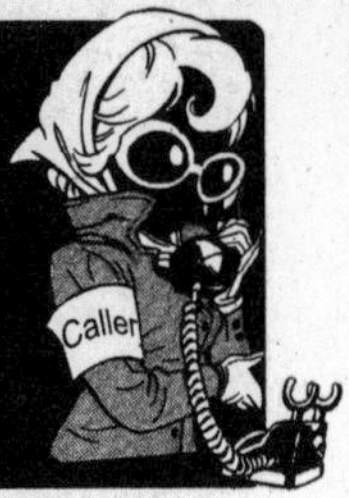
Caller

M.H., Nagano Prefecture and elsewhere

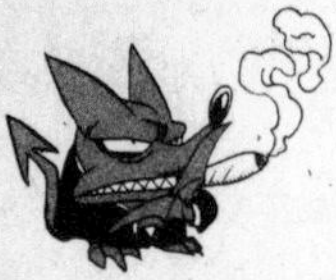

WE'LL ASK 'EM ONE BY ONE.
LET'S START WITH MONTA.

THERE'S NOT MUCH SPACE SO KEEP IT SHORT.

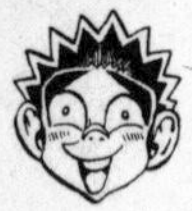

WHAT? MY TYPE?!
I CAN'T BE BOTHERED WITH A QUESTION LIKE THAT WHEN WE'RE ABOUT TO WIN THE TOURNAMENT!! BUT IF I HAD TO SAY...I MEAN, REALLY HAD TO SAY...NOT THAT I'M INTERESTED IN LOVELY-DOVEY...BUT IF I HAD TO SAY...I GUESS SHE'D BE KIND AND...HOW SHOULD I PUT IT?...SMART AND PRACTICAL...LIKE...MAMORI! B-B-BUT I'M NOT POINTING AT ANYONE IN PARTICULAR! HEH HEH... BUT WHEN A MAN'S FIGHTING ALONE, HAVING SOMEONE THERE WITH HIM--

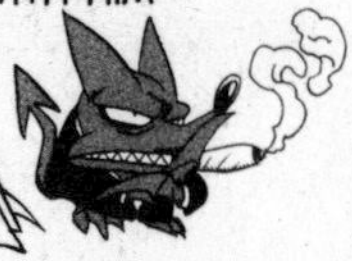

THAT'S IT! WE'RE OUT OF ROOM!

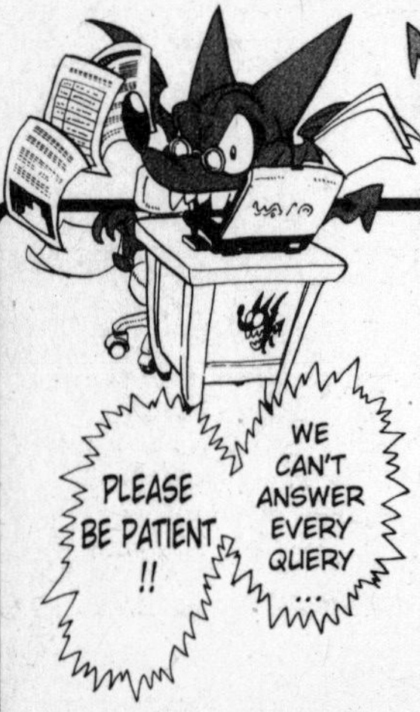
PLEASE BE PATIENT!!
WE CAN'T ANSWER EVERY QUERY...

Send your queries for Devil Bat 021 here!!

Devil Bat 021
Shonen Jump Advanced/Eyeshield 21
c/o VIZ Media, LLC
P.O. Box 77010
San Francisco, CA 94107

Deluxe Biographies
of the Supporting Cast

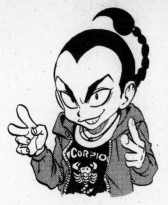

Kanagushi

He's an expert at reading people's intentions from their gestures. Because of this skill, he tends to look down on others.

When his father would lecture him about his attitude, Kanagushi would say, "Shee-hee-hee! It's so easy! I can read people in an instant! Dad, you're thinking about slapping m--. *Ouch!!*"

As is often the case, he got his face slapped. *In life, reading others' intentions is frequently no help at all.*

Jonan Giants Cheerleaders

Compared to these girls, the players are scrawny! The guys do have some grit, because *they're afraid of what the girls will do to them if they lose...*

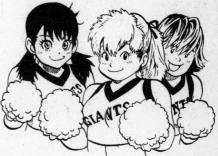

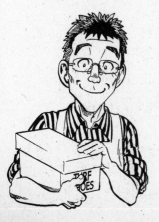

Kimidori Sports

This is a famous old shop in the neighborhood. The owner recently started one of those trendy point-card systems.

You get one point for every ¥1,000 you spend there.* It seems that once you collect 100 points you get an *original postcard*. Needless to say, nobody is collecting.

※¥1,000 is about U.S. $9.
Multiply this by 100.

Tall, Old Guy at the Sumo Tournament

He's the *ozeki* of Deimon Shopping Mall--this being the sumo rank just below yokozuna (the top rank). The old man will go all out against anyone!!

Kids in ***kindergarten*** who've asked him to play sumo have been sent ***flying!*** Afterward, he says, "Easy fight!" and ***roars with laughter!*** To a kid in kindergarten! Well, fair is fair...

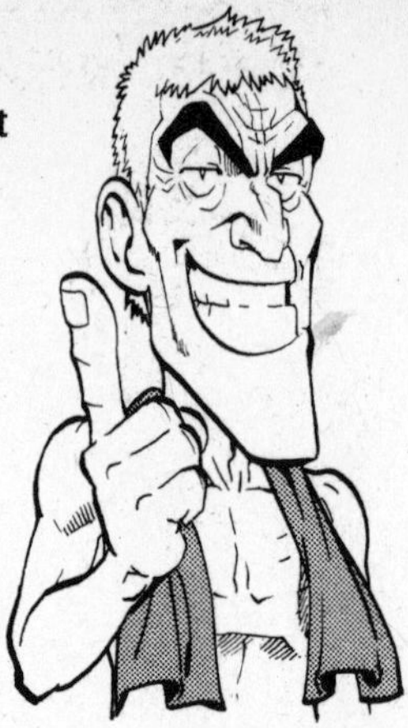

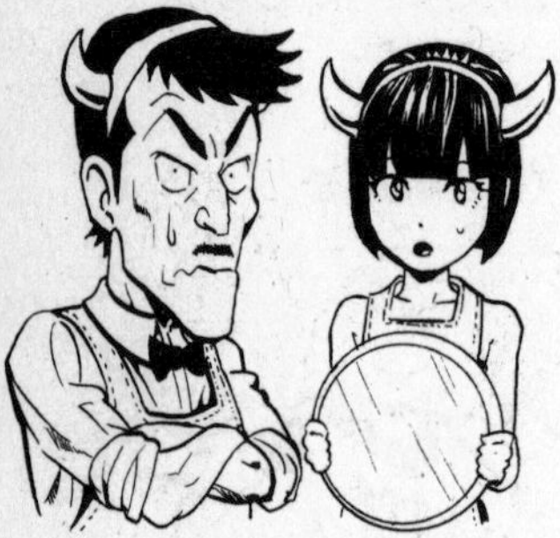

Yakiniku Minotaur

This place is famous for the staff's rigorous morning training. Recently, "jumping dogeza" was added to the program. [Dogeza is a deep bow. See vol. 7, pp. 123-124 for more on this.]

This was so that the staff can beg kids like that pointy-headed boy to leave if he ever comes back for their all-you-can-eat buffet.

Sengoku Samurai Coach

He has a habit of saying, ***"If we lose, I'll commit harakiri!!"*** Not that he ever has, mind you.

Another of his favorite sayings is, ***"My word is my bond!!"*** Not that it ever is, mind you.

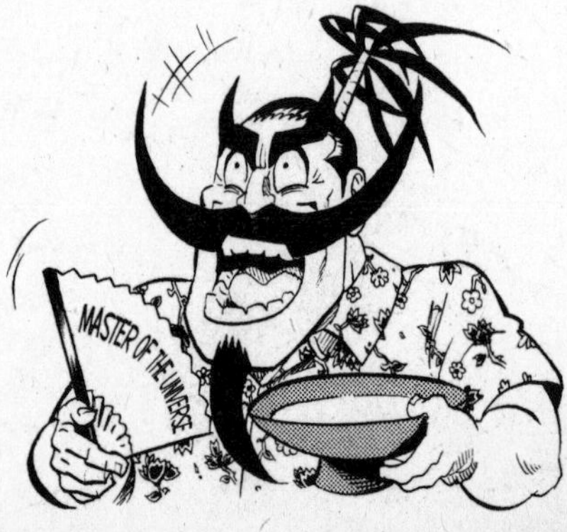
MASTER OF THE UNIVERSE

The Devil Bat Pirates

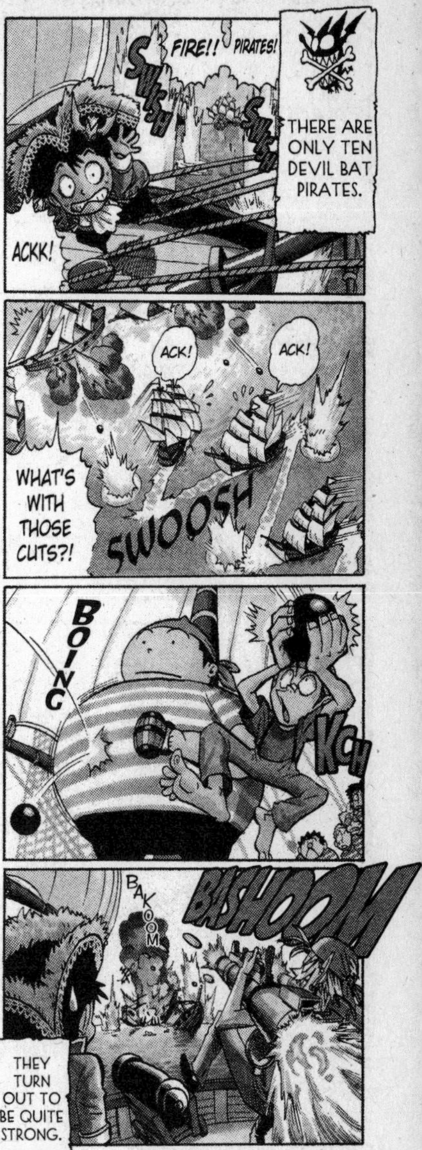
THERE ARE ONLY TEN DEVIL BAT PIRATES.
PIRATES!
FIRE!!
SWISH
SWISH
ACKK!
ACK!
ACK!
WHAT'S WITH THOSE CUTS?!
SWOOSH
KCH
BOING
BAKOOM
THEY TURN OUT TO BE QUITE STRONG.

First published in *Weekly Shonen Jump*, combined issue, nos. 22 and 23 (2003).

The Magician

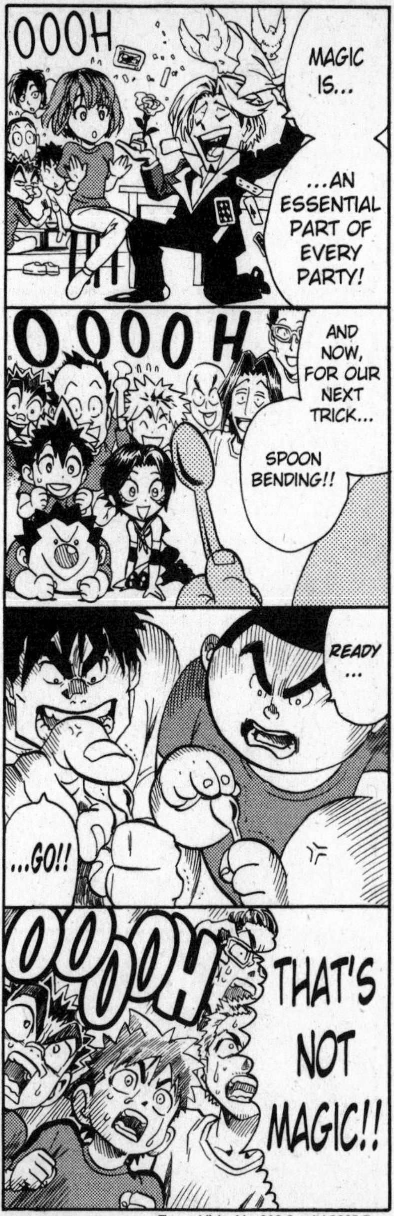
MAGIC IS...
...AN ESSENTIAL PART OF EVERY PARTY!
OOOH
AND NOW, FOR OUR NEXT TRICK...
SPOON BENDING!!
OOOOH
READY...
...GO!!
THAT'S NOT MAGIC!!
OOOOH

First published in *GAG Special 2005 Extra*

The Devil's Present

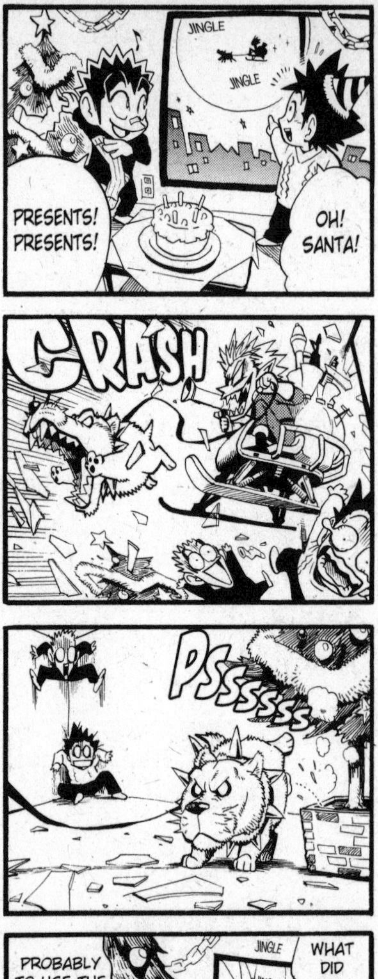
JINGLE
JINGLE
OH! SANTA!
PRESENTS! PRESENTS!
CRASH
PSSSSSS
JINGLE
WHAT DID THEY COME FOR?
JINGLE
PROBABLY TO USE THE *BATHROOM* ...
JINGLE

Santa's Light-Speed Trio

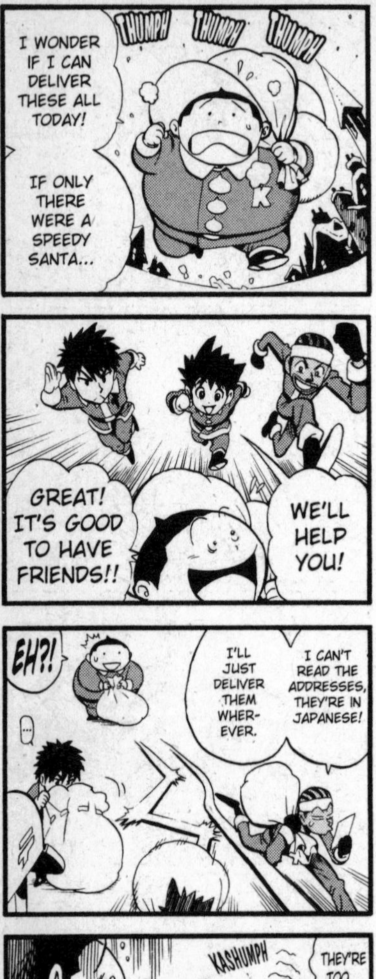
THUMPH
THUMPH
THUMPH
I WONDER IF I CAN DELIVER THESE ALL TODAY!
IF ONLY THERE WERE A SPEEDY SANTA...
WE'LL HELP YOU!
GREAT! IT'S GOOD TO HAVE FRIENDS!!
I CAN'T READ THE ADDRESSES, THEY'RE IN JAPANESE!
I'LL JUST DELIVER THEM WHEREVER.
EH?!
...
THEY'RE TOO... HEAVY...
KASHUMPH
GAAHHH! WHAT A DISASTER!!
CRACK

First published in *Weekly Shonen Jump,* combined issue, nos. 4 and 5 (2004).

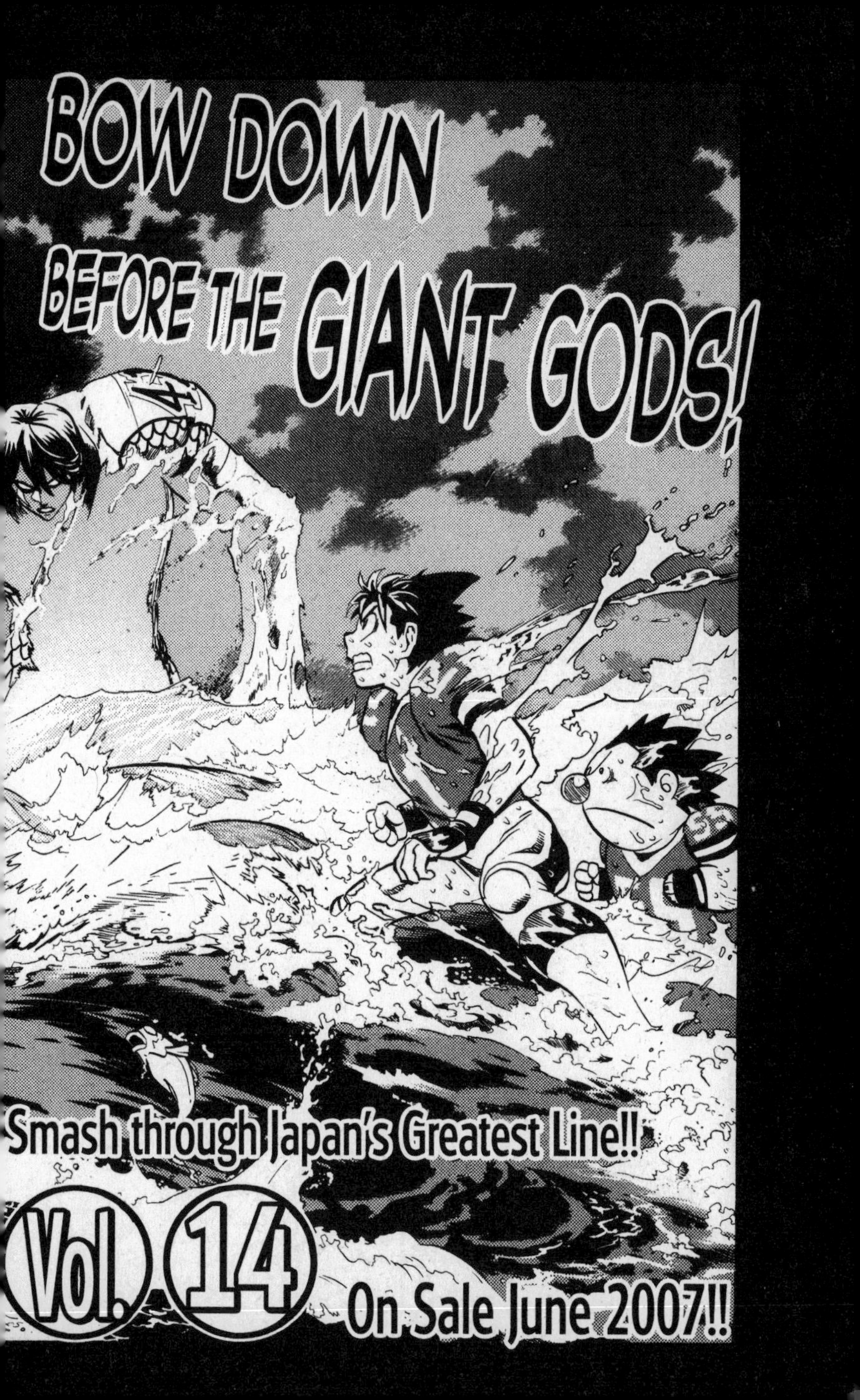

BOW DOWN
BEFORE THE GIANT GODS!
Smash through Japan's Greatest Line!!
Vol. 14
On Sale June 2007!!

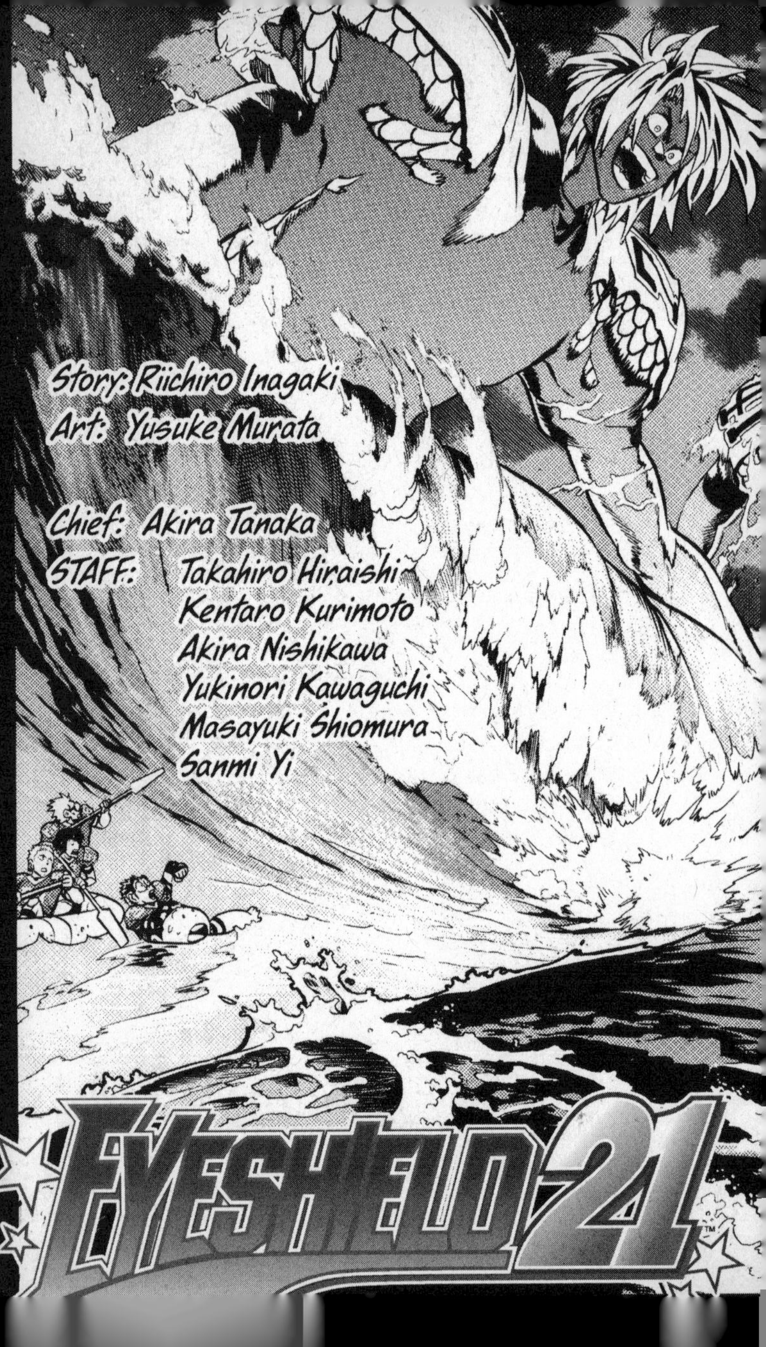
Story: Riichiro Inagaki
Art: Yusuke Murata
Chief: Akira Tanaka
STAFF: Takahiro Hiraishi
Kentaro Kurimoto
Akira Nishikawa
Yukinori Kawaguchi
Masayuki Shiomura
Sanmi Yi
EYESHIELD 21™

EYESHIELD 21
Vol 13: Who Is the Real Eyeshield 21?
The SHONEN JUMP ADVANCED Manga Edition

STORY BY RIICHIRO INAGAKI
ART BY YUSUKE MURATA

Translation/Craig & Hime Kingsley, HC Language Solutions, Inc.
English Adaptation/John Werry, HC Language Solutions, Inc.
Touch-up Art & Lettering/James Gaubatz
Cover and Graphic Design/Sean Lee
Editor/Yuki Takagaki

Managing Editor/Frances E. Wall
Editorial Director/Elizabeth Kawasaki
VP & Editor in Chief/Yumi Hoashi
Sr. Director of Acquisitions/Rika Inouye
Sr. VP of Marketing/Liza Coppola
Exec. VP of Sales & Marketing/John Easum
Publisher/Hyoe Narita

Published by VIZ Media, LLC
P.O. Box 77010
San Francisco, CA 94107

SHONEN JUMP ADVANCED Manga Edition
10 9 8 7 6 5 4 3 2 1
First printing, April 2007

www.viz.com

THE WORLD'S MOST
CUTTING-EDGE MANGA

www.shonenjump.com

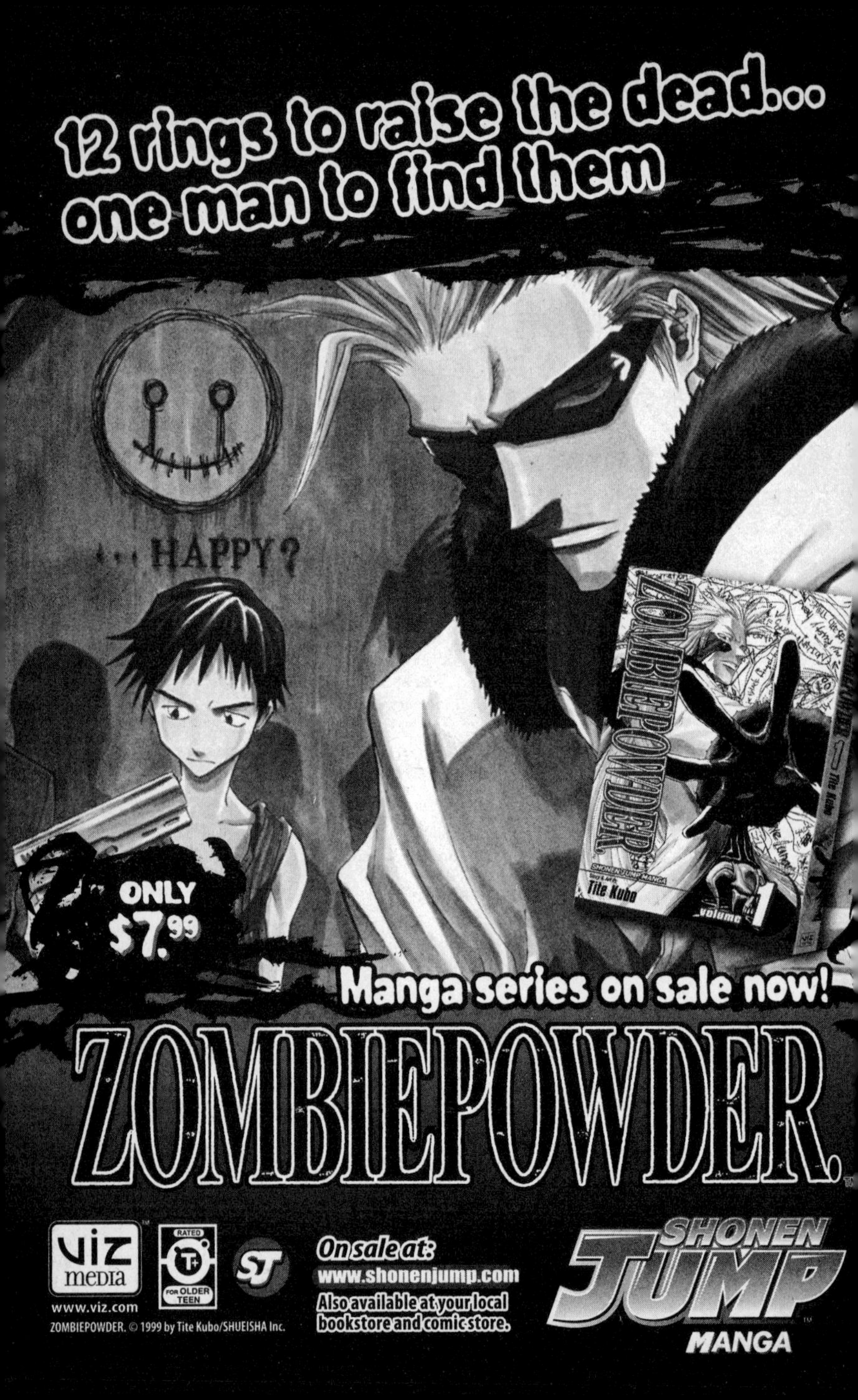

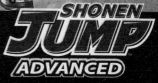

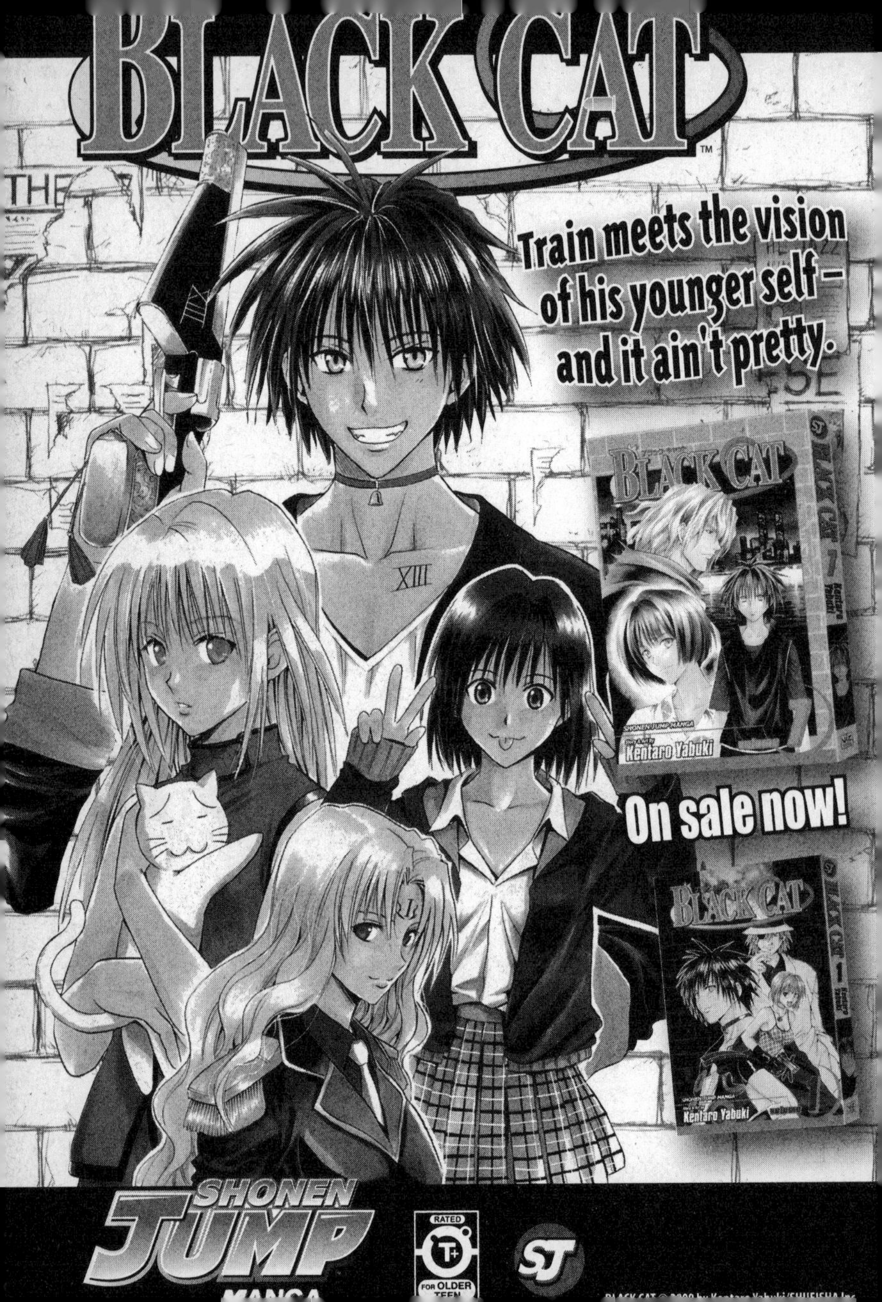

BLACK CAT™
Train meets the vision of his younger self – and it ain't pretty.
BLACK CAT
SHONEN JUMP MANGA
Kentaro Yabuki
On sale now!
BLACK CAT
Kentaro Yabuki
SHONEN JUMP
RATED T+ FOR OLDER TEEN
SJ

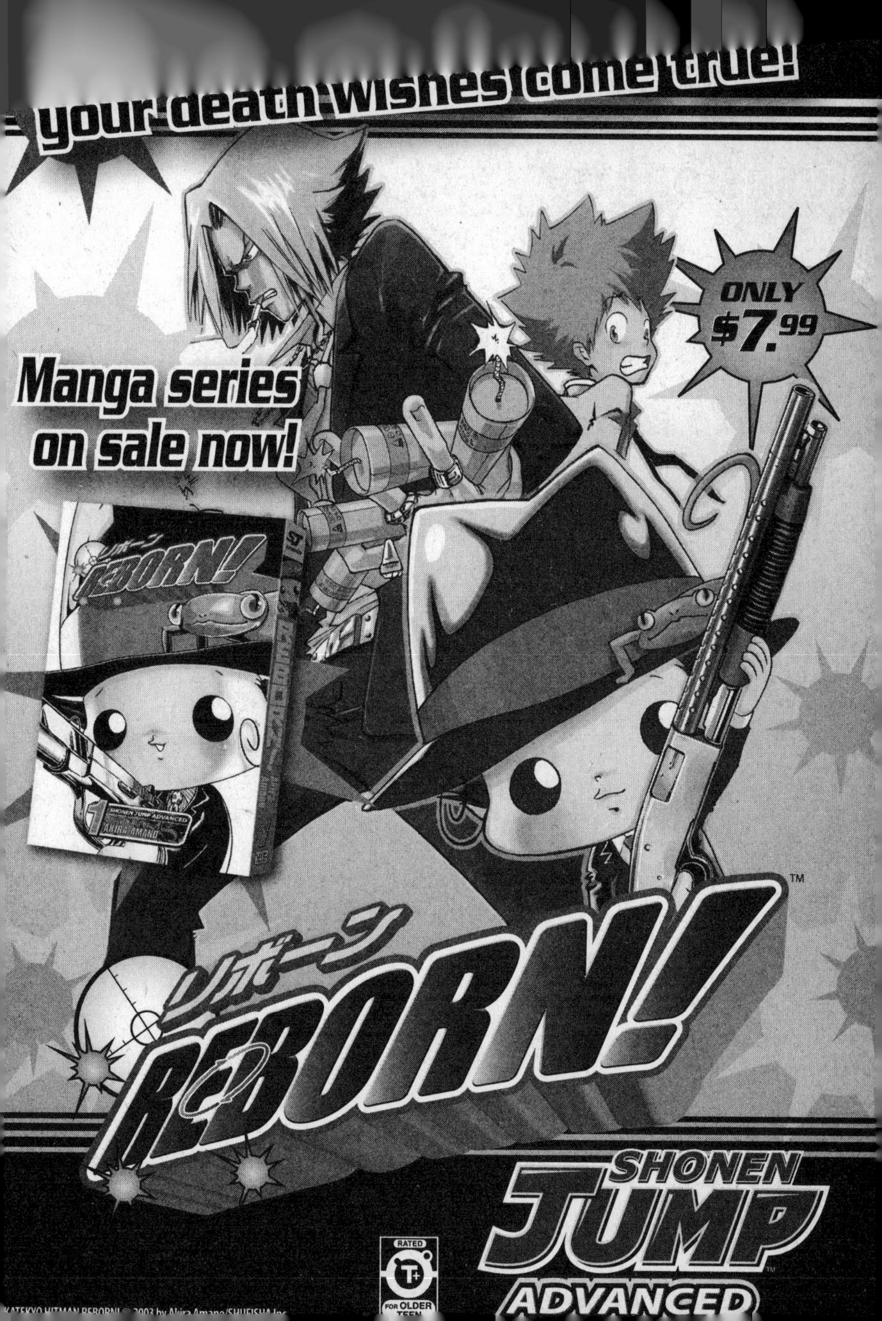
your death wishes come true!
Manga series on sale now!
ONLY $7.99
REBORN!
SHONEN JUMP ADVANCED
AKIRA AMANO
REBORN!™
SHONEN JUMP™ ADVANCED
RATED T+ FOR OLDER TEEN
KATEKYO HITMAN REBORN! © 2003 by Akira Amano/SHUEISHA Inc.

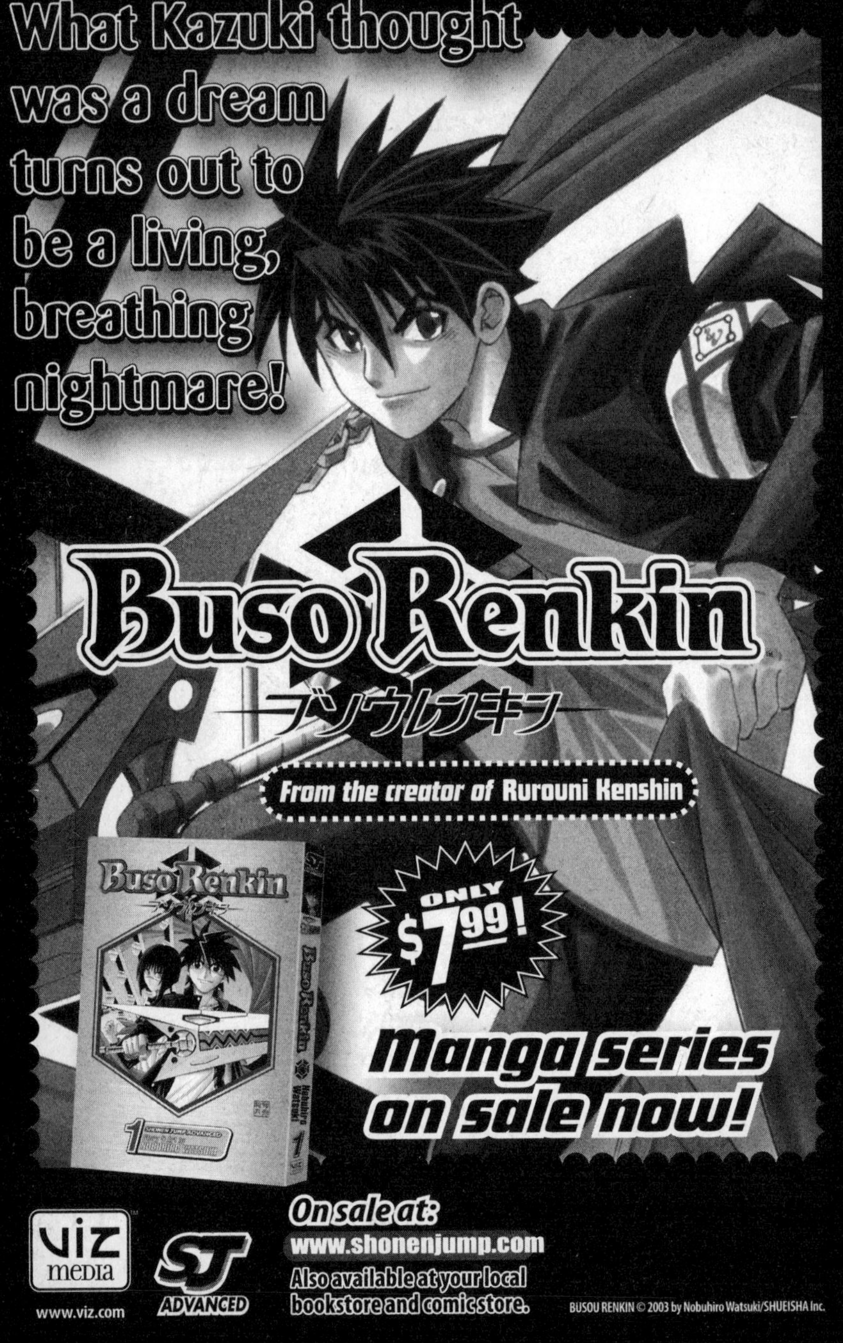
What Kazuki thought was a dream turns out to be a living, breathing nightmare!
Buso Renkin
ブソウレンキン
From the creator of Rurouni Kenshin
Buso Renkin
ONLY $7.99!
Manga series on sale now!
On sale at:
www.shonenjump.com
Also available at your local bookstore and comic store.
viz media
www.viz.com
SJ ADVANCED
BUSOU RENKIN © 2003 by Nobuhiro Watsuki/SHUEISHA Inc.

Tell us what yo SHONEN JUMP manga!

Our survey is now available online.
Go to: www.**SHONENJUMP**.com/mangasurvey

Help us make our product offering better!

THE REAL ACTION
STARTS IN...

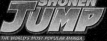

www.shonenjump.com

ADVANCED

VIZ
media

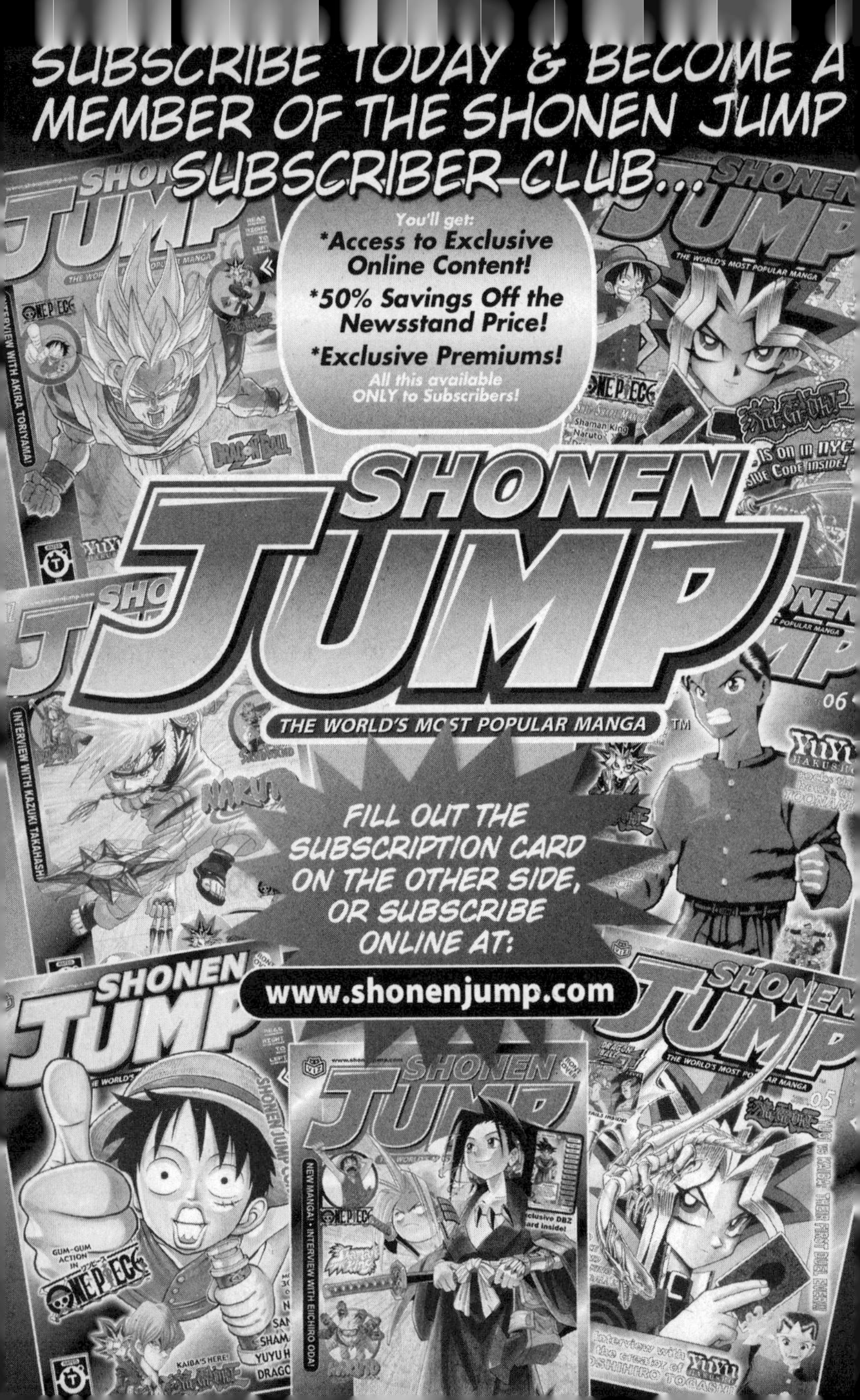
SUBSCRIBE TODAY & BECOME A MEMBER OF THE SHONEN JUMP SUBSCRIBER CLUB...
You'll get:
*Access to Exclusive Online Content!
*50% Savings Off the Newsstand Price!
*Exclusive Premiums!
All this available ONLY to Subscribers!
SHONEN JUMP
THE WORLD'S MOST POPULAR MANGA
FILL OUT THE SUBSCRIPTION CARD ON THE OTHER SIDE, OR SUBSCRIBE ONLINE AT:
www.shonenjump.com